D0152673

Biological Foundations
of Language

Biological Foundations
of Language

Eric H. Lenneberg

Harvard Medical School

with appendices by

Noam Chomsky *and* Otto Marx

John Wiley & Sons, Inc.   NEW YORK LONDON SYDNEY

12 13 14 15

Copyright © 1967 by John Wiley & Sons, Inc.

ISBN 0 471 52626 6

Library of Congress Catalog Card Number: 66–28746
Printed in the United States of America

To
Georg von Békésy
and
G. and B. Mazur

Preface

The study of language is pertinent to many fields of inquiry. It is relevant to psychology, anthropology, philosophy, and medicine. It encroaches upon the humanities, as well as upon the social and natural sciences. We may pursue investigations that concentrate on what man has done with or to specific languages; or we may regard language as a natural phenomenon—an aspect of his biological nature, to be studied in the same manner as, for instance, his anatomy. Which of these approaches is to be chosen is entirely a matter of personal curiosity. This book is concerned with the biological aspects of language.

My intention was to write a theoretical treatise, not a textbook or a survey. I have made no attempt at exhaustive coverage of any of the many fields touched upon. For instance, in the field of physiology much outstanding work has been done on voice and speech mechanisms and on auditory perception. This material is clearly relevant to a general biology of language and certainly ought to be included in any course on this topic. I have omitted this and other similar material because it would not have added much to the *main line* of the argument, because it is readily available to the English-speaking reader, and because the technical detail is difficult to follow if one does not possess prior knowledge of the subject. On the other hand, I did add some detailed discussions of modern biological experiments and theory on the assumption that the student of language is today more likely to come with a background in the social sciences than in biology, and he would, therefore, be unwilling to accept some of the claims made in this book unless they were presented together with the substrate from which they originated.

During the last fifty years, many excellent synopses of language studies have appeared; but biology has been badly neglected in this literature, but for two exceptions. One is B. Naunyn's monograph, *Die organischen Wurzeln der Lautsprache des Menschen* (Bergman, Muenchen, 1925) and the other is C. L. Meader and J. H. Muyskens, *Handbook of Biolinguistics* (Weller, Toledo, 1950). The former is badly out of date, and the latter was written *ad usum scholarum*, and in this capacity it is still of interest; but it does not aim at a distinct theoretical position. Nevertheless, Marx's historical survey in Appendix B makes it clear that there has been an implicit assumption since ancient times that language is somehow dependent upon man's nature. It is only in the last generation or two that behaviorists have openly challenged this position, although even here some ultimate relation to biologically given capacities has never been denied.

This book attempts to reinstate the concept of the biological basis of language capacities and to make the specific assumptions so explicit that they may be subjected to empirical tests. In many instances I have not been able to do more than to formulate questions and to show that they are not spurious. There is no research as yet that provides answers to them. But I hope that I have been able to show what type of investigations might lead to new insights and thus, perhaps, give new directions to old inquiries. A particularly promising approach seems to be the systematic evaluation of patients with various deficits, especially the deaf and the mentally retarded. Modern advances in technology and methodology in behavior research are likely to lead to new knowledge about language function, and thus the patients whose misfortune serves as source material for new studies may, hopefully, eventually profit from the new advances in our understanding of language.

This book must be understood as a discussion rather than a presentation of the biological foundations of language. The exact foundations are still largely unknown. On the other hand, I have considered this book to be the right place to evaluate critically some of the most common claims relating to the biological nature of language. In those instances where I found myself to be in disagreement with widely held opinions, the argument may have taken on a predominantly iconoclastic character, as, for instance, in Chapter six; in other cases the topic seemed to me important enough to warrant a detailed discussion although the data do not lead to new ideas on the nature or origin of language, as, for example, the discussion of peripheral anatomy in Chapter two. However, both the negative and the positive contributions uniformly led me to quite a specific point of view, which I have attempted to summarize in Chapter nine, and which may, some day in the future, become the foundation to a new theory on language.

Ideas do not grow in vacuo. Throughout my fifteen years of residence in the Cambridge area, I have greatly profited from courses taken and given, from conversations, and from general interaction with colleagues and students. I wish to mention particularly Georg v. Békésy, Roger Brown, Jerome Bruner, Noam Chomsky, George Gardner, George Miller, and Peter Wolff. All of them have discussed various aspects of this book with me, and most have read and commented upon several chapters or the entire manuscript. I am also indebted to Hans-Lukas Teuber for critically reading Chapters one and five; to A. H. Schultz and George Erikson for advising me on Chapter two; to Philip Liberman and Arthur House for commenting on Chapter three; to M. Kinsbourne for reading Chapter four; to Charles Gross and Peter Huttenlocher for criticisms of Chapter five; to H. Burla, Hans Kalmus, and Ernst Mayr for reading various versions of Chapter six; and to DeLee Lantz for comments and criticisms on Chapter eight.

Most of my research reported here was carried out under the auspices of The Children's Hospital Medical Center and Harvard Medical School, the Psychological Laboratories, and the Center for Cognitive Studies of Harvard University, and it is a pleasure to acknowledge their generous hospitality here.

Throughout these years, I have enjoyed the financial support of the National Institutes of Health, U. S. Public Health Service, grants MH–02921, M–5268, 1–K–3–MH–21700, and National Science Foundation GS–300. Finally, I would like to express my gratitude to Eleanor F. Rosenberger, who has been responsible for typing and retyping the manuscript, for a gigantic editorial job and for patient library research.

Cambridge, Mass.   E. H. L.
September, 1966

Contents

Biological Foundations
of Language

CHAPTER One

The conceptual framework

I. THESIS: BIOLOGICAL CONSIDERATIONS ARE NECESSARY FOR AN UNDERSTANDING OF BEHAVIOR

Ever since man first mused about his own nature, it has been the gift of language that has surprised him most. If we search through the most primitive and the most ancient evidence of intellectual activity, through myths, magic, or religions, we will find one question that is repeated over and over: from what source comes the power of speech? Answers offered are either of a mystical or rational nature. The first type does not concern us here; the second, which is still prevalent today, is based on the principles of "discovery and rational utilization of inarticulate sounds." Explanations of this type propose that someone discovered certain advantages arising from accidental or instinctive vocalizations, and that one small discovery after another was incorporated into a communication system adopted by an ever-increasing range of individuals. The verbal behavior that came into existence in this manner proved to be so advantageous to those who adopted it in the struggle for survival, that it affected survival rates and natural selection, resulting in a strain that was endowed with "enlarged intellectual capacities," enabling even small children to learn the complicated natural languages as we know them today. A major objective of this monograph is to take issue with this type of formulation and to show that reason, discovery, and intelligence are concepts that are as irrelevant for an explanation of the existence of language as for the existence of bird songs or the dance of the bees.

The explanatory principles which I consider to be potentially fruitful are of a biological nature. This immediately raises a cardinal problem. What does biology have to add to the explanation of behavior such as

1

language, which appears to be acquired by trial and error? Is not learning a psychological rather than a biological phenomenon? Has it not been proved that learning can be explained by a few basic principles which operate in all vertebrates and many invertebrates? Biology, it would seem, deals with the difference between species, whereas psychology (at least the theory of learning) is said to deal with what is "common to all behavior, and all organisms." A biological investigation into language must seem the more paradoxical as it is so widely assumed that languages consist of arbitrary, cultural conventions. Wittgenstein and his followers speak of the *word game,* thus likening languages to the arbitrary set of rules encountered in parlor games and sports. It is acceptable usage to speak of the psychology of bridge or poker, but a treatise on the biological foundation of contract bridge would not seem to be an interesting topic.

The rules of natural languages do bear some superficial resemblance to the rules of a game, but I hope to make it obvious in the following chapters that there are major and fundamental differences between rules of languages and rules of games. The former are biologically determined; the latter are arbitrary. Even if this were not so, we can still reasonably speak in terms of a biology of game-playing. For instance, a zoologist might ask, "What are the homologues of man's *need for play* in animal behavior? What are the specific capacities necessary to enable an animal to play a game of chance, to learn probabilities, to engage in activities that seem to lead to no other reward than being busy or whiling away time? Would a classification of gamelike behavior in animals lead to an interesting taxonomy?" The latter is clearly an ethological problem and thus belongs squarely within the realm of biology.

A biological inquiry into language asks, "Why can only man learn to speak a natural language?" This question is fundamentally different from asking, "In what respect is learning to speak similar to conditioning or operant learning as studied by animal psychologists?" The former question requires an investigation into the specific nature of the species *Homo sapiens;* the latter requires a programmatic disregard of species differences. The former will turn to anatomy, physiology, and developmental studies for an answer (all of which are biological disciplines), whereas the latter will endeavor to discover analogies between stimuli, responses, rewards, and the temporal and spatial relationships between them.

Psychologists and other behavioral scientists have often set up equivalences between natural languages and experimental paradigms. Learning the meaning of a word is said to be like learning to press a bar which will sound the buzzer which represents "food is soon to come"; learning grammar is similar to learning that event A is followed by event B, which in turn is followed by event C. Since these are all accomplishments which many animals can be trained to acquire, some psychologists have asked whether these animals have not in fact learned the essential principles underlying human language. This is a question that must not be answered on the grounds of intuition or common sense, because our understanding of the mechanisms of language is still poor. We do not know intuitively what language is like objectively nor how we manage to communicate with one another. The only way we may judge whether the experimental paradigms have any relevance to natural language at all is to conduct investigations into the nature, structure, and history of natural languages, and then to see whether the empirically determined principles underlying language are, indeed, represented in the experimental paradigms. From this consideration it follows that a biological investigation of language must not only study the organism that speaks but must also investigate the behavior itself—language—much the way the zoologist who studies the badger must study its physique together with its habits in order to give a complete picture of that animal. It is for this reason that some of the material presented in this monograph concerns biological aspects of man and some the biological aspects of language.

The book's fundamental thesis is that behavior, in general, is an integral part of an animal's constitution. Behavior is seen to be an integral part of the organic whole; it is related to structure and function, one being the expression of the other. To put the same thought into its negative form: I do not believe that an animal is like a tool that can be put to just any arbitrary use by a manipulator; I do not believe that anatomy and physiology are comparable to the physical nature of the tool, whereas behavior is like the use to which the tool is put. (The "manipulator" here is either the experimentalist or the vicissitudes of an environment.) Instead, I believe there is evidence that behavior has the same history and the same origin as form and physiological processes; in fact, the division between physiological function and behavioral function is an artifact of our mode of looking at animals, and these functions shade into each other and are, thus, objectively indistinguishable.

This thesis is an anathema in certain circles of behaviorism because it would lead to the conclusion that behavior must always be investigated in terms of specific species, and this proposition runs counter to the belief of many psychologists. On the other hand, if such a thesis *can* be defended, it would at once strengthen the aim of this book: to discover biological principles that explain why a single species displays behavior that is unique in the animal kingdom. To substantiate the thesis, we must inquire to what extent the central nervous system, the peripheral and skeletal structures, and the animal's behavior are interdependent phenomena.

II. FORM AND FUNCTION IN ONTOGENY

There is evidence (1) that the tissues of the brain and the rest of the body constitute an organic, interdependent unit; and (2) that organisms are not programmed for their behavior by an ex-machina force, but instead they develop a program ontogenetically together with nervous and nonnervous tissues.

(1) *Mutual Influence in the Development of Nervous and Other Tissue*

Let us first consider the developmental relationship between nervous and other tissue. Our discussion can be divided into (a) metabolic or trophic relationships and (b) nonmetabolic, particularly mechanical relationships.

(*a*) *Trophic Relationships.* Nervous tissue stands in an intimate relationship to other tissue anatomically contiguous to it. This is shown most clearly by the essential role played by nerves in the process of regeneration. There are a number of studies available which indicate that regeneration of an entire limb in lower vertebrates (fish, lizards, urodele, salamander, larval anuran, and postmetamorphic frog) and probably also in invertebrates is dependent on the presence of nerves in the amputated stump (Singer, 1959, Gutmann, 1964).

In a series of experiments by Schotté and Butler (1944), Singer (1947), and their students, and Nicholas (1949), it has been shown that an amputated limb will not regenerate unless an intact nerve is either present in the remaining stump from the beginning or is transplanted into the cut surface by autograft (however, see Thornton and Steen, 1962). Morphogenesis, that is, an orderly sequence of tissue differentiation and development of the lost appendage, will not ordinarily take place in the absence of living nervous tissue during the very first stage of regeneration. If all nerves are removed from this stump during the earliest period, mitotic activity is dramatically slowed down; eventually some small amount of connective tissue, cartilage, and muscle may form in a disorderly nonfunctional fashion, giving a shriveled and shapeless appearance to the stump. If viable nervous tissue is not present from the start of the amputation but brought into the so-called blastema shortly afterward, regeneration takes place, but the regenerate limb is poorly developed. The nerve need not be present throughout the entire period of regeneration; once the limb has begun to grow and tissues are sufficiently differentiated, the nerve may be removed without impairment of the morphogenetic potency acquired by these tissues during their earliest stage of formation. Singer (1947) has shown that it does not matter for regeneration what type of nerve, whether motor, sensory, or autonomic, is present in the blastema. It is merely the amount of nervous tissue present that controls the regenerative possibilities. Apparently a product of nerve-cell metabolism induces morphogenesis in the blastema.

These studies leave many questions about the biochemistry of embryology and growth unanswered; yet they do give us a glimpse of the complete interdependence and the natural integration of different tissues in the animal body. This impression is further strengthened if we consider some of the other trophic relationships that nerves have to peripheral tissue (for instance, the well-known fact of denervation atrophy). If the axon of a motor neuron is cut, the portion distal of the cut will die promptly, presumably because of its separation from its source of supply of vital substances (Gerard, 1950). But this is not the extent of the degenerative changes following the section of a motor nerve. The muscle innervated by the nerve will also undergo dystrophic changes with an extremely characteristic histological appearance. The loss of muscle substance is not due to a "functional" disturbance, such as the inhibition of nerve impulse transmission (Hamburger & Levi-Montalcini, 1950) nor due to disuse of the muscle; the muscle cannot be saved from atrophy by passive exercise. Indeed, the metabolic interdependence of nonnervous, peripheral tissue and nervous tissue is proven by the fact that the nerves themselves must have anatomic continuity with muscles for proper metabolic function. Severance of nerve from muscle will induce retrograde changes in the body of the neuron (the soma), known as chromatolysis, which is a sign of dysfunction.

Perhaps the most striking evidence for the subtle but definite interdependence of peripheral structures and the central nervous system is provided by the stunted growth resulting from large cerebro-hemispheric and specifically parietal lobe lesions in the neonate human. This phenomenon was described by Macdonald Critchley (1955) and has been generally known to occur in connection with a condition called infantile hemiplegia. The stunting of the body side contralateral to the brain lesion occurs both in congenital and in acquired infantile hemiplegia and is not due to disuse, first, because all tissues in the extremities involved are equally affected and second, because the arrest of growth starts at birth in the congenital cases, that is, before either the affected or the unaffected side *is* actively being used (Holt, 1961). These cases are even more interesting in the present context than the denervation atrophy, because here we see a relation between the highest level of the central nervous system and nonnervous structures of the periphery. Because the cells of the cerebral cortex are separated from those on the periphery by several internuncial neurons, there is an indication of a very subtle control that the higher centers of the central nervous system appear to exercise upon the development of the body as a whole.

(*b*) *Mechanical Relationships.* In addition to the metabolic influences between nervous tissue and other tissue, morphogenesis is controlled by several other factors, some of which are indirectly related to neurophysiology. A good illustration is furnished by the mechanical forces exerted upon growing tissue, particularly bone, which stimulate cell division in certain directions. As muscles are innervated and begin to function, they exert a pull upon the bones to which they are attached and thus help shape the internal structure of this tissue.

It has often been noted (and, unfortunately, frequently been emphasized out of all proportion to its true importance) that the architecture of certain organs is ideally suited to their function. An excellent example of this was provided by D'Arcy Thompson (1942) who wrote, "In all the mechanical side of anatomy nothing can be more beautiful than the construction of a vulture's metacarpal bone. The engineer sees in it a perfect Warren's truss, just such a one as is often used for a main rib in an aeroplane." The fundamental schema of the shape of individual bones and the skeleton as a whole are undoubtedly the result of evolutionary processes including selection and adaptation on a phylogenetic rather than an ontogenetic scale (Hackenbroch, 1957–1962). However, the actual realization of what is only potentially present in the fertilized egg is largely dependent upon factors which are active during ontogenesis. This is best illustrated by the development of the internal structure of bones.

In 1866, a Swiss engineer, Culmann, noted that the internal trusses in the head of a human femur, anatomically known as trabeculae, were oriented in exactly the direction of the lines of maximum internal stress. He drew a diagram of a curved rod showing the lines of stress resulting from the application of a load from above (Fig. 1.1*a*). The model somewhat resembled the head of a derrick which he had just designed, and it is therefore referred to as a crane's head. It bears a striking similarity to a section of the head of the femur (Fig. 1.1*c*). Culmann's idea

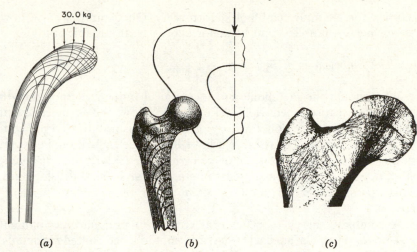

FIG. 1.1. Internal structure of head of human femur. Trabeculae are oriented in the directions of the lines of stress produced by the load bearing on this bone. (*a*) Theoretical lines drawn on a curved rod (after Meyer-Culmann). (*b*) Lines produced on the lacquered surface of natural bone stressed from above (after Küntscher, 1934). (*c*) Thin section of head of femur showing trabeculae (redrawn from a reproduction in Thompson, 1942).

gave rise to J. Wolff's famous theory expressed in his monograph on *The Law of Bone Transformation* (1870), according to which every change in the function of a bone produces changes in its trabecular architecture and external form in conformity with mathematical, static laws. The theory has since been criticized (Küntscher, 1934, 1936), modified (Murray, 1936), and elaborated upon (Evans, 1955, 1957, 1960; Carey, 1929). However, the idea is widely accepted today that muscles, through the tonus already present in early embryonic life, exert essential forces upon the growing bone. These pressures, together with those produced by differential growth of various parts of the embryo, result in stresses and strains which are the prerequisite stimuli for proper bone formation.

It is the influence of muscle tonus upon bone formation that brings this aspect of morphogenesis back to an interaction with the central nervous system. Muscle tonus is, in a sense, the beginning of behavior. Unless tonicity appears in a balanced, centrally regulated sequence, malformations of the outer and inner form of bones and limbs will result (as is indeed encountered in a number of well-known clinical conditions, for example, clubfoot deformities). Once more we see how bones, nerves, muscles, and behavior evolve as an organic entity.

(2) *The Embryology of Behavior*

Why should the metabolic and mechanical influences upon growth be of interest to the behaviorist? For all we know, this is an irrelevant detail of the constructional history of the organism that need not concern the student of behavior. We have had some indication, however, that some primitive precursor of behavior, particularly muscle tonus, is an important factor for at least one aspect of skeletal development. This raises the general question of the embryological history of behavior.

A complete survey of behavioral studies in prenatal development was prepared by Carmichael (1954) and should be consulted for details. In addition to observations on larval behavior in amphibians and pre-hatching behavior in chick embryos, an impressive amount of information exists on prenatal behavior in mammals, ranging from the primitive opossum to human fetuses. There is unanimity among observers that sensory irritability and motor activities come into play as soon as tissues have the differentiation and basic morphology which is characteristic of a given animal. In most mammals this tends to occur roughly toward the end of the first trimester of gestation. Much of the present-day thinking in this connection goes back to the pioneering work of Coghill (1929).

Coghill observed the flexions and, later, the undulating movements in the trunk of the larval *Amblystoma,* which are the behavioral primordium of the mature swimming movements. He demonstrated anatomically that the growth of the nervous system is directly correlated with the emergence of behavior, and he was able to explain certain features of the development of swimming movements (for example, that the movements of the limbs are at first strictly correlated with the gross movements of the trunk and only later assume a degree of independence) on strictly neuro-anatomic grounds. Coghill's over-all conclusions were that behavior (in the animals studied by him and his students) emerged as an integrated but undifferentiated whole involving the entire animal from the start. With further development, a process of individuation of patterns appears which is manifested by the emergence of more specific and more detailed behavioral sequences; but these sequences were considered by him as parts of the behavioral schema as a whole which is potentially present from the beginning.

The concept of the integrated primordial whole, present from the beginning, has not been accepted by all embryologists (Kuo, 1939). Windle (1950) and his group, for instance, had reservations on this point; these workers tended to stress the developmental assembly of initially unrelated reflexes into new and more complex patterns of co-ordination such as locomotion or feeding. When prenatal development of higher animals is considered, the controversy over the assembly view as against the differentiation view is quite academic. A survey of behavior embryology today leads to the following general conclusions.

First, the order in the emergence of sensory and motor capacities, reflexes, and spontaneous motoric events is constant and predictable for any given species. The sequence of events is not dependent upon experience.

Second, the embryological emergence of behavior in mammals cannot be characterized by one simple scheme such as gradual differentiation of a whole or assembly of independently arising component reflexes. Although some aspects of behavior do emerge as undifferentiated patterns with subsequent individuation (for instance, the movements of limbs and digits and, to some extent, of head and trunk), other aspects of behavior are best regarded as a lawful but gradual integration of reflexes that can be observed to function independently before the total integration takes place. The natural history of gait in man is an example of the latter condition. Stepping movements and righting reflexes are present long before the infant is capable of coordinating them for competent stance or locomotion. Coronios (1933) described many similar examples in the course of his observations on the embryological development of behavior in the cat. But in addition to individuation and assembly, we may observe other types of reflex histories that fit neither of these two schemes. For instance, some motor reactions, such as the tonic neck reflex in man, emerge at a specific time only to disappear again in the course of further development. Other reflexes undergo certain transformations in function and appearance, such as infantile startle reactions, whereas still other types of reflexes may merely be suppressed by the appearance of inhibitory mechanisms, but can reappear if the inhibitory mechanisms are abolished; for instance, sucking and rooting reflexes may be seen in patients with advanced degenerative diseases affecting the cerebral cortex, in particular. The embryology of human behavior has been studied by Hooker (1952) and Humphrey (1964) who have also reviewed the recent literature on the subject. In man, certain synergisms, such as grasping, have been observed as early as the eleventh gestational week. After completion of the first trimester, that is, by the fourteenth week, most reflexes seem to be present that can also be observed in the neonate born at term.

Third, species differ considerably in the order of emergence of spontaneous behavior. In most birds, for instance, the embryo may be seen to move before there is any sign of sensory reactivity. In mammals, however, sensory reactivity is very early, and in many species, including man, spontaneous behavior does not become prominent until after peripheral sensitivities have developed. There are, however, enough exceptions to this to discredit the notion that fetal behavior is the result of learning.

The entire developmental process is of a physiological nature. In the earliest stages those metabolic events that have to do with cell division and tissue differentiation are most predominant. With the emergence of tissues differentiated into bone, muscle, and nerves, physiological interactions begin to manifest themselves as mechanical, motor events in addition to the biochemical events. Coordination emerges together with morphology, and a matrix for the animal's future behavioral repertoire is developed, grows and develops into complex synergisms regardless of the "use" the individual will make of it in postnatal or mature life. This is not to imply that the habits of an individual at birth are so predetermined as to dominate completely his adult habits. Many modifications occur after birth in most vertebrates, but the scope of modifiability is always limited by genetic and prenatal events.

III. BEHAVIORAL SPECIFICITY
AND THE PROBLEM OF PLASTICITY

(1) *The Problem*

A discussion of the embryology of behavior is likely to raise more questions than it answers. For instance, how can we explain the results of animal training? A dog can learn to fetch, point, heel, jump, etc., upon his master's commands. Pigeons are trained to run in a figure eight. Rats can learn to press a bar that produces a marble which they must carry to another machine that delivers a pellet of food when the rat drops the marble into a slot. In short, there appears to be an infinite variety of novel tasks certain animals can learn to perform and an even greater number of possible combinations in which we can have an individual associate a certain stimulus with a certain response.

On the other hand, all dogs bark, all pigeons coo, all rats squeak. Behavior that is so universal among all members of one species cannot be the consequence of either training or unique environmental circumstances that produced it.

Here we have grouped behavior in such a way as to make it appear as if there were two entirely different types: one specific to a species, and one the result of plasticity. Although this dichotomy conforms to a popular conception, it is actually untenable. Specificity and plasticity are phenomena that may co-exist. Most behavior of higher animals is in some aspects specific to the species and still be the result of circumstance. Biological factors are ever present, and even the degree of plasticity is an evolutionary phenomenon, the product of biological conditions.

The problems of species-specificity and plasticity of behavior are particularly relevant to investigations of speech and language because, on the one hand, this behavior is specific to the species *Homo sapiens,* and on the other hand, there is an obvious degree of plasticity that accounts for the divergences between modern natural languages. A general discussion of this theme against a background of a wide variety of zoological and physiological phenomena will help us in obtaining a better biological perspective of man and of verbal behavior.

Instead of considering behavior in a complex, molar way, let us concentrate on motor and sensory processes alone. Every animal has biologically given modes of moving and perceiving; its behavior must be dependent on the ways in which it is internally wired, so to speak. How is this internal constitution related to the behavioral patterns we study in psychology? How is plasticity affected by the ways an animal is arranged biologically?

Weiss (1950) and Sperry (1958) have summarized the results of many experiments in which the neuro-muscular connections in animals were surgically rearranged. Various kinds of lower vertebrates were operated on with the general aim of interfering with peripheral motor and sensory mechanisms. For instance, limbs of larval salamanders were transplanted and allowed to regenerate in the "wrong position or wrong side" of the animal; or eyeballs of frogs were severed from the optic nerve and made to regenerate after 180 degree rotation. In all these experiments motor and sensory functions could be restored after surgery, but in each case the behavior was inappropriate to the demands of the situation. After rotation of the eye the frog would jump to the right side in order to catch a fly that was presented to it from the left; or the misplaced limbs of the salamander would make the animal walk backward instead of forward. In no case could the animals operated on learn to overcome the anatomic disarrangement. Experience, purpose, reinforcement, or whatever other mechanisms we might postulate, were of no avail. Here we obtain a picture of highly rigid mechanisms with an apparent absence of plasticity. But let us guard against overgeneralizations.

The lowest immature vertebrates behave as if they had but one (or very few) motor-behavior or perceptive patterns. Even if we switch limbs or sense organs to unnatural positions, the original behavior pattern and sensory integration soon reasserts itself—although it is now useless to the animal. As long as tissues function, they cause the animal to behave in the one and only pattern with which it was endowed.

In higher forms a multitude of patterns emerges. The patterns are no longer indivisible units but may be thought of as consisting of constituents or behavioral components. They are the building stones for the complex patterns which are available and which enter into a great many combinations, thus producing the infinity of tasks for which a higher animal can be trained. But if we examine the motor coordination itself, if we study the sequence in which muscles contract, limbs flex, and trunks rotate, we can often discover species-specificities on the level of motor patterns. Also in perception there are species-specific thresholds and species-specific limits to pattern perception. The greatest degree of specificity is probably found when we make inventories of complex reflexes, since these combine both sensory and motor peculiarities.

Thus specificity is always present, whereas plasticity is a matter of degree. The two phenomena are discovered by different approaches of study. They are not mutually exclusive types of behavior. Nor can plasticity be defined as "dependent upon experience or upon environmental influence" while specificity is not so dependent. All of life is dependent upon environment and may be modified by it. Thus the notion "dependence upon environment" (which by implication is the same as "dependent upon experience") is not a useful criterion for the classification of behavior.

Let us follow the problem of motor coordination further and discuss the concept of plasticity with respect to this aspect.

(2) *Central Regulatory Mechanisms of Motor Coordination*

There are several reasons for assuming that motor coordination, such as for gait, is regulated by a central controlling mechanism. Let us picture this mechanism as consisting, in its most primitive aspects, of spontaneous central nervous system activity, for example, a rhythmic beat related to metabolic processes within the brain (Lindsley, 1957). Lashley (1951) postulated such a central rhythmic activity to account for some of the phenomena discussed under the title of serial order. He conceived of the neural correlates for rapidly following movements as a kind of pacemaker activity, a source which emits spreading waves of facilitation alternating with inhibition, with the whole mechanism providing for a clock or timing device. (For elaborations see Chapters Three and Five.) Let us hypothesize, following the approach of P. Weiss and his students, that it is this central mechanism or its rhythmic activities and modulations that is "nonplastic" because they are inherent in the most intimate organization of the brain, at least of higher organisms. In those animals where the central regulatory mechanism drives a great number of individual coordination patterns (movements used for grooming, pouncing, swimming, or nest-building activities), recombination of movements or partial patterns offers so many possibilities that a picture of nearly infinite variation is created. However, in animals where the central regulatory mechanism drives only a small repertoire of whole coordination patterns, recombination of partial movements is difficult to produce experimentally and, from a behavioral point of view, we are inclined to believe that the animal has a limited learning capacity. This is, in a few words, the hypothesis of this section.

Since central regulatory mechanisms are referred to repeatedly throughout the book, a few more comments are in order. The argument is largely based on Lashley's paper (1951), which should be consulted for fuller documentation and explanations.

The smooth execution of any limb movement requires synergistic interaction of a considerable number of muscles. Most skeletal muscles are arranged into agonist-antagonist pairs. If one muscle contracts, the other has to relax or, more generally, an increase of tonus in one muscle will be accompanied by a proportional decrease of tonus in its counterpart. If this reciprocity is interfered with by diseases such as Parkinsonism, tonic rigidity ensues. In the movement of a limb, an intricate timing mechanism comes into play in which the muscles of, for example, the shoulder-girdle, the humerus and forearm, of the hand, and of the fingers are activated in very rapid succession and with great precision. In addition to the timing mechanism regulating the muscular activities in a single limb, there must be coordinating mechanisms which relate the whole movement of one limb with that of all others, such as in the performance of forward or retrograde ambulation, of swimming, and scratching.

The complexity of the regulatory mechanism may perhaps be made more illustrative if we compare it to a huge train-switching yard (that is, trains of nervous impulses!). Trains are dispatched according to schedules, one schedule for each motor pattern. Each schedule calls for hundreds of simultaneous dispatches as well as a program of staggered dispatches where each successive train must start a fraction of a second after its predecessor.

At one time it was thought that the sequencing of muscular events was the product of a chain of associations; this belief is still widely held today. According to this theory, one motor event comes to be the stimulus for another motor event, these two now determining a third one, and so on. Lashley has shown that such chains of association cannot account for the sequential ordering of motor behavior. There are three major reasons for this: (1) motor events may occur in such rapid succession that there cannot be sufficient time for impulses to be sent from stretch receptors in the muscle to the brain and then back to another muscle which is programmed to be the second in line to contract; (2) certain rhythmic activities can be observed in many animals after far-reaching de-afferentation, that is, severing or blocking of the nerve fibers that carry information from the muscles to the center (v. Holst, 1934, 1937); (3) (this is the most important reason) an individual movement, using again flexion of a limb, is part of not just one but many different coordination patterns. Some animals, for instance, have three or four different types of ambulation. In each type there are different sequences of foot-falls, and the limb as a whole may assume a different style of movement (whipping, slow-lifting, pushing, jerking, etc.). But flexion at a given point is part of each of these various coordination patterns, even though the sequence of motor events is different for each type of gait.

If events A–B–C were simply chained by association, how could we account for the ease with which animals switch back and forth (and without apparent practice or learning) between this pattern and, for example, B–C–A or C–B–A? Chaining by association would let us expect considerably greater habit interference during switching of coordination patterns than is actually observed. Furthermore, it would lead us to expect that any sequence of muscular events could be arbitrarily chained together so that any new coordination pattern could be produced; this is not found to be actually true.

It is this type of argument supported by a wide variety of other biological phenomena that led Lashley to reject the chaining-by-association theory of serial ordering and to assume a different central regulatory mechanism. Instead of repeating the evidence by Lashley, let us turn once more to an analogy for illustration. Consider again the schedules for dispatching trains. The associative chain theory would hold that the movements of individual trains are the signals for movements of other trains. The central mechanism theory holds that neither individual trains nor their movements affect, by themselves, the movements of other trains following them in time. Instead it is the dispatch schedule that regulates the pattern of activities as a whole. Individual trains and their runs may be part of a variety of mutually independent schedules. According to the first theory, an engineer of a train B begins to move after he has seen train A arrive. But according to the second theory engineer B can make no use of the information from A since it may now be part of an entirely different schedule in which B does not follow A; it must await signals from the central switchboard.

(3) *Developmental History of the Central Regulatory Mechanism*

The logical argument offered by Lashley is supported by an impressive array of experimental findings. We have mentioned the experiments on salamander larvae in which limb buds were transplanted to inappropriate sites. If a left forelimb is amputated from a donor animal and transplanted as a supernumerary limb to a host animal where it is allowed to regenerate into the right armpit, the extra limb is soon found to be moving smoothly. No tonic rigidity is noticed, and therefore we must assume that agonist and antagonist muscles receive innervation that is appropriate to the muscle. Interestingly enough, the limb will move at the time that is appropriate for a forelimb to move; since, however, we have changed sides in the process of transplantation, the supernumerary limb will move in the opposite direction from the original limb that is next to it. Thus one limb cancels the effect of the other, and it is possible to have a preparation with totally paradoxical behavior.

What is the nature of this relationship between the limb and the brain? How can reciprocal innervation of muscles and timing of the limb with respect to other limbs be established in a fairly orderly way where there could not have been any neuronal "wiring" for the additional leg? Inspection under the microscope of the regenerated tissues does not reveal any visible order. Nerve fibers seem to have sprouted every which way, and the established connections seem to be entirely random. Could this be a delusion due perhaps to insufficient power of resolution of the light microscope? Is it possible that the nerve sprouts actually find their way to the appropriate muscle because of some unknown biochemical affinity between muscle and nerve? At first this possibility was never entertained. Instead it was thought that muscles were physiologically tuned to specific neuronal messages and simply responded whenever they "heard their name over the public address system." This hypothesis was known as the muscle-resonance theory.

However, Wiersma (1931) disproved the theory by recording electrical potentials from the nerves. Subsequently, the orderly recovery of motor coordination in the transplanted limb was interpreted on the basis of structural connections. There are two essential possibilities here. Either the nervous system is entirely fixed and proper connections are made at the periphery in the way first mentioned, that is, fibers that carry given messages have the capacity of finding their way into the appropriate muscle during regeneration; or the muscles have the capacity of influencing the nerves that grow into them and thus affect the central nervous system retrogradely.

The first of these two possibilities has gained plausibility in most recent investigations (Mark, 1965), although it is still far from established. The second possibility is favored by many of the neuroembryologists who had made the original discoveries on lower vertebrates. In Weiss's own words (1950*b*): It is thought now that "each muscle has a specific biochemical differential, that it projects this differential into the motor nerve fibers that come to innervate it and thus tunes (modulates) the motor ganglion cells to a specificity appropriate for the particular muscle. The ganglion cells have received their specificity by a retrograde influence (modulation) from the muscle itself." Until recently, Sperry (1958) believed that the biochemical influence exerted by the muscle upon the nerve actually induces synaptic changes in the central nervous system. But Eccles et al. (1962) found only limited support for this interpretation, lending credence to Mark's (1965) interpretation, a point of view that is also now favored by Sperry (1963). For an up-to-date review of the entire topic see Weiss (1965).

The importance of the original discovery is that in phylogenetically primitive vertebrates (and probably during fetal stages of most other vertebrates) there is an inescapable *Bauplan* (blueprint) for both the gross form *and* the sensory-motor integration. The surgical rearrangement experiments on lower forms show how difficult it is to interfere with the "preestablished harmony" of the movements of muscles throughout the body which accounts for smooth coordination.

Compare this situation with rearrangement experiments in mammals and *adult* forms of lower vertebrates. If the nerves which normally feed a flexor and extensor pair of muscles, respectively, are interchanged surgically and are allowed to regenerate into the wrong muscle, subsequent coordination becomes disordered and remains so.

The difference in the results of rearrangement between lower and higher forms is not as paradoxical as it might appear at first. Table 1.1 summarizes the situation for easier reference. We discern here the emergence of a specific theme. For all animals examined, rigid plans

TABLE 1.1. *Survey of Research Results with Experimental Rearrangement of Motor and Sensory Mechanisms*

Type of Animal	Motor		Sensory	
	Type of Physiological Rehabilitation	Usefulness of Restored Behavior	Pattern Perception	Usefulness of Restored Behavior
Interference with Anatomy				
Lower, Immature Vertebrates	Good regeneration with myotypic response; coordination and original timing preserved	No behavioral adaptation	Pattern perception possible after regeneration	No behavioral adaptation to inverted image
Higher Mature Vertebrates	Amyotypic regeneration with coordination and timing permanently disarranged	No behavioral adaptation	No regeneration of optic or acoustic nerves	Irreversible blindness and deafness
Subhuman Primates	As above	Question of possible readaptation; never complete and easily disturbed	As above	As above
Extra-Corporeal Disarrangement with Anatomy Intact				
Mammals Including Man and other Primates		Adequate adaptation if subject is allowed active movements	If disarrangement consists of one single and constant transformation (e.g., image inversion) adaptation is almost complete but paradox sensations remain. (For animals reared in diffuse light there is some evidence that learning of pattern perception is tied to certain ages.)	

17

for development of form and motor coordination seem to exist. In primitive forms, tissues are less differentiated or specialized and thus participate in the organization responsible for motor coordination; end organs may influence the structure and function of centers as much as the centers may influence the periphery. The result is preservation of the original plan for integration. In adult and higher forms, tissues become more and more specialized and thus more independent of each other. The motor-integration plan is no longer "inscribed" in tissues other than those directly concerned with coordination, principally the brain. The basic plan or plans (the dispatch schedules) for sensory motor coordination are still as rigidly inherent in the internal organization of the animal but they are stored now in the central nervous system alone. In this context, the dimension of plasticity-rigidity refers exclusively to adaptation and readjustment of internal processes, not to an animal's adaptation to environmental conditions.

The situation for primates and man in particular is not completely clear. Although regeneration is also amyotypic and coordination is either permanently disarranged or at least always remains poor, some central nervous system mechanisms seem to have developed in those forms that enable the individual to make some secondary, partial readjustment. Perhaps this new learning is based on more complex cortical activities—possibly those that are experienced by man as *will*— but these speculations still lack empirical evidence.

The picture would not be complete without at least a superficial reference to the sensory disarrangement brought about by extracorporeal distortions, such as vision through wearing distorting lenses or prisms. Man, and a variety of lower forms, can learn quickly to make a number of adaptive corrections for these distortions (Kohler, 1951). However, the adjustment is not complete. In adjusting motor coordination to distorted visual input, it is essential that the individual goes through a period of motor adaptation, and there is cogent evidence that this is required for a physiological reintegration between afferent and efferent impulses and not simply to provide the subject with "knowledge" of the spatial configurations (Held and Hein, 1958), (Smith and Smith, 1962). Furthermore, man's cognitive adjustment to visually distorted environment is never complete. Subjects who wear image-inverting goggles soon come to perceive the world right-side-up (though at the beginning it was seen upside down). But even after many weeks of relative adjustment, they experience paradoxical sights such as smoke from a pipe falling downward instead of rising upward or snowflakes going up instead of coming down.

The over-all conclusion that must be drawn from the disarrangement experiments are first, that motor coordination (and certain behavior patterns dependent upon it) is driven by a rigid, unalterable cycle of neurophysiological events inherent in a species' central nervous system; second, that larval, fetal, or embryonic tissues lack specialization; this enables these tissues to influence one another in such a way as to continue to play their originally assigned role despite certain arbitrary peripheral rearrangements. Because of this adaptability, species-specific motor coordination reappears again and again regardless of experimentally switched connections. Third, as tissues become more specialized—both in ontogeny and in phylogeny—the adaptability and mutual tissue influence disappears. Therefore, in higher vertebrates peripheral disarrangements cause permanent discoordination. Finally, with advance of phylogenetic history, ancillary neurophysiological mechanisms appear which modify and at times obscure the central and inherent theme—the cyclic driving force at the root of simple motor coordination. More complex storage devices (memories) and inhibitory mechanisms are examples.

With the emergence of more specialized brains, the nature of behavior-specificity changes. Although it would be an inexcusable oversimplification to say that behavior, in general, becomes more or less specific with phylogenetic advance, there is perhaps some truth in the following generalizations. In the lower forms, there seems to be a greater latitude in what constitutes an effective stimulus, but there is a very narrow range of possible responses. Pattern perception, for instance, is poorly developed so that an extremely large array of stimulus configurations may serve to elicit a certain behavior sequence, and thus there is little specificity in stimulability. However, the motor responses are all highly predictable and are based on relatively simple neuromuscular correlates; thus there is high degree of response specificity. With advancing phylogeny, the reverse seems to become true. More complex pattern perception is correlated with greater stimulus specificity and has a wider range of possible motor responses, that is, less response specificity. However, both of these trends in decreasing and increasing specificity are actually related to greater and greater behavioral and ecological specialization. Taxonomists will be quick to point out countless exceptions to these rules. Evolution is not so simple and can never be brought to conform to a few formulas. The statement here is merely to the effect that such trends exist and that, generally speaking, specificity both in stimulation and in responsiveness changes throughout the history of animal life.

In the vast majority of vertebrates, functional readjustment to anatomical rearrangement appears to be totally impossible. Even if the animal once "knew how" to pounce on prey, peripheral-central disarrangement will permanently incapacitate the animal from pursuing the necessities for its livelihood. If the primate order should indeed be proven to be an exception to this rule—and there is little evidence of this so far—then we would have to deal with this phenomenon as an extreme specialization, whose details and consequences are yet to be investigated. There is much less modifiability for those coordination patterns which constitute species-specific behavior than is usually realized, and we must keep in mind that most behavioral traits have species-specific aspects.

This statement is not contradicted by the great variety of arbitrary behavior that is produced by training. Pressing a bar in a cage, pecking at a red spot, jumping into the air at the signal of a buzzer (in short, the infinity of arbitrary tricks an animal can be made to perform) do not imply that we could train individuals of one species (for example, common house cats) to adopt the identical motor behavior patterns of another, such as that of a dog. Although there is perfect homology of muscles, we cannot train a cat to wag its tail with a dog's characteristic motor coordination. Nor can one induce a cat to vocalize on the same occasions a dog vocalizes instinctively, for instance, when someone walks through the backyard. Just as an individual of one species cannot transcend the limits to behavior set by its evolutionary inheritance, so it cannot make adjustments for certain organic aberrations, particularly those just discussed. The nearly infinite possibility of training and retraining is a sign of the great freedom enjoyed by most mammals in combining and recombining individual traits, including sensory and motor aspects. The traits themselves come from a limited repertoire, are not modifiable, and are invariably species-specific in their precise motor coordination and general execution.

In Goethe's words, addressing a developing being:

> Nach dem Gesetz, wonach du angetreten.
> So musst du seyn, dir kannst du nicht entfliehen,
> So sagten schon Sibyllen, so Propheten;
> Und keine Zeit und keine Macht zerstückelt
> Geprägte Form, die lebend sich entwickelt.*

* According to the law that summoned thee.
  Thus must thou be, thy own thou canst not flee,
  Thus spake the sibyls, thus the prophets;
  And neither time nor might can deviate
  Imprinted form alive developing.

IV. GENETIC FOUNDATIONS OF BEHAVIOR

We have constructed a picture of behavior consisting of a fixed matrix (that is, species-specificities delimited by characteristic anatomical and physiological processes), which an individual can never learn to transcend, coupled with varying degrees of freedom for combining existing, built-in skills and traits. If these skills and traits are, indeed, programmed into the individual as is implied here, then we ought to be able to adduce evidence for inheritance of such traits. Moreover, the history of evolution should give us some clues regarding phylogenetic emergence of behavior. Such evidence and clues do exist.

Genetics of behavior were first summarized by Hall (1951) and more recently treated in greater detail by Fuller and Thompson (1960). Genetic influences upon various aspects of behavior have been demonstrated for many species. Several studies were made on the fruitfly. Erlenmeyer-Kimling et al. (1962) bred *Drosophila melanogaster* selectively to produce strains with vastly different geotactic responses (going against or toward the pull of gravity in an appropriate maze). Selective breeding experiments on rats were reported by Rundquist (1933), varying the amount of spontaneous activities in the strains developed; by Tryon (1940), producing maze-bright and maze-dull strains, and by Hall (1951), varying emotionality (as measured by frequency of urination and defecation). It is true that in these experiments it is often not clear exactly what is transmitted genetically. Searle (1949), for instance, pointed out that the behavioral difference demonstrated by Tryon may be a result of a factor of congenital timidity, the dull rats actually being upset about the experimental arrangement, whereas the bright ones are undaunted by the maze. Searle's interpretation may very well be correct, but it does not alter the basic fact that genes do make a difference in the execution of behavior (Fuller and Thompson, 1960). In some instances, the breeds resulting from artificial selection of mates may behave differently from each other because of morphological differentiations (James, 1941). In other instances, morphological changes that are usually inevitable in breeding experiments may be irrelevant to the behavioral changes observed. In this case, physiological processes are altered, thus raising or lowering thresholds of responsiveness.

This was most directly demonstrated by Herter (1936) who showed different thermotactic optima in gray and white mice (where the color of the coat is apparently irrelevant) and by Setterfield et al. (1936), who showed that the inability to taste phenylthiocarbamide is inherited in man as a recessive Mendelian trait. Scott and Charles (1954) make a similar point, extending it generally to the interaction between the genetically given and the environmentally modified. In summarizing their work on dogs, they state: ". . . different thresholds of response to minimal . . . stimulation tend to produce all-or-none responses, and the process of habit formation tends to cause individuals to react one way or the other, producing increasingly clear-cut differences."

This point is very well taken. It seems unlikely that genes actually transmit behavior as we observe it in the living animal because the course that an individual takes in its peregrinations through life must necessarily depend on environmental contingencies which could not have been "programmed and prepared for" in advance. Inheritance must confine itself to propensities, to dormant potentialities that await actualization by extra-organic stimuli, but it is possible that innate facilitatory or inhibitory factors are genetically transmitted which heighten the likelihood of one course of events over another. When put into these terms, it becomes quite clear that nature-nurture cannot be a *dichotomy* of factors but only an *interaction* of factors. To think of these terms as incompatible opposites only obscures the interesting aspects of the origin of behavior.

So much about genetics of behavioral variations within species. The sources cited are only a small sample of the ever-growing field. The studies demonstrate that genetic mechanisms definitely play a role in the development of an individual's behavior. Many problems remain to be solved. This science is young and its major victories have yet to be won.

It is very tempting to generalize from the genetic experiments mentioned to the genetic basis underlying behavioral variations between species. Although there is little doubt among evolutionists that interspecies differences—be they morphological or behavioral—must eventually be explained by genetic mechanisms, it is well to remember that there are no experiments as yet in which new species have been created. Thus, speciation continues to be a problem—one in which we cannot afford to be involved in the present discussion. For our purpose and argument it will be quite sufficient to mention a few points on which there is wide agreement. Probably the most remarkable of these is that every species has a unique behavior repertoire. Furthermore, the behavioral variations within a species tend to be less pronounced than those between species. Thus the morphological differences on which taxonomy was first based are no more distinctive than behavioral differences, and many ethologists have high hopes that behavior by itself may have the same heuristic value in taxonomy as morphology. This is not a necessary consequence of interspecies behavioral variations.

These variations need not have the same evolutionary history as morphology. Theoretically, at least, they may have greater randomness than form in their distribution or they may be more susceptible to selection pressures than form. However this may be, there are several instances in which species were discovered on the ground of behavioral differences with subsequent confirmation by morphological criteria, as well as instances in which species could be confidently grouped into one family primarily on the grounds of a common behavioral trait (Mayr, 1958).

Genetics and evolutionary science point to an inevitable conclusion: behavior must be considered in the context of species, that is, with reference to the specific type of animal that behaves, and thus behavioral science is inseparable from any other biological consideration that concerns that animal.

V. RELATIONSHIP BETWEEN FORM AND BEHAVIOR

When the term *learning theory* is used, it is ordinarily applied to universal aspects of learning. Psychologists who concern themselves with such theories point out sometimes that there are some aspects of behavior to which the theories do not apply, as, for instance, the swallowing mechanisms in pigeons, the peculiarities of a buzzard's flight, or the phonetic differences between meowing and barking. These phenomena are considered to be appropriate subjects for the biologist but not for the behaviorist. The distinction between biological and psychological aspects of behavior may be possible in certain instances, particularly in behavioral phenomena observed in laboratory experiments, but in many more instances there is no way of telling whether a given phenomenon ought to be explained (or investigated) in terms of psychological or biological mechanisms. We have criticized this distinction throughout this chapter, but we must add one more reason for abolishing the distinction.

It is often thought that behavior which is executed by or is dependent upon a peculiar structure typical of a certain type of animal must therefore be biologically based. The grasping movements of an elephant are of no particular relevance to learning theory; they are said to be species-specific and biological! A corollary to this kind of reasoning is that the absence of a special structure or organ should be a criterion for the psychological nature of the behavior. Thus it has been pointed out time and again that man has evolved no special organ for speech, the implication being that we are simply making use of the organs for eating and breathing in our efforts to communicate. This is seriously offered as evidence for the arbitrary, learned, artifactual nature of language.

The reasoning here is poor, however. The relationship between the outer form of an animal to its species-specific behavior repertoire is not always clear. So many factors influence this relationship that no canonical truths about innateness may be inferred from it.

Certainly, there are *some* instances of amazing degrees of adaptation of morphology to an animal's mode of life. Consider, for instance, the streamlining of fishes, the physical characteristics of feathers ideally suited to conditions of flight, or the specialized mechanisms of claws in cats. The first of these is particularly interesting because it developed once more and independently in dolphins and whales. Convergences of this type occur with many different variations and certainly tell us that there must be mechanisms operating in evolution which optimize the functional relationship between form and behavior. The most flawless discussions of this topic are found in D'Arcy Thompson's essay on *Form and Mechanical Efficiency* (1942). Here he applies the principles of engineering to skeletal structures and generally shows how mechanical principles and phenomena and their mathematical description give some objective insight into over-all morphology. It is D'Arcy Thompson's conviction that growth and form are phenomena subject to physical laws, and that optimization of circumstances can frequently be demonstrated in the living form. We would at first assume that D'Arcy Thompson holds the belief that form is always the expression of greatest adaptation to the environment and therefore is of greatest "utility" to the organism, and consequently form and behavior should be demonstrably adapted one to the other. Actually, Thompson did not draw this latter inference. He was one of the greatest critics of Darwinian thought; he was not convinced that form is *explained by utility* to the animal. He believed that mathematics and the laws of natural science are applied to biology as *descriptive tools* but that they do not *explain* ontological problems of life. In his own unexcelled language:

> "It is certain that the question of phylogeny, always difficult, becomes especially so in cases where a great change of physical or mechanical conditions has come about, and where accordingly the former physical and physiological constraints are altered or removed. The great depths of the sea differ from other habitations of the living, not least in their eternal quietude. The fishes which dwell therein are quaint and strange; their huge heads, prodigious jaws, and long tails

and tentacles are, as it were, gross exaggerations of the common and conventional forms. We look in vain for any purposeful cause or physiological explanation of these enormities; and are left under a vague impression that life has been going on in the security of all but perfect equilibrium, and that the resulting forms, liberated from many ordinary constraints, have grown with unusual freedom."

Similar views are expressed by other biologists (Bertalanffy, 1952). Simpson (1949) gives a beautiful example paralleling the great variations of fishes living in the identical environment: the horns of antelopes living in the Belgian Congo. Discussing the variations in shape, he says:

". . . there must be some one type of horn that would be the most effective possible for antelopes, with some minor variations in proportions or shape in accordance with the sizes or detailed habits of the animals. Obviously, not all of these antelopes have the "best" type of horns, and probably none of them has."

Any serious search for correlation between outer form and animal behavior is limited not only by strictly logical considerations such as those of Thompson and Simpson but also by a heuristic problem. The human observer at times is forced to make predictions about what would be useful to a certain way of life, but the prediction may be purely the result of his anthropocentric outlook. For instance, utilitarian considerations would lead us to expect to find spiders with a given anatomy to build quite different webs from what is actually found. Duncan (1949) points out that ghost spiders weave webs out of very short strands, yet have tremendously long legs which, to the human observer, seem to get in the way both during weaving and moving around in the web. On the other hand, orb spiders have very short legs, but they spin very long cables and spokes which force them to make long journeys on which long legs would appear, from our point of view, to be an advantage.

Behavioral traits that have been demonstrated experimentally to be based on genetic differences and that are inherited from generation to generation within a given strain are rarely correlated with morphological differences between such strains. Airedale terriers look different from German shepherds, but there is nothing in their structure that explains why the latter is more prone to assume a "passive defensive reaction" than the former. Nor could we have guessed that pointers can be trained much more easily to retrieve than spaniels from a mere study of their body-build (Krushinskii, 1962).

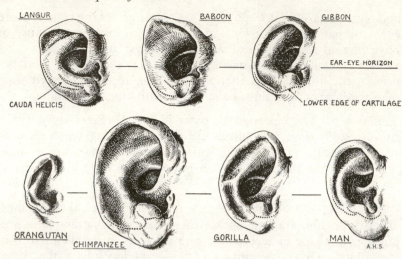

FIG. 1.2. Right auricles of some simians showing variations of a homologous structure that cannot be explained in terms of function. (Adapted from Schultz, 1950; quoted by Lasinski, 1960.)

The same is true of species-specific behavior. The form of spinnerets with their glands does not give any clue to the type of web a spider weaves. From the beaver's anatomy we could not have guessed that he builds dams. The architecture of a bird's nest is, in most instances, unrelated to the animal's morphology. Thus, types of behavior which no one would hesitate to call essentially biologically given are not determined simply by the animal's form.

The reverse is true also. Certain morphological distinctions may exist between species which do not correspond to clearly related behavioral differences. The outer ear in primates is an example (see Fig. 1.2). With the exception of some specialized ear forms of certain prosimians, the auricles of primates developed in a number of directions that have no obvious adaptive value (to the human observer) and no relevance to any of the behavioral characteristics that distinguish these species.

It is clear, therefore, that neither our conviction that tissues and behavior constitute an organismic unity because of their common developmental history nor the established fact that genetic changes and speciation always affect form as well as function makes it necessary to assume a *correlation* between specialized organs and species-specific behavior. There are many types of instinctive behavior which have no structural correlates; and there are many structural distinctions between species which have no behavioral correlates. Thus there is necessarily a historical but not necessarily a causal relationship between gross structure and over-all behavior pattern. This point is important because it emphasizes once more the difficulty, if not complete impossibility, of setting up common sense criteria for the distinction between innate and acquired types of behavior.

A methodological general principle emerges from these considerations. Morphological characteristics of a species may be understood as a specialized form of the general (abstracted) type characteristic of the genus; each genus represents a special modification from the general structural pattern of the superordinate family; each family represents special deviations from the more general structural pattern of the order, etc. On the other hand, the systematics of behavior do not have the same hierarchical relationships. Discontinuities and unique traits are common; specializations of behavior seem to deviate more markedly from general patterns, and in many cases the specializations are so pronounced that the abstraction of general behavior types is impossible or hazardous.

This difference in structural as opposed to behavioral systematics may be entirely due to the limitations of human observation and insight. We can discern, visually, the relationship between forms; but the relationship of behavior escapes our powers of observation more easily. However this may be, it leads to the following methodological principle:

Knowledge of structure alone cannot lead to exact inferences of behavior patterns (only general modes of life); but once behavior patterns are known, we can understand and explain by hindsight certain specializations of morphology.

This is a methodological formulation. It does not give clues to the direction of causality; it does not assert that behavior is prior to form or vice versa.

VI. CONCLUSION

In this chapter we have covered a vast territory citing embryological, anatomical, physiological, and genetic facts pertinent to a great variety of animals. The aim of these excursions was to provide a panorama of the many aspects of the study of behavior and the scientific approaches to this study. We wished to demonstrate the intimate relationship between behavior and biological phenomena in general. We shall, in subsequent chapters, focus on language, but from the foregoing discussions it will be apparent that a biology of language must go far beyond the traditional subjects, namely beyond a demonstration that man is not the only communicating animal, and that certain animal experiments are analogous to language acquisition. Instead, we may expect that language, just as the other types of behavior discussed in this chapter, is determined to a large extent by biological potentialities.

We have come to the following conclusions in the previous sections. The central nervous system and other tissues in the body develop simultaneously and influence one another continuously during morphogenesis. Also, the internal architecture of bones is in part influenced by muscle tonus, which in turn depends on central nervous system activity. As soon as embryonic tissues are sufficiently differentiated, movement and primitive stages of behavior appear, and these develop *pari passu* with further embryonic development. In mammals and most birds, individuals emerge into the world after a complex ontogenetic history in which behavioral differentiation played as important a role as tissue differentiation. Once the individual mammal attains freedom from the intrauterine influence, he is neither a passive tool that may be put to any arbitrary use nor a tabula rasa into which behavior can be arbitrarily inscribed. There are biological limits to its future behavioral repertoire, and these express themselves as species-specificities. Such specificities are ever present and there is no behavior (including language) that is exempt from them. In many animals there is a certain degree of plasticity, but the building blocks of any behavior, however arbitrarily it might have been shaped by exterior forces, remain species-specific reflexes, sensitivities, and motor patterns. Genetic transmission appears to play an important role in the fundamental nature of behavioral building blocks and their propagation through animal populations. There is in certain instances a developmental connection between the morphological characteristics and the behavioral characteristics of a species. However, a simple inspection of form does not ordinarily allow us to predict the complete behavioral characteristics of the animal. But if the animal's behavior is well-known, some of its morphological characteristics can then be related to function.

In our investigations of biological foundations of language we shall examine anatomical and physiological correlates; we shall attempt to follow the emergence of language through growth and maturation; and we shall attempt to see language in the context of the science of evolution. These and related matters must, by necessity, be treated in individual chapters. Yet none of these topics by themselves is likely to give us definitive clues to the biological nature of language. Each produces circumstantial evidence. Only a synopsis of the entire material will give us a picture, however hazy, of the immensely intricate design of the whole.

REFERENCES

Barron, Donald (1950), Genetic neurology and the behavior problem, in *Genetic Neurology*. P. Weiss (ed.), Univ. of Chicago Press, Chicago.

Bertalanffy, L. von (1952), *Problems of Life,* John Wiley and Sons, New York.

Carey, E. J. (1929), Studies in the dynamics of histogenesis: experimental studies of the architecture of human cancellous bone, *Radiology* **13:**127–168.

Carmichael, L. (1954), The onset and early development of behavior, in *Manual of Child Psychology* (2nd ed.), pp. 60–185. John Wiley and Sons, New York.

Caspari, E. (1958), Genetic basis of behavior, in *Behavior and Evolution*. Anne Roe and G. G. Simpson (eds.), pp. 103–127. Yale Univ. Press, New Haven.

Coghill, G. E. (1929), *Anatomy and the Problem of Behaviour*. Cambridge Univ. Press, MacMillan, New York.

Coronios, J. D. (1933), Development of behavior in the fetal cat, *Genet. Psychol. Monogr*. **14:**283–386.

Critchley, Macdonald (1955), *The Parietal Lobes.* Arnold, London.

Duncan, W. (1949), *Webs in the Wind; the Habits of Web-weaving Spiders*. Ronald Press, New York.

Eccles, J. C., Eccles, R. M., Shealy, C. N., and Willis, W. D. (1962), Experiments utilizing monosynaptic excitatory action on motoneurons for testing hypotheses relating to specificity of neuronal connections, *J. Neurophysiol*. **25:**559–580.

Erlenmeyer-Kimling, L., Hirsch, J. and Weiss, Jane M. (1962), Studies in experimental behavior genetics: III. Selection and hybridization analyses of individual differences in the sign of geotaxis, *J. comp. Physiol. Psychol*. **55:** 722–731.

Evans, F. G. (1955), Studies in human biomechanics, *Symposium on Dynamic Anthropometry. Ann. N. Y. Acad. Sci*. **63:**586.

Evans, F. G. (1957), *Stress and strain in bones; their relation to fractures and osteogenesis*. C Thomas, Springfield, Illinois.

Evans, F. G. (1960), Biomechanics: stress-strain phenomena in bones, in *Medical Physics,* Vol. III, pp. 89–93, Otto Glasser (ed.), The Yearbook Publ., Chicago.

Fredericson, E. (1953), The wall-seeking tendency in three inbred mouse strains (*Mus musculus*), *J. genet. Psychol*. **82:**143–146.

Fuller, J. L. (1955), Hereditary differences in trainability of purebred dogs, *J. genet. Psychol*. **87:**229–238.

Fuller, J. L. and Thompson, W. R. (1960), *Behavior Genetics,* John Wiley and Sons, New York.

Gerard, R. W. (1950), Some aspects of neural growth, regeneration, and function, in *Genetic Neurology*. P. Weiss (ed.), Univ. of Chicago Press, Chicago.

Gutmann, E. (1964), Neurotrophic relations in the regeneration process, in *Mechanisms of Neural Regeneration, Vol. 13, Progress in Brain Research*. M. Singer and J. P. Schadé (eds.), Elsevier, Amsterdam.

Hackenbroch, M. (1957–1962), Form and Funktion, in *Handbuch der Orthopaedie*, I–IV, G. Hohmann, M. Hackenbroch and K. Lindemann (eds.), Thieme, Stuttgart.

Hall, Calvin S. (1951), The genetics of behavior, in *Handbook of Experimental Psychology*. S. S. Stevens (ed.), pp. 304–329, John Wiley and Sons, New York.

Hamburger, V. and Levi-Montalcini, Rita (1950), Some aspects of neuroembryology, in *Genetic Neurology*, P. Weiss (ed.), pp. 128–160, Univ. of Chicago Press, Chicago.

Held, R. and Hein, A. V. (1958), Adaptation of disarranged hand-eye coordination contingent upon re-afferent stimulation, *Perceptual and Motor Skills* **8**:87–90.

Heron, W. T. (1935), The inheritance of maze learning ability in rats, *J. comp. Psychol.* **19**:77–89.

Herter, K. (1936), Das thermotaktische Optimum bei Nagetieren, ein mendelndes Art und Rassenmerkmal, *Z. vergl. Physiol.* **23**:605–650.

Holst, E. von (1934), Studien ueber die Reflexe und Rhythmen beim Goldfisch (*Carassius auratus*), *Z. vergl. Physiol.* **20**:582–599.

Holst, E. von (1937), Vom Wesen der Ordnung im Zentralnervensystem, *Naturwiss.* **25**:625–631, 641–647.

Holt, K. S. (1961), Growth disturbances, in *Hemiplegic Cerebral Palsy in Children and Adults*. A report of an international study group, Little Club Clinics in Developmental Medicine No. 4, Medical Advisory Committee of the National Spastics Society, pp. 39–53.

Hooker, D. (1952), *The Prenatal Origin of Behavior*. University of Kansas Press, Lawrence, Kansas.

Humphrey, T. (1964), Some correlations between the appearance of human fetal reflexes and the development of the nervous system, in *Progress in Brain Research: Vol. 4, Growth and Maturation of the Brain*. D. P. Purpura and J. P. Schadé (eds.), Elsevier, Amsterdam.

James, W. T. (1941), Morphologic form and its relation to behavior, in *The Genetic and Endocrine Basis for Differences in Form and Behavior*. C. R. Stockard (ed.), Wistar Institute, Philadelphia.

Kohler, I. (1951), Ueber Aufbau und Wandlungen der Wahrnehmungswelt, insbesondere ueber bedingte Empfindungen, *Oest. Akad. Wiss.*, Phil-Hist. Klasse, Sitzungsber., Vol. 227, No. 1.

Krushinskii, L. V. (1962), *Animal Behavior; its Normal and Abnormal Development*. Consultants Bureau, New York.

Küntscher, G. (1934), Die Darstellung des Kraftflusses im Knochen, *Zentralbl. f. Chir.* **61**:2130–2136.

Küntscher, G. (1936), Die Spannungsverteilung am Schenkelhals, *Arch. f. Klin. Chir.* **185**:308–321.

Kuo, Z. Y. (1939), Total pattern or local reflexes? *Psychol. Rev.* **46**:93–122.

Lashley, K. S. (1951), The problem of serial order in behavior, in *Cerebral Mechanisms in Behavior,* L. A. Jeffress (ed.), pp. 112–136. The Hixon Symposium. John Wiley and Sons, New York.

Lasinski, W. (1960), Aeusseres Ohr, in *Primatologia, Handbook of Primatology, Part II, Vol. I, fasc. 5.* H. Hofer, A. H. Schultz, and D. Starck (eds.), Karger, Basel.

Lindsley, D. B. (1957), Psychophysiology and motivation, in *Nebraska Symposium in Motivation.* M. R. Jones (ed.), pp. 44–105. Univ. of Nebraska Press, Lincoln, Nebraska.

Mark, R. F. (1965), Fin movement after regeneration of Neuromuscular connections: an investigation of Myotypic specificity, *Exp. Neurol.* **12**:292–302.

Mayr, E. (1958), Behavior and systematics, in *Behavior and Evolution.* A. Roe and G. G. Simpson (eds.), Yale Univ. Press, New Haven.

Murray, P. D. F. (1936), *Bones; A Study of the Development and Structure of the Vertebrate Skeleton.* The University Press, Cambridge, England.

Nicholas, J. S. (1949), Problems of organization, in *The Chemistry and Physiology of Growth.* A. K. Parpart (ed.), Princeton Univ. Press, Princeton.

Rundquist, E. A. (1933), The inheritance of spontaneous activity in rats, *J. comp. Psychol.* **16**:415–438.

Schotté, O. E. and Butler, E. G. (1944), Phases in regeneration of the urodele limb and their dependence upon the nervous system, *J. exp. Zool.* **97**:95–121.

Schultz, A. H. (1950), Morphological observations on gorillas, in *The Anatomy of the Gorilla, Henry Cushier Raven Memorial,* pp. 227–254. Columbia Univ. Press, New York.

Scott, J. P. and Charles, M. S. (1954), Genetic differences in the behavior of dogs: a case of magnification by thresholds and by habit formation, *J. genet. Psychol.* **84**:175–188.

Searle, L. V. (1949), The organization of hereditary maze-brightness and maze-dullness, *Genet. Psychol. Monogr.* **39**:279–325.

Setterfield, W., Schott, R. G., and Snyder, L. H. (1936), Studies in human inheritance: XV. The bimodality of the threshold curve for the taste of phenylthiocarbamide, *Ohio J. Sci.* **36**:231–235.

Simpson, G. G. (1949), *The Meaning of Evolution: a Study of the History of Life and of its Significance for Man.* Yale Univ. Press, New Haven.

Singer, M. (1947), The nervous system and regeneration of the forelimb of adult triturus. VI. A further study of the importance of nerve number, including quantitative measurements of limb innervation, *J. exp. Zool.* **104**:223–250.

Singer, M. (1959), The influence of nerves on regeneration, in *Regeneration in Vertebrates.* C. S. Thornton (ed.), pp. 59–78. Univ. of Chicago Press, Chicago.

Smith, K. U. and Smith, W. M. (1962), *Perception and Motion; An Analysis of Space-Structured Behavior.* Saunders, Philadelphia.

Sperry, R. W. (1958), Physiological plasticity and brain circuit theory, in *Biological and Biochemical Bases of Behavior.* H. F. Harlow and C. N. Woolsey (eds.), pp. 401–424. Univ. of Wisconsin Press, Madison.

Sperry, R. W. (1963), Chemoaffinity in the orderly growth of nerve fiber patterns and connections. *Proc. Nat. Acad. Sci.* **50**(4):703–710.

Stockard, C. R. (1941) (ed.), *The Genetic and Endocrine Basis for Differences in Form and Behavior.* Wistar Institute, Philadelphia.

Thompson, D'Arcy W. (1942), *On Growth and Form.* (2nd ed.) Cambridge Univ. Press, London.

Thompson, W. R. (1953), The inheritance of behaviour: behavioural differences in fifteen mouse strains, *Canad. J. Psychol.* **7**(4):145–155.

Thornton, C. S. and Steen, T. P. (1962), Eccentric blastema formation in aneurogenic limbs of ambystoma larvae following epidermal cap deviation, *Develop. Biol.* **5**:328–343.

Tryon, R. C. (1940). Genetic differences in maze learning in rats, in *National Society for the Study of Education, The Thirty-ninth Yearbook.* Public School Publ., Bloomington, Illinois.

Tryon, R. C. (1942). Individual differences, in *Comparative Psychology.* F. A. Moss (ed.), Prentice-Hall, Englewood Cliffs, New Jersey.

Weiss, P. A. (1950*a*), An introduction to genetic neurology, in *Genetic Neurology.* P. A. Weiss (ed.), Univ. of Chicago Press, Chicago.

Weiss, P. A. (1950*b*), Experimental analysis of coordination by the disarrangement of central-peripheral relations, *Physiological Mechanisms in Animal Behavior, Symposia of the Society for Experimental Biology* **4**:92–111. Academic Press, New York.

Weiss, P. A. (1965), Specificity in the neurosciences: A report of an NRP work session, chaired by P. A. Weiss, *Neurosciences Research Program Bulletin* **3**(5):1–64.

Weiss, P. A. and Brown, P. F. (1941), Electromyographic studies on recoordination of leg movements in poliomyelitis patients with transposed tendons, *Proc. Soc. exp. Biol.* **48**:284–287.

Weiss, P. A. and Ruch, T. C. (1936), Further observations on the function of supernumerary fingers in man, *Proc. Soc. exp. Biol.* **34**:569–570.

Wiersma, C. A. G. (1931), An experiment on the "resonance theory" of muscular activity, *Arch. Néerl. Physiol.* **16**:337–345.

Windle, W. F. (1950), Reflexes of mammalian embryos and fetuses, in *Genetic Neurology.* P. A. Weiss (ed.), pp. 221–222. Univ. of Chicago Press, Chicago.

Wolff, J. (1870), Ueber die innere Architectur der Knochen und ihre Bedeutung für die Frage vom Knochenwachstum, *Virchow Arch. Path. Anat.* **50**:389–453.

CHAPTER TWO

Morphological correlates

I. INTRODUCTION

Although anatomy is a fascinating subject and its inclusion in a book such as the present one does not require any apologies, there is at the same time the danger of misunderstanding its role here. The anatomical description of man's speech organs does not lead to insight into the origin of language (see Chapter Six) nor does it provide an explanation of man's capacity for language. As biologists we cannot discern meaning or purpose of specific anatomical developments. Survival of the species, increase of efficiency in various respects, or group cohesiveness may very well be among the biasing principles of natural selection. However, any one of these "ends" might conceivably be achieved by an infinity of means. Why a given phylogeny went one particular way instead of any one of the multitude of theoretically possible other ways is in most instances unknown and speculation on this topic is frequently futile.

Anatomy is a descriptive science. The sounds of language are certainly intimately related to the morphology of the vocal tract. Thus, a description of man's vocal tract may account for certain peculiarities of universal features of speech. A discussion of these relationships does not imply knowledge of causality in the course of evolution.

Our approach will be based on comparative studies. We should like to demonstrate morphological peculiarities of man by comparing all speech-relevant structures to homologous ones in Pongidae (that is, the great apes: chimpanzee and gorilla, which are our closest of kin, and orangutan). Whenever available, we shall also make reference to the gibbons, rounding out the picture of the Hominoidea.

A review of the pertinent literature brings to light rather unexpected

33

gaps in our knowledge of primate anatomy. In many instances, a complete comparison is not possible because of lack of data; in other instances, the facts reported are based on dissections of a single specimen so that artifacts of fixation, age, sex, and individual variations are uncontrolled variables. The presentation, however, has been confined to the most outstanding and generally agreed upon facts.

The anatomical discussions lay no claim to completeness and cannot substitute as a text for instruction on the anatomy of speech organs. (Kaplan, 1960 may be used for this purpose.)

II. PERIPHERY

(1) *Face, Lips and Mouth*

Certain characteristics of man's face have a decisive influence upon speech sounds. Comparative anatomy of the facial musculature is therefore relevant to our inquiry. The authoritative work on facial muscles of primates is by Huber (1931). He demonstrated that all of the muscles of the face were phylogenetically derived from two basic muscular mantles which covered the neck and head of the prototype: the *platysma* (shown in Fig. 2.1 with horizontal orientation) and the *sphincter colli profundus* (shown with vertical orientation).

In Fig. 2.2*a* the sphincter colli is almost entirely preserved; some differentiation over the nose and around the muzzle has, however, taken place already. However, the arrangement is much more primitive

FIG. 2.1. Schema of two principal muscles from which facial musculature is derived. Vertical striae, *sphincter colli;* horizontal striae, *platysma.* (After Huber, 1931.)

than in the simians, of whom one New-World example, spider monkey (*Ateles ater*), is given in Fig. 2.2(*b*). A number of distinct muscles that act on the peri-oral region may now be discerned. The musculature in the corner of the mouth in particular (sometimes called the *modiolus*) shows a degree of complexity, absent in the more primitive forms and undergoing further and further differentiation in the higher ones. On the other hand, much of the posterior part of the *sphincter colli* has disappeared.

Numerous distinct schemas of modiolar anatomy have evolved. Among the apes the muscles around the mouth are more distinct than among monkeys. Three basic patterns have been described; one is peculiar to the gibbon family (*Hylobatidae*) and is illustrated in Fig. 2.2*c*. A quite different basic plan has been observed in the facial

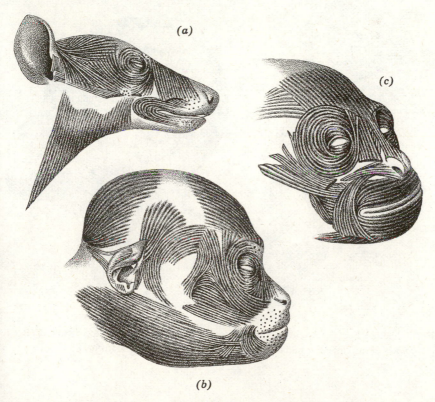

(*a*)

(*c*)

(*b*)

FIG. 2.2. (*a*) Facial muscles of Lemur; (*b*) spider monkey; (*c*) gibbon. (After Huber, 1931.)

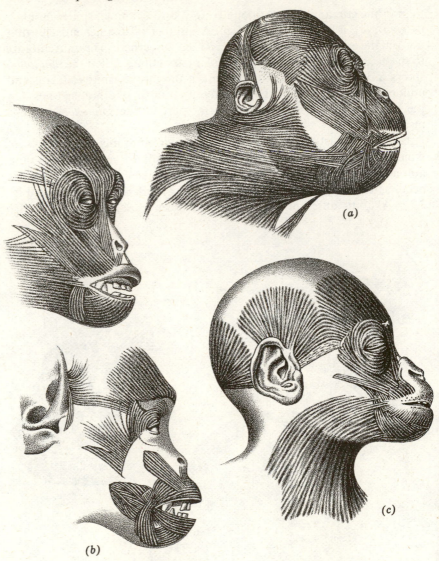

FIG. 2.3. (*a*) Facial muscles of orangutan; (*b*) *above:* chimpanzee, outer layer; (*b*) *below:* chimpanzee, inner layer; (*c*) gorilla infant. (After Huber, 1931.)

anatomy of the orangutan (Fig. 2.3*a*) whereas the chimpanzee and gorilla (Fig. 2.3 *b, c*) show an essential similarity in the schema of the modiolus. According to Lightoller (1925) and Huber (1931), the arrangement of muscles around the corner of the mouth in man is most similar to that in chimpanzee and gorilla. Huber emphasizes, however, that the muscles themselves have undergone further differentiation in man, have grown in shape and anatomical distinctiveness, and show more intricate interlacing than in the great apes (Fig. 2.4). One muscle, *risorius Santorini,* has no undisputed homologue in any subhuman form, and in the muscles of the lips (*orbicularis oris*) the fibers around the oral margin (*pars marginalis*) assume an anatomic prominence not found elsewhere among primates (Duckworth 1910). Clearly, the complexity, size, and number of muscles originating particularly in the corner of the mouth greatly facilitate oral motility in man. The peculiar anatomy of the lips and the shape of the mouth make possible rapid and air tight closure and sudden explosive opening, both being prerequisite for speech articulation.

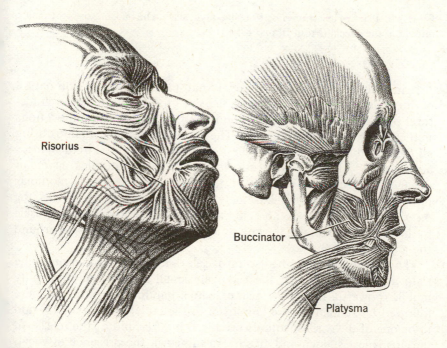

FIG. 2.4. Lower facial muscles in man. *Right:* superficial layers; *Left:* deep layers. (From Braus, 1954.)

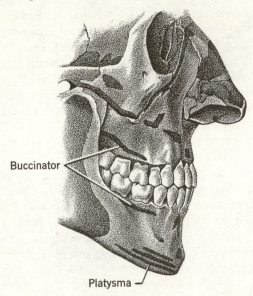

FIG. 2.5. Place of insertion of various facial muscles. The buccinator is the major muscle of the cheek. (From Braus, 1954.)

A most important aspect of facial anatomy is the shape and nature of our cheeks and their relation to the size of the mouth. The architectural peculiarities of man's skull and jaw brought about modifications in the configuration of the cheeks. They cover most of the molars during all comfortable movements of the mouth and under no circumstances are we able to bare all our teeth. In Fig. 2.4 the anatomical layers of the facial muscles are well illustrated. Once the superficial modiolar muscles are removed, the extremely sturdy muscles of the cheeks, the *buccinator*, may be seen, and in Fig. 2.5 the insertion of this muscle in the jaws demonstrates the enclosing nature of the soft tissues around the gap between the jaws.

The topography described so far is relevant to the production of the following speech sounds: the relatively small mouth and the highly mobile, powerful lips allow instantaneous building up of air pressure followed by sudden release employed in the labial stops *p* and *b*, said to be one of the earliest sounds produced by the child. If the release of the lips is less sudden and closure sustained in the presence of vocalization, the sound *m* is produced. The intricate muscular anatomy around and in the corners of the mouth also comes regularly into play during the production of all vowels and labio-dentals such as *f, v, w,* and *wh*.

(2) *Topographical Anatomy of Oral Cavity, Pharynx, and Hypopharynx*

We must now consider the general configuration of the internal organs that are effective during speech and their anatomical relationship to one another.

Man's skull deviates from the skulls of other primates in several respects. Most of the deviations may be attributed to either of two major factors: (1) the increase in volume of the brain and (2) the change in posture and the concomittant shift of the center of gravity of the head. The geometic transformations shown in Fig. 2.6 illustrate these points.

The changes that have taken place affect the entire configuration of the sound-producing structures. Thus the internal geometry of all resonating chambers is altered despite the fact that all bones, muscles, and other soft tissues have homologues among higher primates. Figures 2.7 to 2.11 show some of the alterations, although the exact shape of the tongue and soft palate during lifetime cannot be inferred from these photographs because of fixation artifacts (due particularly to post-mortem shrinkage of interstitial substances). Nevertheless, it is clear that the ratio of height, length, and width of the oral cavity is different

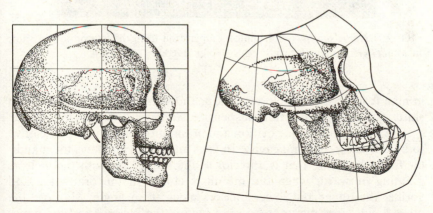

FIG. 2.6. Skulls of man and chimpanzee with coordinates showing the geometric transformations distinguishing the two species. (From Kummer, 1953.) Which of the two coordinate systems is to be drawn with straight lines is an arbitrary decision.

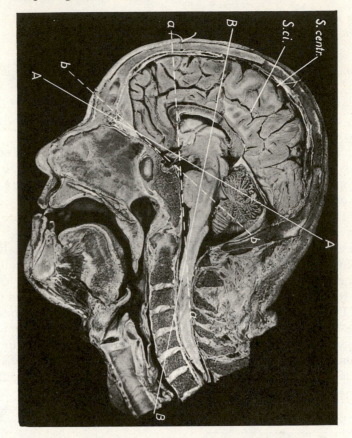

FIG. 2.7. *Homo sapiens* (adult male). Preparation from the anatomical institute in Mainz, Germany. (Reproduced in Hofer, 1965.)*

in man from that of his closest of kin, and there must be concomittant shifts in the relative position, suspension, and attachment of the tongue.

Also interesting is the position and orientation of the incisors relative to tip of tongue and oral cavity. In apes and many monkeys the mandible forms a "shelf" that is anterior to the tongue tip with the incisors pointing outward; when the mouth is closed in the orangutan and gorilla, the upper and lower incisors meet at an angle. Man, on the other hand, gives the impression of having the incisors and the bones

* The cuts for Figures 2.7 through 2.11 were kindly supplied by G. Fischer Verlag, Stuttgart, with the authorization of Prof. H. Hofer, Dr. R. Diepen, and Prof. Dabelow. For explanation of the cross lines in these figures, see Hofer, 1965.

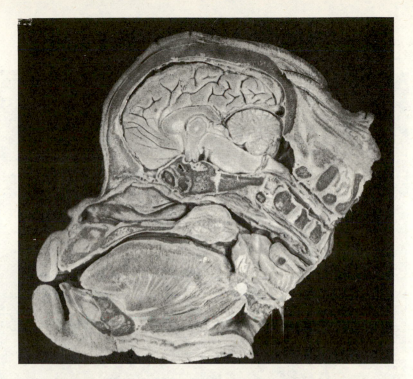

FIG. 2.8. *Pongo pygmaeus* (orangutan), sagittal section of three-year-old animal. (From Hofer, 1965.)*

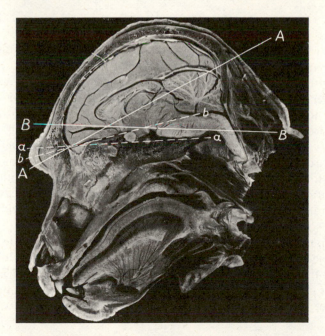

FIG. 2.9. *Macaca mulatta* (rhesus monkey), sagittal section of adult male. (From Hofer, 1965.)*

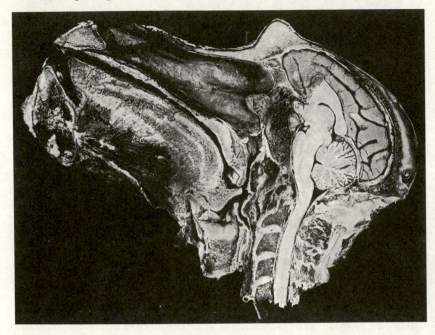

FIG. 2.10. *Papio hamadryas* (baboon), sagittal section of adult male. (From Hofer, 1965.)*

in which they are imbedded pushed into the oral cavity. This flattens out the angle formed by the incisors when the mouth is closed.

According to Schultz (1958), the arch circumscribed by the upper teeth, schematically represented in Fig. 2.12, does not differ basically in man and the other Hominoidea. Nor is the basic plan of the molars and incisors different in any significant way. One deviation in the shape of man's denture is the conspicuous absence of the enlarged canines which are so prominent in most males of most other primate forms. Owing to the great evenness in height and width of all teeth in man, the denture forms an unbroken palisade around the oral cavity. This structural peculiarity is the essential prerequisite for the production of spirant sounds such as *f, v, s, sh, th,* and others.

The position of the epiglottis with respect to the soft palate has been the subject of much discussion in connection with the development of speech. From sagittal sections such as those shown in Figs. 2.7–2.11, we see that in man the epiglottis is located much lower than in most other primates. On the other hand, the epiglottis seems to be in close contact with the soft palate in the lower species and at least in close proximity in the Pongidae. Negus (1929), Kelemen (1938 and 1948), DuBrul (1958), and many others have concluded from this that only man was capable of conducting the glottis-produced sounds through the oral cavity, whereas other primates had the sounds directed through their nasal cavity. Starck and Schneider (1960) have pointed out that these conclusions may not be warranted, and that the basic anatomical facts have not yet been clearly established. The topographical relations become easily disarranged in the process of fixation, and organs often become displaced in the course of anatomical dissections.

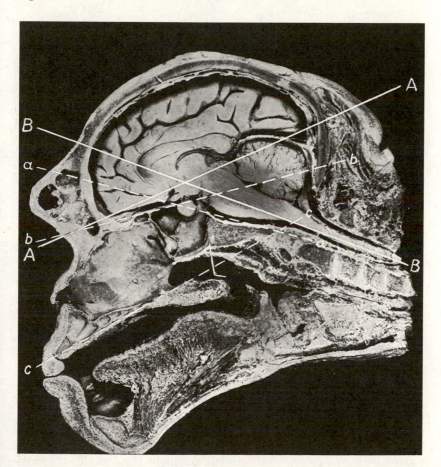

FIG. 2.11. *Pan troglodytes* (chimpanzee), sagittal section of adult femals. (From Hofer, 1965.)*

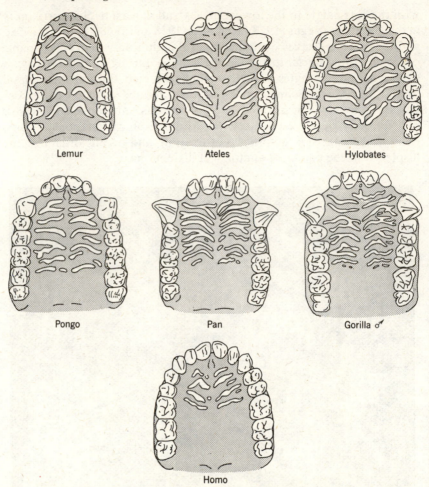

FIG. 2.12. Palates of some primates showing ridges brought to same size. (From Schultz, 1958.)

(3) *Intrinsic Anatomy of the Larynx*

Each species of the Hominoidea has a differently shaped larynx with a great many variations and specializations in the individual mechanisms that are inherent in this intricate apparatus. The most recent survey of all comparative investigations of primate larynges was contributed by Starck and Schneider (1960), who may be consulted for further details. We can only report on a few of the more obviously voice-related differences.

The complex construction and the irregular shape of the larynx make it impossible to find comparable anatomic preparations or diagrams in any literature. Therefore, our pictorial material here is confined to reproducing the few schemata shown in Figs. 2.13 and 2.14, which

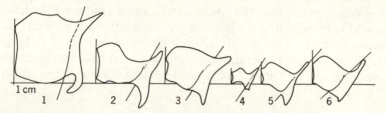

FIG. 2.13. Laryngeal variations: differences in the shape and size of the thyroid cartilage. (1) Gorilla; (2) orangutan; (3) chimpanzee; (4) gibbon; (5) and (6) man, female, and male respectively. (From Stark and Schneider, 1960, due to Kleinschmidt, 1949–1950.)

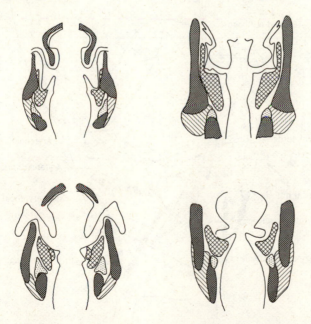

FIG. 2.14. Schematic representation of frontal sections through larynges of apes and man, brought to the same size and showing homology of tissues. *Top left:* orangutan; *top right:* chimpanzee; *bottom left:* gorilla; *bottom right:* man. (After Starck and Schneider, 1960.)

illustrate some of the variability encountered in comparing the voice box of higher primates.

The voice mechanisms of a gibbon were investigated by Némai and Kelemen (1933) among others. The larynx of the gibbon deviates from the basic plan found in the Pongidae and man, thus reflecting its special phylogenetic position. These authors were impressed with the exceptionally well-differentiated system of double vocal cords (homologous to man's true and false cords) as well as with the animal's delicate arytenoid cartilages (for the homologous structure and its function in phonation see Fig. 2.15), which indicate an ability to control and adjust the tension of the cords during phonation. The vocal folds themselves differed markedly in their histological structure from those of other

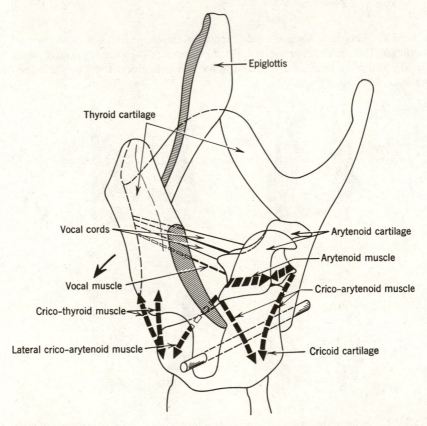

FIG. 2.15. Schematic representation of the human larynx. (From Ranke and Lullies, 1953.)

apes and from man. The two sets of vocal cords explain the peculiar double tones heard in the calls of living gibbons.

The orangutan's larynx was examined by the same authors (Némai and Kelemen, 1929). In their summary, they state that this ape's vocal organ is not capable of producing delicately modulated or controlled sounds. They found the superior structures (*aditus laryngis*) particularly primitive, with a voluminous epiglottis covered by the pendular velum. The arytenoid cartilages were relatively small and most of the cartilaginous material throughout the larynx was more calcified than in man and chimpanzee. Calcification indicates a loss in elasticity of these structures, which should make control of loudness of voice more dependent upon the fluctuating air supply from the lungs. Thus it is probably an impediment in the stabilization of tones. The intrinsic musculature of the larynx was found to be relatively undeveloped and not very strong. The vocal folds themselves were lined with muscle fibers, but the orientation of the fibers was not like that in man.

Kelemen (1948) contributed a histological examination of the chimpanzee's larynx. The chimpanzee also has a double set of vocal folds, but in contrast to both gibbon and man he can articulate each set independently. However, more air pressure is needed to make the false cords vibrate, and so doubletones are heard only after the chimpanzee's vocalization has assumed a certain degree of intensity. The chimpanzee has well-developed aryepiglottic folds which allows him to vocalize not only upon expiration but also upon inspiration, which for man is strenuous and unpleasant. In addition to differences in homologous structures, all apes differ from man in that they have a complex system of air sacs and hollow pouches bulging out from the vocal tract which, according to Kleinschmidt (1938), serve a specialized function during phonation. These structures can be blown up like a balloon, requiring several breaths, perhaps to serve as a reservoir of air supply. The air is expressed from these spaces as in a bagpipe and utilized in phonation (producing a veritable din) without requiring additional respiratory effort.

It is interesting to note that in a certain sense man's vocal apparatus is in several respects simpler than that of the great apes. The geometry of the air spaces and fixed resonance chambers is "streamlined"; there is only one set of functional vocal cords; the vocal cords are mounted in the air tunnel in such a way that, when adducted, they can produce sound only (or primarily) on expiration, instead of allowing both inspiratory and expiratory voice; and the epiglottis has moved so far below the pharynx as to allow the air from the larynx to stream freely

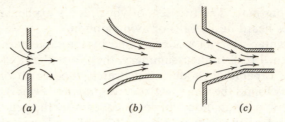

(a)   (b)   (c)

FIG. 2.16. Airflow characteristics in three types of nozzles. The most efficient one is (*b*), and it is analogous to the human larynx. (From Fink and Kirschner, 1959.)

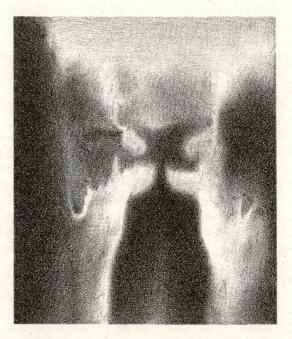

FIG. 2.17. Tomogram of normal larynx while humming at approximately 256 cps. Passage between vocal folds resembles exponential connector of Fig. 2.16*b*. (From Fink and Kirschner, 1959.)

through both nasal and oral cavities. Notice, however, that it is precisely streamlining and simplification which, in many instances in animal morphology, constitute structural specialization for given behavior; for instance, the reduction of toes in the ungulates or appendages in fish. (Of course, this is not the only method of achieving specialization.)

There are two additional structural peculiarities of the larynx which favor phonation in man, but in these instances we are unable to produce any comparative data. First, it has been pointed out by Fink and Kirschner (1959), as shown in Figs 2.16 and 2.17, that

> "the geometrical configuration of the larynx during phonation . . . is such that the internal surfaces are shaped like a nozzle providing optimum flow conditions during respiration. The exponentially curved surfaces constitute a horn functioning as an acoustic transformer between the infra-laryngeal and supra-laryngeal cavities during phonation."

The exponentially curved walls may serve to reduce the high air pressure generated by the lung by accelerating the flow of air with the least loss of energy and the maximum efficiency in excitation of the vibratory organs.

The other structural peculiarity concerns the vocal cords. A study of the articulation of the arytenoid cartilages and the way in which the vocal ligaments and muscles are attached to it (Fig. 2.18) has revealed that the approximation of the vocal folds during phonation causes the vocal muscles to be twisted as shown in Fig. 2.19. Sonesson (1960) hypothesized that this twist contributes to the firmness and tension of the vocal fold during phonation and thus serves to stabilize pitch and volume.

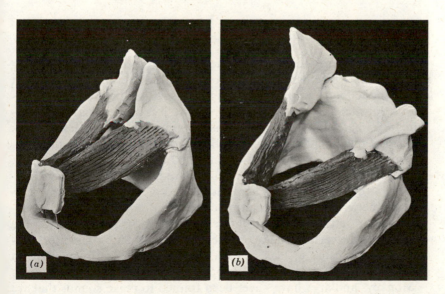

FIG. 2.18. Plasticine model of the glottis. The arytenoid cartilages and the vocal muscles in (a) adducted position; (b) abducted position. (From Sonesson, 1960.)

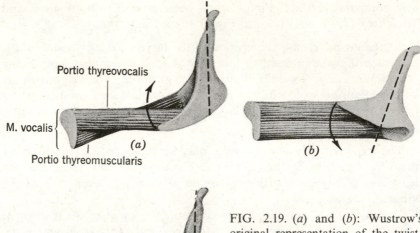

Portio thyreovocalis

M. vocalis {

(a)

Portio thyreomuscularis

(b)

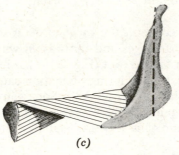

(c)

FIG. 2.19. (*a*) and (*b*): Wustrow's original representation of the twisting of the vocal muscle during adduction; (*c*) Sonesson's modification of the Wustrow hypothesis, based on histological examination of the vocal muscles and their insertion into the arytenoid cartilage. (From Sonesson, 1960.)

(4) *Relationship between Peripheral Anatomy and Speech Sounds*

In Table 2.1 are summarized some of the more commonly occurring speech sounds together with the morphological correlates involved in their production. Anatomical descriptions such as those of the preceding sections tend to be disregarded because it is argued that since sub-human primates have homologous structures, anatomical descriptions tell us nothing about speech. Objections of this kind stem from a misunderstanding of the intention underlying morphological descriptions. The sounds that animals and men make are produced by specific anatomical structures, and thus it would indeed be odd to deny any relationship between the two. Anatomical description, insofar as the purpose is not activated by self-interest alone, ultimately achieves the clarification of certain characteristics of sound-making facilities. Unfortunately, because of lack of data, the description is frequently too poor (the present one included) to obtain this ultimate aim satisfactorily.

Monkeys and apes have never been trained to make sounds that are acoustically similar to human speech sounds (claims to the contrary nothwithstanding). This clearly shows that the phenomenon of struc-

TABLE 2.1.

Groups of Widely Occurring Speech Sounds	Structures Involved in Their Production
p, b, m	Muscular rim in lips; muscles of cheeks; naso-pharyngeal sphincter
f, v, w	Vertical position of incisors; reduced canines; muscles of lips
t, d, n	Position of teeth and alveolar ridge
k, g	Bulging of tongue with ability to raise back
l, r	Blade of tongue with great facility for changing shape of its cross section
Vowels	Muscles in corner of mouth; small mouth; twisting of vocal folds in adducted position

tural homology is irrelevant to our problem. Apparently, there are two essential factors in determining sound-making capacities: (1) the nature of the general structural configuration, including the patterning of geometrical spaces in the vocal tract and the range of movements of articulators; and (2) the physiology of innervation and patterning of motor coordination. (Analogous arguments could be offered for the sensory end of language, but since this aspect has not been treated elsewhere in this book, its discussion is not elaborated here.)

Chapter seven discusses the case studies of children who, for various reasons, have severe articulatory deficiencies. However, these deficiencies need not impair capacity of the children for language acquisition. Certainly, this emphasizes the primary importance of the brain as opposed to peripheral phenomena in the development of language. Furthermore, adult patients with oral pathology [for example, amputation of the tip of the tongue (Brodnitz, 1960), harelip or cleft palate] manage nevertheless to produce sounds that are fair approximations to those of normal speech, thus illustrating the same point. This ability contrasts markedly with that of apes with normal oral configurations and good homologies in structure. Their inability to approximate human sounds would, again, clearly indicate neurophysiological differences that are primary to the anatomical ones.

These arguments are sound, but we must remember that they apply to contemporary, modern creatures. If we look at the development of the individual today, we see an extremely efficient organism which can continue to function competitively even in the face of various handicaps. It is as if the machinery as a whole were put together so well that certain species-specific behavior patterns persist in an individual even if certain supporting or coordinated mechanisms are destroyed or have failed to develop. It also seems likely that there is a hierarchy of importance in the various mechanisms that must work together in the production of speech. Brain function appears to be more basic than peripheral function, and if the former is within normal limits although the latter is not, language can be established more easily than if the reverse holds true.

From the point of view of phylogenetic history, a different sort of argument is in order. During evolution behavior and structure are both in *statu nascendi*. The particular type of behavior and structure that we see in contemporary forms need not have developed simultaneously—one development may have preceded the other. However, in the course of phylogenetic history the various developments exert biasing influences upon one another—the development of structure may affect the direction of behavioral developments and vice versa—and therefore it is not unreasonable to asume that subtle relationships may exist between many aspects of structure and behavior. Of course, it would be objectionable to claim that man's vocal tract has the shape it has "to enable him to make the speech sounds that he makes," just as it is objectionable to make parallel claims with regard to eating, drinking, or breathing. In short, we cannot deny that there is a relationship between the morphology of the vocal tract and the acoustics of speech, and that this relationship has had a long history. There may also have been developmental influences between the two throughout the past, but we have no data to indicate the cause and the effect in this relationship.

III. THE CENTRAL NERVOUS SYSTEM

(1) *Functional Significance of Form in the Central Nervous System*

Thus far, we were able to highlight the structural peculiarities of man's vocal tract by direct comparison with lower primates. In our discussions of the brain we have to depart from this method, first because not enough is known about the anatomical detail of many primate species, and second, because of our ignorance about the physiological significance of morphological variations in the brain. In gross appearance, man's brain is markedly different from that of any other animal, but this general observation cannot easily be related to such a specific behavioral trait as speech. The most outstanding difference is its relative size, as is well-known. Other aspects have been shown by von Bonin (1950), Bok (1959), and others to be direct consequences of the increase in size and weight of the organism. For instance, our brain is more deeply and extensively fissurated than that of most lower forms. This may be explained by the fact that the average thickness of the cerebral cortex remains fairly constant in primates (in absolute measurements!), whereas the total volume of the cortex increases roughly as the cube of the weight of the brain. This proportion can only remain constant at the expense of a smooth surface. Probably, there is a morphogenetic interdependence between the amount of subcortical and cortical brain tissue. With heavy brains, extensive folding on the surface is a developmental necessity.

In other respects, the human brain shows differences which are manifestations of general primate trends. For instance, the cell density of the cortex decreases with phylogenetic ascent, whereas the length and quantity of dendrites increases. This brings about an increase in the axodendritic synapses, an increase in the distance between cell bodies, and a presumable decrease in mutual electrotonic influence.

A parallel trend with a phylogentic history is the appearance of more and more histologically differentiated areas of the cerebral cortex. Man constitutes a high stage in these developments. We must stress, however, that in our search for specializations which are relevant to speech and language, none of these trends is heuristically useful because each is also present, to a greater or lesser extent, in subhuman forms. But it is not at all certain that the types of communication prevalent among such forms may in any sense be regarded as primitive stages of language development. Thus we are forced to look for more specific modifications in man.

Everyone knows that it takes a human brain to acquire a natural language such as English, and this is true of language production as well as comprehension. What is it in the brain that makes language possible? Is it process, structure, or both? *Structure* in connection with the brain has quite a different significance than *structure* in connection with the skeleton or the periphery in general. In the latter, we can observe form and sometimes intuitively relate it to function. Furthermore, peripheral structures have a certain degree of functional autonomy; in the mature individual, they may often be removed without affecting other structures, and they seem to function independently from the rest of the organism (within definite limits!).

In the brain, on the other hand, there are no independent parts or autonomous accessories. In vertebrates, and probably many higher invertebrates, the entire brain is a functionally integrated system with constant, spontaneous, and inherent activities that involve all healthy structures. Electrically "silent" central nervous tissue is abnormal tissue.

In view of this, we cannot expect to find any kind of new protuberance or morphological innovation which deals exclusively with a particular behavior. Any modification on the brain is a modification on the entire brain. Thus species-specific behavior never has a confined, unique, neuroanatomic correlate, but always and necessarily must involve reorganization of processes that affect most of the central nervous system. Yet, the search for correlates in specific regions is not as futile as it may seem after these remarks.

Even though much of the brain of animals might be involved with the task of controlling posture, with ambulation, or with running down prey, it is possible to find loci from where interference by destruction or stimulation with a given type of behavior is maximal. By the same token, it is possible to find loci where stimulation may initiate a complex series of behavioral acts, such as grooming behavior, threat posture, eating movements, etc. Even in these instances the nervous activity is never confined to these loci, but stimulation may either serve as trigger for an automatically running-off series of events throughout the brain or simply constitute an obstacle in the way of proper transmission and circulation of impulses.

With these words of caution, we may proceed with a topographical description of structures in the nervous system that seem to be relevant to speech and language. In this chapter, our remarks refer primarily to the state of affairs in the mature individual.

(2) *The Cortex*

(*a*) *Histological Maps.* A number of aspects of the human cortex have been studied, such as the architecture of its vasculature, the structure of the interconnecting fibers, the density, distribution, nature and stratification of cellular components. Only some of these aspects have been examined to any great extent in subhuman primates. The outlook is further clouded by the fact that the histological descriptions—even in man's cortex—are, in many instances, subjective, resulting in considerable divergence between workers, as first pointed out by Lashley and Clark (1946). Von Bonin and Bailey (1961) have held to strictly objective, descriptive criteria. They have contributed cytoarchitectonic maps of the cortex of several primates, including the macaque, chimpanzee, and man. Figure 2.20 reproduces diagrammatically the most important area differentiations.

The physiological and behavioral significance of the histological differences between areas is still unknown. There are only a few histo-

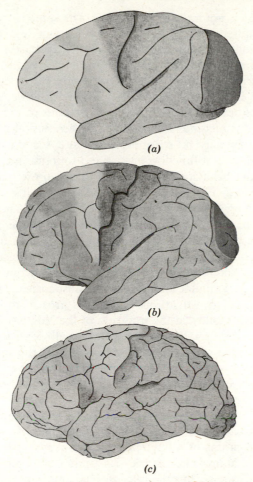

FIG. 2.20. (*a*) histological maps of cortices of Macaca mulatta. (*b*) Pan troglo-dytes (chimpanzee). (*c*) man; all brought to same size. (After von Bonin and Bailey, 1961.)

logically and topographically unique areas to which we can assign corresponding unique motor or sensory roles. For instance, it is universally agreed that the striate area of the occipital pole is the area of primary visual projection. There is no other area in the human cortex which is both histologically distinct *and* unequivocally and uniquely related to one and only one motor or sensory function. The anterior margin of the central sulcus is predominantly related to motor events; the posterior margin is predominantly related to sensory events, but this distribution is not mutually exclusive. The same is true of the other histologically differentiated areas. Never is it possible to assign to them a single function. Conversely, if we draw a map based on our beliefs of functional importance, we find that the "functional" maps are not coterminous with the histological maps, and that a "single function area," in most instances, extends into diverse histological areas.

These difficulties may be due to either or both of the following two sources: first, our methods for discovering behavioral function of any part of the brain may be inappropriate; and second, we cannot be certain that behavioral function has a fixed topographical place on the cortex—that any behavior is elaborated in a definite part.

A comparison of Fig. 2.20 with Fig. 2.22 makes it clear that speech areas are made up of quite different cytoarchitectonic fields. On super-ficial inspection, Broca's area might have some unique characteristics, but even here a closer examination casts doubt on this. In this area, the cortex, according to von Bonin and Bailey (1961), consists of very large cells in the third and fifth cortical layers, and it is surrounded and partly overlapped by dysgranular and homotypical isocortex. The most pains-taking histological investigations of Broca's area were carried out by Kreht (1936), who followed the tradition of the Vogts with their careful description of every detail and variation in cell density and size. Von Bonin's and Bailey's observations were essentially the same as Kreht's, but the latter also occasionally found larger cells in layer VI. The fourth layer in all cortices examined was noticeably sparsely populated with cells. Kreht observed that Broca's area always tended to be different from surrounding areas, but that the cytoarchitecture itself in this region varied greatly from brain to brain. Kreht also investigated homo-logous areas in brains of a few apes and monkeys and found that the cortices of these animals had areas with similar cytoarchitecture as that found in Broca's area. Thus the microscopic anatomical detail does not contribute to our search for histological correlates of speech and lan-guage.

(*b*) *Behavioral Maps.* The mapping of speech areas is based on ob-servations of behavioral derangement in the presence of (α) internal brain disease; (β) of penetrating head injuries (trauma); (γ) surgical excision; and (δ) observations of behavior during electrical stimulation of the exposed cortex during surgery.

(α). From a heuristic point of view, the first type of observation is the most unsatisfactory one because of the many cases in which the exact location of the lesion is only a matter of speculation, and even if these brains should become available for postmortem examination the patient

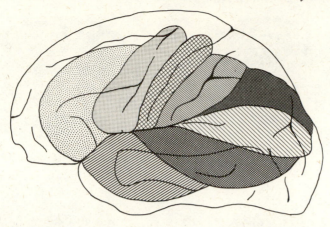

FIG. 2.21. Territory of the middle cerebral artery; fields correspond to various branches. (From Ajuriaguerra and Hécaen, 1949, 1st ed.)

may have died of more widespread disease and destruction in the brain than the lesion which first caused aphasia.

Nevertheless, the vast majority of aphasia patients owe their speech disturbance to internal brain disease, particularly cerebro-vascular accidents, commonly known as strokes. Tissue is destroyed or function is temporarily interrupted because of insufficient blood supply caused by a clot in or rupture of a vessel. The artery most often implicated is the left middle cerebral artery, which runs along the sylvian fissure and sends out branches through the entire lateral face of the hemisphere, as shown in Fig. 2.21. It is precisely because of the vast territorial extent of this artery that behavioral derangement resulting from interference with it gives us the least specific information concerning the localization of the speech and language function. Even when the vascular insufficiency is demonstrated by x-rays of the vascular tree, the exact location of the actual dysfunction remains largely a matter of speculation.

(β). Inferences from traumatic lesions have been drawn repeatedly (Goldstein, 1942, Luria, 1947, Conrad, 1954, Russell and Espir, 1961), resulting in various maps. The extent of the lesion can be determined more accurately in these cases than in internal brain disease, but the fact is frequently overlooked that trauma also causes secondary pathology (particularly hemorrhage and edema) which may have deleterious effects on tissue far beyond the visibly destroyed areas. In Fig. 2.22 the centers of penetrating head injuries to the left hemisphere are shown

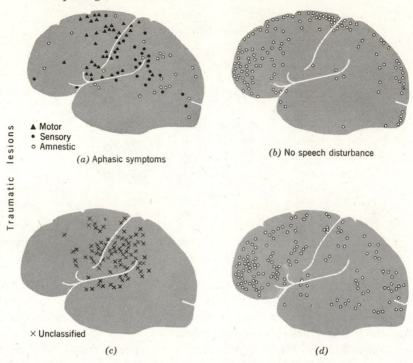

Traumatic lesions

▲ Motor
• Sensory
○ Amnestic

(a) Aphasic symptoms

(b) No speech disturbance

× Unclassified

(c)

(d)

FIG. 2-22. Traumatic lesions to left hemisphere that have and have not caused aphasic symptoms. Each symbol represents roughly the center of the lesion. It must be kept in mind that the extent of the lesion was not indicated in the sources, although it may be a very important variable. Points shown in these diagrams were redrawn from the originals and projected on a uniform hemisphere schema, a process which unfortunately makes some distortion of the originally published data inevitable. [(*a*) and (*b*) after Conrad, 1954; (*c*) and (*d*) after Russell and Espir, 1961.]

with indications of those injuries which caused lasting aphasia and which did not. The subjects were veterans of World War II. To make Russell's and Espir's material comparable to Conrad's, the diagrams had to be redrawn, and in this process some distortions are inevitable because neither the original drawings nor the present mode of representation can be read unequivocally. The distortions, however, occur primarily around the outer margins of these diagrams and are due to the shortened perspective of the curved surfaces. Nevertheless, it is clear that the resulting maps are not identical although correspondences exist.

In Conrad's material, motor-speech deficits predominate on both margins of the central sulcus and extend frontally; linguistic sensory and amnestic deficits predominate in the parieto-occipital areas, but there are a few cases which do not conform to this distribution. Russell and Espir do not indicate the nature of the language deficit in their original data. In both cases, we cannot fail to be impressed with the somewhat random-appearing scatter of lesions and with the overlap between aphasia-producing and aphasia-free lesions. The most striking findings of these recent studies are that there seems to be no more than a statistical relationship between Broca's area and the resultant deficit.

(γ). Surgical excision of limited cortical tissue is a fairly common occurrence in clinical neurology. Penfield and Roberts (1959) have described the outcome of such operations performed on 273 patients who had suffered from focal cerebral seizures caused by earlier injuries, infection, or anoxia of the brain. Over the years, examples of ablations on every part of the cortex have been accumulated, although Broca's area was only excised once and this happened to be a patient with an atypical early history. In all of this material from which tumor cases are excluded, there are very few cases in which the removal of cortical tissue resulted in more than a temporary dysphasic condition, with language function restored within a matter of days or weeks. Many operations in the critical areas had no language disturbance. This is puzzling in view of the consequences of traumatic lesions and cerebro-vascular accidents. We might have expected that in many more cases permanent aphasia had resulted. The explanation must be due to some important differences between the surgical cases and the others. First, patients who come to surgery have had histories of years of abnormally functioning brains manifested by recurrent and uncontrollable seizures. We cannot be sure of the effect that this might have had on localization (using the word here in its loosest terminology). Penfield and Roberts believe that the epileptogenic focus is not the location of the lesion but is adjacent to it. The lesion itself constitutes an irritant which induces abnormal function in structurally healthy tissue. Thus, there may be a systematic "bias" in the localization of function in these brains. The tissue that is surgically removed probably had not been participating in speech function for some years. However, this explanation begs the basic question: why does sudden destruction of tissue interfere irrevocably with language in adult patients, whereas language often remains essentially unaffected in cases where similar destructions were preceded by years (sometimes a lifetime) of sporadic, short, physiological inter-ferences?

The surgical cases do not differ only from traumatic and vascular lesions in terms of abnormal function. The surgical lesion is always

different from the other lesions; it is usually shallower, there is no uncontrolled bleeding, it does not follow the distribution of the vascular
tree, and the healing process is histologically and morphologically different from the events that follow cerebro-vascular accidents and
trauma. With this many differences between the surgical cases and
other cases, it is fair to say that surgical lesions are not commensurable,
and the difference in effects cannot yet be interpreted. However, there
is one lesson we may learn from cortical excisions. The narrow localization theory which holds that engrams for words or syntactic rules are
stored in certain aggregates of cells cannot be in accord with the clinical
facts.

(δ) Electrical stimulation of the exposed cortex during neuro-
surgery is another source of evidence for cortical function-maps. It is
again Penfield and Roberts who have systematized their findings. For
instance, they have published (1959) a cortical map showing points of
stimulation affecting motor speech. From this map it is difficult to
discern any sharply circumscribed area of functional representation.
Roughly, the stimulation map corroborates the impression gained from
the maps of Fig. 2.22 although it does seem as if there were at least
statistical discrepancies between the two types of source-material for
such maps. Penfield and Roberts state that not every stimulation in the
critical area interferes with speech. However, they have not published
maps of the ineffectual stimulations.

If we survey the collected evidence, we cannot fail to be puzzled. Why
do patients who had normal brain function up to the time of catastrophe
sometimes have aphasia from lesions in relatively uncharted areas,
whereas Penfield's patients who had abnormal brain function have
aphasic symptoms when stimulated in the "orthodox" speech areas?
Why is there, in Penfield's patients, such a relatively poor correlation
between the stimulation points (where transient aphasia can be produced) and the cortical excisions in the vicinity of the same areas?
Could this discrepancy be an artifact resulting from the indiscriminate
pooling of cases for the construction of the map? If this were so, we
would have to conclude that there is a great deal of individual variation.

Penfield and Roberts have also published distribution of stimulation
points arranged according to the type of aphasic symptom produced:
complete arrest of speech, hesitation and slurring, distortion and repetition of words, confusion of numbers while counting, and inability to
name objects with retained ability to speak. There is no evidence, however, that any one of these symptoms is correlated with any sharply
delimited cortical area.

Direct stimulation of the cortex may sometimes do more than simply interfere with ongoing speech. It may also elicit fractions of the motor speech act. Penfield and Roberts show a region in which stimulation would occasionally cause the patient to vocalize, namely, either margin of the left (and also the right) Rolandic fissure. The sounds are described as a vowel, and the vocalization will last for the duration of the stimulation; if the patient runs out of breath, he will quickly inhale and continue. The patient is usually aware that he is making sounds, but he is unable to bring this under voluntary control. Besides voicing, pursing of the lips and movements of tongue and jaw may be observed. These movements are not caused by random contraction of one or the other muscle but are well-integrated components such as might enter into chewing, speaking, or swallowing activities.

Interesting as the stimulation experiments are, their relevance to our understanding of the speech mechanism is only limited. Stimulation is a thoroughly abnormal interference with brain function; here nervous activity is initiated on the surface of the cortex from a single anatomic location. In the normal state, however, neuronal activity for speech may consist of modulation of ongoing activity in various parts of the cerebrum, and the modulation is probably initiated by deep structures, starting with ascending impulses that are projected against wide parts of the left parietal and frontal cortex.

(c) *Summary: Language and Cortex.* The discussion leads us to the following conclusions.

Cortical maps of language disorders vary, depending to some extent on the mapping method and on the types of lesions adduced as basic source material.

There is no evidence for an "absolute" language area, but the language function may be localized in statistical terms. Although there is no one area which is necessarily, and exclusively involved in language disturbances in all individuals, there are some regions which are very frequently so involved and other regions which are never involved in either speech or language.

Lesions on either margin of the left Rolandic fissure and convolutions anterior to it frequently interfere with speech production. Comprehension of language is primarily interrupted through lesions in the left parietal lobe and the rostral aspects of the temporal lobe (Wernicke's area).

There is no clear-cut evidence that Broca's area is more specifically related to speech than areas adjacent to it.

The "language maps," established on a statistical basis, are not histologically homogeneous. There is no cytoarchitectural peculiarity of the cortical areas involved in language.

Broca's area consists of large cells in the third and fifth cortical layer, but it is doubtful that this is relevant to language.

The histological maps of cerebral cortices of subhuman primates have somewhat different lines of demarcation than man. This is true of cortical areas which in man have relevance to language; it is also true of Broca's area. The cytoarchitecture of Broca's area is also found in some roughly homologous areas in the cortices of some subhuman primates.

It would be circular or meaningless to state that only man has a cortical speech area, because cortical language maps are based on observation of behavior. We cannot observe language interference in an animal that does not speak. Such an animal, by definition, lacks speech areas.

(3) *Subcortical Structures*

Traditionally, all intellectual functions including speech and language have been thought to be located in the cerebral cortex, and more speculations have been directed to this thin sheet of tissue than toward any other cerebral component. However, there are many other structures that are demonstrably connected with the cortex and with each other (often only by circuitous routes). Every structure of the brain is physiologically active and at least some of the structures have been hypothesized to play a part in the same intellectual functions that are more frequently imputed to the cortex. These speculations have been going on for over a generation. As an example, we may cite Campion and Elliot-Smith (1934) who proposed that thought consisted of cortico-thalamic circulation of impulses. Penfield has suggested the existence of a centrencephalic integrating system, which he has defined as that central system within the brain stem which is responsible for integration of varied specific functions from different parts of the hemispheres. Occasionally, he has defined it even more loosely as that system which includes all those areas of subcortical gray matter, together with their connecting tracts, serving the purpose of intra- and interhemispheral integration. This formulation, as it stands, would include all gray matter beneath the cortex. It reflects our lack of knowledge regarding the cognitive functions of the subcortical ganglia, a state of affairs for which we can hardly hold Penfield responsible. Recently, Penfield has attributed a major role in the execution of speech to a certain part of the centrencephalic system. "It is proposed," he writes (Penfield and Roberts, 1959, p. 207) "as a *speech hypothesis,* that the function of all three cortical speech areas (that is, Broca's, Wernicke's, and the supplementary motor speech area) in man are coordinated by projections of each to parts of the thalamus, and that by means of these circuits, the elaboration of speech is somehow carried out." Penfield finds evidence for this supposition (*a*) in the fact that the superficial excisions performed by him do not cause permanent aphasia, whereas deep trauma and cerebro-vascular accidents do cause aphasia, both as a rule affecting subcortical structures; and (*b*) in the demonstration of fiber tracts running from the so-called speech areas to part of the thalamus. It is well to bear in mind, however, that it has never been demonstrated that all lesions causing irreversible language disorders interrupt those particular cortico-thalamic connections, and the anatomical demonstration of such connections lose some of their language-specific interest seeing that most parts of the cortex are connected to subcortical centers.

The exact cortico-thalamic correspondences in man are not fully known (Feremutsch, 1963; Clark, 1932; Walker, 1938). Our conceptions are based on extrapolations from research on monkeys and apes. According to the most recent and reliable investigations the latero-ventral nucleus of the thalamus sends fibers into those cortical sectors which are most clearly involved with motor speech (together with other motor functions). The temporo-parietal regions of the cortex which are implicated in nonmotor aspects of language are connected by fibers to the latero-posterior nucleus of the thalamus and the pulvinar (see Fig. 2.23).

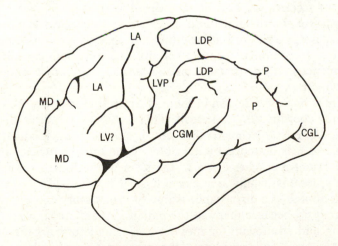

FIG. 2.23. Cortical projections of thalamic nuclei. LV: pars ventralis; LVP: pars ventralis posterior; LA: pars principalis; LDP: pars dorsalis posterior; MD: nucleus medio dorsalis; P: pulvinar; CGM: corpus geniculatum medialis; CGL: corpus geniculatum laterale. (From Feremutsch, 1963.)

Some indications suggest that several other subcortical structures are involved in language and speech. Hartmann-v.Monakow (1965) and Hartmann-v.Monakow and Lenneberg (in preparation) have studied a series of patients with speech and language disorders resulting from surgical diencephalic lesions made in attempts to cure parkinsonism. Some of these patients suffered disorders of expression that were similar to cortically produced motor aphasias. Dr. E. M. Housepian (personal communication) has observed a pure jargon aphasia quite frequently, resulting from either pallidotomy or thalamotomy. These symptoms may last for several weeks before they clear up, although permanent sequelae have been observed in the Hartmann-v.Monakow series. One case of permanent, total language arrest has come to the author's attention through the courtesy of Dr. F. Ervin, and similar cases have also been encountered by other neurosurgeons. Van Buren (1963) has reported "aphasoid" disturbances due to stimulation in the head of the caudate nucleus. He has interpreted the symptom as an arrest of the impulse to speak. These disorders are independent from any cortical lesions, and most of them cannot be predicted on the grounds of cerebral dominance. In Housepian's opinion, some may be due to disruptions in the dorso-lateral thalamic nuclei.

Motor speech disorders may result from either stimulation or lesion of the ventro-lateral nucleus of the thalamus (Guiot et al., 1961, and Housepian, personal communication). The most common symptom is either an acceleration or a slowing down of the rate of speech.

Surgery of the thalamus and its electrophysiological exploration in man has not yet progressed far enough to give us a rounded picture of its precise role in the perception and production of language. However, the evidence is strong that speech and language are not confined to the cerebral cortex.

There is one other region in the mid-brain that may also be involved in motor coordination of speech. This is the gray matter that either surrounds or is adjacent to the ventral side of the aqueduct. On the rostral end it is bounded by the floor of the third ventricle, and in its caudal extent it reaches down to the level of the fourth ventricle. Apparently, lesions in this area cause dysarthria in children more easily than in adults. The disturbance is one of articulatory coordination and not paralysis, because many of the patients so afflicted have no trouble chewing and swallowing or moving the articulatory organs, but they cannot control and coordinate the muscles to make them subserve speech. It is conceivable that a congenital deformity in this region may result in developmental anarthria such as described by Lenneberg

(1962). Perception of language is not involved in these cases, and none of the typical aphasic symptoms is present. Children may acquire a complete understanding of language without ever having been able to produce intelligible words.

The peri-aqueductal gray matter is the anatomical locus of neuro-physiological activity which, in many mammals, regulates coordination of vocalization and facial movements. Thus, there is anatomical homology and, in a sense, physiological homology as well. But the behavioral product is species-specific in each case. Lesions may interfere with coordination for mewing in cats, barking in dogs, and speech-sound-making in man.

The relationship between peri-aqueductal gray matter and vocalization has been known for more than twenty years, but not much attention has been paid to it. As far as I know, the first paper on the subject is due to Bailey and Davis (1942). They placed electrolytic lesions from the aqueduct in a number of cats. If the lesions were small, wild and emotional behavior was observed, including vigorous mewing and hissing; this would last about two days and then subside or in some cases result in extraordinary quietness.

These first reports were followed by further and more precise experimental work (Kelly, Beaton, and Magoun, 1946), again using cats. These authors found that destruction of peri-aqueductal gray matter and adjacent tegmentum beneath the superior colliculi abolished or greatly reduced facio-vocal behavior. They found upon careful examination of the subjects that the deficit was specific to vocalization; they called it pure mutism, perhaps to distinguish it from akinetic mutism, which is due to hypothalamic lesions and is primarily a syndrome of apathy and disinterest. Purring was the only sound that was preserved after peri-aqueductal lesions. More recently, Skultety (1961) reported on similar experiments on dogs with the conclusion that, in order to produce mutism in dogs through peri-aqueductal lesions, "a complete cross-sectional damage of the structure must be accomplished at a level beneath the superior colliculi."

In the absense of experiments on man, we must base our extrapolations on clinical experience. Bailey, Buchanan, and Bucy (1939) described tumors of the lining of the upper fourth ventricle (ependymomas), which is a relatively common neoplasm in children, to be manifested by dysarthria and oculo-motor nerve disturbance. The impact of this evidence is that the mid-brain contains a fairly narrowly circumscribed locus which is of particular importance in motor coordination of speech.

(4) *Lateralization*

The most dramatic difference between the human brain and that of any other vertebrate is the appearance of hemispheric dominance or language specialization. Only in man do we find a behavioral function relatively clearly localized in just one of the two hemispheres.

The phenomenon of laterality affects not only language but also, as is well-known, hand preference (and to some extent also preference in the use of eye, ear, and foot). Although the lateralization of language function cannot be traced phylogenetically for obvious reasons, that of limb-preference could be, at least theoretically. In apes and monkeys and even in some carnivores, it is common that an individual prefers one side of his extremities for a given behavior, but the distribution between right and left preference throughout the species appears to be random. Nor have cortical correlates been discovered for these individual preferences. It has been said of apes, for instance, that either of their hemispheres seems to function like man's right hemisphere; that is, the deficits that result from experimental lesions on either side of a monkey's brain bear similarities to the clinical deficits observed in man following right-hemispheric lesions.

In man, there are even asymmetries of a strictly structural nature, recently reviewed by v. Bonin (1962). They are not very marked and are revealed only through statistics, and their relevance to the asymmetry in function is entirely unknown. The individual measurements need not concern us, but the left hemisphere on almost all quantitative counts yields higher values than the right one.

We have said that normally all parts of the brain interact. If language is primarily localized in the left hemisphere, we might ask what the role of the right hemisphere is with regard to speech and language. Even in the adult individual, where localization is more pronounced than in infancy, the right hemisphere may have some, though lesser, functions in language. Macdonald Critchley (1962) suggests that lesions in the right hemisphere may be followed by any one or more of the following deficits: difficulty with articulation, impairment of creative literary work, hesitations, difficulty in finding words, and difficulty in learning new linguistic material. The common denominator of these symptoms might be called verbal aspects of generally lowered intellectual efficiency. At any rate, there seem to be some language functions that are "reserved" to the right hemisphere.

Lesions in man's left hemisphere, on the other hand, are conspicuous for their interference with verbal activity. Yet they are statistically less likely (Milner, 1962) (Weinstein, 1962) to interefere with general, nonverbal perceptual and cognitive functions than similar lesions in the right hemisphere, particularly in the temporal lobes. The lateralization of function is not present at birth and may be influenced by lesions and disease suffered in early childhood (Chapter four). It is interesting that the corpus callosum, the heavy strand of fiber tracts which most immediately connect the cortices of the two hemispheres, is not essential for the acquisition of speech. Several cases of congenital agenesis of the corpus callosum have been reported in the literature, and it is clear that this deformity need not result in language learning difficulties. It is not known whether it prevents the establishment of cerebral lateralization. (For the relationship between handedness and speech lateralization, see Chapter four.)

(5) *Relative Size of the Brain*

There has been much discussion about man's relatively large brain and its specific relationship to language. Although the thesis of this book would be much strengthened if we could demonstrate a necessary and sufficient connection between these typically human structural and behavioral developments, a closer examination of the various aspects of brain size reveals several unsolved problems.

First, there are problems of measurement. The relevance of average body weight in relation to brain weight is not obvious. For instance, the variance of body weights is much greater than that of brain weights. Even in a single, mature individual, the body weight may fluctuate considerably, whereas the brain weight tends to be quite constant. When different species are compared, additional problems emerge. The weight and volume of the body may vary with density of tissues (especially bones), and this can interfere with the commensurability of the brain-weight/body-weight ratios. For some animals it is advantageous to carry around a great deal of dead or energy-storing tissue, whereas others must travel as lightly as possible. Starck (1965) who has reviewed the recent literature on the encephalization problem has expressed similar criticisms and suggests that intra-cerebral proportions of tissues might provide more important and interesting quotients for taxonomic purposes than the brain-weight/body-weight ratio.

It may also be well to remember that data may be plotted in many different ways. The direct comparison of measurements may often obscure lawful relationships, particularly when these are nonlinear. Dodgson (1962), for instance, has plotted brain-weight/body-weight relationships on double-logarithmic scales (Fig. 2.24) in which an

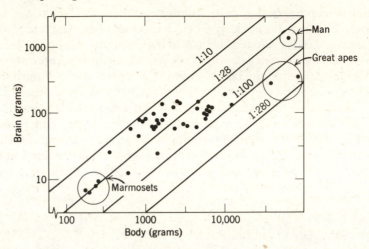

FIG. 2.24. Weight ratios of brain and body of selected primates. (After Dodgson, 1962.)

allometric connection seems to emerge (cf. Chapter six) between brain and body weights that holds for many primates including man. According to this representation, it would seem as if man had kept up with a trend common for the entire order, whereas the great apes were the deviants. However, we should not be so misled by this graph to think that there is nothing peculiar about the dimensions of man's brain. It is of an extraordinary size and is quite obviously capable of functions that differ qualitatively and quantitatively from that of other animals.

A further reason why a simple comparison of a few selected weights is not very revealing is due to the changing proportions of organ weights, including the brain, through growth and development (for details, see Chapter four). The brain-body weight ratios are, for all mammals, different at birth than in maturity. Pertinent data for the primate order have been collected by Schultz (1941) who has shown that it is possible to match a quotient that is typical for mature man by a similar quotient of a subhuman primate but at a more primitive stage of development. Thus the growth histories peculiar to a species are more interesting than the comparison of any single absolute measurement. The growth history of the human brain is quite different from that of other primates.

A second realm of problems concerns the interpretation of the significance of relative and absolute increase in brain size. Man does not only differ from animals in his capacity for language but also in his general cognitive capacities. It may well be that the large-sized brain and the absolute increase in cell number and axodendritic density have increased man's psychological storage capacity, the capacity for simultaneous processing of input and output, and the combinatorial possibilities among specific processes. In modern man, a failure of brain growth, such as in microcephaly, apparently results in lowering of these functions if the condition is severe enough. But it is interesting that language function is comparatively independent (in modern man—the argument must not be extended indiscriminately to fossil forms) from both brain size and variations in cognitive capacities. These phenomena are discussed in greater detail elsewhere in the book. Here we are merely interested in the relationship between brain size and language capacity.

Would it be possible at least to learn to understand a natural language such as English with a brain of markedly different weight and brain-body weight ratio? The answer is *yes:* as far as modern man is concerned, neither the absolute nor relative weight of the brain is the necessary factor for language-learning potentiality. There is a clinical condition, first described and named *nanocephalic dwarfism* (bird-headed dwarfs, as they are sometimes called), by the German pathologist, Virchow, in which man appears reduced to fairy-tale size. Seckel

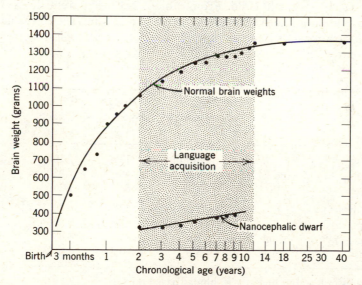

FIG. 2.25. Brain weights determined at autopsy plotted as function of patients' chronological age; data from Coppoletta and Wolbach (1933). *Bottom plot:* various measurements of head-circumference of patient described by Seckel (1960), converted to estimates of brain weight.

(1960) has recently described two such dwarfs and has reviewed the scientific literature on thirteen others. He ascribes the condition to a single-locus recessive gene for dwarfish stature without affecting endocrine organs and function. Adult individuals attain a maximum height of three feet, and about half of the described patients stand not much higher than two and a half feet at adult age; the shortest adult mentioned measured 23 inches.

Nanocephalic dwarfs differ from other dwarfs in that they preserve the skeletal proportions of normal adults. The fully mature have a brain-body weight ratio well within the limits of a young teen-ager. Yet their head circumference and estimated brain weight barely exceeds those of a newborn infant as shown in Fig. 2.25. On microscopic examination, these brains have an unremarkable histological appearance; both the size of individual nerve cells and the density of their distribution is thought to be within normal limits. However, these brains probably differ substantially from normal adult ones in the absolute number of cells. Intellectually, these dwarfs show some retardation for the most part, often not surpassing a mental age level of five to six years. All of them acquire the rudiments of language including speaking and understanding, and the majority master the verbal skills at least as well as a normal five-year-old child. From table 2.2 it is apparent that neither the absolute nor relative weights of brains and bodies reveal the nature of the relationship between speech and its neurological correlates. Apparently, the organization of the brain is more important for lan-

TABLE 2.2.

	Age	Speech Faculty	Body Weight (Kg)	Brain Weight (Kg)	Ratio
Man (m)	2½	Beginning	13½	1.100	12.3
Man (m)	13½	Yes	45	1.350	34
Man (m)	18	Yes	64	1.350	47
Man (dwarf)	12	Yes	13½	0.400[1]	34
Chimp. (m)	3	No	13½	0.400[2]	34
Chimp. (f)	adult	No	47	0.450[3]	104
Rhesus	adult	No	3½	0.090[4]	40

Figures in last four lines are estimates based on:
[1]Seckel (1960)
[2]Schultz (1941)
[3]Schultz (1941)
[4]Kroeber (1948).

guage than its mass, and the entire matter must be discussed in the light of developmental processes and growth. Perhaps growth brings about organization within the brain which does have structural correlates on a molecular level, and in this sense speech and language may have a concrete structural basis. But at the present time, we have no techniques which could demonstrate the structural characteristics of a brain whose owner learned to speak at a normal age to distinguish it from certain brains whose owner had a congenital language disability without other neurological abnormalities.

IV. CONCLUSION

Comparison of man's peripheral anatomy with that of other primates reveals a number of specializations of face and vocal tract. The fact that we can demonstrate homologues of bones and muscles especially in chimpanzee and gorilla does not render a study of anatomy useless in our attempts to understand the biological foundations of speech and language. The general configuration of the vocal tract has undergone geometric transformations in man which have a direct effect upon the acoustics of universal human speech sounds.

The alterations of the vocal tract that are specific to man can hardly be explained as adjustment to a different diet or as peculiar adaptations to any other vital function. Nevertheless, we do not attribute these peculiarities to any primeval need for communication or for making speech sounds, because such teleological arguments are repugnant to the scientific outlook. On the other hand, it is not impossible that some aspect of sound-making efficiency might not have played into the mechanisms of natural selection during the history of the species.

Man's central nervous system presents several innovations. Among them there is at least one that is directly related to language, namely the lateralization of function or, in other words, left-hemisphere dominance. In addition to the right-to-left displacement of function, there is also an antero-posterior polarization within the left hemisphere because anterior lesions disturb predominantly motor aspects of language, whereas the more posterior ones tend to involve predominantly sensory aspects. The histological differentiation of the cerebral cortex and the cortico-thalamic fiber-connections have no clearly demonstrable language specificity. Language and speech are not merely represented in the cortex, but there seem to be language-correlated functions that also involve subcortical and mid-brain structures.

The large size of the human brain cannot be attributed specifically to the exercise of language functions.

In general, it is not possible to assign any specific neuro-anatomic structure to the capacity for language. However, this capacity may be due to structural innovations on a molecular level. Language is probably due to the peculiar way in which the various parts of the brain work together or, in other words, to its peculiar function.

REFERENCES

Ajuriaguerra, J. de and Hécaen, H. (1949), *Le Cortex Cérébral; étude neuro-psycho-pathologique.* Masson, Paris.

Bailey, P. and Bonin, G. v. (1951), *The Isocortex of Man.* Univ. of Illinois Press, Urbana.

Bailey, P., Bonin, G. v., and McCulloch, W. S. (1950), *The Isocortex of the Chimpanzee.* Univ. of Illinois Press, Urbana.

Bailey, P., Buchanan, D. N., and Bucy, P. C. (1939), *Intracranial Tumors of Infancy and Childhood.* Univ. of Chicago Press, Chicago.

Bailey, P. and Davis, E. W. (1942), Effects of lesions of the periaqueductal gray matter in the cat, *Proc. Soc. Exp. Biol. and Med.* **51**:305–306.

Bok, S. T. (1959), *Histonomy of the Cerebral Cortex.* Elsevier, Amsterdam.

Bonin, G. von (1950), *Essay on the Cerebral Cortex.* C Thomas, Springfield, Illinois.

Bonin, G. von (1962), Anatomical asymmetries of the cerebral hemispheres, in *Interhemispheric Relations and Cerebral Dominance.* V. B. Mountcastle (ed.), The Johns Hopkins Press, Baltimore.

Bonin, G. von and Bailey, P. (1961), Pattern of the cerebral isocortex, in *Primatologia; Handbook of Primatology.* H. Hofer, A. H. Schultz, and D. Starck (eds.), Karger, Basel.

Braus, H. (1954), *Anatomie des Menschen, ein Lehrbuch für studierende Ärzte* fortgeführt von Curt Elze (3rd ed.), Vol. I. Springer, Berlin.

Brodnitz, F. S. (1960), Speech after glossectomy, *Curr. Probl. Phoniat. Logoped.* **1**:68–72.

Campion, G. G. and Elliot-Smith, G. *The Neutral Basis of Thought.* Harcourt, Brace and Co., New York, 1934.

Clark, W. E. Le Gros (1932), The structure and connections of the thalamus, *Brain* **55**:406–470.

Conrad, K. (1954), New problems of aphasia, *Brain* **77**:491–509.

Coppoletta, J. M. and Wolbach, S. B. (1933), Body length and organ weights of infants and children, *Am. J. Pathol.* **9**:55–70.

Critchley, M. (1962), Speech and speech-loss in relation to duality of the brain, in *Interhemispheric Relations and Cerebral Dominance,* V. B. Mountcastle (ed.), pp. 208–213. The Johns Hopkins University Press, Baltimore.

Dodgson, M. C. H. (1962), *The Growing Brain; An Essay in Developmental Neurology.* Williams and Wilkins, Baltimore.

DuBrul, E. L. (1958), *Evolution of the Speech Apparatus.* C Thomas, Springfield, Illinois.

Duckworth, W. L. H. (1910), A note on sections of the lips of the primates, *J. Anat. and Physiol.* **44**:348–353.

Feremutsch, K. (1963), Thalamus, in *Primatologia; Handbook of Primatology,* H. Hofer, A. H. Schultz, and D. Starck (eds.), Vol. II, part 2, fasc. 6. Karger, Basel.

Fink, B. R. and Kirschner, F. (1959), Observations on the acoustical and mechanical properties of the vocal folds, *Folia Phoniatrica* **11**:167–172.

Goldstein, K. (1942), *After-effects of Brain Injuries in War; Their Evaluation and Treatment.* Grune and Stratton, New York.

Guiot, G., Hertzog, E., Rondot, P., and Molina, P. (1961), Arrest or acceleration of speech evoked by thalamic stimulation in the course of stereotaxic procedures for Parkinsonism, *Brain* **84**:363–380.

Hartmann-v. Monakow, K. (1965), Psychosyndrome und Sprachstoerungen nach stereotaktischen Operationen beim Parkinson-Syndrom, *Akt. Fragen Psychiat. Neurol.* **2**:87–100.

Heberer, G. (ed.) (1965), *Menschliche Abstammungslehre; Fortschritte der Anthropogenie, 1863–1964.* G. Fischer, Stuttgart.

Hofer, H. (1965), Die morphologische Analyse des Schädels des Menschen, in *Menschliche Abstammungslehre*, G. Heberer (ed.), Fischer, Stuttgart.

Huber, E. (1931), *Evolution of Facial Musculature and Facial Expression.* The Johns Hopkins University Press, Baltimore.

Kaplan, H. M. (1960), *Anatomy and Physiology of Speech.* McGraw-Hill, New York.

Kelemen, G. (1938), Comparative anatomical studies on the junction of larynx and resonant tube, *Acta oto-laryng.* **26**:276–283.

Kelemen, G. (1939), Vergleichende Anatomie und Physiologie der Stimmorgane, *Arch. Sprach-Stimmheilk.* **3**:213–237.

Kelemen, G. (1948), the anatomical basis of phonation in the chimpanzee, *J. Morphol.* **82**:229–256.

Kelly, A. H., Beaton, L. E., and Magoun, H. W. (1946), A midbrain mechanism for facio-vocal activity, *J. Neurophysiol.* **9**:181–189.

Kleinschmidt, A. (1938), Die Schlund-Kehlorgane des Gorillas "Bobby," *Morphol. Jahrb.* **81**:78.

Kleinschmidt, A. (1949–1950), Zur Anatomie des Kehlkopfes der Anthropoiden, *Anat. Anz.* **97**:367–372.

Kreht, H. (1936), Cytoarchitektonik und motorisches Sprachzentrum, *Z. Mikroskopischanat. Forsch.* **39**:331–354.

Kroeber, A. L. (1948), *Anthropology.* Harcourt, Brace and World, New York.

Kummer, B. (1953), Untersuchungen über die Entwicklung der Schädelform des Menschen und einiger Anthropoiden, in *Abhandlungen z. Exakten Biologie.* L. von Bertalanffy (ed.), Borntraeger, Berlin.

Lashley, K. S. and Clark, G. (1946), The cytoarchitecture of the cerebral cortex of *Ateles:* A critical examination of architectonic studies, *J. comp. Neurol.* **85**:223–305.

Lenneberg, E. H. (1962), Understanding language without ability to speak: a case report, *J. Abnorm. Soc. Psychol.* **65**:419–425.

Lightoller, G. S. (1925), Facial muscles, *J. Anat.* **60**:1–85.

Lightoller, G. S. (1928), The facial muscles of three orang utans and two cerco-pithecidae, *J. Anat.* **63**:19–81.

Luria, A. R. (1947), *Traumatic Aphasia: its syndromes, psychopathology and treatment.* Academy of Med. Sci., Moscow.

Milner, B. (1962), Laterality effects in audition, in *Interhemispheric Relations and Cerebral Dominance.* V. B. Mountcastle (ed.), pp. 177–195. The Johns Hopkins University Press, Baltimore.

Myers, R. E. (1962), Discussion E (no title). *Interhemispheric Relations and Cerebral Dominance.* V. B. Mountcastle (ed.), pp. 117–129. The Johns Hopkins University Press, Baltimore.

Negus, V. E. (1929), *The Mechanism of the Larynx.* Wm. Heinemann, London.

Negus, V. E. (1949), *The Comparative Anatomy and Physiology of the Larynx.* Grune and Stratton, New York.

Némai, J. and Kelemen, G. (1929), Das Stimmorgan des Orang-Utan, *Z. Anat. Entw.Gesch.* **88**:697–709.

Némai, J. and Kelemen, G. (1933), Beiträge zur Kenntnis des Gibbonkehlkopfes, *Z. Anat. Entw. Gesch.* **100**:512–520.

Penfield, W. and Roberts, L. (1959), *Speech and Brain-mechanisms.* Princeton Univ. Press, Princeton.

Ranke, O. F. and Lullies, H. (1953), *Gehör, Stimme, und Sprache: Lehrbuch der Physiologie.* Springer, Berlin.

Russell, W. R. and Espir, M. L. E. (1961), *Traumatic Aphasia: a study of aphasia in war wounds of the brain.* Oxford Univ. Press, London.

Schultz, A. H. (1941), The relative size of the cranial capacity in primates, *Am. J. Phys. Anthrop.* **28**:273–287.

Schultz, A. H. (1958), Palatine ridges, in *Primatologia; Handbook of Primatology, Vol. III, Part 1.* H. Hofer, A. H. Schultz and D. Starck (eds.). Karger, Basel.

Seckel, H. P. G. (1960), *Birdheaded Dwarfs: studies in developmental anthropology including human proportions.* C Thomas, Springfield, Illinois.

Skultety, F. M. (1961), Experimental mutism following electrolytic lesions of the periaqueductal gray matter in dogs, *Trans. Am. Neurol. Ass.* **86**:245–246.

Sonesson, B. (1960), On the anatomy and vibratory pattern of the human vocal folds; with special reference to a photo-electrical method for studying the vibratory movements, *Acta oto-laryngologica* Suppl. 156, Lund.

Starck, D. (1965), Die Neencephalisation, in *Menschliche Abstammungslehre.* G. Heberer (ed.), Fischer, Stuttgart.

Starck, D. and Schneider, R. (1960), Larynx, in *Primatologia; Hdbk. of Primatology, Vol. III, Part 2.* H. Hofer, A. H. Schultz, and D. Starck (eds.), Karger, Basel.

Van Buren, J. M. (1963), Confusion and disturbance of speech from stimulation in vicinity of the head of the caudate nucleus, *J. Neurosurg.* **20**:148–157.

Walker, A. E. (1938), *The Primate Thalamus.* Univ. of Chicago Press, Chicago.

Weinstein, S. (1962), Differences of brain wounds implicating right or left hemispheres: differential effects on certain intellectual and complex perceptual functions, in *Interhemispheric Relations and Cerebral Dominance.* V. B. Mountcastle (ed.), pp. 159–176. The Johns Hopkins University Press, Baltimore.

CHAPTER Three

Some physiological correlates

I. AIM OF PHYSIOLOGICAL DISCUSSIONS IN THIS MONOGRAPH

There is no dearth of monographs on the physiology of speech and language (Ranke and Lullies, 1953; Luchsinger and Arnold, 1959; v.d. Berg, 1962). These are comprehensive treatments on the manner in which voice and speech are produced, the acoustics of speech sounds, speech perception, and on neurophysiological correlates. This chapter is not a digest or survey of this material. Instead, we shall concentrate on a few aspects of speech and language selected to illuminate a specific thesis.

Every species has a characteristic way of life, and there are invariably specific behavior patterns that enable it to exploit its own ecological niche. These behavioral peculiarities must be reflected in the animal's physical constitution, particularly in specializations of physiological processes. Digestive processes must undergo modifications to enable one animal to subsist on cadavers, another on plankton, and still another on either a vegetable or a meat diet. Tolerance for high or low temperature or variations in temperature must develop. Sensory processes must be refined to enable members of one species to detect its own mates or to guard against approaching enemies. Specialized protective mechanisms and structural peculiarities are evolved. These may be so effective against the predatory habits of larger carnivores that the animal may have no further need for fast locomotion which, in turn, might have new repercussion on physiological readjustments and eventually result in very sluggish creatures.

A species' successful competition for the occupation of a niche does, in fact, rest entirely on physiological and morphological adaptations. The species can defend its position, so to speak, because its unique physiological specializations and adaptations enable it to exploit a particular environmental circumstance better than its competitors. Therefore, species-specific behavior patterns must necessarily have *some* peculiar physiological correlates. This is even true of those behavioral peculiarities which cannot definitely be called developments that are "useful in the animal's struggle for survival" (as perhaps in the case of the extremely elaborate ritualized behavior and display patterns of certain birds).

Man is not the only vertebrate that makes noises for communicative purposes. But the acoustic nature, the mode of production, and the ethological variables of man's communicative behavior are highly characteristic for the species. Ideally, we would like to follow a strategy similar to Chapter Two and compare physiological correlates of man's behavior with homologous ones in other species. But this is impossible, partly because of lack of data, and partly because of the incomparability of speech with other animal noises (See Chapter Six). Instead, our aim will be to show how dependent speech- and language-production are on specific physiological propensities (demonstrable or inferrable). In this light, the universal, that is, supracultural, features of language will appear to be inextricably intertwined with physiological peculiarities. Whether these peculiarities are specializations evolved by our species only, we cannot say with certainty, but the practical failure of our attempts to train closely related species to utter intelligible words, to use sentences meaningfully, or even to understand sentences out of context makes such an assumption reasonable.

II. RESPIRATION

(1) *Respiratory Adaptations in General*

Respiratory patterns are ideally suited to demonstrate physiological adaptations to species-specific behavior patterns (Krogh, 1959). Insofar as aerobic respiration is concerned, the basic chemical reactions are similar for air-breathing vertebrates; however, there is a wide variety in special metabolic adaptations, regulatory systems, tolerance for oxygen depletion and carbon dioxide accumulation, oxygen requirements during activity, etc. The inhalation-exhalation patterns themselves and the subsidiary functions they serve vary greatly among vertebrates and well illustrate the general phenomenon of physiological adaptations to specific behavior. Consider the panting patterns in dogs which serve cooling rather than gas exchange; some animals have developed mechanisms for inflation which may serve to supply air for sound-making or which may change the animal's shape and come into play during fighting and threatening or may function to change the animal's volume-weight ratio. There are many activities which require special inhalation-exhalation ratios. This is particularly true of air-breathing divers who have to tolerate varying periods of breath-holding (see Table 3.1).

TABLE 3.1. *Maximum Diving Durations for Different Mammals (From Prosser and Brown, 1961)*

	Minutes
Sperm whale	90
Greenland whale	60
Finback whale	30
Harbor seal	15
Beaver	15
Muskrat	12
Man	2.5

In some animals, metabolic requirements may suddenly multiply a hundredfold, as, for instance, during flight, thus necessitating rapid adjustments in the supply of oxygen. It can easily be seen how locomotion, activity cycles, forms of hunting and feeding, the geographical extent of an individual animal's hunting territory, etc., are all dependent on special adaptations of respiratory patterns.

Respiratory patterns cannot be voluntarily adapted to types of behavior that are not indigenous to the species (except within very narrow limits), because of intricate control systems which set the limits to tolerance and prevent the organism from overtaxing itself. Therefore, certain behavioral modifications cannot develop unless respiratory physiology is modified accordingly.

(2) *Respiratory Adaptations to Speech*

The respiratory peculiarities that have evolved and which make it possible to sustain speech are a good illustration of this point. Table 3.2 shows how respiration during speech is significantly altered from its patterns during quiet breathing. Figure 3.1 shows this graphically. Notice that during silent breathing the time for inspiration is just a little shorter than that for expiration; breathing is comparatively shallow and fast; during rest the mechanical work is done primarily by the inspiratory muscles.

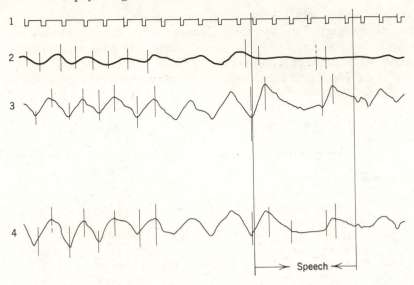

FIG. 3.1. Quiet breathing and breathing during speech in a normal four-year-old girl. (1) Time marker, one second; (2) airflow through nose; (3) chest volume; (4) abdominal expansions. Notice that chest and abdomen move synchronously during quiet breathing but are slightly out of phase during speech. (After Gutzmann reproduced in Ranke and Lullies, 1953.)

The most important (but by no means only) stimulus for the nervous regulation of respiration is the amount of CO_2 accumulation in the blood. As CO_2 concentration rises, it is believed that it activates an inspiratory center located in the medulla. With a further rise in CO_2 an expiratory center is thought to be activated which by reflex blocks the activity of the inspiratory center (Oberholzer and Tofani, 1960). Air may be expelled during expiration either by active contraction of expiratory muscles or by simple relaxation of the inspiratory muscles and elastic recoil of the thoracic cage. Acidosis level drops during expiration because CO_2 is blown off. Inspiration is activated again as soon as CO_2 has once more accumulated sufficiently, and thus the cycle starts again.

During quiet breathing electrical activity of the inspiratory muscles begins and ends with inspiration and is thus synchronous with an increase in chest volume. But during speech the electrical activities of the inspiratory muscles do not cease when expiration begins. Tonus continues during part of the expiratory phase, and thus the activity of these

		Breathing	
		Quietly	During Speech
Air movements	Tidal volume	500–600 cm³	1500–2400 cm³
	I-Fraction = $\dfrac{\text{Time of inspiration}}{\text{Time of inspiration + time of expiration}}$	ca. 0.4	ca. 0.13
	Mean rate of respirations (breaths/minute)	18–20	Range: 4–20
	Expiration	Continuous and unimpeded	Periodically interrupted and against a resistance with increase in subglottal pressure
Motor adjustments	Electrical activity in expiratory muscles	Nil or very low	Very low or nil at the beginning of phonation, then sudden onset and increasingly active toward end of expiration.
	Electrical activity of inspiratory muscles	Active during inspiratory phase and nil during expiration	Active during inspiration and lasting through expiration until suddenly silent when expiratory muscles become active
	Type and coordination of respiratory motorics	Costo-abdominal with good synchronization between costal and abdominal muscles	Primarily costal with slight desynchronization between costal and abdominal movements.
	Airways	Primarily nasal	Primarily oral

muscles is in marked desynchrony with chest-volume changes during speech (Draper, Ladefoged, and Whitteridge, 1959).

During speech respiration is not simply a response to the internal stimuli supplied by metabolic needs but is used to perform work. This is seen in the marked increase of thoracic muscular activities, the building up of subglottal pressure, and the driving of air against a resistance of flow. Since more work is done under these circumstances, it is not surprising that the rate of air-exchange per minute is also increased during speech; however, the manner in which this is accomplished during speech is surprising, because it is a marked alteration of silent breathing patterns observed under no other conditions but speech. The number of breaths per minute is drastically reduced during speech; while inspiration is slightly accelerated, expiration is markedly slowed down, and breathing becomes much deeper. The alterations of breathing during exercise are quite different. The I-Fraction remains fairly constant, and both the rate of breathing and tidal volume change in a predictable fashion—in the healthy subject there would be an increase in both parameters. If a subject is kept physically quiet but made to breathe through a narrow tube which imposes a resistance to the flow of air, the rate of breathing is slowed down and the tidal volume will increase, but the *I-Fraction*, again, is not altered from its original value (Nims, 1949).

Thus, it is quite clear that breathing undergoes peculiar changes during speech. What is astonishing about this is that man can tolerate these modifications for an apparently unlimited period of time without experiencing respiratory distress, as is well demonstrated by the interminable speeches with which many a statesman embellishes his political existence. Cloture is dictated by motor fatigue and limited receptivity in the audience—never by respiratory demands.

Our extraordinary tolerance for breathing adaptations to speech may be appreciated if we think of any other voluntary deviations from the normal breathing patterns. If we deliberately decide to breathe at some arbitrary rate, for example, faster than "normal," we at once experience the symptoms of hyperventilation (that is, lightheadedness, giddiness, and other associated symptoms); similar phenomena may result from blowing through a tube while submerged in water, or when learning to play a wind instrument, or during singing instruction. In fact, the latter two occupations require careful instruction and training in proper breathing, whereas speaking for hours continually seems to come all too naturally to many a three-year-old.

The exact chemical changes in the blood which accompany respiration during speech are not known (but see Lambertsen, 1963; Perkins,

1963; Rahn, 1963). If we look at a typical speech respiration curve it is likely that at the beginning of an utterance, CO_2 is retained somewhat longer than during quiet breathing, whereas toward the end, when active expiration takes place, CO_2 is expelled slightly faster than ordinarily; however, the rate of gas exchange in the course of a minute must correspond exactly to the metabolic needs, for otherwise we would be uncomfortable. Thus, the tolerance which we assume must have developed refers to relatively short periods during which pCO_2 deviates slightly from the normal range. On the other hand, we must assume the existence of sensitive, controlling mechanisms that regulate ventilation in an autonomous fashion during speech, thus preventing hyper- or hypoventilation over longer periods. This latter point can be well-appreciated if one tries to speak (perhaps in a whisper) only during inspiration; at the same time, in order to keep up a good flow of conversation, endeavor to exhale as fast as possible. Now we have reversed the I-Fraction. Theoretically, it must be possible never to transgress the limits of CO_2 tension as encountered during normal speech and also to keep the rate of ventilation to the exact requirements over a period of a minute. This experiment will cause discomfort within a few minutes, and attempts to prolong it for, say twenty minutes or half an hour, might well induce detrimental changes of consciousness.

I believe it is fair to say that we are endowed with special physiological adaptations which enable us to sustain speech driven by expired air. Consider now the morphology of our larynx. The glottis is peculiarly adapted to phonation upon expired air, in contrast to the vocal cords of certain other primates which are so constructed that they can phonate upon inspiration as well as expiration (Kelemen, 1961). Man can also produce sound with inspired air (Hartlieb, Luchsinger, and Pfister, 1960), but control for pitch, timbre, and loudness is very poor in addition to the strain and discomfort that it causes. (In whistling, however, we produce sounds equally easily during inhalation or exhalation.) Thus there is both anatomical and physiological facilitation for phonation during speech. It is impossible to say whether we speak the way we do because of these facilitatory circumstances or whether these circumstances have developed during evolution in response to natural selection pressures. Does the ass who makes noise with inspiration and expiration *ee-ah* so efficiently because nature has given him the organ with which to do it or did it happen the other way around? Perhaps we had better not pursue the question.

During silent breathing the principal muscular work is from increasing the volume of the thoracic cage, producing negative pressure which will cause air to be inhaled. This is done by the inspiratory muscles. After a given volume of air is inhaled, these muscles relax suddenly, allowing the thorax to contract through the elastic recoil of its tissues. Expiratory muscles come into play only during forceful expiration with exercise. In this situation air flows in and out at varying speed. If silent breathing is against a flow-resistance, air becomes periodically compressed, with the pressure varying constantly. In the course of speech production, however, Draper, Ladefoged, and Whitteridge (1957, 1959, 1960) have shown that the mean subglottal pressure may remain fairly constant during phonation of a steady sound, which they have demonstrated is accomplished by particular synergisms—coordination between inspiratory, expiratory, and abdominal muscles. At the beginning of phonation (that is, while air is already escaping), the tonus of the inspiratory muscles continues (Fig. 3.2), from which it must be inferred that these muscles at first prevent the thorax from slumping back too fast and thus seem to be counteracting the elastic contractile forces (called relaxation pressure by Draper et al.). At a certain point, the inspiratory muscles suddenly relax, and some expiratory muscles come into action at once; gradually other expiratory muscles become active until the speaker has to catch his breath. Now the expiratory muscles become electrically silent and inspiratory muscles take over again. The regulation of air pressure is in itself a complex mechanism. Apparently it is fully developed by the time an infant begins to babble in utterances of multiple syllables, roughly during the sixth or seventh month of life.

The over-all "breathing economy" during conversation was investigated by Goldman-Eisler (1955, 1956a, 1956b). In these articles the relationship of respiratory variables to the rate of speaking was studied by listening for inhalation noises on tape recordings. Figure 3.3 gives representative examples of the findings. Theoretically the following variables are involved: breathing rate, tidal volume, amount of air expended per syllable, and rate of articulatory organs producing words. The first two variables are dependent upon each other so that one of them (for instance, tidal volume) may be ignored here. From acoustical and laryngological considerations we know that normally the amount of air per syllable is well-correlated to loudness, and since in ordinary conversations and psychiatric interviews (which was the source of some of Goldman-Eisler's material) variations in loudness are not outstanding, we may assume this factor to be a constant. From these findings it becomes clear that of the two independent variables, rate of breathing and rate of speaking, the former is considerably more subject to variation than the latter. Most subjects speak at a surprisingly constant rate, but some vary in their rate of speech patterns. (Incidentally, the true rate of articulatory movements cannot be inferred from these figures since hesitation pauses are clearly responsible for much of the variation observed.) The rate of breathing appears to be well-correlated with physiological and emotional stress factors; clearly it may vary independently and without affecting the rate of speaking. In other

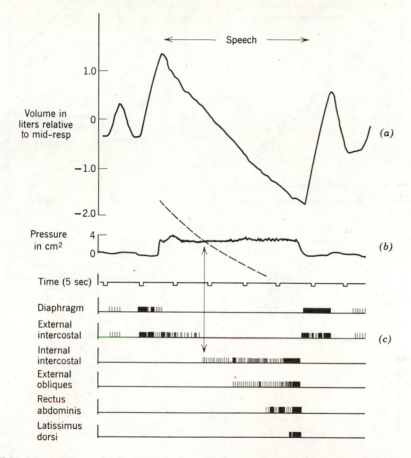

FIG. 3.2. (*a*) Record of variations in volume of the lung; (*b*) oesophageal pressure; (*c*) diagrammatic representation of muscular activity accompanying pressure and volume changes. The dashed line which has been superimposed on the pressure record indicates the relaxation pressure associated with the corresponding volume of air in the lungs. It is equal to zero when the amount of air in the lungs is the same as that at the end of a normal breath. The arrows indicate the moment when the relaxation pressure is no longer greater than the mean pressure below the vocal cords. At this moment, the external intercostal activity ceases, and the activity of the internal intercostals commences. (From Draper et al., 1959.)

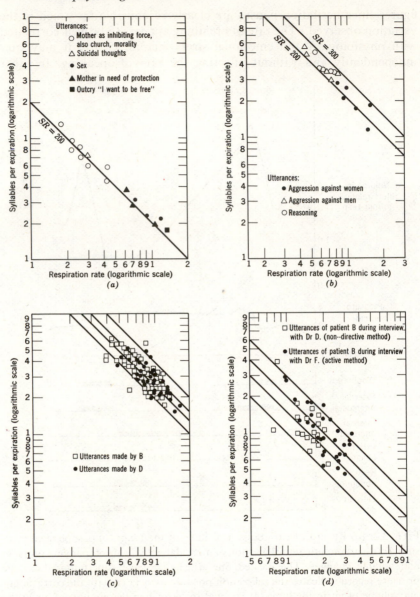

FIG. 3.3. Syllables-per-breath is plotted as a function of breathing rate. If artic-ulatory rate were entirely constant for one person, points would fall on a straight line. This is approximated in (*a*). Breathing rate varies with topic of conversation. Similarly, in (*b*). The two persons in (*c*) and the patient in (*d*) show greater varia-tion in speech rate than those at the top. (From Goldman-Eisler, 1955 and 1956.)

words, during phonation at conversational loudness, air is expended at a constant rate and articulatory movements are also fairly constant in production rate. But the required air may be supplied by breaths that vary in length and depth. (The I-Fraction, however, remains characteristic for speech and is fairly constant.)

A point of considerable speculation has been the central locus of neural regulation of breathing during speech. It has often been said that during speech the control of respiration "is switched" from the mesencephalic center to the cerebral cortex, but this must be an oversimplification. Since speech and breathing are complexly integrated and since speech and language probably involve cortical activities, we may infer that the breathing rhythm during speech is modulated by impulses from the cortex. However, there is no evidence that neural activity in the respiratory centers at lower levels are blocked during speech, and thus the term *switching* is ill-chosen.

(3) *Other Motor Changes Indirectly Related to Respiratory Adaptations*

The principal adaptations are summarized in Table 3.3. In Chapter two we have pointed out that the geometry of the naso-velo-pharyngeal

TABLE 3.3. *Other, Indirect Motor Adaptations to Speech Respiration*

Structure	Breathing	
	Quietly	During Speech
Vocal folds (during inspiration, subject at rest)	Abducted; opening roughly triangular	Maximally abducted and retracted; opening roughly pentagonal
Vocal folds (during expiration, subject at rest)	As above, but slightly narrower	Constant alternation: adduction, tight adduction, and relaxed abduction
Subglottal space immediately below the edge of the cords	Somewhat irregularly shaped	Apparently exponentially curved*
Soft palate	No movements	Alternation between quiet relaxation and retraction

* Based on Fink and Kirschner, 1959; their conclusions and interpretations have not been universally accepted.

space has a unique configuration in man and that this deviation from the rest of the primate order may be related to man's unique posture. A consequence of this morphological peculiarity is that parting of the lips lets air stream simultaneously through oral and nasal cavities. However, during speech air is intermittently shunted either through the mouth, the nose, or both simultaneously, and muscular mechanisms exist to effect these movements quickly and efficiently. The nature of these movements is shown in Figs. 3.4 and 3.5. They have been thoroughly investigated by Björk (1961). Figure 3.5 is a demonstration of the relative speed, accuracy, and timing which integrates palatal movements into the speech event as a whole. Whether there are homologous mechanisms in lower primates is not clear (Müller, 1955). At any rate, the physiology of their movements in deglutition and phonation has apparently not been investigated.

When the vocal folds are spread apart during quiet breathing, the larynx constitutes a tubular air tunnel with somewhat irregularly shaped walls. The shape of the walls is altered during phonation and, as Fink and Kirschner (1959) have noted, some regularities are introduced in the subglottal space that favor the aerodynamics of sound production by reducing subglottal turbulence and thus increasing the efficiency in utilization of air flow. When the cords are brought together for phonation, their medial edge becomes sharpened, their superior surface flattens and forms a shelf, whereas the inferior surface is arched exponentially as shown in Fig. 15 of Chapter 2. Pressman and Kelemen (1955) state that "the advantage of such a curve inferiorly is twofold: (1) it thins out the medial mass of the cord without narrowing it or depriving it of a wide lateral attachment, thereby improving its vibratory characteristics; (2) because it is dome-shaped, the pressure of air converges from below to a point in the midline where the cords are thinnest. Under these circumstances, the free margins of the cords can, during phonation, be more easily blown apart by the pressure of expired air." *

Kainz (vol. III, 1954) who summarized all respiratory and motor changes accompanying speech, also cites a difference between the position of the vocal folds during inhalation while the individual is quiet and during phonation. In the former, the muscles are relatively relaxed, forming a roughly triangular opening in cross section; whereas during speech, further retraction of the cords takes place to increase the available space, thereby facilitating rapid inspiration. During exhalation the cords are thought to assume a similar position as during inhalation as long as breathing is quiet and under relaxed conditions (which is

---

* Not all students of laryngeal mechanisms agree with these statements and perhaps further investigations are indicated before uncritical acceptance.

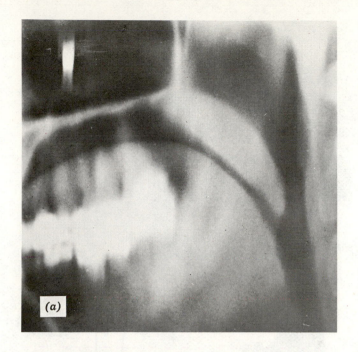

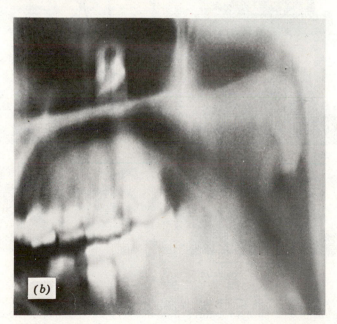

FIG. 3.4. X-rays of palate and velum: (*a*) at rest; (*b*) while uttering a nasalized *a*. (From Björk, 1961.)

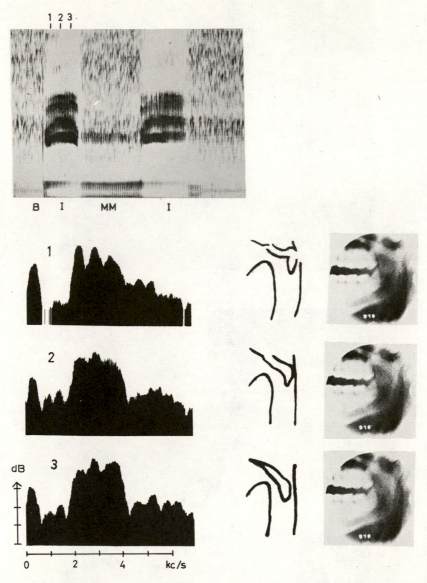

FIG. 3.5. Movement of velum during speech. The test word is /bimmi/. *Top:* spectrogram of utterance with three time-markers, 1, 2, 3; *bottom left:* power spectra at times 1, 2, 3; *middle:* outline of velum as shown in x-rays to the right. (From Björk, 1961.)

not the case during laryngoscopy), whereas they are subjected to a rapid succession of adduction (during phonation), abduction (during unvoiced sounds), and tight adduction (during the production of glottal stops—which are lacking in some languages).

Throughout phonation, the cords are brought together but not so tightly as to prevent them from vibrating when air is blown through them from below. The individual vibrations themselves are probably not the result of neurogenic muscular twitches as proposed by Husson and his followers, but, as is generally agreed now, depend on simple maintenance of muscle tonus, tissue elasticity of the vocal folds, and air pressure.

III. SPEECH PRODUCTION

Speech production poses a number of very important physiological problems which are best appreciated if we consider this activity under the following headings: *first,* the problem of discrete articulatory events; *second,* the problem of rate of articulation; and *third,* the problem of ordering articulatory events.

(1) *Discrete Articulatory Events*

It is not immediately obvious that there are discrete events in the flow of speech. In fact, there has been considerable controversy in this connection, especially among phonologists. The ancient scribes and grammarians evidently felt that language consisted of phonetic *units* which led to the invention and eventual wide acceptance of the alphabetic type of script. In recent times, however, linguists, seeing speech signals projected on cathode-ray screens, were unable to find dividing marks between speech sounds in the wave form; this suggested that segmentation might be an artifact of our perception. But the problem is much more complicated and cannot be decided upon definitively. The reality of segmentation depends primarily on the level or mode of our investigations. From a psychological point of view, phonetic discreteness must have a perceptual reality, for otherwise linguists would not be able to make phonetic transcriptions of languages of illiterate societies, particularly in cases where the linguist does not speak the language himself. Trained field workers do this with excellent interobserver reliability. Even from a physical, acoustic point of view, discreteness must be more than an artifact. There is at least one form of display, namely sound spectrography, in which there are clear discontinuities indicating that there are certain events with definable beginnings and ends, for instance, signals bounded by silences, or vowel phonemes preceded and followed by stop phonemes. In the context of physiology, the perceptual and acoustic events are of less concern to us than the motor events, that is, the contraction and relaxation of muscles. Even here the beginning and end of activity are not self-evident phenomena. During a waking state most muscles have a low level of tonicity, even when relaxed, and it is merely a matter of instrumentation to detect this. When a muscle contracts there is a very dramatic increase in electrical potentials, but this might be displayed graphically in such a way as to make the rise appear gradual (for instance, by running the polygraph paper at high speed), thus obliterating the beginning. When we think of the entire musculature of the speech apparatus in activity, we realize that there is a continuous waxing and waning in states of contraction throughout these muscles. However, if we think of the waxing and waning of tonus as being either above or below some arbitrary level, we can simplify the situation considerably. Operational definitions for states of contraction are very easy: a criterial voltage is chosen, and if the recorded potentials exceed it, the muscle is said to be contracted. What the voltage should be need not concern us here. The digital approach is a necessity in many motor physiological investigations.

(2) *Rate of Articulatory Events*

How fast does one speak? Clearly there can be no simple answer; yet there are some trends which disclose remarkable constancy, at least in the rate of articulatory movements. Goldman-Eisler (1954) has shown that for utterances above a certain length, (roughly 100 syllables or more), those who speak English talk at a fairly constant rate, about 210 to 220 syllables per minute (these figures include hesitation pauses). If the utterances are shorter, much higher rates are regularly observed because few or no hesitation pauses are included. Most adults are capable of producing syllables at rates up to 500 syllables per minute. These higher rates occur particularly if the speaker uses common phrases or clichés. Apparently, the most important factor limiting the rate of speech involves the cognitive aspects of language and not the physical ability to perform the articulatory movements. We may not be able to organize our thoughts fast enough to allow us to speak at the fastest possible rate. In addition, there is a practice factor. Certain words must be used a few times before they can be produced with ease. In the conversations of daily life, however, new words are introduced relatively rarely into discourse, so that this factor is ordinarily minimized and may be ignored. Furthermore, the necessary practice for smooth production requires merely a few seconds, provided the new word can be produced in accordance with phonological rules familiar to the speaker. The picture is different if words belonging to a foreign phonological system are to be uttered, for in this case the underlying formative rules will have to be learned before words can be uttered smoothly.

Goldman-Eisler's data came from tape-recorded conversations, so that the syllable count is based on what the investigator heard—or thought he heard. When we listen to recorded speech, we cannot hear every detail. When a Britisher enunciates *medicine,* he may actually articulate only two syllables; but the American listener may count it as three. Even if speaker and listener have the same dialect, a fast-speaking subject may introduce abbreviations not commonly heard; on occasion he may, for instance, pronounce telephone with syncopation of the second *e.* Furthermore, syllable counts give no direct evidence of the rate at which articulatory organs *move.* For example, in English, drawn-out vowels are usually diphthongized so that even a single phoneme may consist of unexpected tongue movements (or, according to some linguists, a single grapheme may actually represent two phonemes).

In view of these difficulties, the following discussion serves merely to sketch the problem. The figures used here are based on estimates. We have made some syllable and phoneme rate counts based on tape-recordings of three radio newscasts, each by a different speaker. The rate of articulation was remarkably similar for the three speakers, yielding syllables-per-second counts of 5.7, 5.9, and 6. We may convert these figures into phonemes-per-second by multiplying with a factor of 2.4, obtaining an over-all average of roughly 14 phonemes per second. This figure is in accordance with findings by Stetson (1951) and Hudgins and Stetson (1937).

. We cannot state exactly the number of muscles that are necessary for speech and that are active during speech. But if we consider that ordinarily the muscles of the thoracic and abdominal walls, the neck and face, the larynx, pharynx, and the oral cavity are all properly coordinated during the act of speaking, it becomes obvious that over 100 muscles must be controlled centrally. Since the passage from any one speech sound to another depends ultimately on differences in muscular adjustments, fourteen times per second an "order must be

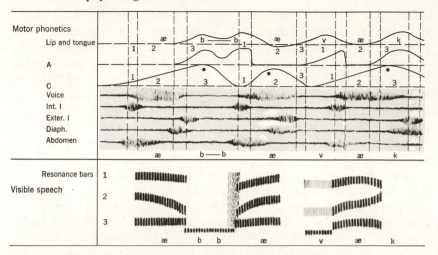

FIG. 3.6. Earlier observations on the relationship and timing of certain muscular activities and sound production. (After Stetson, 1951.)

issued to every muscle," whether to contract, relax, or maintain its tonus. From Fig. 3.6 it is clear, however, that the readjustment does not occur simultaneously for all muscles but that various groups of muscles have characteristic timing; some are active shortly before the acoustic onset of a phoneme, some during, and some shortly after. Thus we gather that the rate at which individual muscular events occur (throughout the speech apparatus) is of an order of magnitude of several hundred events every second. It is evident that the activation of so many muscles in such a short time span cannot depend on volition alone. There must be some automatisms—whole trains of events that are "preprogrammed" and run off automatically. Automatic sequences such as these are called *synergisms;* they form the basis of all motor phenomena in vertebrates. The physiology of speech production would be very simple if every phoneme were associated with one and only one pattern of muscular interaction. However, this is not what we find. The muscular activity associated with one phoneme is influenced by the phonemes that precede and follow it. Thus the motor patterns that we must investigate here are complex motor configurations that extend over relatively long periods, as in the duration of a syllable or word.

The intricacy of the problem becomes apparent if we draw an analogy between the sequence of events during speech and in drumming with the fingers on a table top. Both proceed at a rapid rate, but when we drum out a melody with our fingers, it does not matter in which order each finger falls on the table. The easiest is to use a single order, letting the small finger always be the first and the index always the last. But in speech production the order of activation and precise timing is of paramount importance.

(3) *Ordering of Articulatory Events*

The problem of order in speech and language is not confined to articulation. We can speak of an order of events at the level of perception of acoustic phenomena, of articulation, and of nerve impulses. The perceptual order of speech sounds need not be identical with the order of acoustic correlates (we may ignore or fail to hear certain acoustic phenomena); the order of acoustic events need not be identical with the order of motor or articulatory events (movements occur that do not produce sound or sound-changes); the order of central neuronal events may be different from the order of peripheral motor events. (Certain nervous impulses must be initiated in advance of others because traveling time to the periphery is longer for some pathways than others.)

Figure 3.7 shows the spectrogram of a male speaker saying the words "Santa Claus." No matter how carefully or how often we listen to these tape-recorded words played back at the original speed, we always hear a clear-cut sequence of phones, one beginning at the termination of the previous one. However, the graphic representation demonstrates that, acoustically, phones overlap. The initial portion of a vowel may bear the acoustic clues of the stop-consonant preceding it; the last portion of the lateral /1/ may have the vowel coloring of the next sound; or, in general, vowels and consonants influence each other acoustically (Delattre et al., 1955; Stevens and House, 1963). Thus the onset of a phone is different when defined acoustically than perceptually, with the acoustic onset often preceding the perceptual one.

There are many articulatory events, or more generally, motor events, that leave no trace on spectrograms. Figure 3.6 based on work by Stetson shows this very clearly. Before the onset of phonation, muscles in the abdominal and thoracic wall and in the larynx have to assume certain positions, with some of these events preceding the onset of sound by 100 milliseconds (msec) and more. Also during those silent periods which appear as short blanks on spectrograms a great many movements are performed, particularly by the tongue, which must get into position for alveolar or palatal stops (*d, t, g, k*) or which gets ready for the production of the next vowel.

The order of correlated neuronal events may yet be different from

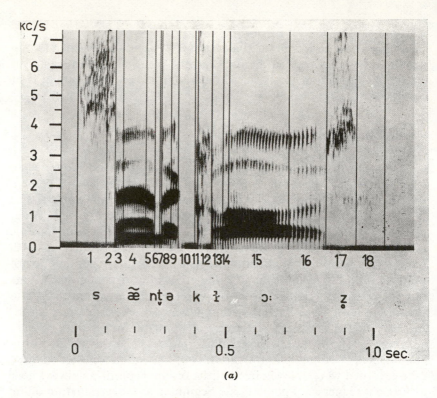

(a)

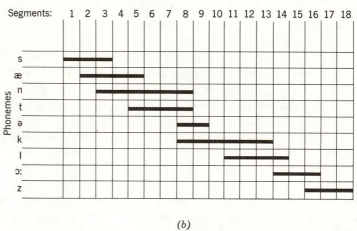

(b)

FIG. 3.7. Perceptually, speech sounds seem to follow one another like a train of independent speech segments. Acoustically, however, there is considerable overlap. (*a*) Spectrogram of the words *Santa Claus*. Vertical lines mark acoustically differentiated segments. (*b*) Assignment of phonemes to acoustic segments. (From Fant and Lindblom, 1961.)

94

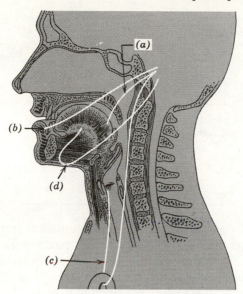

FIG. 3.8. Schematic illustration of the different lengths of nerves supplying selected muscles essential for articulation. (*a*) Branch of the trigeminal nerve innervating muscles of the jaw; (*b*) branch of the facial nerve innervating muscles in the lips; (*c*) the recurrent nerve (which branches off the vagus) supplying the muscles of the larynx; (*d*) hypoglossal nerve supplying the muscles in the tongue.

the three orders discussed so far, although we are entering a realm in which we are almost entirely reduced to speculation. The reason for suspecting a neuronal firing order that is different from the order of motor events is the anatomy of the peripheral nerves that innervate the respective muscles. Figure 3.8 shows diagrammatically the course of some of the nerves that are relevant to this discussion. There is considerable difference in the length of these nerves; notice especially the circuitous course of the recurrent nerve which is more than three times as long as the nerve that innervates a certain muscle of the jaw. The conduction time of impulses does not merely depend upon the distance of peripheral nerve that must be traversed but also upon the diameter of the nerve fibers (the smaller the fiber, the slower the conduction). It is possible to measure the average length of the peripheral nerves and also to make microscopic studies of cross sections of these nerves and to measure the size of the diameters of fibers. This has been done (Auriti, 1954; Krmpotić, 1958 and 1959), and it has been found that nerves involved in speech muscle innervation vary considerably in their composition of fibers. It is customary to express fiber-composition of

TABLE 3.4. *Length and Fiber Caliber of Selected Nerves Innervating Speech Organs (after Krmpotić)*

Cranial Nerve	Length in cm	Fiber Caliber in μ		
		Max.	Min.	Mean
V: branch to internal pterygoid (jaw)	9.7	12	5	9.5
VII: branch to upper lip	26.4	15	8	10.3
X: Recurrent (larynx)	31.7	9	1	5.4

a nerve in terms of a caliber spectrum (a statistical frequency distribution of diameter sizes). Table 3.4 shows a few figures taken from the work of Krmpotić, indicating that there is always some overlap in the distributions but that there are, nevertheless, marked differences among the various nerves. It is interesting that the longest nerve, the recurrent, has statistically the smallest fibers which thus aggravates the timing problem, introducing delays from two independent factors.

Krmpotić, who has been specifically interested in the problem of differential innervation time, has computed so-called neuromuscular indexes for all major muscles involved in speech. These indexes are simply the ratio of the average length of the nerve to the mean size of fiber diameter. Since there is still some uncertainty about the physiological interpretation of these determinations, we need not be concerned here with the details. Suffice it to say that the anatomy of the nerves suggests that innervation time for intrinsic laryngeal muscles may easily be up to 30 msec longer than innervation time for muscles in and around the oral cavity.

Considering now that some articulatory events may last as short a period as 20 msec, it becomes a reasonable assumption that the firing order in the brain stem may at times be different from the order of events occurring at the periphery.

A concrete example will clarify the point. Let us take the words *obtain* and *optimal*. If we make spectrograms of these words and measure the durations of the first three phones, we get values such as these:

	First vowel	Duration of the labial stop	Duration of the aspiration
Obtain	90 msec	170 msec	50 msec
Optimal	110 msec	160 msec	20 msec

Among the acoustic cues for the distinction of certain voiced and unvoiced stops are the duration of the preceding vowel and the duration of the silence during which the lips are closed. Our perceptual acuity is highly sensitized to these and similar temporal factors and, by the same token, our motor coordination is precise enough to time articulation with sufficient precision to bring about these distinctions. In the previous example the duration of the first vowel differs by only 20 msec and that of the labial stops by only 10 msec, and in the second instant, the duration of the aspiration (the only part of the /t/ we hear) lasts only 20 msec. Recent investigations carried out at the Haskins Laboratories have shown that a great variety of phonetic distinctions are entirely dependent upon timing factors of onset, duration, and cessation of voice where magnitudes well below 20 msec are of the essence. (See also the time relationships in the data reported on by Liberman, Delattre, Cooper, 1952; Schatz, 1954; and Liberman, Delattre, Gerstman, and Cooper, 1956.)

It is clear that there must be considerable precision in timing if laryngeal mechanisms are to be integrated with oral ones. In addition, there are hundreds of muscular adjustments to be made every second (that is, a new neuromuscular event every few milliseconds), from which we begin to see the magnitude of the timing-ordering problem.

In view of the above we are hardly surprised that we may encounter patients with lesions in the central nervous system who have difficulty in keeping elements of speech and language in the right order. An important theoretical discussion on this subject was contributed by Jakobson and Halle (1956). Patients who have this problem speak very slowly and indicate to the examiner that speaking constitutes a great effort of concentration; they behave as if they had to "think of the right order." Even so, they will constantly mix up individual sounds; *is* may become *si, task* may become *taks, syllable* may become *syballel* and they are very hard to understand.* Generally, they tend to anticipate sounds that should come at a later time. The difficulty may occur as frequently as every few seconds, which means it will occur in every other word, since their rate of production is markedly slowed down. The improper anticipation of sounds is usually not the patient's only problem of ordering. He will also show a pathological propensity for spoonerism, entire words and phrases being switched around or produced in advance. The patient's intention is frequently made known to the examiner because the patient is fully aware of his difficulty and can often make a fresh start and repeat the intended sentence once more

---

* These are examples from a tape recording made by the author of a patient described further in Chapter Five. This type of metathesis is not necessarily of a phonemic nature.

and correctly. In severe cases the corrected sentence will show new mistakes.

IV. PROBLEMS ARISING FROM RATE AND ORDERING

Karl Lashley (1951) was the first to recognize clearly the problems raised by the fast rate of movements and the ordering of motor events; the solution presented here is essentially similar to his.

We have postulated some automatisms that are responsible for the fast sequence of movements in speech (as well as many other types of motor behavior). What might the nature of such automatism be? Could it be an associative sequential process? Disregarding for the time being our inability to define *association* neurophysiologically, from a logical point of view, let us see whether temporal association might account for the facts. The formal characteristic of the associational automatism to be considered is that events occur in chains. For instance, a stimulus is followed by a response; the response then acts as a new stimulus (perhaps because the subject has heard himself say something or feels his own muscles move) which in turn elicits another response; this again becomes a stimulus which is followed by a response, and thus a chain reaction is produced. Generally speaking, any one event is triggered by one or more events that had preceded it. For instance, in the application of this principle to phonology, one phoneme is thought to heighten the probability of producing a given other one (by virtue of earlier temporal contiguity in the experience of the organism); but once a phoneme has been produced, it cannot be modified, logically, by phonemes yet to come. Thus this model (let us call it the sequential chain model) may account for modifications or occurrences "down stream," namely as consequences of earlier articulatory or phonological events; however, it is unable to account for the phenomenon of anticipation. Nevertheless, articulatory anticipation is a reality as indicated by the pathological example cited previously, and there are cogent physiological reasons that force us to adopt a model that can account as easily for anticipation in articulatory output as modification due to earlier occurrences.

The reality of anticipation is best seen in the fact that a given initial sound, say $/k/$ has different acoustic qualities (in English) if followed by an $/i/$ than when followed by an $/u/$. Chomsky (1957) has also shown that a sequential chain model is incapable of accounting for almost any aspect of syntax (see Chapter Seven and Appendix), but here we are more concerned with physiological reasons for rejecting the sequential chain model.

Lashley was aware of the physiological nature of the problem and discussed it in considerable detail. He advanced an argument against chain association which has been referred to frequently but which, by itself, could be explained away by proposing certain theoretical constructs. He argued that the motor events in certain fast skills, such as playing the piano or snapping the fingers, follow one another at such a fast rate that there would be no time for neural messages to go from the periphery to the brain and there elicit the next response. From Table 3.4 we may deduce that this argument also holds to a certain extent for the rate of speech movements. But auditory feedback greatly speeds up reafferentation and thus minimizes the time problem even though it does not eliminate it. Theoretically, however, this aspect of the problem is not unsurmountable if we assume, as we believe mediation theory does, that the sequential association is between events entirely contained within the brain. Suppose nervous event A triggered nervous event B, both in the cortex of the left hemisphere; now the conduction time between these cortical events would be negligible. This assumption is neurologically naive (see Chapter Five) and it also does not overcome other, more fundamental objections to the associational model, namely to explain every speaker's ability to anticipate events yet to come.

We may illustrate the problem in this way: let us think of a speech act (such as repeating any given word) as an assembly of four distinct processes as shown in Fig. 3.9. In the first process acoustic energy variations are received and analyzed into language-function units called phonemes. The details of this process need not concern us here. In the second process an inventory is made of all the muscles which enter into the production of each speech sound. (These processes are, of course, not "real physiological events" but theoretical stages that help us visualize the complications of speech production.) A more detailed diagram of the second process is shown in Fig. 3.10. Each column

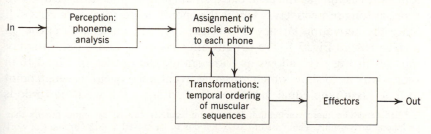

FIG. 3.9. Block diagram of some hypothetical processes involved in the imitation of a given string of phonemes.

| | String of phones | | | | | |
	I	II	III	IV	V	VI
a	+	+	+	0	+	0
b	0	+	+	+	0	+
c	+	+	0	+	+	0
d	+	0	0	+	+	+
e	+	0	+	+	0	+
f	0	+	0	0	+	+

(Row label at left: *Muscles*)

FIG. 3.10. Schema of a catalogue indicating which muscles are to be contracted (+) in order to produce a given speech sound. This is essentially the same as the process of "assigning muscles to each phone" in Fig. 3.9.

represents one speech sound. Each row corresponds to a specific muscle, labeled from *a* to *f*. Naturally, there are many more muscles involved in the speech act, just as an utterance consists usually of more than six speech sounds. This is merely a schema. A plus sign means contraction, zero means relaxation. If we assume silence and relaxation of all muscles before and after the production of each sound (for the sake of discussion), the matrix indicates that in order to produce sound I it will be necessary to contract muscles *a, c, d,* and *e,* for sound II muscles *a, b, c, f,* etc.

If the respective muscles are to be ready to contract simultaneously, that is, the motor action is to come in time to produce a given sound, impulses to some of the muscles will have to be fired earlier than others. Suppose we grouped all muscles into classes, *alpha, beta, gamma, delta,* in accordance with the time it takes impulses to reach them from the brain stem; the *alpha* class of muscles has an activation latency that is four times as long as the *delta* class, and *beta* and *gamma* three and two times as long respectively.* This is the operation performed in Fig. 3.11. Since the activation latency is constant for each muscle, all entries in a given row in Fig. 3.10 are equally affected by it. The classification of muscles in Fig. 3.11 allows us to rearrange the entries of Fig. 3.10 in such a way as to show which muscular event must occur at which point in time (assuming equal duration of all sounds). All we need to do is

* Differences in muscle activation latency are actually caused by more factors than peripheral arrival time. The mass of tissue that has to be moved and the amount of work that must be performed by each contraction varies greatly throughout the vocal apparatus and produces latencies, for instance, in the respiratory muscles, of up to 100 msec.

to shift each row leftward by a given factor, and now we have a matrix in which the columns are consecutive time segments. This matrix indicates that if a string of sounds I to VI is to be produced consecutively and if the muscles fall into latency classes as shown to the left of the matrix, then the first neuronal event to occur is the firing of impulses for contraction of muscle *e* during time segment 1; the next event, during time segment 2, is contraction of muscles *b* and *c,* but relaxation of *e.* During the following time segment, muscles *b, c, d,* and *e* must be contracted, but not *f;* and so forth down the dimension of time, that is, down the columns from left to right.

The operation performed in Fig. 3.11 corresponds to the third schematic process of Fig. 3.9 called temporal ordering of muscular sequences. Notice that in Fig. 3.11 the columns have shifted their labels from Speech sounds to Time segments. Thus each cell entry which tells us something about individual muscles has lost its "phonic denomination." If we want to label each individual plus sign in terms of its "phonic role," we must refer to Fig. 3.10, that is, to the earlier process of assignment of muscles, and by going back and forth between the process of muscle assignment and temporal ordering, Fig. 3.10 and Fig. 3.11, we can produce a third matrix, namely the one shown in Fig. 3.12. This matrix is a summary statement of the previous one, but the cell entries are now labeled with their phonic denomination. In this new arrangement, we have disregarded the top-to-bottom order within

Muscles grouped by activation latency				Time segments								
α	β	γ	δ	1	2	3	4	5	6	7	8	9
			a				+	+	+	0	+	0
b				0	+	+	+	0	+			
	c				+	+	0	+	+	0		
		d				+	0	0	+	+	+	
e				+	0	+	+	0	+			
		f				0	+	0	0	+	+	

FIG. 3.11. The muscular contractions in Fig. 3.10 arranged according to the sequence of activation. This is essentially the same as the process of "temporal ordering" of Fig. 3.9.

Time segments

1st	2nd	3rd	4th	5th	6th	7th	8th
e_I	b_{II}	b_{III}	a_I	a_{II}	a_{III}	d_{IV}	a_V
	c_I	c_{II}	b_{IV}	c_{IV}	b_{VI}	f_V	d_{VI}
		d_I	e_{IV}		c_V		f_{VI}
		e_{III}	f_{II}		d_{IV}		
					e_{VI}		

FIG. 3.12. The sequence of muscular contractions specified in Fig. 3.11, identified by their speech-sound-pertinence. This is the result of cross-reference between the processes of muscle assignment and ordering of Fig. 3.9.

each column, because we merely want to state what the neuronal firing order is on some given level in the brain. Within each column, events are assumed to be practically simultaneous.

We may pause to ask whether the necessity for temporal ordering due to differences in activation latencies is a trivial "engineering" problem or one that involves interesting indications of subtle brain functions. It would be trivial, for instance, if the differences in latency could simply be compensated for by building-in such fixed "delay circuits" that there could be simultaneous neuronal firing instruction on a "high level" in the brain, but the delays on a "lower level" would cause the short latency impulses to be held back until the long latency impulses have traversed most of their route. Probably the situation is more complicated. The synergisms involved in mastication and swallowing, in respiratory adjustments, in whistling, or sucking, or blowing, and in speaking do not make use of the identical set of muscles. Mastication involves only the oral cavity; swallowing, the back of the tongue and pharyngeal structures but not the lips; it is only speech that requires precise temporal integration of laryngeal musculature with those of the face and mouth. Phylogenetically, mastication is undoubtedly an older synergism than speaking, and if there were any built-in "delay-circuits," they would regulate the timing of the motor activity for eating and respiration rather than speech. It is very doubtful that the entire branchial physiology is adjusted to the timing requirements of speaking; but even if it were, we would have to postulate as high a degree of neurophysiological specialization due to speech as is necessary for the other postulation (that is, that the brain is capable of programming speech-specific temporal order formations). In either case, we must assume special circumstances because of speech. Figure 3.12 makes it clear that sequential association cannot be the generating process of speech events. Notice the events that precede the contraction of muscle *a* in the fourth time-segment. There is a total of seven prior muscular contractions, four of which actually belong to sounds that have not yet occurred. Even the sequencing of the three others, *e, c,* and *d* in segments 1, 2, and 3, respectively, depends upon anticipation, because it requires knowledge of the total complement of muscles that go into the production of the first sound I. Thus, on the grounds of muscular physiological speculations, it is evident that even the simplest sequential order of events requires a hierarchic plan in which events are selected, not in response to prior events, but as an integration of all elements within units of several seconds duration. This is even true of the motor assembly in the production of a single speech sound. In Fig. 3.13 a diagram shows the difference between the sequential chain-model, which is associative and the plan-model which is nonassociative.

Figure 3.12 shows clearly how speech-sound correlates might be ordered haphazardly with respect to time. At one point, the brain is busy with sound I, next with sound I and II, then with sound I, II, and III, then with sound I, II, and IV (in two different ways), then only with II and IV, but next we are back to III among other sound correlates, and so on. Here the input order of phonemes (that is, the sequence in which the individual heard the speech sounds which are eventually to be reproduced) has to be thoroughly rearranged in the process of reproduction.

The situation depicted here was highly idealized by making a number of assumptions that are not met by the real situation. Reality is in many ways more complex, but in one way there is also simplification. There are restrictions to the freedom of sound combinations, for example, imposed by phonological structure of natural languages. For instance,

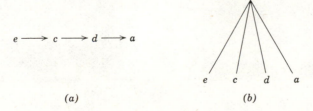

(a)   (b)

FIG. 3.13. Two proposed models to account for the sequencing of muscular events underlying the production of speech sounds; (a) sequential chain model: order is determined by preceding events only; (b) order is superimposed by a prior program.

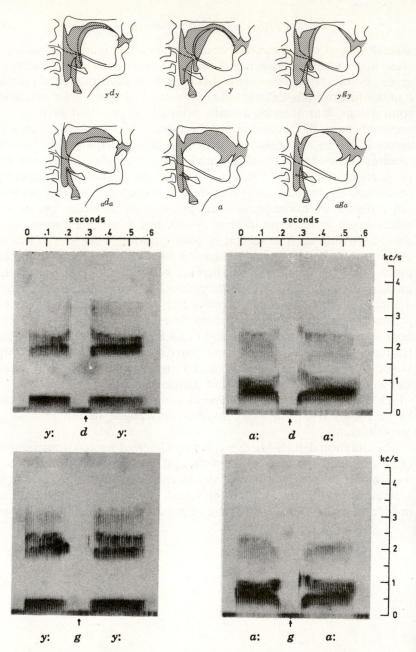

FIG. 3.14. Tracings from x-ray moving films showing the influence of vocalic environments upon the place and manner of production of the stops *d* and *g*. Arrows under the spectrograms show the precise moments at which the pictures were taken. (From Öhman, 1963.)

104

in English, utterances that begin with an *f* sound cannot be followed by a *t* sound. In German, the final stop consonant must be unvoiced; in Portuguese, vowels preceding the *nt* cluster are nasalized, and so on. But the basic problem of temporal ordering and the need to explain anticipation is not affected by these simplifications.

Actual X-ray studies of speech illustrate the importance of the articulatory preplanning. Figure 3.14 based on research by Öhman (1963), shows the position of the tongue at the moments marked by arrows on the accompanying spectrograms. The position and shape of the tongue at the time we hear the stop consonant *d* is different for various vocalic environments. The same is true of the palatal stop *g*.

The most important complication, not properly represented so far, arises from the hierarchical interdependence of all speech events on virtually all levels of analysis, from muscular ordering to word and phrase ordering. The total time required for the activation of all muscles that enter into the production of a single speech sound may be as much as twice as long as the duration of the sound itself. This is represented in diagrammatic form in Fig. 3.15a. If we now consider a cluster of short phones, the interdigitation of individual motor events belonging to different phones again becomes apparent. Figure 3.15b is merely a simplification of Fig. 3.12. Such interdigitation of fragments of a higher unit is characteristic of all sequencing in speech and language. On the lowest level, muscular contractions belonging to different speech sounds intermingle and therefore their sequencing cannot be programmed without considering the order of the speech sounds to

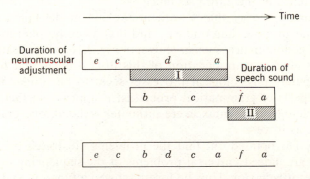

FIG. 3.15. In many instances, the physiological events necessary for the production of speech-sounds precede the occurrence of that sound. The time required for preparation and production of a given sound may take as much as twice the time of the duration of the sound itself. If two such sounds follow close upon each other (as in consonantal clusters), the physiological events (*a* to *f*) of each sound are intermingled in time as diagrammatically shown here.

which they belong. But the choice and sequencing of speech sounds cannot take place without knowledge of the sequence of morphemes to which the sounds belong. This is not only evident from the material presented in Fig. 3.14 but also from rules of morphophonemics. The definite article *the* is pronounced with a /ə/ vowel if it is followed by a consonant but with /i/ if followed by a vowel. Examples of this type occur frequently in all languages. On the next higher level, the level of morphemes, we encounter again the phenomenon of intermingling of elements and an impossibility to plan the sequence without insight into the syntactic structure of higher constituents. Examples of discontinuous, intermingling morphemes are the *is, -ing* of the gerund, or the *has, -ed* of the past participle. (For more powerful arguments of this point see Chomsky's appendix.) On a still higher level, the level of immediate constituents, we find a similar phenomenon which is best illustrated by turning our attention to our understanding of sentences. Consider the first two words of the sentences:

The floor is brown.

The floor is waxed.

These words are understood to be the subject of the sentences. However, in the sentence:

The floor is waxed once a week by charwomen.

the same words are at once understood as the object of the sentence. The mechanism of understanding is essentially no different from the mechanism of planning a sentence for production. This example illustrates also that the highest syntactic elements cannot be ordered without knowledge of the entire sentence.

In summary, we see that a sequential chain model fails to account for the facts in more than one way and that a central plan model with hierarchical dominance, such as shown in Fig. 3.16, is more satisfactory. The most interesting implication of this discussion is that formal aspects of purely physiological processes seem to be similar to certain formal aspects of grammatical processes; it appears, in fact, as if the two, physiology and syntax, were intimately related, one grading into the other, as it were.

Lashley has pointed out that the problems illustrated by the study of syntax are indeed universal problems of the sequencing of any patterned motor behavior. Thus he foreshadowed a fundamental theme of this book: the foundations of language are ultimately to be found in the physical nature of man—anatomy and physiology—and that language is best regarded as a peculiar adaptation of a very universal physiological process to a species-specific ethological function: communication among members of our species.

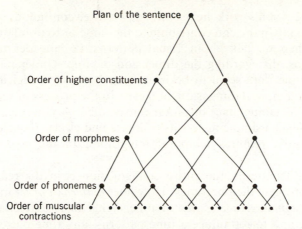

FIG. 3.16. Speech and language units have a hierarchic arrangement; because of the interdigitation of the muscular correlates, the sequential order can be programmed only if the order of phonemes is known. The order of phonemes can only be determined after the order of morphemes is determined. The order of morphological units is dependent upon the entire structure of phrases, and this, in turn, is dependent upon the structure of the sentence.

V. THE PROBLEM OF THE ORGANIZING PRINCIPLE: RHYTHM

The production of speech and the understanding of language may be sustained for several hours without any interruptions longer than a few minutes. Within one minute of discourse as many as 10 to 15 thousand neuromuscular events occur. The facility for production or reproduction of this multitude of overlapping and closely timed activities cannot possibly have been acquired by a simple rote-learning procedure or by any other direct "stamping in" method (Miller, Galanter, and Pribram, 1960). There must be some organizing principle that underlies the perception of speech and language as well as the intricacies of timing and ordering during production. What is that general, organizing principle? Lashley, perceptive also in this respcet, proposed a rhythmic phenomenon as an explanatory construct. He was, however, vague and had no empirical evidence to back up this working hypothesis. A similar solution suggests itself for reasons quite unsuspected by Lashley.

The sequence of speech sounds that constitute a string of words is a sound pattern somewhat analogous to a mosaic; the latter is put together stone after stone, yet the picture as a whole must have come into being in the artist's mind before he began to lay down the pieces. In the progress of his work, he may put down three contiguous stones, each of which may in the end contribute to the same or to unrelated pictorial units. When we talk about visual patterns we consider only spatial dimensions, disregarding the dimension of time. Under most circumstances, time does seem to be irrelevant. Yet, physiological processes do have a temporal dimension, and even in the process of seeing, which strikes us as taking place instantaneously, time plays a role. The identification of such simple figures as triangles and circles requires time and consequently, requires temporal integration in the central nervous system.

In sound patterns, the entire configuration is in the realm of time and the problem then becomes: How does *pattern* or *order* in time differ from *randomness* or *disorder* in time. What is it that enables us to recognize and to reproduce a time pattern—any time pattern?

In music it is well-known that it is possible to recognize melodies by finger tapping, or even head nodding; and after listening to ten seconds or more of finger tapping, we can discriminate fairly well between random tapping and patterned tapping. Behaviorally, patterned tapping can be memorized and is recognizable and reproducible; random tapping is not. The essential nature of a time pattern is an underlying pulse or beat. In the extreme case of order in time, the simplest pattern is the unadulterated pulse such as the tick-tock of a metronome. We can complicate this simple pattern by temporal modulation such as skipping a beat regularly or introducing additional taps between beats where those extra taps must occur at fractional periods of the time unit. The underlying pulse is the carrier on which the rhythmic pattern can be "fastened." It is its indispensable ingredient in much the same way as a figure may only be recognized against a ground. Notice that of all the information contained in a melody none is as indispensable for recognition as that concerning time. We may eliminate variations in pitch, loudness, or timbre and still recognize the melody, but if we destroy the internal temporal relationships without distorting the other variables, the melody becomes at once unrecognizable (cf. also Sachs, 1953).

We have been talking here primarily of sound patterns. But our observations are actually applicable to *all temporal* patterns whether they are perceived through our ears, our eyes, our skin, or our sense of proprioception. In any medium, temporal pattern means a carrier pulse with modulations. Let us call the carrier pulse simply the *rhythm*.

If speech is a patterned temporal phenomenon, and if such phenomena are based on underlying rhythms, is articulation rhythmic?

(1) *The Rhythmic Nature of Articulation*

A rhythm may be marked by equidistant pulses or by simple oscillations. A special case of the latter is the periodic alternation between two states, say sleep and wakefulness, or facilitation and inhibition. The rhythm underlying speech seems to be based on rhythmic alternations between states, although we cannot yet say what the origin or nature of these states might be. Because of our ignorance of the true physiological basis of these states, we must be content with thinking of them as purely theoretical constructs. Let us say they are states of initiation and execution of motor patterns (or cycles of activation and inhibition).

An analogy might illustrate the point. Take once more the drumming of our fingers upon a table top. We can make the taps follow one another in rapid succession, and with practice we may learn to tap without introducing a longer pause or louder tap at the time we start with the small finger again. Nevertheless, the tapping is organized in terms of a single motor pattern of the hand; for every four taps we have to repeat that pattern. If we tap simultaneously with both hands we have two such patterns going on at the same time, and the individual taps from the right and the left hand will intermingle in their temporal sequence. Ordinarily we can hear the tapping rhythm (that is, the grouping by fours), but in some cases the rhythm may no longer be recognizable. However, even in these cases, there are statistical means by which the underlying rhythmicity could be demonstrated. Each motor pattern is somewhat similar to fundamental motor patterns that underlie speech, probably corresponding to syllables.

Let us hypothesize that there is a basic periodicity of approximately six cycles per second.* Since we are not dealing with a mechanical device, we must expect some variations within and among individuals. It is, therefore, safer to hypothesize a rate of 6 ± 1 per second. Thus, one-sixth of a second is taken to be a time unit in the programming of motor-speech patterns. With this assumption, a great variety of phenomena may be explained. The basic facts pertaining to them are well-established, but so far individual, unrelated explanations have been offered for each of them. A single hypothesis concerning an underlying rhythm brings them all together. We shall discuss each under a separate heading.

(*a*) *Delayed Feedback.* Normally we hear our voice at practically

* I am indebted to A. W. F. Huggins for valuable suggestions regarding the following paragraphs.

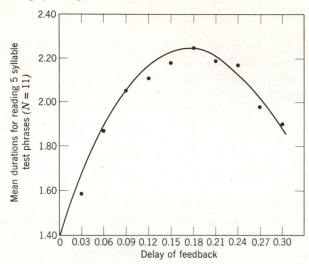

FIG. 3.17. Delayed auditory feedback: the degree of perturbation, expressed in terms of number of seconds it takes to read test sentences, plotted as a function of the magnitude of the delay. Time in seconds. (Based on data by Black, 1951.)

the same time as it is produced. Speech may be seriously disrupted if a delay is artificially introduced between the time we actually speak and the time the corresponding sounds reach our ears. This phenomenon is often called the Lee effect. J. W. Black (1951) studied the relationship between the length of the delay and the degree of speech interference. He measured the latter in terms of the time it took subjects to read certain test material. In Fig. 3.17 this variable is plotted as a function of the delay time. It appears that there is a critical delay that maximizes interference. The greatest interference occurs with a delay of about 180 msec ($\frac{2}{11}$ sec.). The curve found by Black is more or less what we would expect from the rhythm hypothesis.

Let us arbitrarily characterize the activation phase as a sudden peak and the execution phase as a gradual slope as in the functions shown in Fig. 3.18, Curve I (the exact shapes are immaterial for the argument); I(*a*) shows the time of speech production and (*b*), (*c*), and (*d*) show the artificially delayed arrival times of the speech sounds at the ear. In I(*b*) the feedback is delayed by about 40 msec and in I(*d*) by about 165 msec. During the activation phase, the most rapid readjustments in the geometrical spaces of the vocal tract can be made, roughly corresponding to the times in which consonants are produced and/or lips and tongue are set in preparation of vowels; the execution phase is then primarily taken up by the vowel sounds themselves. Thus, the acoustic signals of the activation phase are rapid transitions in the speech wave. When these signals are perceived aurally, they may be assumed to serve as cues for the initiation of the next cycle.

By introducing delays into the feedback loop, the cues for the beginning of the next cycle are delayed by an equal amount of time, thereby prolonging the execution phase. The behavioral correlate of this is the

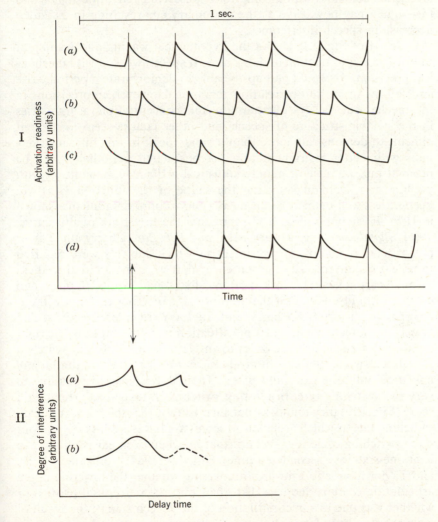

FIG. 3.18. I. Hypothetical changes in the readiness for adjusting articulatory organs. II. Speech interference waxes and wanes as a function of auditory delay time. (For explanation see text.)

drawing out of vowels; this is the most characteristic aspect of speech under delayed auditory feedback. As the delay is increased, the duration of the cycle also is increased accordingly until the delay becomes so long that the signal of the first activation phase arrives at the ears at the same time as the motor apparatus is ready to produce the signal of the second activation phase. At this point, the activation phase of *production* coincides with the auditorily perceived activation *signal,* and this signal may now serve as the customary cue resulting in a sudden decrease in speech interference.

Curve II of Fig. 3.18 shows the hypothetical waxing and waning of interference as a function of delay time. If speech worked with mechanical precision, we would perhaps be able to demonstrate a periodic rise and fall, as in an autocorrelation function. However, imprecisions in the mechanism, factors of attention and concentration, asymmetries in the syllabic structure of speech, and other factors seem to make it difficult to demonstrate more than a single peak in this function. Perhaps with better instrumentation the postulated periodicity may be brought out. Because of mainly statistical artifacts concomitant with pooling and averaging of data, the shape of the function II(*a*) will become less well-defined, resulting in a curve approximating that shown in II(*b*). Presumably, Fig. 3.17 represents the first peak of this curve.

(*b*) *Signal-switching Between Right and Left Ear.* Cherry and Taylor (1954) have reported an experiment in which subjects were required to repeat instantaneously the sentences that were transmitted to them through earphones. This task is often called "shadowing." Subjects can do this without difficulty if the auditory signal comes through without changes or distortions. Cherry and Taylor were interested in seeing how fast a subject could direct his attention from the input to the right ear to that of the left ear. In order to answer this question they switched the speech signal alternatively from one ear to the other, so that at any one time only one ear could listen. Their device made it possible to vary the switching rate. In plotting switching rate against articulation score (Fig. 3.19) they found, rather surprisingly, that there is a "critical" switching rate at which articulation scores are lowest. That rate is about three switching cycles per second (that is, when each ear is allowed to hear one-sixth of a second at a time). Huggins (1964) duplicated Cherry and Taylor in an effort toward discovering whether the lowering of the articulation score is due to a disturbance in the perceptual process or whether it is due to some mutilation of the speech signal; the result of his work favors the latter alternative, although some switching of attention does seem to be taking place. His subjects varied a great deal in the amount of disturbance they experienced from the switching, and

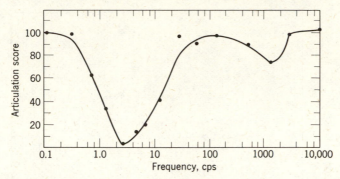

FIG. 3.19. Articulation score for continuous speech, switched periodically at various frequencies from one ear to the other in one subject. For each ear, the proportion of the period occupied by speech is 50%, the remainder being silence. (From Cherry and Taylor, 1954.)

there were few with articulation scores as dramatically lowered as in the subjects reported by Cherry and Taylor. This particular difference between Huggins' results and those obtained by Cherry and Taylor may be due to a number of factors that were not controlled in either of these studies; these factors need not concern us here. Huggins did confirm, however, that there is a critical switching rate, and this rate was constant for all subjects and the same as the one reported by the first authors. When the switching becomes too fast, subjects tend to concentrate on the input of their dominant ear, and therefore the switching, at certain critical rates, may have the effect of essentially interrupting the signal periodically. Nevertheless, Huggins' subjects obtained greater accuracy in their shadowing task when the signal was switched from ear to ear than when presented with nothing but the interrupted speech of one ear. These are merely technical details. Cherry and Taylor, as well as Huggins, were confronted with the magical one-sixth of a second as a basic time unit in speech production. The connection is further clarified by the next point.

(c) *Rate of Interruptions.* Periodically interrupted speech is unintelligible if the interruptions occur with certain frequency. Intelligibility is lowest at a rate of 3 ± 1.5 interruptions per second, that is, when listeners are allowed to hear about 165 msec of speech at a time (with a lower limit of 110 msec and an upper limit of 300 msec). If the interruption rate is outside these limits, intelligibility is much improved, as shown in Fig. 3.20. These curves differ from the results of somewhat similar experiments reported by Miller and Licklider (1950), but the discrepancy must be due to the difference in stimulus materials used.

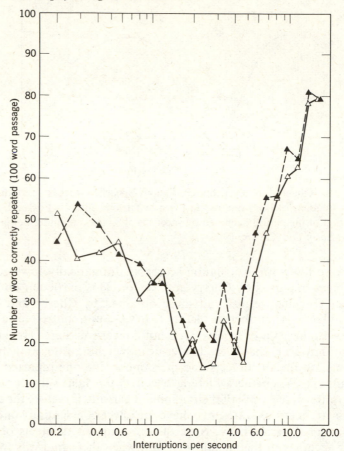

FIG. 3.20. Ability to repeat sentences played back from a tape recorder plotted as a function of the rate of interruptions. The proportion of the duration of silence to the duration of speech heard is always 1:1. The two curves correspond to supplemental tapes. Where there were interruptions in one tape, there was speech in the other. (After Huggins, 1963.)

Miller and Licklider required subjects to identify monosyllabic words, whereas Huggins used connected discourse. Recitation of monosyllabic words lengthens each syllable beyond the duration of the same syllable in connected discourse (cf. also Ahmend and Fatehchand, 1959).

The critical interruption rate and the critical switching rate are easily explained if we assume speech to be constituted of basic units of one-sixth of a second duration. If the interruptions have approximately the same duration, it should be easy to blot out periodically speech-significant units. Thus there is a methodic interference with the intimate texture of articulation. If the interruptions are longer but come less frequently, longer trains of periodic units are eliminated, but trains of similar duration are left intact, making the understanding of some words possible. If the interruptions are six per second, that is, each stretch of speech heard lasts one-twelfth of a second, the rhythmic unit is not sufficiently obscured to make speech unintelligible.

(*d*) *Rate of Syllable Production.* Since the time of the ancient grammarians and inventors of scripts there has been awareness of some rhythmically occurring events in speech, namely the syllable. Stetson and many other phoneticians considered the syllable to be the "true basic unit" of speech. Completely objective definition of the syllable has never been achieved, however, perhaps because of the failure to recognize that this unit is of a physiological nature instead of an acoustic or linguistic one. A physiological correlate of the syllable may be what Stetson called the breath pulse. If the contraction of the thorax during speech is graphically recorded, we may occasionally see trains of little steps on the downward (expiratory) slope of the curve. Frequently our perceptual impression of syllable boundaries is synchronous with these steps. The reason for this is clear: many syllables have a vowel-core delimited by consonants or silence, and most consonants either retard or stop the flow of air and are thus obstacles to the smooth contraction of the thoracic wall. Stetson observed that the rate of breath-pulses clusters around six per second. Hudgins and Stetson (1937) found that the "relative speed of articulatory movements" is also from 5.5 to 7.5 per second. In this case, nonsense syllables such as pa-pa-pa-pa and ta-ta-ta were measured. These measurements check with my own observations on the rate of syllable production in radio newscasters, where the definition of syllable is based on intuition (which, however, has high interobserver reliability). I have also duplicated Hudgins's and Stetson's observations on nonsense syllables with essentially the same results as theirs, the only exception being that subjects between the ages of eight to about thirty could speed up production to eight and occasionally even nine syllables per second for the duration of a few seconds; the rate slowed down to about six per second if the alternating movements were to be sustained over more than three or four seconds. Direct measurements on the duration of speech sounds (Harris, 1953; House, 1961; Lehiste and Peterson, 1961; Peterson and Lehiste, 1960) make the assumption of a basic time unit plausible; however, because of the way in which these measurements were made, they afford only indirect evidence for our hypothesis.

The four points discussed so far concern various aspects of speech production per se. When discussed from the point of view of rhythmicity they seem to be closely related, although these connections were not originally apparent. This lends credence to the hypothesis of a fundamental speech rhythm. The temporal unit of 160 plus or minus 20 msec also appears to play a role in general psychological, and neurophysiological processes.

(*e*) *Psychological Correlates.* Thought is, naturally, a temporal phenomenon, and insofar as there are discrete parts of thought, we can inquire into the rate of production of these parts. This might become a tour de force if we attempted to apply the notion to complex gestalten of thought; but as long as we limit ourselves to thinking about digits or letters, the approach is reasonable. We may run a very simple experiment using our own rates of thinking about numbers or silent counting. Just take a stop watch and count mentally as fast as you can and see how many numbers per second you can count on the average. If we simply count from one to ten over and over, seven digits per second is a high average and somewhat fatiguing to reach. A more comfortable rate that may be sustained for longer periods is six per second. The same is true of letters. In other words, simple *psychological* trains of events appear to move at rhythmic rates similar to observable motor events such as tapping a finger on the table or saying papapa at its fastest but still comfortable speed.

(*f*) *Neurological Correlates: EEG.* When rhythms of the central nervous system are discusssed, our thoughts turn at once to the electroencephalogram. A wide range of rhythms may be recorded extracranially, the rate depending primarily on the state of wakefulness and attentiveness of the subject. Waves with frequencies of less than three per second and up to forty per second are frequently observed in the adult. There is still much to be learned about the origin, nature, and significance of brain waves. At present, there is only one safe conclusion that may be drawn, namely that rhythmic activity is a fundamental property of the vertebrate brain.

The early encephalographers, who analyzed records of brain waves by unaided, visual inspection of the polygraph tracings, were impressed by a dominant nine to ten per second rhythm (called alpha rhythm by its discoverer, Berger) which appeared during states in which the subject was awake but inattentive. This rhythm could be seen primarily in recordings from the occipital region, that is, over the visual projection area. The occipital alpha rhythm does not seem to fit into the range of rhythms that are relevant to speech. However, powerful instruments have become available by means of which we can make various types of mathematical, statistical analyses of the output voltages from electro-

encephalographic amplifiers. With the aid of these instruments, period-
icities have been discovered that had been so masked by "electrical
noise" that they could not have been visualized by direct inspection
of the tracings. There is evidence now that there is a dominant rhythm
more anteriorly which has a slower frequency than that recorded from
the occiput (see Fig. 3.21 from Brazier, 1960). Over the temporo-
parietal region a steady rhythm of about 7 cps has now been identified;
notice that this cortical region is more closely related to the speech
areas than the occipital region. We do not yet know whether there are
several distinct simultaneous rhythms or whether the same rhythmic
phenomenon manifests itself with one frequency in the occiput and
with other frequencies in other areas.

It is also interesting to note that children do not begin to develop
speech until their brains have attained a certain degree of electrophysiological maturity, defined in terms of an increase with age in the
frequency of the dominant rhythm. Only when this rhythm is about
7 cps or faster (at about age two years) are they ready for speech development.

(g) *Neurological Correlates; Pacing of Speech During Thalamic
Stimulation.* Deep electrical stimulation in the basal ganglia and thalamus is frequently performed in the course of surgical treatment of
thalamic pain or certain extrapyramidal motor disorders. Guiot,
Hertzog, Rondot, and Molina (1961) have reported that electrical stimulation in a particular place in the thalamus (the ventrolateral nucleus

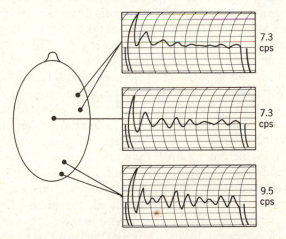

FIG. 3.21. Autocorrelograms of EEGs run simultaneously from bipolar temporal
leads, a unipolar lead from the vertex and bipolar occipital leads. Analyses made
in 5 msec steps of delay. (From Brazier, 1960.)

near its contact with the internal capsule) frequently interferes with the rate of speaking. Both slowing to the point of total arrest and acceleration of speech have been observed. The latter is the more interesting for our discussion. It is a behavioral derangement which may occur in complete isolation, that is, without any other observable motor manifestation or abnormal subjective experience. The patient is conscious and cooperative during part of the operation. He is encouraged to maintain spontaneous conversation and, failing this, is asked to count slowly at a rate of about one digit per second. If acceleration occurs with electrical stimulation, it may be sudden and immediate, or it may be a quick speeding up, the words at the end being generated so rapidly as to become unintelligible. It is significant that under conditions of evoked acceleration the shortest observed intervals between digits are about 170 msec.

Acceleration, uncontrollable by the patient, is occasionally associated with parkinsonism and goes under the name of tachyphemia.

(2) *Final Comments on Speech Rhythmicity (Cultural, Individual and Biological Variations)*

We have proposed that a rhythm exists in speech which serves as an organizing principle and perhaps a timing device for articulation. The basic time unit has a duration of one-sixth of a second. If this rhythm is due to physiological factors rather than cultural ones, it should be then present in all languages of the world. But what about the rhythm of Swedish, Chinese, or Navaho which sound so different to our English-trained ears? What about American Southern dialects which seem more deliberate than the dialect of Brooklyn, New York; and the British dialects which seem faster than American ones? These judgments are based on criteria such as intonation patterns and content of communications, which have little in common with the physiological considerations here. We are concerned with a potential underlying metric of speech movements. The rise and fall time in intonation patterns (non-tonal languages) are much slower than the phenomenon discussed here, usually extending over two seconds and more. With proper analysis, they may well reveal themselves to be multiples of the much faster basic units discussed above. On the other hand, the pitch-phonemes (also known as tonemes) are likely to fall within the same metric as other phonemes. Nor does our ability to speak slowly or fast have any bearing on the "six-per-second hypothesis," because it should be possible to make different use of the time units available. There most likely is more than one way of distributing a train of syllables over the rhythmic vehicles.

On the other hand, physiological factors would allow for individual differences because organisms vary one from the other. Moreover, the underlying rhythm may be expected to vary within an individual in accordance with physiological states and rates of metabolism. Such within-subject variations would, of course, be subtle, and detection would require statistical analysis of the periodic phenomena involved.

The statistic necessary to prove or reject our hypothesis is quite simple. At present the only obstacle is the necessity of making observations and measurements of hundreds of thousands of events. Suppose we programmed an electronic computer to search the electrical analogue of a speech signal for that point in time at which any voiceless stop is released, and then measured the time lapse between all such successive points. From these data we can make histograms (bar-charts) showing the frequency distribution of all measurements. Since our hypothesis assumes that the variable *syllable-duration-time* is not continuous and that there are time quanta, the frequency distribution should be multi-modal; and since the basic time unit is predicted to be 160 ± 20 msec, the distance between the peaks should be equal to or multiples of this unit.

In a previous section of this chapter we have demonstrated certain formal properties of the ordering of speech events. In the discussion of rhythm we have added some temporal dimensions to those events. The rhythm is seen as the timing mechanism which should make the ordering phenomenon physically possible. The rhythm is the grid, so to speak, into whose slots events may be intercalated.

It has long been known that the universally observed rhythmicity of the vertebrate brain (Bremer, 1944; Holst, 1937) or central nervous tissue, in general (Adrian, 1937; Wall, 1959) is the underlying motor for a vast variety of rhythmic movements found among vertebrates. If our hypothesis is correct, the motor mechanics of speech (and probably even syntax) is no exception to this generalization, and in this respect, then, speech is no different from many other types of animal behavior. In man, however, the rhythmic motor subserves a highly specialized activity, namely speech.

VI. SUMMARY

Language, as any other type of behavior, is seen as a manifestation of intricate physiological processes. In higher mammals the processes have many common denominators, but they have also undergone modifications in accordance with specializations in behavior. Respiration, which is in many ways identical in a wide variety of species, shows particularly well forms of adaptations to species-specific behavior patterns. Some such adaptations have been described for the execution of speech and vocalization.

From examination of speech production, the following points emerged:

(1) The neuromuscular correlates of speech sounds are muscular contraction patterns among one and the same set of muscles.

(2) In most instances, physiological events precede the acoustic events of speech sounds.

(3) For individual speech sounds, the duration of physiological events may be twice as long as the duration of acoustic events.

(4) Hence, the sequential arrangements of muscular events require preplanning with anticipation of later events; therefore, the occurrence of some events is contingent upon other events yet to come, which may be adduced as proof that sequencing on a neuromuscular level is not accomplished by an associative mechanism.

(5) The interdigitation of muscular correlates of phones is mirrored also on higher levels of segmentation. Thus ordering-phenomena on all levels of speech and language appear to be related and to exhibit striking formal similarities.

On the neuromuscular level the interdigitation phenomenon poses a problem of timing owing to the fast rate of sound production. Throughout the duration of individual speech sounds, muscles must be activated (or de-activated) at such rapid succession that a neuronal firing order must be assumed that functions with an accuracy of milliseconds. This can be accomplished only by automatisms consisting of intricate time-patterns. Patterning in time (in contrast to temporal disorder) is based on an underlying rhythmic metric. The hypothesis is advanced that the temporal patterns on which the neuromuscular automatisms are based have at their roots a physiological rhythm consisting of periodic changes of "states" at a rate of 6 ± 1 cps. Indirect evidence is cited that articulation itself reflects such a basic rhythm. There are also psychological and neurological rhythms or basic temporal units and their possible relationship to the speech rhythm is discussed.

REFERENCES

Adrian, E. D. (1937), Synchronized reactions in the optic ganglion of *Dytiscus,* *J. Physiol.* **91**:66–89.

Ahmend, R. and Fatehchand, R. (1959), Effect of sample duration on the articulation of sounds in normal and clipped speech, *J. Acoust. Soc. Am.* **31**:1022–1029.

Auriti, G. (1954), Istologia del ricorrente umano, *Clin. otorinolar.* Nos. 6/5 (cited by Krmpotić, 1959).

van den Berg, J. (1956), Direct and indirect determination of the mean subglottic pressure, *Folia Phoniatrica* **8**:1–24.

van den Berg, J. (1962), Modern research in experimental phoniatrics, *Folia Phoniatrica* **14**:81–149.

van den Berg, J.; Zantema, J. T., and Doornenbal, Jr., P. (1957), On the air resistance and the Bernoulli effect of the human larynx, *J. Acoust. Soc. Am.* **29**:626–631.

Björk, L. (1961), Velopharyngeal function in connected speech, *Acta Radiologica,* Supplementum 202.

Black, J. W. (1951), The effects of delayed side-tone upon vocal rate and intensity, *J. Speech Hearing Dis.* **16**:56–60.

Brazier, M. A. B. (1960), Long-persisting electrical traces in the brain of man and their possible relationship to higher nervous activity, in *The Moscow Colloquium on Electroencephalography of Higher Nervous Activity,* H. H. Jasper and G. D. Smirnov (eds.), *EEG Journal Suppl.* **13**:347–358.

Bremer, F. (1944), L'activité "spontanée" des centres nerveux, *Bull. Acad. Roy. de Méd. de Belgique* **9**:148–173.

Cherry, E. Colin and Taylor, W. K. (1954), Some further experiments upon the recognition of speech, with one and with two ears, *J. Acoust. Soc. Am.* **26**:554–559.

Chomsky, N. A. (1957), *Syntactic Structures,* Mouton, The Hague.

Delattre, P. C., Liberman, A. M., and Cooper, F. S. (1955), Acoustic loci and transitional cues for consonants, *J. Acoust. Soc. Am.* **27**:769–773.

Draper, M. H., Ladefoged, P., and Whitteridge, D. (1957), Expiratory muscles involved in speech. *J. Physiol. (London)* **138**:17P, (Proc. Physiol. Soc., July, 1957, Oxford).

Draper, M. H., Ladefoged, P., and Whitteridge, D. (1959), Respiratory muscles in speech. *J. Speech Hearing Res.* **2**:16–27.

Draper, M. H., Ladefoged, P., and Whitteridge, D. (1960), Expiratory pressures and air flow during speech. *Brit. Med. J.* Vol. I, June 18, 1837–1843.

Faaborg-Andersen, K. (1957), Electromyographic investigation of intrinsic laryngeal muscles in humans, *Acta Physiol. Scandinav.* **41,** Suppl. 140.

Fairbanks, G. (1955), Selective vocal effects of delayed auditory feedback, *J. Speech Hearing Dis.* **20**:333–346.

Fant, G. and Lindblom, B (1961), Studies of minimal speech and sound units, *Speech Transmission Lab; Quarterly Progress Report,* **2:**1–11. Royal Institute of Technology, Stockholm.

Fink, R. and Kirschner, F. (1959), Observations on the acoustical and mechanical properties of the vocal folds, *Folia Phoniatrica* **11:**167–172.

Flanagan, J. L. (1958), Some properties of the glottal sound source, *J. speech hearing Res.* **1:**99–116.

Goldman-Eisler, F. (1954), On the variability of the speed of talking and on its relation to the length of utterances in conversations, *Brit. J. Psychol.* **45:**94–107.

Goldman-Eisler, F. (1955), Speech-breathing activity—a measure of tension and affect during interviews, *Brit. J. Psychol.* **46:**53–63.

Goldman-Eisler, F. (1956a), The determinants of the rate of speech output and their mutual relations, *J. Psychosomatic Res.* **1:**137–143.

Goldman-Eisler, F. (1956b), Speech-breathing activity and content in psychiatric interviews, *Brit. J. Med. Psychol.* **29:**35–48.

Goldman-Eisler, F. (1961), The significance of changes in the rate of articulation, *Language and Speech* **4:**171–174.

Guiot, G., Hertzog, E., Rondot, P., and Molina, P. (1961), Arrest or acceleration of speech evoked by thalamic stimulation in the course of stereotaxic procedures for Parkinsonism, *Brain* **84:**363–381.

Harris, C. M. (1953), A study of the building blocks in speech, *J. acoust. Soc. Am.* **25:**962–969.

Hartlieb, K., Luchsinger, R. and Pfister, K. (1960), Ein Vergleich der exspiratorischen mit der inspiratorischen Stimmgebung mit Verwendung der differenzierten Klanganalyse, *Folia Phoniatrica* **12:**241–260.

Holst, E. von (1937), Vom Wesen der Ordnung im Zentralnervensystem, *Naturwissenschaften* **25:**625–31, 641–47.

House, A. S. (1961), On vowel duration in English, *J. acoust. Soc. Am.* **33:**1174–1178.

Hudgins, C. V. and Stetson, R. H. (1937), Relative speed of articulatory movements, *Arch. Néerl. Phonét. Exper.* **13:**85–94.

Huggins, A. W. F. (1963), *Distortion of the temporal pattern of speech: interruption and alternation,* unpublished Ph. D. dissertation, Harvard University.

Huggins, A. W. F. (1964), Distortion of the temporal pattern of speech: interruption and alternation, *J. acoust. Soc. Am.* **36:**1055–1064.

Jakobson, R. and Halle, M. (1956), *Fundamentals of Language,* Mouton, The Hague.

Kainz, F. (1954), *Psychologie der Sprache,* Vol. I–V, 1941, 1943, 1954, 1956, Ferdinand Enke, Stuttgart.

Kelemen, G. (1961), Anatomy of the larynx as a vocal organ: evolutionary aspects, *Logos* **4:**46–55.

Krmpotić, J. (1958), Anatomisch-histologische und funktionelle Verhältnisse des rechten und des linken Nervus recurrens mit Rücksicht auf die Geschwindigkeit der Impulsleitung bei einer Ursprungsanomalie der rechten Schlüsselbeinarterie, *Arch. Ohr.- Nas.- Kehlk. Heilk.* **173:**490–496.

Krmpotić, J. (1959), Données anatomique et histologiques relatives aux effecteurs laryngo-pharyngo-buccaux, *Rev. Laryngol.* (Bordeaux) **11**:829–848.

Krogh, A. (1959), *The Comparative Physiology of Respiratory Mechanisms* (2nd ed.), Univ. of Penn. Press, Philadelphia.

Ladefoged, P. (1960), The regulation of sub-glottal pressure, *Folia Phoniatrica* **12**:169–175.

Ladefoged, P. (1961), Speech production, *Speech Transmission Laboratory Quarterly Progress and Status Report,* Oct. 15, pp. 16–21. Royal Institute of Technology, Stockholm.

Lambertsen, C. J. (1963), Factors in the stimulation of respiration by carbon dioxide, in *The Regulation of Human Respiration,* D. J. C. Cunningham and B. B. Lloyd (eds.), pp. 257–276, Blackwell, Oxford.

Lanz, T. v. and Mayet, A. (1959), Zur Morphologie der Nervenendigungen am quergestreiften Muskel: Untersuchungen am M. Thyreoarytaenoideus des Menschen, *Z. Anat. Entw. Gesch.* **121**:116–129.

Lashley, K. S. (1951), The problem of serial order in behavior, in *Cerebral Mechanisms in Behavior,* L. A. Jeffress (ed.), John Wiley and Sons, New York.

Lehiste, I. and Peterson, G. E. (1961), Transitions, glides and diphthongs, *J. acoust. Soc. Am.* **33**:268–278.

Lenneberg, E. H. (1962), A laboratory for speech research at the Children's Hospital Medical Center, *New Engl. J. Med.* **266**:385–392.

Liberman, A. M., Delattre, P. C., and Cooper, F. S. (1952), The rôle of selected stimulus-variables in the perception of the unvoiced stop consonants, *Am. J. Psychol.* **65**:497–516.

Liberman, A. M., Delattre, P. C., Gerstman, L. J. and Cooper, F. S. (1956), Tempo of frequency change as a cue for distinguishing classes of speech sounds, *J. Exp. Psychol.* **52**:127–137.

Luchsinger, R. and Arnold, G. E. (1959), *Lehrbuch der Stimm- und Sprachheilkunde.* Springer, Vienna.

Miller, G. A. and Chomsky, N. A. (1963), Finitary models of language users, in *Handbook of Mathematical Psychology,* Vol. II, R. D. Luce, R. R. Bush and E. Galanter (eds.), pp. 419–491. John Wiley and Sons, New York.

Miller, G. A., Galanter, E., and Pribram, K. (1960), *Plans and the Structure of Behavior,* Holt, Rinehart and Winston, New York.

Miller, G. A. and Licklider, J. C. R. (1950), The intelligibility of interrupted speech, *J. acoust. Soc. Am.* **22**:167–173.

Müller, E. (1955), Zur Physiologie der Gaumensegelbewegung beim Schlucken und Sprechen, *Archiv. Ohr.- Nas.- Kehlk. Heilk.* **167**:472–477.

Nims, L. F. (1949), Anatomy and physics of respiration, in *A Textbook of Physiology,* 16th ed., J. F. Fulton (ed.), pp. 782–799. Saunders, Philadelphia.

Oberholzer, R. J. H. and Tofani, W. O. (1960), The neural control of respiration, *Handbook of Physiology.* J. Field (ed.), Section I: Neurophysiology, Vol. II, pp. 1111–1129, Am. Physiol. Soc., Washington, D.C.

Öhman, S. (1963), Speech production: coarticulation of stops with vowels, *Speech Transmission Laboratory Quarterly Progress and Status Report.* Royal Institute of Technology, Stockholm, **2**:1–8.

Perkins, J. F. (1963), Arterial CO_2 and hydrogen ion as independent, additive respiratory stimuli: support for one part of the gray multiple factor theory, in *The Regulation of Human Respiration,* D. J. C. Cunningham and B. B. Lloyd (eds.), pp. 303–318. Blackwell, Oxford.

Peterson, G. E. and Lehiste, I. (1960), Duration of syllable nuclei in English, *J. acoust. Soc. Am.* **32:**693–703.

Potter, R. K., Kopp, G. A., and Green, H. C. (1947), *Visible Speech.* D. Van Nostrand Co., New York.

Pressman, J. L. and Kelemen, G. (1955), *Physiology of the Larynx.* Am. Acad. of Opthalmol. and Otolaryngol. Also in *Physiol. Rev.,* **35,** No. 3.

Prosser, C. L. and Brown, F. A. (1961), *Comparative Animal Physiology* (2nd ed.), Saunders, Philadelphia.

Rahn, H. (1963), Lessons from breath holding, in *The Regulation of Human Respiration.* D. J. C. Cunningham and B. B. Lloyd (eds.), pp. 293–302. Blackwell, Oxford.

Ranke, O. F. and Lullies, H. (1953), *Gehör, Stimme und Sprache.* Springer, Berlin.

Sachs, C. (1953), *Rhythm and Tempo: a study in music history.* W. W. Norton, New York.

Schatz, C. D. (1954), The role of context in the perception of stops, *Language* **30:**47–56.

Stetson, R. H. (1951), *Motor Phonetics: a study of speech movements in action.* For Oberlin College, North-Holland, Amsterdam.

Stevens, K. N. and House, A. S. (1963), Perturbation of vowel articulations by consonantal context: an acoustical study, *J. speech hearing Res.* **6:**111–128.

Wall, P. D. (1959), Repetitive discharge of neurons, *J. Neurophysiol.* **22:**305–320.

CHAPTER Four

Language in the context of growth and maturation

I. CHARACTERISTICS OF MATURATION OF BEHAVIOR

Why do children normally begin to speak between their 18th and 28th month? Surely it is not because all mothers on earth initiate language training at that time. There is, in fact, no evidence whatever that any conscious and systematic teaching of language takes place, just as there is no special training for stance or gait. Superficially, it is tempting to assume that a child begins to speak as soon as he has a need for it. However, there is no way of testing this assumption because of the subjectivity of the notion of need. We have here the same logical difficulties as in testing the universality of the pleasure principle as the prime motivation.

To escape the inevitable circularity of the argument we might ask: Do the child's needs change at 18 months because his environment regularly changes at that time, or because he himself undergoes important and relevant changes? Society and parents do behave somewhat differently to an older child, and thus there are some environmental innovations introduced around the time of the onset of speech; yet the changes of the social environment are to a great extent in response to changes in the child's abilities and behavior. Quite clearly the most important differences between the prelanguage and postlanguage phases of development originate in the growing individual and not in the external world or in changes in the availability of stimuli. Therefore, any hypothesis that pivots on an assumption of need may be restated: the needs that arise by eighteen months and cause language to develop are primarily due to maturational processes within the individual. Since needs *per se* can be defined only in a subjective and logically circular manner, it is futile to begin an inquiry into the relevant factors of speech development by the adoption of a need-hypothesis. Instead, we must try to understand the nature of the maturational processes. The central and most interesting problem is whether the emergence of language is due to very general capabilities that mature to a critical minimum at about eighteen months to make language, and many other skills, possible, or whether there might be some factors specific to speech and language that come to maturation and that are somewhat independent from other, more general processes.

Unfortunately, the importance and role of maturation in the development of language readiness cannot be explored systematically by direct experiment, and we are reduced to making inferences from a variety of observations and by extrapolation. The difficulty is that we cannot be certain what kind of experiments or observations to extrapolate from. Behavior is far from the monolithic, clear-cut, self-evident phenomenon postulated by psychologists a generation ago. Different aspects of behavior make their emergence at different periods in the life cycle of an individual and for a variety of causes. Furthermore, the spectrum of causes changes with species.

The hallmarks for maturationally controlled emergence of behavior are the following: (1) regularity in the sequence of appearance of given milestones, all correlated with age and other concomitant development facts; (2) evidence that the opportunity for environmental stimulation remains relatively constant throughout development, but that the infant makes different use of such opportunities as he grows up; (3) emergence of the behavior either in part or entirely, before it is of any immediate use to the individual; (4) evidence that the clumsy beginnings of the behavior are not signs of goal-directed practice.

Points (1) and (2) are obvious and need no elaboration. Point (3) is commonplace in the embryology of behavior. A vast array of motor patterns may be observed to occur spontaneously or upon stimulation in embryos long before the animal is ready to make use of such behavior. The so-called *Leerlaufreaktion* or vacuum activity observed by ethologists is another example of emergence of behavior at given developmental stages and in the absence of any use or externally induced need-fulfillment (for details see Hess, 1962; Lorenz, 1958).

Point (4), the relatively unimportant role of practice for the emergence of certain types of behavior with maturation, has been amply demonstrated in animals by Carmichael (1926, 1927), Grohmann (1938), and by Thomas and Schaller (1954). Similarly, children whose legs had been immobilized by casts (for correcting congenital hip deformations) at the time that gait normally develops can keep perfect equilibrium and essentially appear "to know" how to walk when released from the mechanical handicap even though their muscles may be too weak during the first weeks to sustain weight over many steps.

Generally, there is evidence that species-specific motor coordination patterns (*Erbkoordination*) emerge according to a maturational schedule in every individual raised in an adequate environment. The emergence of such patterns is independent of training procedures and extrinsic response shaping. Once the animal has matured to the point at which these patterns are present, the actual occurrence of a specific pattern movement may depend upon external or internal stimuli (for instance, certain hormone levels in the blood) or a combination of the two (Lehrman, 1958a and 1958b).

The aim of these comments is to direct attention to *potentialities* of behavior—the underlying matrix for behaving—instead of to a specific *act*. If we find that emergence of a certain behavior may be partially or wholly attributed to changes within the organism rather than causative changes in the environment, we must at once endeavor to discover what organic changes there are. Unless we can demonstrate a somatic basis, all our speculations are useless.

The four characteristics of maturationally controlled emergence of behavior will now be employed as touchstones, so to speak, in discussing whether the onset of language may reasonably be attributed to a maturational process.

II. EMERGENCE OF SPEECH AND LANGUAGE

(1) *The Regularity of Onset*

The onset of speech consists of a gradual unfolding of capacities; it is a series of generally well-circumscribed events which take place between the second and third year of life. Certain important speech milestones are reached in a fixed sequence and at a relatively constant chronological age. Just as impressive as the age constancy is the remarkable synchronization of speech milestones with motor-developmental milestones, summarized in Table 4.1.

The temporal interlocking of speech milestones and motor milestones is not a logical necessity. There are reasons to believe that the onset of language is not simply the consequence of motor control. The development of language is quite independent of articulatory skills (Lenneberg, 1962); and the perfection of articulation cannot be pre-

TABLE 4.1. *Developmental Milestones in Motor and Language Development*

At the completion of:	Motor Development	Vocalization and Language
12 weeks	Supports head when in prone position; weight is on elbows; hands mostly open; no grasp reflex	Markedly less crying than at 8 weeks; when talked to and nodded at, smiles, followed by squealing-gurgling sounds usually called *cooing*, which is vowel-like in character and pitch-modulated; sustains cooing for 15–20 seconds
16 weeks	Plays with a rattle placed in his hands (by shaking it and staring at it), head self-supported; tonic neck reflex subsiding.	Responds to human sounds more definitely; turns head; eyes seem to search for speaker; occasionally some chuckling sounds
20 weeks	Sits with props	The vowel-like cooing sounds begin to be interspersed with more consonantal-sounds; labial fricatives, spirants and nasals are common; acoustically, all vocalizations are very different from the sounds of the mature language of the environment
6 months	Sitting: bends forward and uses hands for support; can bear weight when put into standing position, but cannot yet stand with holding on; reaching: unilateral; grasp: no thumb apposition yet; releases cube when given another	Cooing changing into babbling resembling one-syllable utterances; neither vowels nor consonants have very fixed recurrences; most common utterances sound somewhat like ma, mu, da, or di

128

TABLE 4.1 (*Continued*)

8 months	Stands holding on; grasps with thumb apposition; picks up pellet with thumb and finger tips	Reduplication (or more continuous repetitions) becomes frequent; intonation patterns become distinct; utterances can signal emphasis and emotions
10 months	Creeps efficiently; takes side-steps, holding on; pulls to standing position	Vocalizations are mixed with sound-play such as gurgling or bubble-blowing; appears to wish to imitate sounds, but the imitations are never quite successful; beginning to differentiate between words heard by making differential adjustment
12 months	Walks when held by one hand; walks on feet and hands—knees in air; mouthing of objects almost stopped; seats self on floor	Identical sound sequences are replicated with higher relative frequency of occurrence and words (mamma or dadda) are emerging; definite signs of understanding some words and simple commands (show me your eyes)
18 months	Grasp, prehension and release fully developed; gait stiff, propulsive and precipitated; sits on child's chair with only fair aim; creeps downstairs backward; has difficulty building tower of 3 cubes	Has a definite repertoire of words—more than three, but less than fifty; still much babbling but now of several syllables with intricate intonation pattern; no attempt at communicating information and no frustration for not being understood; words may include items such as thank you or come here, but there is little ability to join any of the lexical items into spontaneous two-item phrases; understanding is progressing rapidly

TABLE 4.1 (*Continued*)

At the completion of:	Motor Development	Vocalization and Language
24 months	Runs, but falls in sudden turns; can quickly alternate between sitting and stance; walks stairs up or down, one foot forward only	Vocabulary of more than 50 items (some children seem to be able to name everything in environment); begins spontaneously to join vocabulary items into two-word phrases; all phrases appear to be own creations; definite increase in communicative behavior and interest in language
30 months	Jumps up into air with both feet; stands on one foot for about two seconds; takes few steps on tip-toe; jumps from chair; good hand and finger coordination; can move digits independently; manipulation of objects much improved; builds tower of six cubes	Fastest increase in vocabulary with many new additions every day; no babbling at all; utterances have communicative intent; frustrated if not understood by adults; utterances consist of at least two words, many have three or even five words; sentences and phrases have characteristic child grammar, that is, they are rarely verbatim repetitions of an adult utterance; intelligibility is not very good yet, though there is great variation among children; seems to understand everything that is said to him
3 years	Tiptoes three yards; runs smoothly with acceleration and deceleration; negotiates sharp and fast curves without difficulty; walks stairs by alternating feet; jumps 12 inches; can operate tricycle	Vocabulary of some 1000 words; about 80% of utterances are intelligible even to strangers; grammatical complexity of utterances is roughly that of colloquial adult language, although mistakes still occur
4 years	Jumps over rope; hops on right foot; catches ball in arms; walks line	Language is well-established; deviations from the adult norm tend to be more in style than in grammar

dicted simply on the basis of general motor development. There are certain indications for the existence of a peculiar, language-specific maturational schedule. Many children have learned a word or two before they start to toddle, and thus must be assumed to possess a sufficient degree of motor skill to articulate, however primitive; yet the expansion of their vocabulary is still an extremely slow process. Why could they not rapidly increase their lexicon with "sloppy" sound-symbols much the way a child with a cleft palate does at age three? Similarly, parents' inability to train their children at this stage to join the words *daddy* and *by-by* into a single utterance cannot be explained on the grounds of motor incompetence, because at the same age children babble for periods as long as the duration of a sentence. In fact, the babbled "sentence" may be produced complete with intonation patterns. The retarding factor for language acquisition here must be a psychological one, or perhaps better, a cognitive one and not mechanical skill. About age three manual skills show improved coordination over earlier periods, but dexterity is still very immature on an absolute scale. Speech, which requires infinitely precise and swift movements of tongue and lips, all well-coordinated with laryngeal and respiratory motor systems, is all but fully developed when most other mechanical skills are far below their levels of future accomplishment. The evolvement of various motor skills and motor coordinations also has specific maturational histories; but the specific history for speech control stands apart dramatically from histories of finger and hand control.

The independence of language development from motor coordination is also underscored by the priority of language comprehension over language production. Ordinarily the former precedes the latter by a matter of a few months (especially between the ages of 18 to 36 months). In certain cases this gap may be magnified by many years (Lenneberg, 1964). Careful and detailed investigations of the development of understanding by itself have been undertaken only in more recent years (Brown and Bellugi, 1964; Ervin, 1964; Ervin and Miller, 1963). The evidence collected so far leaves little doubt that there is also an orderly and constant progression in this aspect of language development.

The development of children with various abnormalities provides the most convincing demonstration that the onset of language is regulated by a maturational process, much the way the onset of gait is dependent upon such a process, but at the same time the language-maturational process is independent of motor-skeletal maturation. In hypotonic children, for instance, the musculature in general is weak, and tendon reflexes are less active than normal. Hypotonia may be an isolated phenomenon that is quickly outgrown or a sign of a disease such as muscular atrophy, which would have unfortunate effects on the child's future motor development. Whatever the cause, the muscular development alone may be lagging behind other developmental aspects and thus disarrange the normal intercalation of the various processes. Here, then, speech and language emerge at their usual time while motor development lags behind.

On the other hand, there are some children with normal intelligence and normal skeletal and motor development whose speech development alone is markedly delayed. We are not referring here to children who never learn to speak adequately because of acquired or congenital abnormalities in the brain, but rather of those who are simply late speakers, who do not begin to speak in phrases until after age four, who have no neurological or psychiatric symptoms which can explain the delay, and whose environment appears to be adequate. The incidence of such cases is small (less than one in a hundred), but their very existence underscores the independence of language-maturational processes from other processes.

There are also conditions that affect all developmental processes simultaneously. These are diseases in which growth and maturation are retarded or stunted through a variety of factors (for instance, of an endocrine nature as in hypothyroidism); or retardation may be due to an intracellular abnormality such as the chromosomal disorder causing mongolism. In these cases all processes suffer alike, resulting in general "stretching" of the developmental time scale, but leaving the intercalation of motor and speech milestones intact (Lenneberg, Nichols, and Rosenberger, 1964). The preservation of synchrony between motor and speech or language milestones in cases of general retardation is, I believe, the most cogent evidence that language acquisition is regulated by maturational phenomena.

The evidence presented rules out the possibility of a direct, causal relationship between motor and speech development. Normally, growth and maturation proceed at characteristic rates for each developmental aspect. In the absence of specific retardations affecting skills or organs differentially, a picture of consistency evolves such as represented in Table 4.1 or in the many accounts of normal human development (McGraw, 1963; Gesell and Amatruda, 1947).

The use of the word *skill* brings out another interesting aspect of the emergence of speech. With proper training probably everybody could attain some proficiency in such diverse skills as roller-skating, sketching, or piano playing. However, there are also vast individual differences in native endowment and considerable variation with respect to the age at which training is most effective. Perfection can rarely be expected before the teens. The establishment of speech and language is quite different; a much larger number of individuals show equal aptitude, absence of the skill is rare, and onset and fluency occur much earlier, with no particular training required.

Nevertheless, individual differences in time of onset and reaching of various milestones exist and must be accounted for. The rate of development is not constant during the formative years, and there may be transient slowing in the rate of maturation, with subsequent hastening. This is hardly surprising in view of the complex interrelation of intrinsic and extrinsic factors that affect development. Nevertheless, there is a remarkable degree of regularity in the emergence of language. Figure 4.1 illustrates the regularity in the attainment of three major language-developmental levels and Fig. 4.2 illustrates the sudden increase in vocabulary size, particularly around the third birthday.

In a survey of 500 middle and lower-class children in the Boston area, examined in connection with an epidemiological study, we found that nine out of ten children had acquired all of the following verbal skills by the time they reached their 39th month; ability to name most

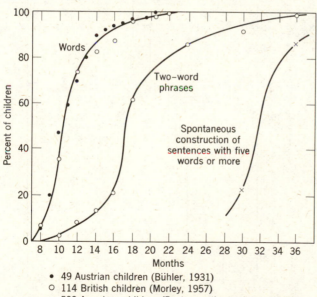

• 49 Austrian children (Bühler, 1931)
○ 114 British children (Morley, 1957)
× 500 American children (Boston, author's observation)

FIG. 4.1. Emergence of various developmental milestones in the acquisition of language.

objects in the home, fair intelligibility, ability to comprehend spoken instructions, spontaneous utterance of syntactically complex sentences, and spontaneity in oral communication. The field observations were made in the child's home by specially trained social workers who worked with a screening test and a schedule of questions. Any child who was found or suspected to fall short of these standards was referred, by the social worker, to my office where he was examined by a speech

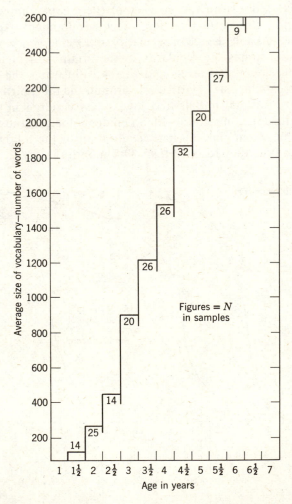

FIG. 4.2. Average vocabulary size of ten samples of children at various ages. (Data based on Smith, 1926.)

TABLE 4.2. *Distribution of Causes for Failing Language Screening Test (Given to 500 children at about the third birthday)*

	Number
(1) Uncooperative child but, upon more intense examination, apparently normal speech development (health good, environment adequate)	7
(2) Poor articulation, but otherwise normal onset of language milestones (health good, environment adequate)	29
(3) Various types of speech defects associated with psychiatric conditions	9
(4) Speech defects associated with other behavioral disorders due to gross environmental abnormalities	2
(5) Speech defects associated with central nervous system disease	3
(6) Delayed onset of speech, unexplained (health good, environment adequate)	4

therapist, an audiologist, and by myself. Fifty-four children were thus referred and found to fall into the classifications shown in Table 4.2.

Differences in age at onset become much less dramatic if we scrutinize these statistics. Of 486 children who were free from nervous or mental disease and were raised in an adequate environment (all children in the sample except those of groups 3, 4, and 5) only 33 (less than 7%) were below the norm of attainment.

(2) *The Relation of the Environment to the Age of Onset*

It is obvious that a child cannot acquire language unless he is exposed to it. Apart from this trivially obvious point, the role of the environment is not immediately clear. There are two major problems: (1) How are the infant's eventual capabilities for language acquisition affected by environmental variations during his prelanguage life; (2) what influence does the environment have upon the age at which language capabilities appear? We must emphasize once more that we are concerned with potentialities, not actually occurring behavior. Many of the earlier studies failed to make this distinction. Subnormal speech habits may not be used as evidence for subnormal capacity. Most language tests assess the quality of existing language development but they do not tell us if the children tested are actually not capable of taking advantage of existing stimulation. It is a reasonable assumption that in most instances an initially poor language environment does not cripple the child's basic potentialities forever. If the social environment is enriched early enough, he will at once improve his language habits. The important point here is that intuitively the notion can be accepted that language potentialities do develop regularly and in spite of certain environmental deprivations. A closer look at the empirical investigations support precisely this view.

In many countries families consist of many children where the birth of one is quickly followed by the birth of another. The social environment of the first child is clearly different from that of a subsequent child. This makes possible empirical research into the relation between age at attainment of certain milestones and social environment. Morley (1957) contributed statistics showing that the age of emergence of single words, of phrases, and of intelligible speech is no different for first than for subsequent children.

Even for single or first children the environment is not always the same. Mothers vary greatly in their attitudes toward their children. Some use baby talk; others are very silent. Some mothers bring a natural maternal warmth and certainty to the nursery, and others are ill at ease with their first child. Some children are welcome additions, but others are not. Further statistics compiled by Morley indicate that variables such as "mother's ability to cope," loss or temporary absence of either parent, or socioeconomic class are not predictive of the age of emergence of various milestones in speech development.

Morley's findings are not contradicted by studies which report differences in speech habits of children of the upper, middle, and lower class (Bühler, 1931; Irwin, 1948; and many others). These are usually cross-sectional studies in which nature and quality of speech is compared with a norm but the age of onset of certain speech phenomena is not determined. Morley found that the language habits which emerged at the common time soon showed signs of impoverishment in the underprivileged, and unintelligibility occurred more commonly in second and subsequent children than in first. Thus the influence of the environment upon speech habit is undeniable, even though the onset of speech habits is relatively unaffected.

The differences observed in the speech habits of upper and lower class children are actually difficult to evaluate because of the many covarying factors. For example, the influence of malnutrition and of diseases that delay development is higher among poorer children who may also be emotionally less amenable to testing situations than those from more carefree homes. In attempts to estimate the child's vocabulary by means of flash cards, an assumption is made that the relative frequency of occurrence of words in the vocabularies of the upper and lower class is identical. This is not necessarily valid.

The role of environment is documented most drastically by the studies on the development of children in orphanages (Brodbeck and Irwin, 1946; Goldfarb, 1943; Dennis and Dennis, 1951; Fisichelli, 1950; McCarthy, 1954). Without considering the old question of the possible difference in biological stock between this and the general population, there is no denying that the institutional life leaves its mark on speech and language habits. On the other hand, Goldfarb (1945) and Dennis and Najarian (1957) have given an illustration of covert processes in the unfolding of potentialities. Children reared in orphanages are frequently below average in speech and motor development when tested at three but when retested at six or seven are found to have caught up with the control population. As soon as their environment is enriched, perhaps through greater freedom to move around, they are able to make use of the greater stimulus availability.

Lenneberg, Rebelsky, and Nichols (1965) have studied emergence of vocalization during the first three months of life as it relates to the parents' speech and hearing. Children of congenitally deaf parents (deaf father and mother) were compared with children born to hearing and normally speaking parents. Among the six deaf families studied, five of the babies had normal hearing but in one case the baby was born deaf. Twenty-four-hour tape recordings were made bi-weekly in the child's home and compared qualitatively and quantitatively. The environment of the two groups of children differed in two ways: (1) the amount, nature and occasion of adult vocalization heard by the babies differed significantly, and (2) the baby's own vocalizations could never be responded to by a deaf mother who, we discovered, could not even tell whether her child's facial expressions and gestures were accompanied by silence or noise. The babies born to hearing parents appeared to vocalize on the occasions of adult vocalization, whereas the babies born to deaf parents did not. Nevertheless, they made as much noise and went through the same sequence of vocalization development with identical ages of onset (for cooing noises) as the control group.

We have also been able to observe older hearing children born to deaf couples, although I have not undertaken a statistical study. These observations, on a dozen children in five families, leave no doubt that language onset is never delayed by this dramatically abnormal environment, even though the quality of vocalization of the preschool children tends to be different; children very soon become "bilingual" in the sense that they use normal voice and speech for hearing adults and abnormal voice and "deafisms" for their parents.

How universal in human society is the onset of speech? Do cultural attitudes toward child-rearing influence the emergence of speech, or are there languages that are either so complicated that no one can master oral communication until puberty, or so primitive that the entire system is learned by every child before he begins to toddle? There are many studies on child development in primitive cultures and most authors have described every minute deviation from the norm of western society. Strangely enough, the onset of speech has rarely been a subject of a detailed study in the anthropological literature (but see Austerlitz, 1956; Kroeber, 1916). Apparently no field worker has even been struck by any discrepancies between the vocalizations or communicative behavior among the children of "primitive" and "western" man. I have investigated this problem further with the cooperation of several students in anthropology (Samuel Putnam, Mary Ann Whelan, and Eleanor Crocker) who made direct field observations among the Dani of Dutch New Guinea, the Zuni of the American Southwest, and the Bororo of Central Brazil.

In these investigations, children were given tests of sensory-motor development such as coordination for reaching, nature of the grasp, and the ability to walk, stand on one leg, or throw a ball. Tape recordings were made of the vocalizations of the babies before they appeared to possess the common language, as well as of their utterances throughout their physical development to age three. In addition, information was obtained from native informants about the linguistic competence of the various children studied, their fluency, types of mistakes in articulation, syntax, and choice of words, and information was gathered on the parents' attitude toward their children's speech development. In some instances, the chronological age of the child studied was not known, and therefore neither the motor nor the language achievements could be compared directly with the age of emergence in American children. But the chronological age was not as important as the question of whether developmental progress, gauged upon the emergence of definite motor skills, marked also the beginning and major milestones of the child's speech development, and whether the concordance between speech and motor development observed in western children were also found in children of these cultures. As far as we can judge from the analysis of the material, the answer is clearly yes. The first words appear at about the time that walking is accomplished, and by the time a child is able to jump down from a chair (or its equivalent), tiptoe, or walk backward three yards, he is reported by the informants to be communicating fluently, even though certain inaccuracies and childlike usages seem always to persist for a longer period. Anthropologists have pointed out that the label "primitive language" is misleading when applied to any natural living language. The developmental studies here support the view that no natural language is inherently more complicated or simpler to learn by a growing child than any other language.* There seems to be no relation between progress in language acquisition and culturally determined aspects of language.

In summary, it cannot be proved that the language environment of the growing child remains constant throughout infancy, but it can be shown that an enormous variety of environmental conditions leaves at least one aspect of language acquisition relatively unaffected: the age of onset of certain speech and language capabilities. Thus, the emergence of speech and language habits is more easily accounted for by assuming maturational changes within the growing child than by postulating special training procedures in the child's surroundings.

(3) *The Role of Utility in the Onset of Speech*

There is evidence, although only of a circumstantial nature, that language does not emerge as a response to an experienced need, as a result of discovery of its practical utility, or as a product of purposive striving toward facilitated verbal communication. I have made tape recordings of the spontaneous noises made during play by congenitally deaf children. In two instances, periodic sample recordings were made of deaf children born to deaf parents; samples began during the first month of life. Sixteen other deaf children were recorded between their second and fifth year. Usually, follow-up recordings are available throughout an 18 month period. All 18 children vocalized often during concentrated play; the quality of their voices was quite similar to that of hearing children, and in certain respects the development of their vocalizations was parallel to that observed in hearing children, although the deaf did not develop words. Nevertheless, cooing appeared at about three months, babbling sounds were heard at six months and later, and laughter and sounds of discontent seemed identical with those of the hearing population. It was particularly interesting to note that many of the deaf children, during their spontaneous babbling, would produce sounds that were well-articulated speech sounds such as pakapakapaka. This does not imply that there was no difference between the deaf and hearing children over six months. The deaf had a tendency to

* Slobin (1966) reports that several aspects of Russian morphology and syntax are not learned by the Russian child until after entering school. However, he informed the author in personal conversation that the forms acquired later are rarely used (or even used wrongly) in colloquial discourse.

engage in certain types of noise more persistently, whereas the hearing would tend to go frequently through a wide range of different types of babbling sounds, as if to run through their repertoire for the sheer pleasure of it. No precise quantitative measurements of amount of vocalization could be made on the children after the first three months, but subjectively the hearing children were much more vocal in the presence of others than the deaf.

A healthy deaf child two years or older gets along famously despite his total inability to communicate verbally. These children become very clever in their pantomime and have well-developed techniques for communicating their desires, needs, and even their opinions. There is no indication that congenital peripheral deafness causes significant adjustment problems within the family during preschool years. This observation has an important bearing on the problem of motivation for language acquisition. Language is extremely complex behavior, the acquisition of which, we might have thought, requires considerable attention and endeavor. Why do hearing children bother to learn this system if it is possible for a child to get along without it? Probably because the acquisition of language is not, in fact, hard labor—it comes naturally—and also because the child does not strive toward a state of perfect verbal intercourse, normally attained only two years after the first beginnings.

(4) *The Importance of Practice for the Onset of Speech*

Closely related to the question of utility is the problem of practice. Do cooing and babbling represent practice stages for future verbal behavior? We have every indication that this is not so. Occasionally the natural airways above the voice box become narrowed because of swelling in connection with disease, and an opening must be made into the trachea below the larynx for insertion of a tube through which the patient can breathe. This prevents the patient from making sounds, since most of the expired air escapes before it can excite the vocal cords. I have examined a 14-month-old child who had been tracheotomized for 6 months. A day after the tube had been removed and the opening closed the child produced the babbling sounds typical of the age. No practice or experience with hearing his own vocalizations was required.

Comparable observations may be made on children (not older than 24 months) who are admitted to a hospital because of severe physical neglect by the parents. On admission they are characteristically apathetic, unresponsive babies who seem to be grossly retarded in their motor, social, and sound development. After a few weeks of hospital care, they become less reserved, begin to relate to the nursing staff, and make all the noises that are heard in infants of comparable age. If the neglected child is over three or four years of age, environmental deprivation will have contributed to severe emotional disturbance often more typical of psychotic conditions (Davis, 1947). However, some children with psychoses, regardless of whether parental neglect was a contributing factor, give excellent demonstrations of subclinical language development. There are children who fail to communicate with the world around them, including their own parents, and who give an impression of muteness and incomprehension from their second year of life on. Yet in response to treatment, or even spontaneously, some will often snap out of their state of isolation and almost miraculously begin to talk fluently and in accordance with their age level (Luchsinger and Arnold, 1959, and own observations). Practice is, of course, not the same as learning. It is fair to say that these children have not practiced speech and language in the same manner as normal children might, but we cannot say that they have not undergone years of learning. They simply did not choose to respond.

(5) "Wolf Children"

It is difficult to refrain from referring to the stories of children supposedly reared by wolves and other cases of extreme neglect. Yet a careful analysis of this literature is convincing that even the most fundamental information is usually missing in the descriptions or omitted from the case reports. The children are invariably discovered by well-meaning but untrained observers, and the urgency for getting help to the victims is so overwhelming that the scientifically most important first months are the least well-documented. The nature of the social and physical environment is never clear and the possibility of genetic deficiencies or congenital abnormalities can never be ruled out. One child reported by Davis (1947) was discovered at age six without speech, but was said to have made very rapid progress, going through all the usual baby language stages, and within a period of nine months had attained complete mastery of speech and language. In the same article, a comparable case is described, also discovered at age six but who only began to speak at age nine. At the time of her death at ten and one-half, she could name people and communicate her needs by a few sentences. The behavioral descriptions of this child point to severe psychosis and feeble-mindedness. Descriptions of children supposedly reared by wolves or growing up in forests by themselves are plentiful, but none is trustworthy (Koehler, 1952). Singh and Zingg (1942) have collected the entire material, and an excellent commentary may be found in Brown (1957). The only safe conclusions to be drawn from the multitude of reports is that life in dark closets, wolves' dens, forests, or sadistic parents' backyards is not conducive to good health and normal development.

It is impossible to say why some children are capable of overcoming the insults inflicted upon their early health, whereas others succumb to them. The degree and duration of neglect, the initial state of health, the care provided for them after discovery, and many other factors are bound to influence the outcome; in the absence of information on these points, virtually no generalizations may be made with regard to human development.

We started by developing criteria for the distinction of behavioral emergence due to changes of capacity within the growing individual (regularity in onset, differential use of environmental stimulation with growth, independence from use, and superfluousness of practice). Applying these criteria to language and assuming the existence of an adequate environment we have found strong suggestions that the appearance of language is primarily dependent upon the maturational development of states of readiness within the child.

III. AGE LIMITATIONS TO LANGUAGE ACQUISITION

Analogous to the question of how old must a child be before he can make use of the environment for language acquisition is the question of how young must an individual be before it is too late to acquire speech and language. There is evidence that the primary acquisition of language is predicated upon a certain developmental stage which is quickly outgrown at the age of puberty.

(1) *Age and Recovery from Traumatic Aphasia*

The most revealing evidence for an age limitation of language acquisition is provided by adventitious language disorders. The chances for recovery from acquired aphasia are very different for children than for adult patients, the prognosis being directly related to the age at which insult to the brain is incurred. To illustrate this difference, let us first describe the recovery patterns for adult patients.

The patient with aphasia has not, strictly speaking, lost his language habits the way we may "lose" a poem, once memorized and now forgotten. Nor is he in a cognitive state that is comparable to the 20-month-old infant before the advent of language learning. Usually, there is evidence that language is not lost but that its proper organization, in either the expressive or the receptive process or both, is interfered with. He cannot organize his cognitive activities to recruit, integrate or inhibit the many partial processes, which when consolidated are prerequisite for speaking and understanding. Yet, shreds of the earlier language behavior usually persist, although there are some patients who can say no more than a few words, and sometimes even these few utterances may be unintelligible jargon.

In contrast to normal small children, the adult patient does not relearn language. Neither training nor conditioning procedures are guarantees for the restoration of language to the patient with a well-established aphasia. This is understandable because his problem is not that he does not know language but that he can no longer make use of language that he has learned. A patient with aphasia has not lost other, more general abilities to learn; he is not demented and not psychotic; he may continue to make new associations, to build up new expectations, to make new inferences and, generally, to give signs that his nonspecific learning capacities have not come to an end. Thus, the language disorder is not a learning impairment.

Aphasias acquired during adult life, that is, after the age of eighteen, may recover within a three-to-five months period. There are reasons to believe that this is due to physiological restoration of function rather than a learning process. Symptoms that have not cleared up by this time are, as a rule, irreversible.

There are a few clinical exceptions to this picture (Woodward, 1945, and two cases alluded to in Marks, Taylor, and Rush, 1957). Speech disturbances resulting from anoxic states often disappear more gradually with recovery periods extending over a year or more. Furthermore, aphasia is often accompanied by emotional depressions. If this is the case, speech rehabilitation may work wonders by instilling confidence and by encouraging the patient to explore all his remaining potentialities; he may learn to compensate for certain losses by recruiting skills not ordinarily part of the speech and language act. The five-months-rule previously mentioned holds true for the basic capacities for verbal communication.

When aphasic symptoms subside in the adult patient, he does not traverse the infant's stages of language learning. There is no babbling, single-word stage followed by a two-word-phrase stage. There is no semantic overgeneralization nor a gradual emergence of the more complex grammatical constructions. Dysarthria (which in most instances is caused by quite different pathology from aphasia) does not have the characteristics of unintelligibility in childhood, and the overcoming of dysarthria is not a gradual differentiation into contrasting phonemes. Recovery from aphasia and dysarthria means arrest of interference with established habits. This is very different from the emergence and assembly of speech and language phenomena throughout the synthesizing process of language acquisition.

We must now turn to the likelihood of recovery from aphasia and the incidence of permanent, irreversible aphasic symptoms in traumatized adult patients. For this type of inquiry, we are primarily dependent upon published case material.

Generally speaking, evaluation of the literature on aphasia is extremely difficult. The individual clinical picture cannot be understood unless over a dozen variables are known. Some of these concern the etiology and pathology; others the symptoms per se; others have to do with the reliability and accuracy of the history; still others with environmental conditions. In the compilation of published case reports, we find that authors differ enormously in their thoroughness of reporting. Usually, a few arbitrary facts are reported, with a constantly changing choice of emphasis, sometimes even differing from patient to patient within the same article. This makes it difficult to compare cases with assurance of commensurability. The worst kind of article is that in which various statistics are presented for a given population, giving in one table a breakdown of ages, in another a breakdown of pathologies, in still another a breakdown of recovery histories. By reshuffling patients into different classifications, the actual connections and correlations among the many variables are totally obliterated, so that we can no longer judge what facts of the history are related to what aspects of the condition and treatment.

A further difficulty arises from the lack of uniform definition of terms. A term such as "recovery" is often used when partial *improvement* is meant; "loss of language" could mean either *paucity of utterances,* or *lack of comprehension,* or *difficulty in production,* etc. "Learning to speak" usually means return to a *status quo* without signs of actual learning or relearning. "Agrammatism" may mean *telegraphic style* in a patient for whom speaking requires an inordinate effort and who reduces his utterances to the barest minimum for intelligibility; on the other hand, it may mean fluent speech with many grammatical mistakes. There is virtually no term that has not been used in a number of different senses.

TABLE 4.3 *Clinical Course of Left-Sided Trauma in 88 War Veterans*

	Number	*Percent*
Aphasia cleared within 3 months or less	29	32
Permanent aphasic residues	26	30
Slow and protracted improvement; final status not reported	5	6
Initial aphasia cleared but permanent associated symptoms	7	8
Clinical course not reported	7	8
No aphasia	14	16

Based on Russell and Espir, 1961.

Generalizations on aphasia must essentially be based on our own clinical experience. Reference to the literature is made here primarily to take the discussion out of the realm of mere anecdotal accounts. We rely only on published case histories that contain a great many relatively well established facts.

In Table 4.3 we have summarized the clinical course of aphasic war veterans whose histories were reconstructed from reports published by Russell and Espir (1961). The majority of these young men have *either* temporary aphasias (three months duration or less) *or* lasting residual aphasic symptoms. Only five of the 88 had histories which might possibly have been characterized by slow and continuous improvement over years. Actually, this was stated explicitly for only one of these patients; but the description of the other four makes slow recovery at least possible. In no case in this group did the aphasia seem to disappear entirely after the prolonged recovery period.

The recovery history for aphasias caused by stroke is essentially the same as that caused by trauma. Whether the proportion of recoveries is identical in the two populations is difficult to ascertain because of the many additional differences between the stroke patients and the war veterans.

Compare now aphasia in childhood. We shall only consider children who had been in possession of language before the catastrophe and who suffered a one-sided lesion.

The aphasic symptoms seen in the adult traumatized patient may also be observed in children with comparable lesions. The only possible exception is the so-called fluency aphasia or "logorrhea" in which the patient is either unable or unwilling to inhibit his flow of speech, producing a continuous train of semantically disconnected phrases or sentences. This symptom is rare or perhaps altogether absent among pediatric patients. Otherwise, the general characterization of aphasia as interference with existing verbal habits also applies to this group. However, there are other important differences between children and adult aphasics. If the aphasia occurs early in life, for example, at age four, two processes intermingle so intensely during the recovery period that a rather different clinical picture emerges. The two processes are the interference phenomena caused by the lesion and the extremely active language-learning process that may not be inhibited at all by the disease or may only very temporarily have come to an arrest, soon to be reinstated.

In patients between four and ten years of age, the symptoms are similar to adult symptomatology but there is an extraordinary difference in the prognosis in two ways: the overwhelming majority of these children recover fully and have no aphasic residue in later life (even though some individuals may always retain minor cognitive or perceptual deficits that may or may not be related to language, Teuber, 1950, 1960); and the period during which recovery from aphasia takes place may last much longer than in the adult. Instead of the adult trend toward a five months period of improvement, children may show steady improvement over a period of several years, but usually not after puberty.

In Table 4.4 I have compiled 17 published case reports together with eight reports on children either examined personally in Children's Hospital Medical Center of Boston (CHMC) or whose record was made available to me. Only those published reports were included in which the exact age at injury and some information on the rate, progress, and residue of recovery was given and the pathology was lateralized. Apparently, aphasia runs a different course before the end of the first decade than after it. Neither in these cases nor in those published cases omitted here because of incomplete information on recovery is there any record of permanent residue from acquired unilateral, aphasia-producing lesions incurred during early childhood. If language had developed before the onset of the disease and if the lesion is confined to a single hemisphere, language will invariably return to a child if he is less than nine years old at the time of the catastrophe.*

If aphasia strikes the very young during or immediately after the age at which language is acquired (between 20 to 36 months of age), the recovery is yet different. Cerebral trauma to the two or three year old will render the patient totally unresponsive, sometimes for weeks at a time; when he becomes cognizant of his environment again, it becomes

* But compare note on page 187!

TABLE 4.4. *Recovery from Aphasic Symptoms*

Patient's Age at Insult (Years)	Residual Deficit Remained After:			Etiology or Pathology	Comments	Source and Identification of Case
	3 months	1 year	2 or more years			
$1\frac{8}{12}$	+	+	0	Trauma, L hemisphere worse than R	Complete speech loss; new onset 16 months later. L hemispherectomy at 12 followed by aphasia clearing within 9 months postoperative	Basser (1962) 28
2	+	+	0	Diphtheria with convulsions		Basser (1962) I
$2\frac{4}{12}$	+	0	–	Measles followed by right-sided spasm and hemiplegia		Bateman (1890)
3	+	+	0	Trauma followed by CVA, left		CHMC 63
4	+	0	0	Trauma, L forehead		Gutmann (1942) TP
4	?+	?0	–	Abscess, L temporal lobe with operative evacuation to internal capsule	Last follow-up 8 weeks postoperative. Child steadily improving but speech not yet normal	Brunner and Stengel (1932)
5	+	+	0	Sudden hemiplegia of unknown origin		Basser (1962) XII

TABLE 4.4. (continued)

Patient's Age at Insult (Years)	Residual Deficit Remained After:			Etiology or Pathology	Comments	Source and Identification of Case
	3 months	1 year	2 or more years			
6	+	0	0	Ruptured aneurysm, left		CHMC 34
6	0	0	0	Sudden hemiplegia of unknown origin		Basser (1962) I
6	0	0	0	Trauma, left side		Gutmann (1942) AC
6	0	0	0	Trauma, left side		Gutmann (1942) JK
6	+	–	–	Meningo-encephalopathy	Satisfactory improvement reported but follow-up not clear	Branco-Lefèvre (1950) MR
6	+	0	0	Trauma, left temporo-parietal		André-Thomas et al. (1935)
7	+	0	0	CVA R. hemisphere (confirmed by arteriogram)		CHMC 39
7	+	0	0	Unknown	Comprehension and expression deteriorating over 3 months period, followed by slow improvement over 9 months	Poetzl (1926)

No.				Cause	Outcome	Source
8	+	0	0	Trauma, left temporal		CHMC 00
8	+	+	0	CVA, left		CHMC 51
9	+	+	+	?, Convulsions with hemiplegia	Permanent residue	Basser (1962) III
10	+	0	0	Trauma, left		Gutmann JJ
11	+	+	0	Trauma, left, probably followed by CVA		CHMC 63
11	+	+	+	Left otogenic abscess	Mild permanent residue: hesitation and grammatical mistakes	Gutmann (1942) JW
12	+	?0	?0	Trauma, left	No follow-up but substantial though slow improvement reported	Branco-Lefèvre (1950) AJ
14	+	+	+	Trauma, left	Slight aphasic symptoms, permanent; marked agraphia and alexia, permanent	Branco-Lefèvre (1950) MCS
15	+	+	+	Tumor, left parietal	Receptive aphasia preoperative; jargon aphasia postoperative, clearing within 9 months; other aphasic symptoms unchanged 2 years postoperative	CHMC 14
18	+	+	+	Trauma, left temporo-parietal	Marked aphasia, permanent	CHMC 70

+ = reported present
– = reported absent
? = report not clear
0 = no specific report but restoration of language is implied in article.
CHMC = Children's Hospital Medical Center, Boston (unpublished case)

clear that whatever beginning he had made in language before the disease is totally lost, but soon he will start again on the road toward language acquisition, traversing all stages of infant vocalization, perhaps at a slightly faster pace, beginning with babbling, single words, primitive two-word phrases, etc., until perfect speech is achieved. In the very young, then, the primary process in recovery is *acquisition,* whereas the process of symptom-reduction is not in evidence.

Between the age of three and four, language learning and language interference may compete for a few weeks, but within a short period of time, the aphasic handicap is overcome. In patients older than four and younger than ten, the clinical picture is that of a typical aphasia which gradually subsides. At the same time, the child appears to have no difficulty expanding his vocabulary and learning new and complex grammatical constructions.

By the time of puberty, a turning point is reached. Aphasias that develop from this age on or that have not had time to clear up completely by this stage, commonly leave some trace behind which the patient cannot overcome. These youngsters characteristically regain language and can carry on a conversation; but there will be odd hesitation pauses, searching for words, or the utterance of an inappropriate word or sound sequence that cannot be inhibited. Emotional tension magnifies the symptoms, making their aphasic nature very obvious. In the middle teens the prognosis for recovery rapidly becomes the same as that for the adult patient.

Before we can accept these clinical findings as pertinent specifically to language (they may reflect merely a general facility to adjust to disease and handicaps during childhood), it is necessary to adduce evidence that the difference between childhood aphasia and adult aphasia is related to (1) speech specific lateralized lesions in the brain, and (2) that it reflects a potential for speech-specific physiological readjustment which ceases to function after puberty.

(2) *Age of Lateralization of Speech Function in the Brain*

We have previously referred to the phenomenon of cerebral dominance; ordinarily the left hemisphere is more directly involved in speech and language functions than the right, though the lesser hemisphere is not passive with respect to verbal communication. How obligatory is this lateralization with its shift of language function to the left hemisphere? Important clues to this problem are given by a study of massive lesions to either of the hemispheres incurred in early life.

TABLE 4.5. *Lesions Before Onset of Speech*

	Onset of Speech		
	Normal	Delayed	Never
Left hemisphere	18	15	1
Right hemisphere	19	15	4

Based on Basser, 1962.

Basser (1962) has contributed the most important study in this respect. His data are shown in Tables 4.5 and 4.6. Apparently, there is a period in infancy at which the hemispheres are still equipotential. In roughly half of the children with brain lesions sustained during the first two years of life, the onset of speech development is somewhat delayed; however, the other half of this population begins to speak at the usual time. This distribution is the same for children with left hemisphere lesions as with right ones, indicating that during the first two years of life cerebral dominance is not yet well established. A lesion in the left hemisphere is apparently sufficient cause to confine the language function to the right side. At the beginning of language development both hemispheres seem to be equally involved; the dominance phenomenon seems to come about through a progressive decrease in involvement of the right hemisphere. If, however, the left hemisphere is not functioning properly the physiological activities of the right hemisphere persist in their earlier function.

From Table 4.6 it is clear that by the time the child has matured into the stage at which language acquisition is possible and from that time on, left-sided cerebral dominance is manifest in a large proportion of children. Left-sided lesions result in speech disturbances in 85% of the cases, whereas right-sided lesions disturb speech only 45% of the time. All speech disturbances, as mentioned previously, are overcome in less than two years' time. In the adult, right-sided lesions cause aphasia only

TABLE 4.6. *Lesions after onset of speech and before age 10*

	After Catastrophe Speech was:	
	Normal	Disturbed
Left hemisphere	2	13
Right hemisphere	8	7

Based on Basser, 1962.

in about 3% of all patients; most of these patients are left-handed (further discussion and literature in Ajuriaguerra, 1957, and Zangwill, 1960).

(3) *Hemispherectomy: (the Effect of Removal of an Entire Hemisphere)*

At times it becomes necessary to remove an entire hemisphere surgically. This is most frequently done on patients with uncontrollable seizures originating from one hemisphere, but occasionally it is also performed in the surgical treatment of large, infiltrating tumors (Laine and Gros, 1956). Again we are indebted to Basser (1962) for a complete survey of the literature and a substantial contribution of case histories from his own practice. The material is summarized in Table 4.7. We see that the consequences of a left hemispherectomy depend upon the age at which the original insult was incurred. If the child had a lesion in infancy, regardless of side, speech function was eventually confined to the healthy hemisphere, so that when the diseased hemisphere had to be removed later in life, it caused no aphasia. In this group, (lesions acquired in childhood), about 80% of the operations were performed sometime after age ten and the remainder in adult life.

TABLE 4.7. *Hemispherectomy*

Lesions Acquired	Hemisphere Operated On	Speech Not Affected or Improved Postoperatively	Permanent Aphasia
Before teens*	Left	49	3 (had aphasia before operation)
	Right	38	5 (had aphasia before operation)
During puberty† (single case)	Left	Slow improvement	Some residue to end of life (27 months postop.)
Adult*	Left	None	6 (1 had aphasia before operation)
	Right	25	None

* Based on Basser, 1962.
† Hillier, 1954 and personal communication.

However, patients who acquired their lesions in later life, and who had hemispherectomy subsequently, had permanent aphasic symptoms if the operation was done on the left side and no aphasia if it was on the right side.

There is only one case where the lesion was acquired during the early teens (Hillier, 1954), and a left hemispherectomy was performed at age fourteen. According to personal communication from Dr. Hillier this patient had a global aphasia following the operation but within eight months could make himself understood fairly well, although gross speech deficits remained. He lived for another 19 months during which no further speech improvements were noted, and it became clear that a stable language deficit had been established. He died 27 months after his hemispherectomy due to recurrence of tumor (glioblastoma multiforme) which had invaded the brainstem.

III. PRELIMINARY SUMMARY

The outlook for recovery from aphasia varies with age. The chance for recovery has a natural history. This natural history is the same as the natural history of cerebral lateralization of function. Aphasia is the result of direct, structural, and local interference with neurophysiological processes of language. In childhood such interference cannot be permanent because the two sides are not yet sufficiently specialized for function, even though the left hemisphere may already show signs of speech dominance. Damage to it will interfere with language; but the right hemisphere is *still* involved to some extent with language, and so there is a potential for language function that may be strengthened again. In the absence of pathology, a polarization of function between right and left takes place during childhood, displacing language entirely to the left and certain other functions predominantly to the right (Ajuriaguerra, 1957; Hécaen and Ajuriaguerra, 1963; Teuber, 1962). If, however, a lesion is placed in either hemisphere, this polarization cannot take place, and language function together with other functions persist in the unharmed hemisphere.

Notice that the earlier the lesion is incurred, the brighter is the outlook for language. Hence we infer that *language learning* can take place, at least in the right hemisphere, only between the age of two to about thirteen. That this is probably also true of the left hemisphere follows from observations on language development in the retarded and in the congenitally deaf, discussed subsequently.

A unique pathological study of congenital aphasia was reported by Landau, Goldstein, and Kleffner (1960). This was a child who died of heart disease at age ten. This patient, in contrast to the cases discussed so far, had not begun to develop speech until age six or seven. At that time, he was enrolled in a class for congenitally aphasic children at the Central Institute for the Deaf. By age ten, the authors report, he had acquired considerable useful language. A postmortem examination of the brain revealed bilateral areas of cortical destruction around the sylvian fissure in the area of the central sulcus, together with severe retrograde degeneration in the medial geniculate nuclei deep in the brain. The authors conclude that "Language function therefore appears to have been subserved by pathways other than the primary auditory thalamocortical projection system." I am citing this case to illustrate the far-reaching plasticity of the human brain (or lack of cortical specialization) with respect to language during the *early* years of life. There is clinical evidence that similar lesions in a mature individual would have produced severe and irreversible defects in reception and production of speech and language.

The implication of this discussion is that the brain at birth and during the subsequent maturation process may be influenced in its normal course of organization which usually results in the specialization of areas. This is not a tabula rasa concept of the brain which would propose that any arbitrary reorganization is possible.

Postnatal cerebral organization has recently been demonstrated in cats (Scharlock, Tucker, and Strominger, 1963) who ablated auditory cortex in neonate kittens with control ablations on mature cats. When the kittens matured, they had no difficulty in learning to make auditory discriminations, which the older individuals after an identical postoperative waiting period could no longer perform. Comparable investigations on other sensory or motor functions and different cortical locations have been reported by Benjamin and Thompson (1959), Brooks and Peck (1940), Harlow, Akert, and Schiltz (1964), Doty (1953), and others. In short, various kinds of postnatal cortical ablations leave no or very minor deficit whereas comparable ablations in later stages of development result in irreversible symptoms.

(4) *Arrest of Language Development in the Retarded*

The material reviewed might give the impression that the age limitation is primarily due to better recovery from disease in childhood and that the language limitations are only a secondary effect. This is probably not so. In a study by Lenneberg, Nichols, and Rosenberger (1964), 54 mongoloids (all raised at home) were seen two to three times a year over a three-year period. The age range was from 6 months to 22 years.

The appearance of motor milestones and the onset of speech differed considerably from individual to individual, but all made some progress —although very slow in many cases—before they reached their early teens. This was true of motor development as well as of speech. In all children seen in this study, stance, gait, and fine coordination of hands and fingers was acquired before the end of the first decade. At the close of the study 75% had reached at least the first stage of language development; they had a small vocabulary and could execute simple spoken commands. But interestingly enough, progress in language development was only recorded in children younger than fourteen. Cases in their later teens were the same in terms of their language development at the beginning as at the end of the study. The observation seems to indicate that even in the absence of gross structural brain lesions, progress in language learning comes to a standstill after maturity. Figure 4.3 is a graphic illustration of the empirical findings.

(5) *The Effect of Sudden Deafness on Language at Various Ages*

The study of acquired deafness during childhood and in later life gives further insight into the importance of age and language acquisition. The most common cause of sudden and total loss of hearing is meningitis. The virulence of the disease may be such that many a child falls ill and is left without hearing practically overnight. Throughout childhood sudden acquisition of deafness has an immediate effect upon voice and speech, and, before the age of six, also on language habits. Within a year or less the small child, say up to about four years of age, will have lost the ability to control his voice and articulatory mechanisms for ordinary speech sounds, and will develop noises and habits very similar or even indistinguishable from those heard and seen in the congenitally deaf. Their education has to be relegated to special teachers in the schools for the deaf. Both these populations, those who become deaf before and those after the onset of speech, sound and behave like the congenitally deaf children. But those who lose hearing after having been exposed to the experience of speech, even for as short a period as one year, can be trained much more easily in all language arts, even if formal training begins some years after they had become deaf. On the other hand, children deafened before completion of the second year do not have any facilitation in comparison with the congenitally deaf (based on personal observations). It seems as if even a short exposure to language, a brief moment during which the curtain has been lifted and oral communication established, is sufficient to give a child some foundation on which much later language may be based.

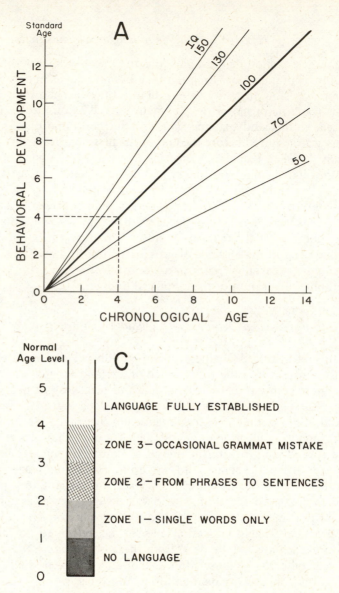

FIG. 4.3. Ideally, IQ-figures should remain constant throughout life as shown in *A;* in reality, however, they tend to fluctuate and the test-retest discrepancies are most marked in exceptionally high and low cases. In the mentally retarded, the IQ tends to decay fairly predictably as shown in *B*. The acquisition of language proceeds through fixed developmental stages shown as zones in *C*. *D* shows the empirically determined relationship between nonverbal IQ and language development. After age twelve to thirteen, language development tends to "freeze." (Data based on a follow-up study of 61 mongoloid children and 23 children with other types of retarding disease.)

156

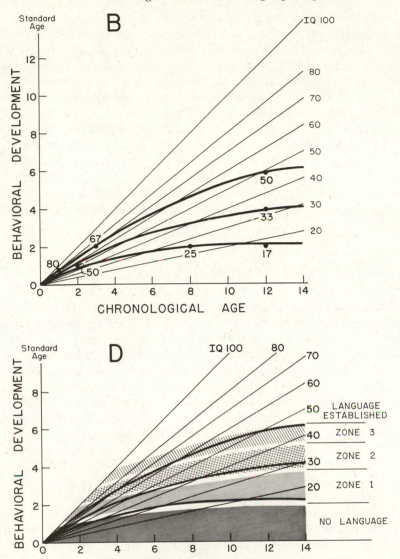

The effect of deafness thus complements our knowledge obtained from the effects of acquired aphasia. Although the prognosis for recovery from aphasia gets worse and worse with advancing age after ten, the prognosis for speech habilitation in the deaf improves directly with the advance of age at onset of the disorder.

Fry (1966) presents material that stresses the paramount importance of age in the establishment of optimal speech habits. He has recorded utterances of British children whose audiograms would indicate profound hearing loss, but whose quality of voice, intonation patterns and articulation are far superior to anything that is achieved either in America or the European continent. Fry's explanation is that these children were provided with hearing aids during earliest infancy (age two) and were given intensive sound training long before school started. In America children are also given hearing aids and sound training but the latter does not begin seriously until age four or even later, and the hearing aids are often given little attention until school begins. If these findings can be verified on a larger scale it would indicate an even shorter span of the critical age for optimal speech acquisition than assumed here.

IV. CONCOMITANTS OF PHYSICAL MATURATION

Language cannot begin to develop until a certain level of physical maturation and growth has been attained. Between the ages of two and three years language emerges by an interaction of maturation and self-programmed learning. Between the ages of three and the early teens the possibility for primary language acquisition continues to be good; the individual appears to be most sensitive to stimuli at this time and to preserve some innate flexibility for the organization of brain functions to carry out the complex integration of subprocesses necessary for the smooth elaboration of speech and language. After puberty, the ability for self-organization and adjustment to the physiological demands of verbal behavior quickly declines. The brain behaves as if it had become set in its ways and primary, basic language skills not acquired by that time, except for articulation, usually remain deficient for life. (New words may be acquired throughout life, because the basic skill of naming has been learned at the very beginning of language development.) In Fig. 4.4 we have a diagrammatic representation of the factors that limit the acquisition of the individual's first and primary language.

A few comments are in order regarding the state of the brain during the initial period for language acquisition. I must stress, however, that this is not an attempt to discover the specific anatomical or biochemical basis of language development *per se*. The specific physiology of language is unknown and, therefore, it would be futile to look for any specific growth process that would explain language acquisition. Never-

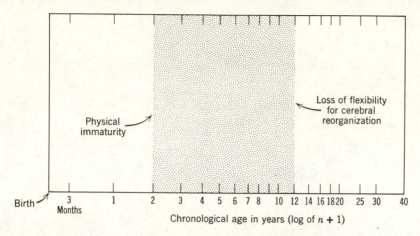

FIG. 4.4. Factors which limit the acquisition of primary language skills.

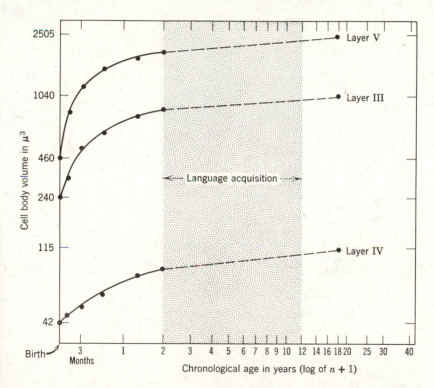

FIG. 4.5. Neurons in the cerebral cortex grow in volume with age. The broken lines between age two and eighteen indicate that no measurements were made on brains of children who died between these ages. (Redrawn from Schadé and van Groenigen, 1961.)

159

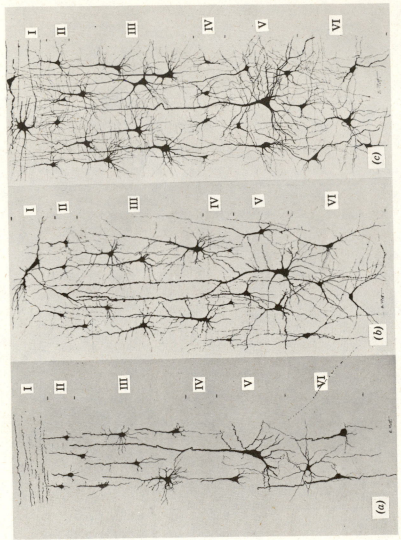

FIG. 4.6. Postnatal development of human cerebral cortex around Broca's Area (FCBm); camera lucida drawings from Golgi-Cox preparations. *a*: newborn; *b*: 1 month; *c*: 3 months; *d*: 6 months; *e*: 15 months; *f*: 24 months. Inspection of original sections shows an even more dramatic increase in density of neuropil between 15 and 24 months. (From Conel, 1939–1959.)

160

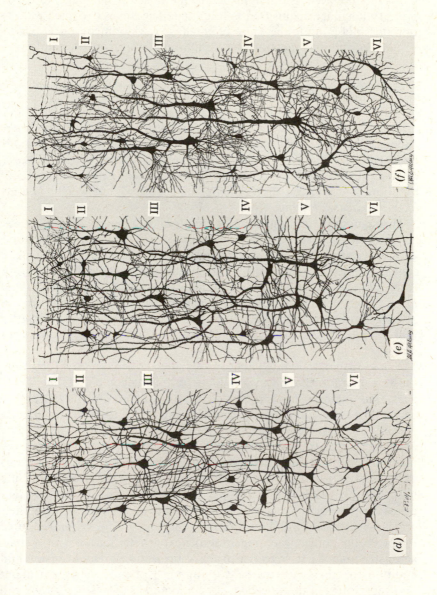

161

theless, it may be interesting to know in what way the brain, particularly the cerebral cortex, is different before the onset of language and after primary language acquisition is inhibited. The answer to such a question does not point to the cause of language development, but it tells us something about its substrate and its limiting or prerequisite conditions.

(1) *Structural Changes in the Brain*

In Chapter two (Morphological Correlates) we saw how the brain undergoes a very rapid weight increase during the postnatal period. During the first two years of life there is roughly a 350% weight increase, whereas at the end of the next ten years the weight gain is merely 35%. By about age fourteen the brain has reached its adult weight and no further increases are registered.

Throughout infancy the number of individual neurons probably does not increase because microscopic examination of cortical nervous tissue never reveals cell divisions (mitotic figures). Nevertheless, we have conclusive evidence that neurons themselves grow considerably during early infancy. Extensive studies by Schadé and van Groenigen (1961) have shown that, for instance, pyramidal cells of the middle frontal gyrus gain in volume rapidly during the first two years (Fig. 4.5); after that the growth rate decreases markedly, and little change occurs after puberty.

The growth of individual neurons may be verified directly. Figure 4.6 shows camara lucida tracings made from microscopic sections of cortices. The material for this research comes from Conel's laboratory where the most monumental research on the maturation of human cortex has originated (Conel, 1939 to 1963). The major change that evidently occurs during the period of expansion of the brain is the interconnection of cells. Processes grow out from the cell body (axons and dendrites) and eventually form a dense net of interconnecting branches. De Crinis (1934) was the first to show that no, or few, dendrites are present in the cortex of the neonate and that the time of their appearance varies in different parts of the cortex. He recognized three major cortical areas, each reaching dendrogenetic maturity at a characteristic time. First were the primary projection areas of vision and audition together with the sensory-motor Rolandic strips. At about two years, most of the so-called association areas and Broca's area, and finally a certain portion of the frontal lobe and the medial region of the parietal lobe develop. The last stage of dendrogenesis is attained, according to De Crinis, by the fourth year. This earlier work will have to be verified further by the detailed methods of Conel and the statistical investigations as first used by Sholl (1956), Bok (1959), and Schadé and van Groenigen (1961).

Schadé and van Groenigen also have contributed data on the packing density of neurons. As the brain expands, the distance between the cell bodies increases, and thus the cell density decreases. This is the concomitant or perhaps even the histological prerequisite for the increase in dendritic arborization. Figure 4.7 shows how the packing density decreases at a rapid rate during the first two years, at a very slow rate thereafter, with complete stabilization after the early teens. Also the so-called gray-cell coefficient, that is, the ratio of the volume of cortical

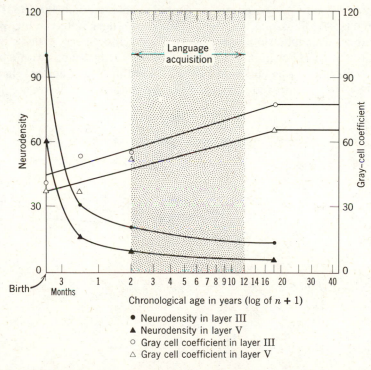

FIG. 4.7. As the cerebrum expands with advancing age, the nerve cells in the cortex become less crowded, and the neurodensity (number of cells times 10^3 per cubic millimeter) decreases. The gray-cell coefficient was computed by dividing the volume of gray matter by the volume of nerve cells contained in it. The rising curves indicate that the distances between the cells increases with age and are increasingly filled with dendrites and neuropil, resulting in dense arborization. (Based on data by Schadé and van Groenigen.)

gray matter to the volume of nerve cells contained in it, was computed, and this parameter also reaches an asymptote at or around puberty.

Thus, there is ample evidence that age two is the beginning of a period of slowed-down structural growth; it is preceded by a period during which growth had gone on at a very rapid pace, and followed by a period of absence of growth.

(2) *Changes in Chemical Composition of the Brain*

Neurochemical investigations of maturational changes of the brain are of a much more recent date than anatomical researches, and, therefore, we have only a few indications of development in these terms. Figures 4.8 and 4.9 based on data published by Folch-Pi (1955) and Brante (1949), illustrate the trend of major changes noted so far. Work by other investigators, notably Kety (1955) and Sperry (1962), could be cited in corroboration of the same point, but the details would carry us too far afield. The curves of Fig. 4.8 show that the structural changes with age in the cortex are accompanied by changes in relative composi-

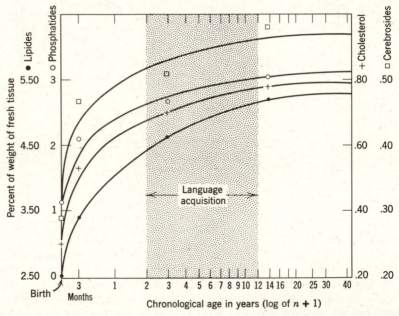

FIG. 4.8. Chemical composition of human cerebral cortex plotted as a function of chronological age. (Based on data by Brante, 1949, and Folch-Pi, 1955.)

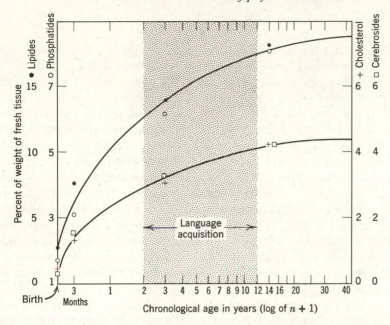

FIG. 4.9. Chemical composition of human cerebral white matter plotted as a function of chronological age. (Based on data by Brante, 1949, and Folch-Pi, 1955.)

tion of brain tissue. Again age two and the early teens mark the beginning and end of a period, characterized by very slow approximation of the final state. Turning to Fig. 4.9 we see that the old problem of myelinization rate is now being solved through more quantitatively oriented analyses. At one time it was thought that the development of behavior could be correlated with progress of myelinization. These endeavors were particularly stimulated by Flechsig's myelogenetic theory (summarized by Flechsig, 1927) and further supported with work initiated by the Vogts (1911). Criticism of these theories was strong from the beginning. Kaes (1907) was the first to show that myelinization as a whole is a continuous process. Although its rate decreases rapidly after two or three years, there is a constant and steady increase from infancy to old age. Nevertheless, the more detailed work by Brante (1949) and Folch-Pi (1952, 1955) now shows that in the development of white matter there are some components (cholesterol and cerebrosides) that show a relative growth that follows the curves illustrated in Fig. 4.9 whereas other components, lipids and phosphatides, gain in percentage even after puberty and probably throughout life.

(3) *Electro-Physiological Changes*

Considering the large amount of work in general neurophysiology, it is surprising to see how little attention has been devoted to the problem of maturational changes of the brain with respect to process and function. There is only one area in which changes with age have been investigated systematically, namely electroencephalography. In this field the changes were so obvious that it must have been difficult to overlook them. Contributions were made by Lindsley (1936), Bernhard and Skoglund (1939), Henry (1944), Dreyfus-Brisac and Blanc (1956), and many others. Figure 4.10 is based on an important article by Smith (1941) in which he confirmed earlier observations that the dominant rhythm of brain waves changes its frequency with age. He described the occipital and central alpha rhythms which show a growth curve very similar to the growth curves obtained from the measurements mentioned previously. Of particular interest with respect to language development is the growth curve of the central alpha rhythm. Here the change in rate of growth is most marked around the two-year level, and it is clearly the central rhythm which is more directly relevant to language activities than the occipital waves. In Fig. 4.11, extrapolated from

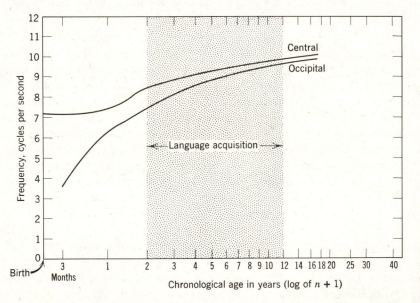

FIG. 4.10. Dominant frequency of brain waves as a function of age. (Redrawn from Smith, 1941.)

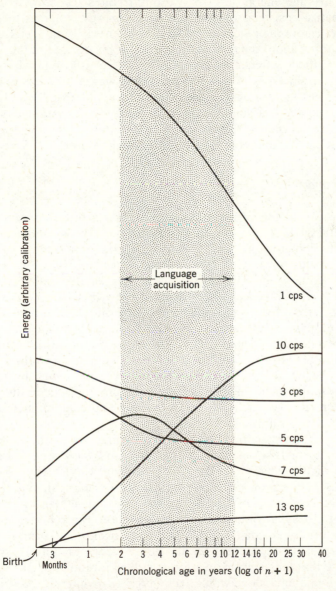

FIG. 4.11. Average amplitude of various brain waves as a function of age. (Based on data by Gibbs and Knott, 1949.)

167

data published by Gibbs and Knott (1949), we see variations with age in the average energy level of various frequencies. Low frequencies (less than 6 cps) tend to lose in average energy, whereas higher frequencies (more than 8 cps) tend to gain in energy with age. The graph says nothing about the relative frequency of occurrence of these waves. Actually, the low frequencies, particularly 1 cps is rare in adults except during certain types of sleep. Notice that waves of 7 cps undergo a peculiar change during the age of two to about five. Except for the lowest frequency, a stable state is reached for all parameters by the middle teens, whereas the two years preceding the onset of speech are certainly most different in terms of energy distribution.

(4) *Summary*

If we survey the various maturation curves, those concerned with structural growth, those with biochemical changes, and those with neurophysiological changes, we notice a common trend. The significance of this for a study of language acquisition is simply this: the curves define what is meant by maturation of the brain. All of the parameters of brain maturation studied show that the first year of life is characterized by a very rapid maturation rate. By the time language begins to make its appearance about 60% of the adult values of maturation are reached. Then the maturation rate slows down and reaches an asymptote at just about the same time that trauma to the left hemisphere begins to have permanent consequences. Thus, by the time primary language acquisition comes to be inhibited, the brain can also be shown to have reached its mature state, and cerebral lateralization is irreversibly established.

The question remains of what is the significance of the coincidence between these brain-maturational phases and the onset and gradual decline of the capacity for language learning. Could they be entirely spurious? The infant's obvious incapacity to learn all but the most primitive beginnings of language during his first fifteen months is, at least intuitively, attributable to a general state of cerebral immaturity. The maturational data for the end of the critical period is more difficult to interpret. If it were not for the consequence of different types of evidence that language acquisition is indeed inhibited at this time, the maturational data alone would lack much of its interest. As it is, however, we may think of these data as contributing to the diverse circumstantial evidence that puberty marks a milestone both for the facility in language acquisition and a number of directly and indirectly related processes in the brain. We are, therefore, suggesting as a working hypothesis that the general, nonspecific states of maturation of the brain constitute prerequisites and limiting factors for language development. They are not its specific cause.

This hypothesis leads to a rather revealing generalization. Since the various aspects of cerebral maturation are so highly correlated, we may think of maturation of the brain as a relatively unitary phenomenon (perhaps as shorthand for the sake of the following demonstration). As the brain matures, the growing infant successively attains various developmental milestones such as sitting, walking, and joining words into phrases. In Fig. 4.12 we see these milestones as developmental horizons

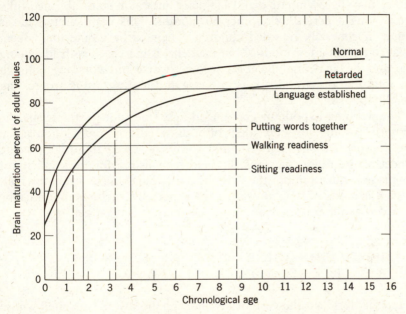

FIG. 4.12. On the ordinate, we have combined all the parameters of brain maturation, discussed earlier, into a single factor. Retarded children presumably attain the maturational values later in life than normal children. Attainment of brain maturation is correlated with behavioral achievements shown here as "horizons." A comparison of the growth curves of normal and retarded children explains why the relative distances among the various milestones becomes greater with advancing age. Normally, a child begins to join words together about 15 months after he is ready to sit up; in a retarded child it may take 24 months to achieve this. It takes about two years to acquire the general basis for language establishment once a normal child has begun to put words together. In a retarded child it may take five years or more to acquire the same facility in language.

signifying the breadth of the maturational accomplishments; that is, sitting or walking are not the only developmental achievements of these various periods but, at the same time, there is a whole spectrum of sensory and motor development, and sitting or walking are merely their most outstanding characteristic. Figure 4.12 shows that if the normal maturation function is slowed down, developmental horizons are reached later and, most importantly, the spacing between the milestones becomes more prolonged without altering the order of sequence. Normally 12 to 14 months elapse between sitting and putting words together, and language is fully established within another 20 months. But in the retarded, the lapse between sitting and putting words together may be 24 months, and language may not be established fully for as long a period as another 60 months. This is precisely what is found in generally retarded children. Their earliest milestones seem delayed by just a few months, but the delay is increased with advancing age, and the lag behind the norm becomes worse and worse even though the retarding disease may be stationary and maturation is progressing steadily but slowly.

The working hypothesis expounded here does not postulate specific "criteria" or any absolute values of brain weight or composition as the *sine qua non* for language. It is not so much one or the other specific aspect of the brain that must be held responsible for the capacity of language acquisition but the way the many parts of the brain interact. Thus it is mode of function rather than specific structures that must be regarded as the proper neurological correlate of language.

V. GROWTH CHARACTERISTICS OF THE HUMAN BRAIN AND THEIR POSSIBLE RELATIONSHIP TO LANGUAGE ACQUISITION

In Chapter Two the case of a nanocephalic dwarf was cited whose estimated brain weight and brain-body-weight ratio was thought to be about that of a three-year-old chimpanzee. From this similarity it was concluded that *individual* measures of weight give us no clue to the problem of why dwarfs learn to speak, whereas chimpanzees do not.

Instead of comparing individual measurements, taken out of the context of growth and maturation, let us now compare man, dwarf, and chimpanzee in terms of their developmental *histories*. Maturation is a much more dramatic event in the human brain during childhood than in the chimpanzee's brain during the comparable period. Consider the ratio of the weight of the brain to the weight of the entire body. This ratio does not change appreciably after maturity, although it cannot remain completely constant because the body weight of a young adult slowly increases with advancing age. At birth, however, the ratio is about six to seven times the value of adulthood, and it decreases gradually throughout infancy and childhood. In Fig. 4.13 brain-body-weight ratios are shown as a function of "adjusted age." Direct comparison between man and chimpanzee in terms of age in years would distort the picture because of the difference in life span of the two forms. Since we are interested in maturation, the time it takes each form to reach puberty is taken as unity, that is, the first 14 man-years are equated to the first 8 chimpanzee-years and this period is divided into four equal subperiods. Young adulthood is defined as the age at which no further growth of long bones is recorded. (The weight determinations for man in Figure 4.13 come from Altman and Dittmer, 1962.)

Man's brain-maturational history is unique among primates (cf. also Schultz, 1956). All lower forms approach the adult condition at a relatively quicker pace than man. On the other hand, except for man's first six months, there is no brain-weight index value that is unique to man. Man's adult index value is about 2.2; in a chimpanzee that value is

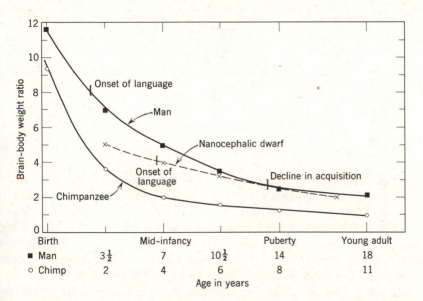

FIG. 4.13. Brain body-weight ratio as a function of maturational stage. The adult proportions are attained in man much more gradually than in the chimpanzee. Notice that developmental facts in this condition are more revealing than the individual measurements given in Table 2.2 of Chapter two. (Based on tables published by Altman and Dittmer, 1962.)

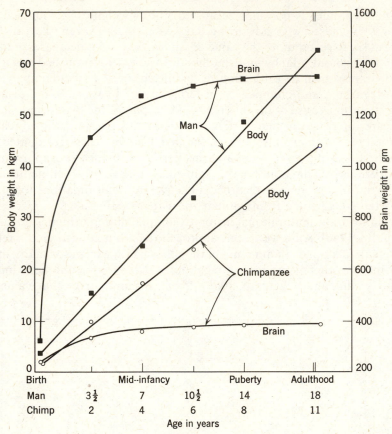

FIG. 4.14. Weight increases as a function of maturational stage.

attained shortly before mid-infancy. At the end of the first childhood-quarter, the chimpanzee's index is 3.5, which is the same as man's at the close of the third-quarter. The measurements themselves are not different, but the developmental stage at which these values are attained is. When we discussed the nanocephalic dwarf, we were comparing a form near puberty with a form shortly before mid-infancy, and hence the values for both brain and body could be matched. But the present material points to a fundamental difference between dwarf and chimpanzee, namely their developmental history. The dwarf quickly approaches the human curve and merges with it by puberty.

So far we have discussed the growth rate of the brain relative to growth rate of the body. In comparison to lower primates, man's brain remains large throughout life. We obtain yet a different view if we compare the growth rate of the brain *per se*. In Fig. 4.14 we see the absolute weight increases of brain and body, plotted separately, as a function of adjusted age. Man's body increases at a faster rate than the chimpanzee's but the difference is not very startling. The growth curves of the brains look very different, however. During the first quarter of childhood, man's brain gains about 800 gm as against 110 in the chimpanzee. This form of presentation is difficult to interpret. Instead of looking at the absolute values, let us compare the rate of growth in terms of relative increase. Figure 4.15 is more interesting because it tells us how large the weight gain is from quarter to quarter in terms of the final value. Now we see that the body-weight gain, in terms of percentage of adult weight, is nearly identical in man and chimpanzee. But the brain-weight gain in terms of percentage is very different during the first quarter, then it becomes closely similar during the second, and it is virtually the same during the second half of childhood. Notice that

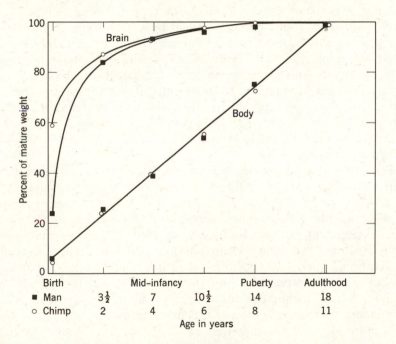

FIG. 4.15. The same data as in Fig. 4.16, but weights are expressed in terms of per cent of mature weight. The parameter is now *rate* of growth. Notice that the rate of body-weight increase is practically identical in man and chimpanzee, whereas the rate of brain-weight increase is quite different during the first quarter of the maturational histories.

at birth man's brain weight is only 24% of the adult weight, whereas the chimpanzee starts life with a brain that already weighs 60% of its final value. During the first quarter, the chimpanzee's brain gains only 30%, whereas man's gains 60%.

What conclusions may be drawn from these differences? We do not have the maturational data for chimpanzee brains that we have for human brains, but it is interesting to note that in man growth characteristics of the brain weight are closely paralleled in time by growth of microscopic structures, growth in chemical compounds, and by growth in electrophysiological parameters. There is always rapid acceleration in the first quarter and attainment of the adult condition by puberty. By extrapolation, we may assume that the maturational events of the chimpanzee brain during childhood differ from those in man in that at birth his brain is probably much more mature and all parameters are probably more stabilized than in man. This would indicate that the facilitation for language learning is not only tied to a state of flux but to a maturational history that is characteristic for man alone.

We should not suppose that we might be able to train a chimpanzee to use a natural language, such as English, simply by delaying the animal's physiological development. When physiological delay occurs in man (as in mongolism) it also protracts his speech development. The onset of speech is regulated by maturational development of certain physiological and perceptual capacities which are probably lacking or take on different forms in lower primates. Maturational retardation cannot induce growth of the basic biological matrix for cerebral language organization.

Pertinent to man's prolonged maturational history is the hypothesis that man constitutes a "fetalized" version of a more generalized primate developmental course. Kummer (1953) presents much evidence to show that man's development is not simply a slowed-down version of ape development, but runs a course all its own. The cross-species comparison shows that man's brain has a peculiar and species-specific maturational curve. Add to this our earlier observations that man is unique among vertebrates in the functional asymmetry of neurophysiological process within the adult brain. Only man has hemispheric dominance with lateralization of function and marked preference with respect to side in the use of limbs and sensory organs. Notice that cerebral dominance and dexterity are not present at birth but regularly emerge in the course of early development and are thus clearly tied to maturational processes. We have, indeed, cited evidence that laterality is a process of innate organization and polarization which is inevitable in the normal course of development, but which may be blocked, so to speak, within certain age limits by destruction of tissue in either hemisphere. We would like to propose that lateralization is a phenomenon of growth and development in man.

The development of language, also a species-specific phenomenon, is related physiologically, structurally, and developmentally to the other two typically human characteristics, cerebral dominance and maturational history. Language is not an arbitrarily adopted behavior, facilitated by accidentally fortunate anatomical arrangements in the oral cavity and larynx, but an activity which develops harmoniously by necessary integration of neuronal and skeletal structures and by reciprocal adaptation of various physiological processes.

VI. FURTHER COMMENTS ON THE "CRITICAL PERIOD" FOR LANGUAGE ACQUISITION

At first sight it might be tempting to relate the age-limited potential for language acquisition to a variety of other types of emergence of animal behavior that depend upon stimulation during a short period of the animal's infancy. Most important in this connection is the phenomenon of *imprinting* (Gray, 1958), a highly specialized type of behavioral development investigated most closely in certain birds. It occurs during early infancy at a specific developmental stage, usually a few hours or days after hatching. The chick will follow that moving object to which it is exposed during the critical period, and it will continue to follow that object during most of its "childhood." The response is established very rapidly and indiscriminately to essentially anything that moves at a given speed and is within certain limitations of size. The response resists extinction to a high degree, but it is not completely irreversible. Eventually it will be overshadowed or displaced by other responses. Failure to develop imprinted responses during infancy may cause behavioral abnormalities in the adult, and such a bird's behavior cannot be normalized by later training, (Hinde, 1961; Hess, 1962).

Age-limited emergence of behavior has also been described in mammals (Thorpe, 1961). It is possible that many types of social organizations among animals are based on somewhat similar mechanisms, the most elementary of which is infant-mother relationship (Bowlby, 1953; Ahrens, 1954; Scott, 1963). The inference we may draw from this material is that many animal forms traverse periods of peculiar sensitivities, response-propensities, or learning potentials. Insofar as we have made such a claim for language acquisition, we have postulated nothing that would be extraordinary in the realm of animal behavior.

But at the same time we must sound a warning. Merely the fact that there are critical periods for the acquisition of certain types of behavior among a number of species *does not imply* any phylogenetic relationship between them. Age-linked emergence of behavior may be due to such a variety of factors that this phenomenon by itself is of limited heuristic value when it comes to tracing evolutionary origins of behavior. In the case of language, the limiting factors postulated are cerebral immaturity on the one end and termination of a state of organizational plasticity linked with lateralization of function at the other end of the critical period. We do not know whether these or similar factors are responsible for limitations of critical periods in the case of other animals.

Do the time limitations postulated for language acquisition function across the board for all types of human learning? Probably not: there are many skills and tasks that are much better learned during the late teens than in early childhood and a great deal of general learning has no age limitation whatever. Nevertheless, an accurate answer to the question is very difficult. For instance, our ability to learn foreign languages tends to confuse the picture. Most individuals of average intelligence are able to learn a second language after the beginning of their second decade, although the incidence of "language-learning-blocks" rapidly increases after puberty. Also automatic acquisition from mere exposure to a given language seems to disappear after this age, and foreign languages have to be taught and learned through a conscious and labored effort. Foreign accents cannot be overcome easily after puberty. However, a person *can* learn to communicate in a foreign language at the age of forty. This does not trouble our basic hypothesis on age limitations because we may assume that the cerebral organization for language learning as such has taken place during childhood, and since natural languages tend to resemble one another in many fundamental aspects (see Appendix A), the matrix for language skills is present.

Would cerebral lateralization of function develop in the absence of language acquisition? If we were dealing with a laboratory animal, we could perform a number of decisive experiments to answer this important question. As it is, we must be satisfied with inconclusive but suggestive evidence. A total absence of language development is nowadays seen only in the worst cases of feeblemindedness and chronic childhood psychosis. Hand preference is poorly developed in the amented, probably a reflection of their extremely retarded state of development. Reliable surveys of hand preference in psychotic children are not available, but it is my impression that right-handedness may be observed in all of those psychotic children whose motor milestones are attained at normal age. In this population, however, we can never be certain about the degree of covert language acquisition. As mentioned earlier, unwillingness to communicate is not necessarily a sign of absence of language.

Congenitally deaf but otherwise healthy children whose language acquisition is delayed to their first years in school, say age seven, have a normal incidence of right-handedness which seems to emerge at the usual time and which is firmly established between four and five years. However, the diagrams of Fig. 4.16 show that hand preference is not an unfailing guide to knowledge about cerebral dominance. There is a

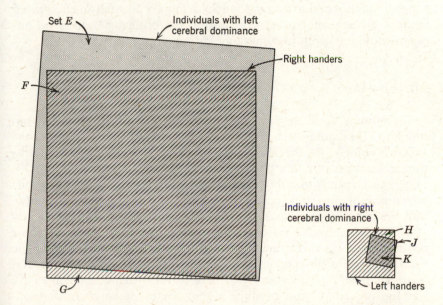

FIG. 4.16. Set diagrams illustrating the relationship between handedness and cerebral dominance (defined here as cerebral lateralization of the language function). The geometrical proportions are not drawn accurately. Notice that there are more individuals with left cerebral dominance than there are right handers. On the other hand, there are more left handers than there are individuals with clealy right cerebral dominance. Set *E* consists of individuals who are either left handers *or* have no hand preference. Set *G* consists of right-handed people in whom cerebral dominance is not well-established or whose cerebral dominance is predominantly in the right hemisphere (rare). Most individuals belong to Set *F*: right handed with left cerebral dominance. Half of the individuals in the set of left handers have right cerebral dominance (Set *K*) and half have either left dominance or bilateral cerebral representation (Set *H*). Set *J* consists of the very rare individuals who are not clearly left handers but who have definite right cerebral dominance.

small percentage of right-handers who have been found to have poorly established cerebral lateralization. Perhaps a relatively large percentage of the congenitally deaf falls into this category. Militating against this possibility is the fact that aphasia with right-sided paralysis has been reported in congenitally deaf persons, (Critchley, 1938; Douglas and Richardson, 1959; Grasset, 1896; Tureen et al., 1951). None of these four patients had had oral speech before their stroke; all four used sign language and finger spelling, and in all of them, manual language communication was disordered by left-hemisphere lesions. From these cases and the deaf population as a whole we may conclude that even delayed exposure of the child to language and a definitely unusual and decreased amount of language stimulation during the critical period is no impediment to left cerebral dominance formation.

VII. SUMMARY AND CONCLUSION

The notion "need" explains nothing (1) because of its subjective nature and (2) because if the infant's "needs" change in the course of the first two years of life, they do so because of his own growth and maturation and not because of arbitrary extrinsic factors.

We must assume that the child's capacity to learn language is a consequence of maturation because (1) the milestones of language acquisition are normally interlocked with other milestones that are clearly attributable to physical maturation, particularly stance, gait, and motor coordination; (2) this synchrony is frequently preserved even if the whole maturational schedule is dramatically slowed down, as in several forms of mental retardation; (3) there is no evidence that intensive training procedures can produce higher stages of language development, that is, advance language in a child who is maturationally still a toddling infant. However, the development of language is not caused by maturation of motor processes because it can, in certain rare instances, evolve faster or slower than motor development.

Primary language cannot be acquired with equal facility within the period from childhood to senescence. At the same time that cerebral lateralization becomes firmly established (about puberty) the symptoms of acquired aphasia tend to become irreversible within about three to six months after their onset. Prognosis for complete recovery rapidly deteriorates with advancing age after the early teens. Limitation to the acquisition of primary language around puberty is further demonstrated by the mentally retarded who can frequently make slow and modest beginnings in the acquisition of language until their early teens, at which time their speech and language status becomes permanently consolidated. Furthermore, according to Fry, the profoundly deaf must receive sound training and prosthetic aid as close to age two as possible to develop good speech habits. The reverse is seen in acquired deafness where even short exposure to language before the onset of deafness improves prognosis for speech and language, with the outlook becoming better in proportion to the length of time the patient had been in command of verbal skills.

Thus we may speak of a critical period for language acquisition. At the beginning it is limited by lack of maturation. Its termination seems to be related to a loss of adaptability and inability for reorganization in the brain, particularly with respect to the topographical extent of neurophysiological processes. (Similar infantile plasticity with eventual irreversible topographical representation in the brain has been demonstrated for many higher mammals.) The limitations in man may well be connected with the peculiar phenomenon of cerebral lateralization of function, which only becomes irreversible after cerebral growth-phenomena have come to a conclusion.

The specific neurophysiological correlates of speech and language are completely unknown. Therefore, emergence of the capacity for language acquisition cannot be attributed directly to any one maturational process studied so far. But it is important to know what the physical states of the brain are before, during, and after the critical period for language acquisition. This is the prerequisite for the eventual discovery of more specific neural phenomena underlying language behavior. We find that in almost all aspects of cerebral growth investigated about 60% of the mature values are attained before the onset of speech (roughly at two years of age, when speech and language become rapidly perfected), whereas the critical period comes to a close at a time when 100% of the values are reached. This statement must not be mistaken for a demonstration of causal relationship between the variables involved. It merely suggests what structural and physiological substrates there might be that limit the capacity for cerebral organization and reorganization.

Species differ in their embryological and ontogenetic histories. Brain-maturation curves of *Homo sapiens* are different from those of other primates. Man's brain matures much slower, and there is evidence that the difference is not merely one of a stretched time-scale, but that there are intrinsic differences. Thus man is not born as a fetalized version of other primates; the developmental events in his natural history are *sui generis*. The hypothesis is advanced that the capacity for language acquisition is intimately related to man's peculiar maturational history

TABLE 4.8. *Summary Survey*

Age	Usual Language Development	Effects of Acquired, Lateralized Lesions	Physical Maturation of CNS	Lateralization of Function	Equipotentiality of Hemispheres	Explanation
Months 0–3	Emergence of cooing	No effect on onset of language in half of all cases; other half has delayed onset but normal development	About 60–70% of developmental course accomplished	None: symptoms and prognosis identical for either hemisphere	Perfect equipotentiality	Neuro-anatomical and physiological prerequisites become established
4–20	From babbling to words					
21–36	Acquisition of language	All language accomplishments disappear; language is reacquired with repetition of all stages	Rate of maturation slowed down	Hand preference emerges	Right hemisphere can easily adopt sole responsibility for language	Language appears to involve entire brain; little cortical specialization with regard to language though left hemisphere beginning to become dominant towards end of this period
Years 3–10	Some grammatical refinement; expansion of vocabulary	Emergence of aphasic symptoms; disorders tend to recover without residual language deficits (except in reading or writing). During recovery period, two processes active: diminishing	Very slow completion of maturational processes	Cerebral dominance established between 3–5 years but evidence that right hemisphere may often still be involved in speech and language	In cases where language is already predominantly localized in left hemisphere and aphasia ensues with left lesion, it is possible to re-	A process of physiological organization takes place in which functional lateralization of language to left is prominent. "Physiological redundancy" is gradually reduced and polarization of activities between right and left hemisphere is established. As long

180

Age						
	aphasic interference and further acquisition of language	functions. About 1/4 of early childhood aphasias due to right-hemisphere lesions			establish language presumably by reactivating language functions in right hemisphere	as maturational processes have not stopped, reorganization is still possible
11–14	Foreign accents emerge	Some aphasic symptoms become irreversible (particularly when acquired lesion was traumatic).	An asymptote is reached on almost all parameters. Exceptions are Myelinization and EEG spectrum	Apparently firmly established but definitive statistics not available	Marked signs of reduction in equipotentiality	Language markedly lateralized and internal organization established irreversibly for life. Language-free parts of brain cannot take over except where lateralization is incomplete or had been blocked by pathology during childhood
Mid-teens to Senium	Acquisition of second language becomes increasingly difficult	Symptoms present after 3–5 months postinsult are irreversible	None	In about 97% of the entire population language is definitely lateralized to the left	None for language	

and the unique degree of lateralization of function. Table 4.8 presents the argument in tabular form.

REFERENCES

Ahrens, R. (1954), Beiträge zur Entwicklung des Physiognomie- und Mimikerkennens, *Z. exp. Angew. Psychol.* **2**:412–454; 599–633.

Ajuriaguerra, J. de (1957), Langage et dominance cérébrale, *J. Français d'Oto-Rhino-Laryngol.* **6**:489–499.

Altman, P. L. and Dittmer, D. S. (eds.) (1962), *Growth Including Reproduction and Morphological Development,* Federation of American Societies for Experimental Biology, Washington, D.C.

André-Thomas, Sorrel, E. and Sorrel-Dejerine, Mme., Un cas d'aphasie motrice par traumatisme craniocerebral chez l'enfant. *Rev. Neurol.* **63**:893–896.

Austerlitz, R. (1956), Gilyak nursery words, *Word* **12**:260–279.

Basser, L. S. (1962), Hemiplegia of early onset and the faculty of speech with special reference to the effects of hemispherectomy, *Brain* **85**:427–460.

Bateman, F. (1890), *On Aphasia, or Loss of Speech, and the Localisation of the Faculty of Articulate Language.* (2nd ed.) Churchill, London.

Benjamin, R. M. and Thompson, R. F. (1959), Differential effects of cortical lesions in infant and adult cats on roughness discrimination, *Exp. Neurol.* **1**:305–321.

Bernhard, C. G. and Skoglund, C. R. (1939), On the alpha frequency of human brain potentials as function of age, *Skandinav. Arch. f. Physiol.* **82**:178–184.

Bok, S. T. (1959), *Histonomy of the Cerebral Cortex.* Elsevier, Amsterdam.

Bowlby, J. (1953), Critical phases in the development of social responses in man and other animals, in *Prospects in Psychiatric Research; the proceedings of the Oxford Conference of the Mental Health Fund.* J. M. Tanner (ed.), Blackwell, Oxford.

Branco-LeFèvre, A. F. (1950), Contribuição para o estudo da psicopatologia da afasia em criança, *Arq. Neuropsiquiat.* (São Paulo) **8**:345–393.

Brante, G. (1949), Studies on lipids in the nervous system; with special reference to quantitative chemical determination and topical distribution, *Acta Physiol. Scand.* 18 Suppl. 63.

Brodbeck, A. J. and Irwin, O. C. (1946), The speech behavior of infants without families, *Child Development* **17**:145–156.

Brooks, C. and Peck, M. E. (1940), Effect of various cortical lesions on development of placing and hopping reactions in rats, *J. Neurophysiol.* **3**:66–73.

Brown, R. W. (1957), *Words and Things.* Free Press, Glencoe, Illinois.

Brown, R. W. and Bellugi, U. (1964), Three processes in the child's acquisition of syntax, in *New Directions in the Study of Language,* E. H. Lenneberg (ed.), M.I.T. Press, Cambridge, Massachusetts.

Brunner, H. and Stengel, E. (1932), Zur Lehre von den Aphasien im Kindesalter, *Z. Neur. Psychiat.* **142**:430–450.

Bühler, C. (1931), *Kindheit und Jugend* (3rd ed.) Hirzel, Leipzig.

Carmichael, L. (1926), The development of behavior in vertebrates experimentally removed from the influence of external stimulation, *Psychol. Rev.* **33**:51–58.

Carmichael, L. (1927), A further study of the development of behavior in vertebrates experimentally removed from the influence of external stimulation, *Psychol. Rev.* **34**:34–47.

Carmichael, L. (ed.) (1954), *Manual of Child Psychology.* John Wiley and Sons, New York.

Conel, J. LeRoy (1939–1963), *The Postnatal Development of the Human Cerebral Cortex.* Volumes I through VI. Harvard Univ. Press, Cambridge, Mass.

Critchley, MacD. (1938), Aphasia in a partial deaf-mute, *Brain* **61**:163–168.

Davis, K. (1947), Final note on a case of extreme isolation, *Am. J. Sociol.* **52**:432–437.

De Crinis, M. (1934), *Aufbau und Abbau der Grosshirnleistungen und ihre anatomischen Gründe,* Karger, Berlin.

Dennis, W. and Dennis, M. G. (1951), Development under controlled environmental conditions, in *Readings in Child Psychology,* W. Dennis (ed.), Prentice-Hall, Englewood Cliffs, New Jersey.

Dennis, W. and Najarian, P. (1957), Infant development under environmental handicap, *Psychol. Monogr.* **71,** No. 7, Whole No. 436F.

Doty, R. W. (1953), Effects of ablation of visual cortex in neonatal and adult cats, *Abstracts Comm. XIX Int. Physiol. Congr.,* p. 316.

Douglas, E. and Richardson, J. C. (1959), Aphasia in a congenital deaf-mute, *Brain* **82**:68–80.

Dreyfus-Brisac, C. and Blanc, C. (1956), Electro-encéphalogramme et maturation cérébrale, *Encéphale* **45**:204–241.

Ervin, S. M. (1964), Imitation and structural change in children's language, in *New Directions in the Study of Language,* E. H. Lenneberg (ed.), M.I.T. Press, Cambridge, Mass.

Ervin, S. M. and Miller, W. R. (1963), Language development, *Child Psychology,* 62nd Yearbook, National Society for the Study of Education. Univ. of Chicago Press, Chicago, Ill.

Fisichelli, R. M. (1950), *A study of prelinguistic speech development of institutionalized infants.* Unpublished Ph.D. dissertation, Fordham University. Quoted by McCarthy, 1954.

Flechsig, P. (1927), *Meine myelogenetische Hirnlehre mit biographischer Einleitung.* Springer, Berlin.

Folch-Pi, J. (1952), Chemical constituents of brain during development and in maturity, in *The Biology of Mental Health and Disease, The 27th Annual Conference of the Milbank Memorial Fund,* Hoeber, New York.

Folch-Pi, J. (1955), Composition of the brain in relation to maturation, in *Biochemistry of the Developing Nervous System; Proceedings of the First International Neurochemical Symposium,* H. Waelsch (ed.), Academic Press, New York.

Fry, D. B. (1966), The development of the phonological system in the normal and deaf child, in *The Genesis of Language: a psycholinguistic approach*. F. Smith and G. A. Miller (eds.), M.I.T. Press, Cambridge, Mass.

Gesell, A. and Amatruda, C. S. (1947), *Developmental Diagnosis; normal and abnormal child development, clinical methods and pediatric applications* (2nd ed.), Hoeber, New York.

Gibbs, F. A. and Knott, J. R. (1949), Growth of the electrical activity of the cortex, *EEG & Clin. Neurophysiol.* **1**:223–229.

Goldfarb, W. (1943), The effects of early institutional care on adolescent personality, *J. Exp. Educ.* **12**:106–129.

Goldfarb, W. (1945), Effects of psychological deprivation in infancy and subsequent stimulation, *Am. J. Psychiat.* **102**:18–33.

Grasset, J. (1896), Aphasie de la main droite chez un sourd-muet, *Le Progrès Médical,* Series 3, Vol. 4, No. 44, p. 281.

Gray, P. H. (1958), Theory and evidence of imprinting in human infants. *J. Psychol.* **46**:155–166.

Grohmann, J. (1938), Modifikation oder Funktionsregung? ein Beitrag zur Klärung der wechselseitigen Beziehungen zwischen Instinkthandlung und Erfahrung, *Z. Tierpsychol.* **2**:132–144.

Gutmann, E. (1942), Aphasia in children, *Brain* **65**:205–219.

Harlow, H. F., Akert, K., and Schiltz, K. A. (1964), The effects of bilateral prefrontal lesions on learned behavior of neonatal, infant, and preadolescent monkeys, in *The Frontal Granular Cortex and Behavior*. J. M. Warren and K. Akert (eds.), McGraw-Hill, New York.

Hécaen, H. and Ajuriaguerra, J. de (1963), *Les Gauchers, Prévalence Manuelle et Dominance Cérébrale*. Presses Universitaires de France, Paris.

Henry, C. E. (1944), Electroencephalograms of normal children, *Monograph, Society for Research in Child Development*, **9,** No. 3.

Hess, E. H. (1962), Ethology: an approach toward the complete analysis of behavior, *New Directions in Psychology*. R. W. Brown, E. Galanter, E. H. Hess, and G. Mandler (eds.), Holt, Rinehart and Winston, New York.

Hillier, W. F., Jr. (1954), Total left cerebral hemispherectomy for malignant glioma, *Neurology* **4**:718–721.

Hinde, R. A. (1961), The establishment of the parent-offspring relation in birds, with some mammalian analogies, in *Current Problems in Animal Behavior,* W. H. Thorpe and O. L. Zangwill, Cambridge University Press, Cambridge, England.

Irwin, O. C. (1948), Infant speech, *J. Speech and Hearing Disorders* **13**:224–225, 320–326.

Kaes, T. (1907), *Die Grosshirnrinde des Menschen in ihren Massen und in ihrem Fasergehalt*, Gustav Fischer, Jena.

Kety, S. S. (1955), Changes in cerebral circulation and oxygen consumption which accompany maturation and aging, in *Biochemistry of the Developing Nervous System; Proceedings of the First International Neurochemical Symposium*, H. Waelsch (ed.), Academic Press, New York.

Koehler, O. (1952), "Wolfskinder," Affen im Haus und Vergleichende Verhaltens-forschung, *Folia Phoniatrica* **4**:29–53.

Kroeber, A. L. (1916), The speech of a Zuni child, *Am. Anthrop.* **18**:529–534.

Kummer, B. (1953), Untersuchungen über die Entwicklung der Schädelform des Menschen und einiger Anthropoiden, *Abhandlungen zur exakten Biologie,* fasc 3, L. v. Bertalanffy (ed.), Borntraeger, Berlin.

Laine, E. and Gros, C. (1956), *L'Hémispherectomie,* Masson, Paris.

Landau, W. M., Goldstein, R., and Kleffner, F. R. (1960), Congenital aphasia; a clinicopathologic study, *Neurology* **10**:915–921.

Lehrman, D. S. (1958*a*), Induction of broodiness by participation in courtship and nest-building in the Ring Dove *(Streptopelia risoria), J. comp. physiol. Psychol.* **51**:32–36.

Lehrman, D. S. (1958*b*), Effect of female sex hormones on incubation behavior in the Ring Dove *(Streptopelia risoria), J. comp. physiol. Psychol.* **51**:142–145.

Lenneberg, E. H. (1962), Understanding language without ability to speak: a case report, *J. abnorm. soc. Psychol.* **65**:419–425.

Lenneberg, E. H. (1964), Speech as a motor skill with special reference to non-aphasic disorders, in *The Acquisition of Language,* Monograph of the Society for Research in Child Development. U. Bellugi and R. Brown (eds.), Serial No. 92, Vol. 29, No. 1.

Lenneberg, E. H., Nichols, I. A., and Rosenberger, E. F. (1964), Primitive stages of language development in mongolism, in *Disorders of Communication Vol. XLII: Research Publications,* A.R.N.M.D. Williams and Wilkins, Baltimore, Maryland.

Lenneberg, E. H., Rebelsky, F. G., and Nichols, I. A. (1965), The vocalization of infants born to deaf and to hearing parents, *Vita Humana* (Human Development) **8**:23–37.

Lindsley, D. B. (1936), Brain potentials in children and adults, *Science* **84**:354.

Lorenz, K. Z. (1958), The evolution of behavior, *Scientific American* **119**, No. 6, December, 67–78.

Luchsinger, R. and Arnold, G. E. (1959), *Lehrbuch der Stimm- und Sprachheil-kunde* (2nd ed.), Springer, Wien.

Marks, M., Taylor M., and Rusk, H. A. (1957), Rehabilitation of the aphasic patient, *Neurology* **7**:837–843.

McCarthy, D. (1954), Language development in children, in *Manual of Child Psychology.* L. Carmichael (ed.), pp. 492–630.

McGraw, M. B. (1963), *The Neuromuscular Maturation of the Human Infant.* Hafner, New York.

Morley, M. (1957), *The Development and Disorders of Speech in Childhood.* Livingstone, London.

Peiper, A. (1961), *Die Eigenart der Kindlichen Hirntätigkeit* (3rd ed.), G. Thieme, Leipzig.

Poetzl, O. (1926), Ueber sensorische Aphasie im Kindesalter, *Z. Hals- N.-Ohrenhlk.* **14**:190–216.

Russell, W. R. and Espir, M. L. E. (1961), *Traumatic Aphasia,* Oxford University Press, Oxford, England.

Schadé, J. P. and Groenigen, W. B. van (1961), Structural organization of the human cerebral cortex; maturation of the middle frontal gyrus, *Acta anat.* **47**:74–111.

Scharlock, D. P., Tucker, T. J., and Strominger, N. L. (1963), Auditory discrimination by the cat after neonatal ablation of temporal cortex, *Science* **141** (Sept. 20):1197–1198.

Schultz, A. H. (1956), Postembryonic age changes, in *Primatologia: Handbook of Primatology,* Vol. I. H. Hofer, A. H. Schultz, and D. Starck (eds.), pp. 887–964. Karger, Basel.

Scott, J. P. (1963), The process of primary socialization in canine and human infants, *Monograph of the Society for Research in Child Development,* Serial No. 85, Vol. 28, No. 1.

Sholl, D. A. (1956), *The Organization of the Cerebral Cortex.* Methuen, London.

Singh, J. A. L., and Zingg, R. M. (1942), *Wolf Children and Feral Man.* Harper, New York.

Slobin, D. I. (1966), The acquisition of Russian as a native language, in *The Genesis of Language: a psycholinguistic approach.* F. Smith and G. A. Miller (eds.), M.I.T. Press, Cambridge, Mass.

Smith, J. R. (1941), The frequency growth of the human alpha rhythms during normal infancy and childhood, *J. Psychol.* **11**:177–198.

Smith, M. E. (1926), An investigation of the development of the sentence and the extent of vocabulary in young children, *Univ. Iowa Stud. Child Welfare,* Vol. 3, No. 5.

Sperry, R. W. (1961), Cerebral organization and behavior, *Science* **133**:1749–1757.

Sperry, W. M. (1962), The biochemical maturation of the brain, in *Mental Retardation,* L. C. Kolb, R. L. Masland, and R. E. Cooke (eds.), A.R.N.M.D., Vol. 39, Williams and Wilkins, Baltimore.

Teuber, H.-L. (1950), Neuropsychology, in *Recent Advances in Diagnostic Psychological Testing: a critical summary,* Chapter 3, pp. 30–52, C Thomas, Springfield, Illinois.

Teuber, H.-L. (1960), Perception, in *Handbook of Physiology, Section 1: Neurophysiology,* Vol. 3, Chapter 65, pp. 1595–1668, American Physiological Society, Washington, D.C.

Teuber, H.-L. (1962), Effects of brain wounds implicating right or left hemisphere in man: hemisphere differences and hemisphere interaction in vision, audition, and somesthesis, in *Interhemispheric Relations and Cerebral Dominance,* pp. 131–157. V. B. Mountcastle (ed.), Johns Hopkins Press, Baltimore.

Thomas, E. and Schaller, F. (1954), Das Spiel der optisch isolierten, jungen Kaspar-Hauser-Katze, *Naturwiss* **41**:557–558.

Thorpe, W. H. (1961), Sensitive periods in the learning of animals and men: a study of imprinting with special reference to the induction of cyclic behavior, in *Current Problems in Animal Behavior,* W. H. Thorpe and O. L. Zangwill (eds.), Cambridge University Press, Cambridge, England.

Tureen, L. L., Smolik, E. A., and Tritt, J. H. (1951), Aphasia in a deaf mute, *Neurology* **1**:237–244.

Vogt, O. (1911), Die Myeloarchitektonik des Isocortex parietalis, *J. Psychol. Neurol.* **18**: (Suppl. No. 2) 379–390.

Woodward, F. R. (1945), Recovery from aphasia; report of two cases, *Bull. Los Angeles Neurol. Soc.* **10:**73–75.

Yakovlev, P. I. (1962), Morphological criteria of growth and maturation of the nervous system in man, in *Mental Retardation,* A.R.N.M.D., Vol. 39, pp. 3–46, Williams and Wilkins, Baltimore, Maryland.

Zangwill, O. L. (1960), *Cerebral Dominance and its Relation to Psychological Function.* Oliver and Boyd, Edinburgh.

Note: Since the time of my original research for this chapter two recent articles have come to my attention that are relevant to the neurological material covered here. They are Alajouanine, T. and Lhermitte, F., Acquired aphasia in childhood. *Brain* (1965) **88:**653–662; and Penfield, W., Conditioning the uncommitted cortex for language learning, *Brain* (1965) **88:**787–798. Although there are some discrepancies both in facts and in interpretation between these articles and the material presented here, there appears to be perfect agreement on the basic issue, namely that the prognosis for acquired aphasia in childhood is definitely better than for similar pathology in the adult.

CHAPTER Five

Neurological aspects of speech and language

The literature on aphasia—*aphasiology,* as it has been called recently —is enormous, and facts and fancy are freely interspersed. No attempt shall be made to review this material; good discussions may be found in Adams (1958), Brain (1961), Schuell et al. (1964), Kainz (1943), Penfield and Roberts (1959), Weisenburg and McBride (1935). It is important, however, to assemble here the main clinical findings and to attempt to fit them into the general picture of language as a biological phenomenon.

Many classificatory schemes of aphasic symptoms, clinical syndromes, and underlying pathology exist, and many authorities have strong feelings about the usefulness of one or another such scheme. Since we are not concerned here with clinical applications, the material has been arranged in a slightly unconventional way in order to facilitate orientation and cross reference. The captions used do not imply any preference for or criticism of any of the existing classifications.

I. CLINICAL SYMPTOMS OF SPEECH AND LANGUAGE DISORDERS

(1) *General Characteristics of the Patient with Aphasia*

We shall be concerned here primarily with adult patients whose communication through the medium of natural language has been disturbed as a consequence of insults to the brain. The disorders may have come on suddenly, as in cerebro-vascular accidents (stroke), or traumatic lesions (mechanical destruction of tissue), or gradually, as in any other

188

disease of the brain. In the case of vascular accidents, there is no pain but a sudden, catastrophic modification of certain skills. Characteristically, the patient notices that the right side of his body does not move at will (although this does not always occur) and that he cannot express himself when he wishes to describe his problems. If the disease process is arrested, symptoms usually reach a certain height and then regress to varying degrees. There may be just a barely noticeable improvement or complete recovery. In the majority of cases, symptoms become stabilized within a period of roughly five months after the arrest of the disease. Whatever language function has not been restored within this period may essentially be considered as a permanent residue of dysfunction. There are certain exceptions to this rule. Language disorders due to damage from sudden anoxic states or from certain intoxications such as carbon monoxide have a slightly better prognosis, improvement sometimes taking place over periods of years.

Often there are more general psychological deficits in addition to the language disorder, such as confusion, perseveration, memory lapses, flight of associations and ideas, difficulty in concentration, difficulty in suppressing irrelevant thoughts, and emotional lability. It may not be easy, in some cases, to distinguish between these more general abnormalities and specifically aphasic symptoms. However, intellectual deterioration is not a necessary concomitant of acquired language disorders.

In many cases the clinical course of the aphasic patient is hampered by unfavorable psychological attitudes. This is not surprising, for it must be frightening to know that something has happened in one's brain that causes profound behavioral alterations. Some patients do not recognize their own deficits (anosognosia). Thus, a person may be completely unaware that his utterances are always and only gibberish and that he does not understand anything that is being said to him (evidenced by the fact that he cannot follow the simplest commands, answer questions, or even understand those answers that are made to what seems to be a question on his part). Quite commonly the aphasic patient is, understandably, depressed, discouraged, and fatigued. It is especially due to this psychological substrate that speech rehabilitation should be attempted soon after the occurrence of aphasia.

If motivation can be improved early during the convalescence, a more favorable attitude may be created, and the patient might be taught to make the best use of his residual communicatory skills. This is, in fact, the most likely reason why occasionally a person who is suddenly given speech therapy after years of deep aphasia may respond relatively well to such treatment. His language remnants are being recruited, as it were, and the realization that a certain degree of language communication is again possible will combat the psychological depression and increase motivation for seeking contact with the world around him.

The patient's psychological conditions and basic motivation are also an important determinant for his language behavior in stressful situations. Occasionally, it happens that two behavioral disorders overlap: in addition to the aphasia there may be a disorder of volition, which results in a state of muteness or pathological lack of initiative for communication. When this occurs, a patient may regularly perform poorly during routine neurological examinations as well as on formal aphasia tests. Yet he is neither malingering nor psychotic. There appears to be neurogenic interference with something we might call the activating system for language. When this is the case, the patient surprises the hospital ward personnel by sudden and unexpected ability to express himself reasonably well when put under emotional stress.

Once I studied a patient who had been admitted to the hospital with what seemed to be a stroke. His recovery was very imperfect, and after several weeks on the ward he was still showing signs of a severe, predominantly expressive communication-disorder. On the day that he was told that arrangements had been made for him to be discharged to his sister's home, he became very agitated and could suddenly express himself fairly well, conveying to the medical staff that this was one place he definitely did not desire to go. Further social work investigations revealed that serious frictions existed between the patient and his sister's family, and new arrangements had to be made. When the patient was returned to the ward, his communication difficulties reappeared at once. Apparently there was a critical level of activation at play.

As a general rule we may say that in those aphasics whose volition for language is pathologically depressed, heightened stress increases language ability. However, patients with indications for high motivation for oral communication, as a rule, do worse under stress. The latter condition is much more common.

It is often held that the biological roots of language lie in the emotional apparatus of man. Some support for this notion may be seen in the fact that very often the expressive disorders of language are less severe in emotional discourse than in propositional discourse. For instance, sudden, passionate exclamations may still occur at a time when the patient can no longer use language to explain something or to ask polite questions. Interestingly enough, this may not be simply attributed to generalized disorders of thought. A number of intelligence tests have been described in which aphasics do as well as nonaphasics (Alajouanine and Lhermitte, 1964; Zangwill, 1964. For contrary evidence, however, see Teuber, Battersby, and Bender, 1952, and Weinstein et al., 1955). The exact mechanisms responsible for this are unknown.

Following is a more detailed description of symptoms. It is rare that any one of them occurs in complete isolation.

(2) *Receptive Disorders*

This type of language disorder is usually called sensory aphasia, which is a somewhat misleading term because there is no evidence that the patient's perceptual threshold for hearing is different after the aphasia from what it was before. The deficit consists of an inability to recognize or understand words or spoken language. The afflicted person reports that he can hear speech and he knows that he is being talked to, but he cannot make out what is being said. He may spontaneously explain that "words don't separate" or that "everything sounds like a foreign language." With careful tests, we can sometimes demonstrate that individual speech sounds appear as unfamiliar acoustic phenomena. In extreme cases, the patient is completely unable to repeat any utterance or word, even though he may use the same words or phrases spontaneously. Sometimes his receptivity improves a little if he is spoken to very slowly, one word at a time and with unusual loudness. When he does repeat one or the other word, it is frequently distorted; often just the phonemic stress is reproduced accurately. In less severe cases only one word is repeated out of a longer sentence, and then used in an entirely different context.

Patients with severe receptive disorders usually have other communication problems, although these may be less evident. Most patients show a superfluency (described subsequently), difficulty in focusing attention on words spoken to them, and some impairment of reading —or at least concentration on reading. The basic reading mechanism need not be disturbed. Kleist (1962) believes that receptive disorders may be classified into phonemic deafness, word deafness, name deafness and sentence deafness, and that each of these functions has distinct anatomical correlates. This is an extreme view shared by few contemporary neurologists.

(3) *Expressive Disorders*

(*a*) *Subfluency.* Here the flow of speech is severely hampered. The articulation of every word apparently requires an enormous effort and concentration. Words are produced slowly and with pauses between them. Utterances are reduced to telegram style. Speaking appears to require such an effort that every attempt is made to communicate by one word utterances. Examination of these patients reveals that their voices and respiratory mechanisms are intact and that individual movements of tongue, lips, or other articulatory organs may be performed quite well, although some slowing down is very common, such as in the production of the sounds *papapapapa* or *tatatatata*. However, the slowed-down rate of alternating tongue or lip movements cannot explain the extreme impediment during speech itself. If it were simply a matter of slowing down, the patient might be expected to speak fluently but at a much reduced rate. Furthermore, there are some rare cases in which the fluency of speech is markedly hampered, whereas the rate of saying *papapa* is barely, if at all, altered.

Apparently, a more central and speech specific mechanism is disturbed than general motor coordination of articulatory organs. Thus, these patients have no difficulty chewing or swallowing or controlling their saliva. We can hardly escape the impression that this problem consists of an inability to "plan for the motor events" that are necessary for speech. Patients report, and give clinical evidence, that they know what they wish to say (they do not grope for words), but they cannot guide the motor integration that is specific to speech. They are usually attentive, well motivated, and eager to communicate.

(*b*) *Superfluency*. The flow of speech is markedly increased and, apparently, can not be inhibited or "phrased" in accordance with the rules of either grammar or common, social interaction. In ordinary conversation of healthy individuals, utterances are not always couched in syntactically complete sentences; but in the patient with superfluency, syntax is even more mutilated. Utterances consist of an interminable flow of phrases, unfinished or improperly begun sentences, and clichés. The patient jumps from thought to thought and topic to topic, and if he asks a question at all, he fails to wait for answers. Usually the substance of the communication can not be understood. It is difficult to decide how much of this condition ought to be attributed to a dysfunction of language and how much to a peculiar difficulty in ordering thoughts. Often there is a particular word or phrase that recurs again and again as if the patient could not rid himself of one particular line of associations. If he can understand language and is asked a question, he will begin by answering but is incapable either of confining himself to a short answer or of finishing the answer before he is off to quite irrelevant topics.

(*c*) *Semantic Disturbances*. These are probably the most common symptoms. A never-ending variety of different manifestations may be found. There may be an inability to name colors or to name numbers;

or words are substituted that are inappropriate in the context of the sentence but are semantically related to the word that was apparently intended. If the patient spoke more than one language before the disease, he may slip foreign words into his utterances. Often entirely inappropriate words are uttered within a sentence, and then efforts are made to correct this, resulting in a train of semantically related but inappropriate words. When objects are shown and the instruction is to name them, the patient may start with a neologism which is then corrected to a word that exists in English but is not correct for the object though a semantic connection is discernible: (knife), "that's a bilk, a bite yes, meat bite." Henry Head (1926) spoke of semantic aphasia, a term which has fallen into disrepute among neurologists because it does not comprise symptomatology characteristic of a specific clinical condition. Some degree of semantic disturbance is encountered among all types of aphasia, although not every patient may be thus disturbed. Nevertheless, Head's discussion is very detailed and still of interest.

(*d*) *Difficulty in Word Finding.* This is the most common symptom in this category. A patient may audibly grope around for the appropriate word by first telling the examiner how the object whose name he forgot is used, what it is for, or with what it is usually associated. Sometimes he may give a list of words that are somehow related to the correct one and occasionally the word may become available in this devious way. Even if the patient cannot think of the right name, he is usually able to recognize the correct word when given a list of words to choose from. Once he hears the right word, he can immediately repeat it and use it in a grammatically correct sentence. It is also interesting that, typically, these patients may be unable to think of such a word as "watch" when they are asked to name that object, but immediately after the test they may say spontaneously to the examiner, "Give me back my watch!" This general condition is called, at times, *anomia,* implying a loss of names for things. Usually, it is quite clear that names have not been "lost" but cannot always be made available at will. It seems to be a recruiting or activating difficulty rather than a loss in the sense of a return to a state of ignorance with respect to one or the other word. Nor can it be said that it is a "simple" memory defect. Patients with memory defects need not have word-finding difficulties and vice versa.

(*e*) *Paraphasic Disturbances.* This is a wastebasket category of symptoms not sharply distinguishable from semantic disturbances. However, nonsense words are produced more frequently and often exclusively. For instance, I knew a patient whose original language had been English and who had known no other language but whose entire vocabulary, after her stroke, consisted of the words, "Oh, nay, konossopay." She would use these words with varying intonation and stress patterns, all of them recognizably of an American-English character, and also she could use these words in all combinations. She did not seem to have psychiatric disease. Considering the circumstances, she managed to communicate remarkably well!

This symptom is called *jargon* aphasia, and some authorities consider it as a condition distinct from those symptoms more commonly called paraphasic. However, it appears to me that it is just a difference in degree. In the more typical instances of paraphasias, the patient apparently knows the right word but has only the approximate phonemic representation. He is shown a bird and calls it a bit, a birt, a bilt; he may even ask the examiner to correct him because he knows the sound configuration is odd. Here, the speech sounds are recognizable English, but they seem to have been thrown together helter-skelter.

A phenomenon of the same nature but of a different scale are the *agrammatisms*. (Again not ordinarily called paraphasia but grouped here together under one head because of my belief that all of these derangements belong to the same symptom complex.) Utterances are exactly as the name implies, ungrammatical. A few illustrations make further elaboration unnecessary: "I haven't been headache troubled not for a long time." "A kind of little ver (bird), machinery, a kind of animal do for making a sound." (Both quotations from Brain, 1955.) "He is speeching it, there and then, straight away for me, there." ". . . that I shall have lesson with the lungage of the hear itself." (Quoted by Ross et al, 1964) "That is a dark." "Well, I thought thing I am going to the . . . tell is about my operation and it is not about all I can tell is about the preparation the had was always the V . . . time was when they had me to get ready that is they shaved off all my hair was and a few odd parts of pencil they pr . . . quive me in the fanny." (Quoted by Penfield and Roberts, 1959.) The latter is a written document but is very reminiscent of transcripts of tape-recorded utterances.

(*f*) *Fixation on Phrases.* Many patients have one or two phrases which they produce fluently and correctly but which they repeat at all times, appropriately or inappropriately (more frequently the latter). Their discourse may be entirely confined to such phrases or they may slip the phrase into almost every statement they make.

(4) *Disorders of Manner of Production*

These symptoms are distinguished from those discussed previously in that the patient has no difficulty in understanding speech and that his utterances are standard English in terms of fluency, grammar, and content. However, utterances are affected in their physical aspects in one of the following three ways:

(*a*) *Errors of Order.* There is a pathological propensity for spooner-isms on the level of phonemes, words, and sometimes even whole phrases. The following short sample from a transcribed tape recording is a good illustration.

> "I am taking (pause) ah (pause) Sherriks ah Sherring's mixture (laugh)—it's easier for me to (pause) stalk—talk staccato and break-ing up each word (pause) into sentences—breaking up sentences into words provided they have ah (pause) not many syllables. Ah, syllable is hard. (pause) Precise words that I have trouble with are Republican and epics—epis—(pause) copalian."

This patient was a sixty-year-old lady who had been a successful journalist and an accomplished public speaker, active to the day of her stroke which had occurred about three months before this tape was made. During the examination it was evident that she was painfully aware of her difficulty. Her awareness is also reflected in the transcript. Notice that the hesitation pauses tend to occur immediately before or while she commits a mistake of order. Most of the mistakes are antic-ipations of units yet to come. Thus the *k*'s in *Sherriks* is clearly a pre-mature occurrence of the *x* in *mixture;* the *st* of *stalk* is an anticipation of the *st* in *staccato.* Next she interchanged *words* and *sentences.* In the last line, there is an example of true metathesis: *cs* instead of *sc.*

In contrast to previous discussion of aphasic symptoms, there is good reason to assume here that we are not dealing with a generalized con-fusion of thoughts but that the disorder is fairly specific to language. The ordering of speech sounds is not a conscious procedure as may be gathered from the utterances of confabulating, delirious, or totally confused patients who have no difficulty whatever in producing words with perfect phonemic sequences. Furthermore, the patients with or-dering difficulties tend to correct and edit their own utterances fre-quently. It is curious that patients with this type of aphasic symptoms often (but not necessarily) make similar mistakes in their written documents.

(*b*) *Dysarthria.* Under this term we shall discuss all impairments of articulation. Some neurologists prefer to reserve this term for disorders that are symptomatically and etiologically quite distinct from aphasia. All agree that any type of dysarthria may be seen as an isolated symp-tom and that the manifestations become more distinct the more pe-ripherally the lesion is located. Although aphasia refers essentially to content, dysarthria refers exclusively to manner of production. It is common to see aphasia without dysarthria and even more common to see dysarthria without aphasia. Dysarthria caused by cortical lesions tends to produce speech reminiscent of someone talking with a hot potato in his mouth. Acoustic contrasts are poorly defined but otherwise the articulatory flow is normal. Lower lesions cause more distinct interferences with the articulatory process. Alterations of rate are most common. Usually the patient speaks markedly more slowly, although fluently. Measurements on sound-spectrograms indicate that the slowing down is due to a decrease in the rate of movement of articulatory organs which is in contrast to slow discourse of a neurologically healthy person. In the latter, slowness is primarily produced by increasing pauses and extending vowels while the rate of movement during transition of speech sounds is statistically no different from that in fast speakers.

Less common are lesions that seem to cause an acceleration in the rate of speech. The patient has the subjective impression that he is unable to slow down the flow of speech; articulation seems to run away with him, and he is forever trying to catch up. * His utterances give us the impression that he produces speech sounds at top speeds, but what he is saying is unintelligible. Through the courtesy of Dr. Norman Geschwind (Veterans' Administration Hospital, Jamaica Plain, Boston, Massachusetts), I have had an opportunity to examine the speech of one such patient in great detail. His spontaneous communications were for the most part unintelligible. Although he seemed to be hurrying along, he did not stutter. When asked to count or recite the alphabet he produced about five to seven units per second, which corresponds to the normal upper limit for sustained speech, although it sounds very fast. When asked specifically to say the same thing at a slower rate, he could not do it; he also reported, "I cannot slow down." He had observed himself that the only way for him to control his rate of articulatory production was to sing, which he would do with pathos if not sonority. (It had to be well-learned songs, however. He could not convey his prose through improvised melodies.) When he was asked to recite the words of the song without the melody, he seemed to be speeding up again and became unintelligible. When samples of his tape-recorded speech were analyzed spectrographically and listened to again and again, it became clear that the rate of articulatory movements was

*These symptoms are distinct from the aphasic superfluency in that only the articulatory components are speeded up relative to the content of communications. In the former case, articulation is frequently within normal limits, but there is a lack of inhibition of word production.

barely higher than average, but that the emission of language-relevant units was markedly slower. Thus, his lips or tongue would move at approximately normal rate producing additional but irrelevant sounds within a word.

His production of phonemes (using the term in its abstract sense: a language-symbol) and morphemes was slower than his uncontrolled articulatory movements, interspersing his utterances with duplications or triplications of stops. It is a temporal dissociation between rate of language and rate of speech. The latter, which may be regarded as the vehicle for the former, in this case goes wild, so to speak, and runs away from the former. It is as if the "speech-pace-maker" were disinhibited (cf. Chapter Three).

Closely related to disturbance of rate is that of *rhythm*. Here the speech rate is not uniformly transformed by constant and steady slowing down, but the rate of articulation changes rapidly within utterances. Characteristically, speech begins normally or perhaps even slower than usual, and very suddenly accelerates giving the utterance a staggering or sometimes "explosive" pattern. Sometimes changes in rate may themselves be rhythmical; the regular, though slight, waxing and waning of rate (and usually also of volume) gives discourse a monotonous impression, somewhat reminiscent of a class of fourth-graders reciting a poem with exaggerated *scanning*. Since this is a typically cerebellar symptom, it is never seen in conjunction with aphasia.

In some conditions, such as parkinsonism, there may be a dramatic impoverishment of all articulatory movements. Instead of the required rapid changes in the spatial geometry of the vocal tract, a relative rigidity of musculature allows for practically no changes in the oral configuration resulting in monotonous inarticulate utterances. In these cases, the dysarthria is merely a concomitant of a condition that affects all facial and oral movements.

(c) *Discoordinations*. In discoordination the precise timing between the actions of the respiratory, laryngeal, and oral apparatus is out of order. Air may be supplied when it is not called for, causing an over-aspiration of sounds, or there may be insufficient breath at the onset of a vowel, for instance, allowing sounds to fade out momentarily. The glottis may close or open at an inappropriate time, changing consonants from voiced to unvoiced sounds or vice versa or, in some cases, there may be transient interruptions of all sounds somewhat reminiscent of certain types of stuttering. These symptoms can only be demonstrated with the aid of instruments such as sound-spectrography, tape-loops and polygraph recorders.

Marginally relevant are also the *dysphonias,* in which the voicing mechanism is disturbed. This is not likely to be due to central nervous system disease; the most frequently occurring cases are due to peripheral lesions which are not under discussion here.

A curious though rare disorder is sometimes seen in connection with chorea and athetosis (that is, central nervous system disorders producing involuntary movements). Sounds may be emitted involuntarily, in some cases one every few minutes. They are essentially random and uncontrolled productions. Patients cannot inhibit these acoustical emissions, which are regularly accompanied by other choreo-athetoid movements and jerks. During sleep all of this activity ceases.

(5) *Other Language-Related Disorders*

Patients may lose the ability to read (alexia); this affliction may occur in relative isolation, although careful testing will always bring out a plethora of other, less prominent deficits in the realm of either perception or recognition, and some subtle language abnormalities can usually also be demonstrated. The subjective experience seems to be analogous to word-deafness and it is, indeed, sometimes called word-blindness. The difficulty is not due to a generalized breakdown in pattern perception, although complexity of pattern may be a partially controlling variable. The identification of single letters is usually not impaired and two- to three-letter words can be read correctly if presented in isolation. But the same word in a paragraph can no longer be recognized. It seems as if the multiplicity of stimuli produces confusion, and the patient can no longer suppress momentarily irrelevant stimulus configurations—he cannot regard them one at a time and in the right order.

A similar symptom in the realm of writing (*agraphia*) also exists, and this deficit too may occur as the most outstanding disorder. The incapacity for writing may be more conspicuous than all other deficits, but aspects of reading (at least comprehension) and language in general are always affected to some extent. An adventitious, pure loss of either reading or writing faculties in otherwise normally functioning individuals is extremely rare. The written documents of a patient with *agraphia* may bear remarkable similarities to aphasic speech; letters may be well formed, but they may not spell any recognizable word; or words may be quite legible, but they do not add up to intelligible sentences.

Most cases of aphasia beyond a certain degree of severity are also accompanied by reading and writing difficulties.

II. THE UNDERLYING PATHOLOGY

Aphasic symptomatology can only be evaluated intelligently in the light of the underlying disease processes. For the present discussion it will be useful to classify lesions into two groups: localized and diffuse. Both types of pathology may produce aphasic pictures.

(1) *Localized Lesions*

(*a*) *Cerebro-Vascular Accidents.* In times of peace this is the most common cause of aphasia, and it is therefore well to go into some detail here. Strokes are either due to thrombosis (occlusion of a vessel due to a fixed clot), embolism (a clot traveling in the stream of the arterial vasculature until it is arrested by the narrowing lumen of the branching vessel), or hemorrhage (rupture of a vessel and spilling of blood into tissue, which soon becomes a large clot-mass or hematoma).

In each case, the tissue further downstream is deprived of its blood supply and dies (infarct and necrosis), resulting in a series of pathological changes: the vessels in the infarcted area become more permeable; water transgresses into the tissue, causing it to swell up (edema) and bringing insult to the entire brain, often resulting clinically in a state of stupor or even coma. The necrotic tissue degenerates; liquefaction (brain-softening) sets in, and as some compensatory changes in collateral vessels take place—mostly an increase in collateral arterial blood supply and venous drainage—the general edema subsides, and the patient regains consciousness. The damage is now confined more to the bloodless area, which degenerates further. In severe cases, after liquefaction a cavitation may take place which again may change the gross architecture within the cranial vault.

In order to see how these events may cause aphasia, it is necessary to turn to the anatomy of the cerebral vessels. Usually, it is occlusions in the territory of the left middle-cerebral-artery that cause language disorders. Figure 5.1 shows the distribution of the major branches of this artery over the surface of the cortex. These major divisions send smaller arterial branches deep into cerebral matter as shown in Fig. 5.2. The anatomical configuration makes it clear that vascular accidents cause lesions that can never be confined to the hypothetical cortical speech areas and that subcortical areas are invariably destroyed as well.

The recovery pattern in aphasia may also be best understood by reference to the anatomy of the vasculature. It has been pointed out in

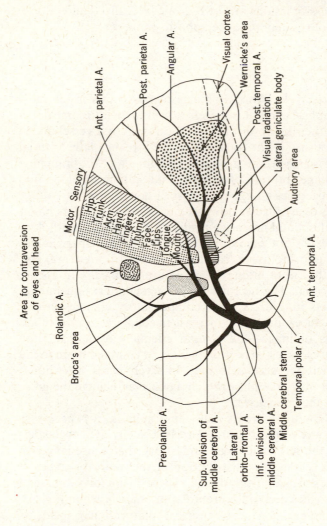

Area for contraversion
of eyes and head

Rolandic A.

Broca's area

Prerolandic A.

Sup. division of
middle cerebral A.

Lateral
orbito–frontal A.

Inf. division of
middle cerebral A.

Middle cerebral stem

Temporal polar A.

Ant. temporal A.

Motor Sensory

Hip
Trunk
Arm
Hand
Fingers
Thumb
Face
Lips
Tongue
Mouth

Ant. parietal A.

Post. parietal A.

Angular A.

Visual cortex

Wernicke's area

Post. temporal A.

Visual radiation

Lateral geniculate body

Auditory area

FIG. 5.1. Diagram of the lateral aspect of the left cerebral hemisphere, showing branches and distribution of the middle cerebral artery. (From Fisher, Karp and Adams; see Adams, 1958.)

200

earlier chapters that remission of symptoms occurs essentially within the first five months after arrest of the disease. In fact, the most dramatic recovery takes place during the first four weeks, but further improvement may be expected for another few months. These events may be explained by various physiological processes none of which has, unfortunately, been verified empirically. I prefer either of the following two explanations although some neurologists give preference to other explanations.

The considerable swelling of brain tissue that is contiguous to the infarcted area may incapacitate physiological function in large parts of the brain. Normal function may be restored when the edema subsides.

Another physiological explanation concerns the adjustment of collateral blood supply.

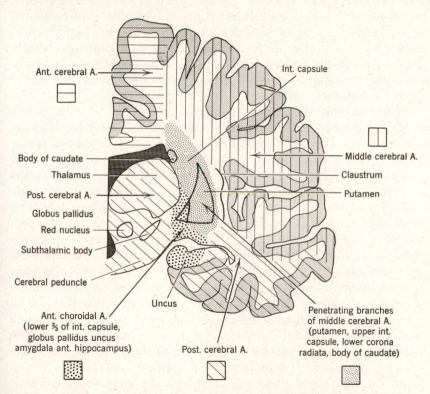

FIG. 5.2. Diagram of a cross section of the cerebral hemisphere to show the deep and superficial territories of the major cerebral vessels. (From Fisher, Karp and Adams; see Adams, 1958.)

Most portions of the cerebrum can receive blood from more than one arterial branch. Thus it is possible that an area in the brain can become ischemic (receives diminished blood supply) without becoming necrotic. As one artery is obstructed by a clot, blood is pumped with relatively greater pressure into another artery, which becomes dilated and is soon capable of negotiating more blood than usual. Thus, blood is sent by devious routes into the ischemic areas, which "revive"; and at least partial recovery is thereby established. Figure 5.3 shows diagrammatically the collateralization of the middle cerebral artery. Most of its territory may also be reached via the anterior cerebral artery.

Notice that reference to the basic anatomy of the vascular system of the brain relieves us from having to explain the recovery from aphasia by such mysterious processes as the taking over of function by other nervous tissue, not ordinarily engaged in the now lost function. Even in animal research it is very difficult to prove that such vicarious action of various parts of the brain can occur after maturation has been reached, and we must, therefore, be cautious in our speculations about man. (This point must not be confused with the freedom of organization in immature, growing mammalian brains mentioned briefly in Chapter Four, Growth and maturation.)

In a hydrodynamic, or preferably, a hemodynamic model, "taking over" is explained in a mechanistic way: if the flow of blood is obstructed in one direction, it will take new routes and/or change its rate of flow proportionately to its pressure. We do not have to imply a *deus ex machina* who opens or closes gates or switches relays. In this model no portion of the brain is said to take over functions, but it is merely claimed that tissue is temporarily "out of order" because of decreased blood supply, yet it is capable of recovering its complete and normal function given a return to the physiological status quo. The proponents of the taking over notion are logically in a more difficult situation. How can the mechanism of speech be forced from one region of the brain to another? We do not know what *will, consciousness,* or *purpose* might be physiologically or anatomically. Yet we do know that they are all intimately related to neurons and their supportive cells within the brain case. If these cells and their interaction are irreversibly damaged, these mysterious processes must be affected as well. There is nothing with a will of its own outside the brain that can decide or will that a particular part of the brain ought to change its activity to serve this or that purpose.

(*b*) *Tumor.* In adult patients space-occupying lesions produce relatively rarely isolated aphasic symptoms, and if they do, they tend to

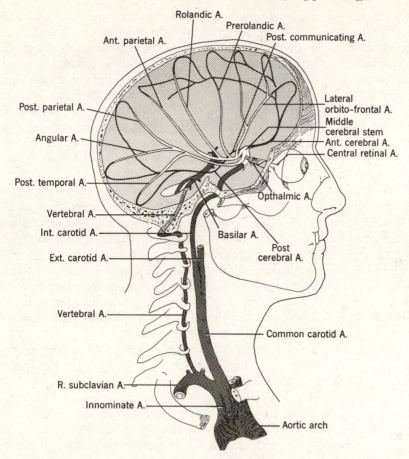

FIG. 5.3. Diagram of arrangement of major cerebral arteries. Notice connection between carotid and basilar arterial systems through the posterior communicating artery. The middle cerebral artery is also connected with the anterior and posterior cerebral arteries through subarachnoid interarterial anastomoses. (From Fisher, Karp and Adams; see Adams, 1958.)

occur fairly late in the history of the neoplastic growth. The negative findings here are theoretically more interesting than the positive ones.

Sometimes the tumor mass is encapsulated in a membrane and is a sharply defined and strictly localizable lesion. In these instances damage results mostly from pressure created within the intracranial vault. In other tumors nervous tissue is destroyed locally and replaced by an ever-increasing mass of tumor cells. The lesion may not be sharply defined because cells infiltrate in surrounding tissue and, again, cause generalized increase in pressure. The pressure is not merely due to the uncontrolled growth of new cells but also to concomitant vascular disturbances. The veins in the immediate vicinity of the tumor are compressed by the local expansion, thus increasing the capillary pressure in this area which, in turn, sets the stage for further local swelling and edema. Many brain tumors grow quite slowly, sometimes over a period as long as ten years. Because of this relatively slow evolvement, certain adjustments to the intracranial pressure may develop although the leeway is limited.

It is interesting that in some cases aphasia is seen only as a consequence of the surgical treatment of brain tumors rather than as the presenting symptom of the disease. It would be tempting to attribute this fact to the slow growth rate of the lesion, but such an assumption would again lead to a hypothesis of vicarious functioning of tissue. A more plausible explanation might be that the surgical excision extends over wider territory than the mass and that nervous impulses may still be transmitted through tissue that has been partially invaded by tumor cells. Perhaps it is also relevant that most tumors of the brain originate in proliferations of glial cells rather than neurons.

Certain mesencephalic tumors cause dysarthria as do certain cerebellar neoplasms. They are quite common in children, and the speech defect may be an isolated first sign of disease.

(c) *Abscess.* This is another focal, inflammatory lesion which, because of its swelling, may cause generalized intracranial pressure. It develops much more rapidly than brain tumors and may cause reactions in tissue immediately surrounding it. In contrast to tumor, however, the pathology in the neighborhood of the lesion is reversible and, in the case of surgical treatment, less nervous tissue needs to be destroyed.

(d) *Trauma.* Traumatic lesions during peacetime are often accompanied by fractures of the skull and/or, in the case of closed head injuries, by extensive vascular damage between and beneath the meninges. It is important to remember that in none of these cases may we expect to find limited and sharply defined destruction of tissue.

Penetrating gunshot wounds sustained during war do produce occasionally more limited lesions, but even here the investigator has no knowledge of possible secondary disturbances due to bleeding, infection, or degeneration of cells and their fibers. Furthermore, these head injuries are rarely confined to our assumed speech areas. Thus, inferences from this material must be made cautiously.

(e) *Other Focal Lesions.* It is, of course, impossible here to describe the pathology of all possible lesions in the central nervous system, even though a great many of them are capable of affecting speech and language. Some diseases which show scattered lesions throughout the cerebrum at the time of death may begin with small destructions of tissue, for example, in the cerebellum or diencephalon where they produce characteristic interference with articulation.

(2) *Diffuse Lesions*

Aphasia may be produced by diseases that affect nerve cells throughout the brain. Cellular destruction may follow a criterion of cell size (such as in carbon monoxide poisoning which affects large cells more readily than small ones), or the distribution of lesions may appear to be random, as in the case of the *presenile dementias,* for instance, Alzheimer's Disease. A description of the latter will suffice as an illustration of this general point. Alzheimer's Disease is a markedly premature aging of the brain. It has an insidious onset and, by definition, occurs during or before the fifth decade of life. It runs a course of gradual exacerbation until death occurs some ten years after onset. The clinical findings show a general intellectual deterioration, including disturbance of thought, memory, and practical judgment. In addition, there may be distinct symptoms of aphasia, apraxia, or agnosia. At autopsy there is diffuse brain atrophy with shrinkage in all convolutions; the gray matter is more affected than the white, and there is a tendency for the pathology to be more marked frontally than posteriorly. On histological examination, there is a loss of nerve cells throughout the cortex, apparently due to a microscopically visible intracellular degenerative process. There also are fine spherical depositions of amorphous material to be seen everywhere in the cortex, known as "senile plaques." This pathology shows that aphasic symptoms may ensue from a general reduction in the total cell population, particularly of the cortex, even though the main pattern of transcortical and subcortical fiber connections is largely intact.

III. CLINICAL SYNDROMES

We have given a fairly detailed account of the symptomatology and have described the nature of lesions that may cause combinations of those symptoms. Ideally, we should now relate the location of lesions to specific syndromes. Many such attempts have been made but it is fair to say that the results have never been satisfactory, and there is no scheme that is acceptable to all neurologists. Nielsen (1946) who is an exponent of the localizationist school of thought reports, for instance, only 25 cases of expressive aphasia in 43 cases of verified destruction of Broca's area. In his ten cases of temporal lobectomy, nine cases have receptive disorders, and all have paraphasic derangements, but there seems to be no more than random association of this type of lesion with reading and writing disorders and difficulties in spontaneous speech. In seven cases of supramarginal parietal lobe lesions and adjacent lesions of superior temporal lobe, both reading and writing is always disrupted, but there was no constant combination of receptive and expressive disturbances.

Generally speaking, we may say that expressive disorders result more frequently from anterior lesions, whereas more posterior lesions implicate receptive skills. It is quite possible that there is considerable individual variation in the cortical topography of language representation and that, therefore, the locus of a lesion is the immediate cause for a given combination of symptoms in one patient; but if the functional organization differs from one patient to the next, clinical-pathological correlations become difficult. Fortunately, clinical diagnoses need not be made exclusively upon an inventory of speech and language derangements. When other signs and symptoms are taken into account, a diagnosis may be made that is quite specific with respect to place. Furthermore, some aphasic symptoms have greater diagnostic value than others, particularly if they definitely predominate over other language disturbances. Thus, word-deafness may be attributed to lesions in the superior middle temporal lobe; speech monotony (not to be confused with dysprosody; see Monrad-Krohn, 1947) to lesions of the basal ganglia; alterations in rate to diencephalic disorders and changes in rhythm to cerebellar disorders.

The position advocated here is not so much an "antilocalizationist" one but an emphasis on individual variations on the one hand and on the possibility of bringing about similar symptoms by different lesions on the other.

IV. THEORETICAL INTERPRETATIONS

(1) *Interference vs. "Loss"*

This survey of the clinical picture of language and speech disorders makes it evident that there is not a single type of pathology in man that furnishes us with unequivocal data concerning the problem of language localization. In some cases, we cannot be certain of the exact extent of the destruction of tissue; in others pathological processes are so diffuse that any effort at localization becomes futile; in still other cases, there are surgical, and therefore entirely known lesions, but the patient population is atypical because a large percentage has had abnormal brains in structure, function, or both since early life. Nevertheless, a study of clinical manifestations can be revealing as long as we keep the entire gamut of symptoms, their combinations, and their pathological correlations in mind and avoid basing our speculations on merely a few particular aspects of language disorders.

The most striking common denominator in aphasia is the ubiquitous evidence that the patient has not literally "lost" language; that is, he is not returned to a state of no language such as an animal or even a person who forgot everything he once knew in a foreign language. We can usually demonstrate that an aphasic still understands *some* statements, recognizes *some* words, or knows basically "how language works." The few utterances that he can still produce are clearly patterned after *some* aspects of the patient's mother tongue. In the literal sense of the word, the patient's language skills are merely interfered with; there are disturbances of cerebral function. Neither discrete words nor discrete grammatical rules are neatly eliminated from the store of skills.

Although this phraseology might appear as academic pedantry, there are practical consequences. If we say the aphasic person has lost parts of language, we would naturally assume that he can simply relearn them, much the way an infant does and that the condition for teaching ought to be the same as or comparable to a foreign-language course. But careful observation of the recovery process during the critical postmorbid period, makes it very plain that the patient does not start with specific lexical or grammatical lacunae, but that some basic physiological processes relating to activating, monitoring, or processing of speech are deranged. If there is clinical improvement, it is not due to the acquisition of new vocabulary or grammatical rules, but to release from inhibitory factors, to faster acting memory, to better controlled organization of elements, etc. Thus the distinction between *loss of language* and *interference with skills* leads to different approaches in rehabilitation and management of patients with aphasia.

The distinction between loss and interference has yet another implication. The severity-scale of language disorders has frequently been regarded as the mirror image of stages of language acquisition. Complete inability to speak or understand, the severest form of aphasia, is supposed to be congruent to the speechlessness of the infant at 10 months; a very mild aphasia would correspond to the last stage of language perfection in the child, and there are supposed to be similar correspondences for all intermediate stages. But the empirical study of language acquisition in the child and language interference in disease do not confirm this assumption. The infant's first emerging patterns of language acquisition are global, undifferentiated aspects which gradually unfold until the fully differentiated rules, lexical items, and phonological skills are established. The history of development is one in which the grammatical apparatus becomes more and more complex; accretion is by way of a progressive differentiation of language mechanisms. In disease, however, the grammatical apparatus does not gradually return to undifferentiated stages, and the regression is not one in which formerly distinct language mechanisms become amalgamated again; an aphasic patient never makes the grammatical mistakes heard in children. His mistakes tend to be grammatical nonsequiturs. We must remember that this disturbance is physiological, and there can only be interference with the fully established complexities that normally enable the speaker to produce coherent discourse.

(2) *The Problem of Neurological Correlates*

It would be intellectually satisfying if we could deduce the nature of the brain mechanisms of language from a careful survey of neurological disorders. Unfortunately, this is not possible. To appreciate the difficulties fully it is necessary to discuss briefly the relationship between *general* behavioral variables and some recent findings in the field of neurophysiology and neuro-anatomy.

When the psychologist studies behavior he might propose certain theoretical categories which appear self-evident to him; for instance, the meaning of *memory, associations, stimulus-response,* and *concepts* may not need to be questioned within the framework of research of a strictly behavioral science. They might be considered phenomena that have psychological reality. And so they do—in the psychological laboratory. However, these categories do not have clear-cut neurological correlates. For example, what the behaviorist might call a class of equivalent stimuli may be an enigma to the neurologist. The psychologist's definition of simple memory trace does not define any one clearly understood neurological process. The occurrence of associations between two stimuli are observable phenomena to the student of behavior but not to the student of the brain. On the other hand, many of the simple processes of the neurophysiologist have very poorly definable behavioral characteristics. This lack of congruence between behavioral and neurological sciences is probably not due to any true discordance between the nature of the nervous system and behavior—after all, the latter is entirely mediated by the former—but must be a consequence of the theoretical apparatus that have been built up by each science without knowledge of the other. As a result, we often search in vain for neurological correlates of phenomena that seem to be entirely obvious to the behaviorist but only because he is used to thinking about behavior in a peculiar and sometimes arbitrary conceptual frame.

The critical remarks that follow must not be interpreted as a return to the Goldsteinian pessimism that studies of the brain can tell us nothing specific about behavior nor as a reactivation of an indiscriminate mass-action notion which states that it would be hopeless to search for specific functions of any given brain structure and that it is only quantity of tissue that counts in the elaboration of behavior. Nor do we wish to bring out the stale controversy between the localizationists and the holists. Too much has been learned about specific brain functions during the last three decades to consider seriously the idea that any component of the brain lacks specific physiological function. The questions are merely, what are these functions and can they be discovered through gross observations on whole, complex behavior patterns?

(*a*) *Connections and Associations.* The discrepancy between behavior theories and neurological theories may be illustrated by considering a few specific concepts. For instance, the terms *connections* and *associations* occur in both literatures, but their meanings do not remain the same. Failure to recognize this may lead to wrong inferences. The early behaviorists thought of connections as the neurological correlate of associations. An organism comes to relate event *A* with event *B,* and it was assumed that some connection is established, maybe by a growth process, between two anatomical loci. We do not yet know whether this is so or not; but the establishment of connections that are being investigated experimentally by neurologists at present and that have recently led some students (Sperry, 1963) to state that a very strict connectionism is being reintroduced into neurological theory is of a different nature. Attardi and Sperry (1963) and Gaze, Jacobson, and Székely (1965) have begun to show that end-organ cells and internuncial and central neurons and their fiber connections bear a structurally fixed and orderly relation to each other. Surgical rearrangement of these connections in immature or primitive vertebrates cannot be accomplished because the original connections reestablish themselves through regenerative processes.

In mature and higher vertebrates the surgical rearrangement results in most cases in permanent perceptual and motor dysfunction. In fact, training, artificial pairing of stimuli or any other extracorporeal manipulation *fails* to foster demonstrable anatomical restructuring. There are many variations to this theme. Generally speaking, it is clear now that peripheral and central tissues influence each other in their growth and function to produce a unique assembly and modus operandi. If this natural connectivity is altered, dysfunctions result. Some theorists may feel that the connectionism discussed here is irrelevant to discussions of learning and behavior. We do not wish to argue for or against this position. But *if* behavioral "connectionists" were to search for corroborative data produced by the new neuro-anatomical "connectionism," they would actually find results that are more likely to contradict their own theories of connections than to support them.

Let us turn briefly to the concept of associations. It is well known that we can pair a neutral stimulus such as a geometric pattern to a constitutionally "meaningful" stimulus such as the smell of food in such a way that the neutral stimulus will come to elicit part of the response pattern that was formerly reserved for the "meaningful" or unconditioned stimulus. Here a visual stimulus becomes associated to an olfactory stimulus. What is the neurological correlate of this association? No one knows: it is still easier to say what it is not than what it may be. For instance, it is probably not any form of transcortical structural connection. Several attempts have been made to sever fiber connections after associations between two sense-modalities had been established experimentally (Evarts, 1952; Sperry, 1958) in order to bring about surgically the original state of neutrality of the conditioned stimulus. If associations between stimuli simply depended upon patency of transcortical pathways, it should be possible to sever the association surgically without however impairing at the same time the integrity of perception. If we leave aside for the moment the fiber-connections between the two hemispheres and confine the argument to transcortical connections within each hemisphere, then it may be said that so far no one has succeeded in this strategy.

Lesions can disrupt behavior by either disrupting the perceptual or the motor process, but it has not been possible to produce an animal whose perceptual and motor functions are demonstrably unaffected by the surgery but in whom a specific type of experimental association has become an impossibility. The anatomical demonstration of an associative bond would require that an animal has normal pattern perception and acuity in say both the visual and auditory modality but can no longer make associations between the two. It is not clear why experimental efforts in this direction have been negative. Perhaps some day there will be techniques to accomplish surgically pure disconnection of experimental associations, but at present the neurological nature of association is unknown.

Nevertheless, the term *cortical association areas* have been widely accepted by neuro-anatomists. Strictly speaking, the term association in this context is a metaphor taken over from psychological theory, rather than a descriptive term of the demonstrated function of these tissues. Destruction of association cortex does not abolish a modality-specific type of behavioral associations in animals. Nor do destructions of these areas prevent any specific type of future associations (that is, leaving the animal intact in every other respect). In fact, in certain parts of the association areas lesions have no clear behavioral effect whatever. There are areas, especially in higher primates, which have most tenaciously defied our efforts to reveal their role in the elaboration of grossly observable behavior. This is not to imply that these areas have no specific function. Such an assumption runs counter to our picture (or beliefs) of the evolution of structures. But their function is still poorly understood.

All areas of the cortex and the two hemispheres are interconnected by short and long fibers which have been traditionally called association fibers. Essentially, the same argument remains here with respect to association areas. The very prominent fibers that connect the hemispheres, collectively called *commissures,* have been thought for some time to have no function in behavior whatever. In a series of brilliant experiments, Sperry (1961) and his students (Myers, 1956; Downer, 1959; Trevarthen, 1960; see also Thompson, 1965) have been able to show that these commissures are indeed the pathways for neural signals that mediate acquired behavior. But it is important to realize that the messages that apparently go across these connections are fully elaborated "schedules" or "instructions" for performance. There is still no evidence for fibers that serve to bring together some simple percepts such as might have been expected from the psychologist's paired-stimuli experiments. Mishkin (1954; in press) and Mishkin and Pribram (1954) have recently demonstrated that ipsilateral transcortical fiber connectivity does play a role in visual perceptual integration. Experiments of this kind may eventually tell us more about the specific function of various fiber systems. But at the same time these results render more untenable than before any kind of naive expectation to discover direct neurological correlates of behavioral association.

(*b*) *Perceptions.* If there are difficulties in interpreting the behavioral function of the so-called association areas, our position is barely more favorable when it comes to the interpretation of primary projection areas (Creutzfeldt, 1961; Lindsley, 1961). Again, it is easier to say what these areas are not, than what they are or what precise function they serve. For instance, they are definitely not store houses for "perceptions." It may be possible to interfere with the process of perception by placing lesions in primary projection areas, but it is not possible to remove surgically a specific percept. Nor is it clear what happens when a lesion does interfere with perception (Teuber, 1961; Weinstein et al., 1955; Weiskrantz, 1961; Diamond et al., 1962).

The topography of sensory end-organs on the periphery bears a lawful relationship to the topography of cortical cells in projection areas. Thus there are correspondences between the retina and the area striata, between the distribution of touch-receptors over the skin and neurons in certain areas of the cortex, and it has also been said that sound-sensitive end-organs have topographical correspondence in certain areas of temporal cortex. These findings do not lead inescapably to the conclusion (as might have been thought at first) that the perception of a pattern is due to the arousal of an impulse pattern in the primary projection area that is isomorphic with the stimulation pattern as it is projected, for instance, on the retina. In fact, we have every indication that this is not so. Pattern perception is not abolished either by partial ablations of primary projection areas (although mild impairment may ensue) nor by making multiple, crisscrossing lesions or vertical incisions through such an area (Sperry and Miner, 1955, and Sperry, Miner and Myers, 1955). As long as only a small portion of the projection area is spared, and it does not seem to matter which portion, perception and recognition seem to be fairly unaffected.

Although we have no knowledge of the physiological processes that constitute pattern perception, we do know that these cortical areas cannot properly be regarded as the final reception station for input stimuli. It is possible to record peripherally evoked responses from the cortex, but, in addition, there are reasons to believe that afferent impulses are reflected caudad as cortico-fugal impulses where they seem to project upon midbrain structures (Jasper et al., 1952; Thompson, 1965). Thus, we may be fairly certain that physiological processes of pattern perception are not confined to horizontal activity at the level of the cerebral cortex.

Teuber (1961) has pointed out that there is good evidence that traumatic lesions of the primary visual projection area in man may lead to isomorphic scotomata, demonstrable through perimetry, but that the patient is capable, nevertheless, of perceiving and reporting visual patterns presented tachistoscopically, thus indicating that he can perceive "across the scotoma."

Let us use the word "engram" to denote a neurophysiological correlate of a percept. (For the present argument it will not matter that we cannot define either *engram* or *percept* physiologically.) The investigations reported previously make it clear that an "engram" cannot be anything that is horizontally integrated in the primary projection areas of the cortex. Instead, we may think of it as neuronal activity that proceeds in a vertical direction, such as impulses that circulate between diencephalic structures (perhaps the thalamic nuclei) and cortical cell assemblies. There is some corroboration for such a view because all sensory projection areas have fiber connections to the thalamus, and thus cell fields of the cortex have congruent fields in the thalamus (although this match is far from being a cell to cell correspondence). Furthermore, sensory activity can also be interfered with from these lower centers but the nature of the ensuing deficit is usually not identical with deficits resulting from cortical lesions.

Considerations of this kind make it clear that the cerebral cortex alone cannot be (either by virtue of its architecture or its function) the exclusive locus of neurological correlates of the psychologist's behavioral categories. Cortical projection areas do not contain percepts nor are any other cortical areas the depositories of thoughts; whatever the nature of the signals that travel through transcortical fibers, they cannot be identified with the phenomenal content of experience. The cortex is closely integrated with the rest of the brain and functions in coordination with other cerebral structures.

(*c*) *Storage.* The notion that certain aspects of behavior are stored in specific parts of the brain has received some superficial support from electrical stimulation experiments. However, upon closer examination we are immediately led away from such a simple hypothesis. It is possible, for instance, to evoke by direct electrical stimulation of various parts in the brain, well-organized coordination patterns which are recognizable parts of the animal's spontaneous behavior, such as the assumption of a threat-position together with the customary vocalizations and showing of teeth (Hunsperger, 1956), or the entire sequence of movements used for drinking, or parts of courtship patterns. In primates, smooth skeletal movements may be produced (for example, lifting and extending of the arm), or a human subject may report sensations such as tingling in the fingers, memories, tastes, short hallucinations.

It is important to remember that an AC current delivered to the cerebral cortex, for instance, must· be a very different physiological phenomenon from the nervous activity that is normally the background to action. It must have very different physical characteristics from the normal impulse patterns in the stimulated area, and probably it spreads out from the point of stimulation to tissue in its vicinity in a rather un-natural fashion. Experimental electrical stimulation is at best a crude interruption of normally encountered states. Therefore, our ability to produce well-coordinated and timed sequences of movements that seem very similar to those coordination patterns seen in a cat drinking or in a rooster courting, cannot be attributed to our ability to replicate, impulse by impulse, the nervous pattern upon which that behavior is founded. The current is just a single and very simple event. It appears more reasonable to assume that the stimulus eliminates or interferes with a factor that normally inhibits the spontaneous unwinding of a built-in mechanism. It triggers a chain of events but does not cause it.

This interpretation is largely corroborated by attempts to localize behavior by ablation experiments. The surgical destruction of those punctate loci from which some specific behavior patterns may be elicited through electrical stimulation does not always abolish that behavior. It is not even generally true that such a lesion will necessarily raise the threshold for triggering by stimulation from other points (Hassler, 1961). In fact, the total abolishment of a behavior pattern through destruction of specified, small portions of tissue, especially cortical tissue, is difficult to achieve. A lesion may interfere with behavior, and thus we may construct maps of loci of optimal interference, but a lesion that virtually "cuts out" a specific type of behavior is not easy to produce experimentally. (But see Bard, 1933, and Bard and Macht, 1958). It is hard to escape the conclusion that the nervous activity that mediates specific behavior patterns and experiences is never confined to any one cerebral locus. Behavior must be the product of interaction and integration of functions of many components of the brain.

It may also be instructive to consider the effects of brain lesions upon memory (Hassler, 1962; Milner, 1962; Milner and Penfield, 1955). Remembrances that had once been well-established cannot ordinarily be eradicated by lesions. The patient may not be able to think of certain things at a given time, that is, to recruit memories at will, or he may not be able to organize his memories with respect to his personal history; he may not know whether something has just happened this morning or twenty years ago, but there are no lesions that render him perma-nently and irreversibly ignorant of his entire past. On the other hand, there are lesions (bilateral hippocampal) that prevent man from *forming* memories so that it becomes very difficult to build up new remem-brances. This interference with the formation of memories can also be brought about by generalized alterations of the normal physiological function of the brain through pharmacological agents, brain concussion, or electro-convulsive shock. This results in a state clinically known as retrograde amnesia. There is a total gap in the history of the patient's flow of past experience. He cannot remember any of the events that preceded the catastrophe by a variable stretch of time, in some cases up to several hours. The physiological disturbance seems to be capable of wiping out memory traces that have not yet become consolidated as permanent remembrances.

From these facts we obtain a picture in which permanent memories are not locally defined, structural alterations but probably intercellular activities that are not confined to such specific parts of the brain that they could be surgically eradicated. It clearly takes time for memories to become firmly established, and this may, according to the most recent speculations on the subject (Fair, 1965), be due to intracellular, molecular alterations. Firm evidence of this point is still lacking, but there are theoretical models available now according to which we may conceive of molecular changes taking place within cells that are located over wide areas in the brain and causing changes in the interaction between cells. Thus, the idea that memories are activities that need not be confined to specific anatomical loci may be reconciled with the earlier assumptions of structural changes. We are now merely postulating that the restructuring may take place within cells instead of between them.

(*d*) *Processing.* The central nervous system and all its tissues are always in a state of activity. Stimulation, processing input, and responding are not signaled by a change from a passive to an active state. Instead there are alterations of rates and rhythms in the firing patterns of cells. All aspects of behavior may be considered to be based upon modulation of activity in neuronal nets. Nervous tissue that has become temporarily inactivated, as, for instance, in the spreading depression of Leão (1944), is not capable of receiving or processing input even though all cells remain viable (Russell and Ochs, 1963). Thus, any kind of pattern or "engram" that becomes established in the brain and that corresponds to a memory trace, a concept or percept or an acquired skill or reaction could be described as an essentially temporal pattern played upon the endogenous activity of cells and cell aggregates. This fact is in danger of being overlooked because of present-day preoccupation with recording from single cells and with the important discovery that even single cells, both on the periphery (Maturana et al., 1960) and in higher centers (Hubel and Wiesel, 1962 and 1963; Jung, 1960), are highly selective in their responsiveness. But there is ample evidence that peripheral stimulation, no matter how confined it might be, evokes responses in more than single cells. Further, the total central responses outlast the duration of the peripheral stimulus as if a complex and interacting system were thrown out of equilibrium and requires time for the establishment of a new equilibrium or steady state.

Time pattern and temporal coding are not difficult to imagine. Music and speech are patterns that exist entirely in time and time-coded signals of patterns that are usually displayed spatially are familiar to us from Morse code, in which every letter of the alphabet is changed into a "linear" time pattern. G. v. Békésy (1960 and 1965) has shown how in the nervous system spatially arranged end-organs stimulated simultaneously may give rise to temporally encoded patterns and vice versa. Through the ubiquitous convergence, dispersion, and collateralization of nerve fibers and their axodendritic interconnections, we may assume a constant interchange of patterns from spatial to temporal coordinates.

Nor is it difficult to imagine how an intrinsically active system may become the medium or carrier of temporally coded signals. Frequency modulated radio broadcasts are a good example. Spontaneous rhythmic activities of ganglia and even individual cells and fibers have been studied for many years now. It is entirely conceivable that these oscillations may serve a function that is analogous to the FM carrier frequency. (For a recent animal experiment indirectly involving time functions of brain activity see Overton, 1964.)

Let us return now to the effect of lesions. The temporal patterns that we envision are not elaborated by single cells or small cell assemblies. They are changes in activities, temporally staggered in various parts of the brain, with the effects spreading at characteristic rates from structure to structure. Of course, the proper temporal patterning requires a medium through which to spread as well as points of relay. Lesions may thus interfere with the elaboration, propagation, or modulation of temporal patterns and thus result in severe behavioral deficits. At the same time, since the temporal patterning extends through so many structures of the brain, it should be very difficult to completely eradicate a specific type of behavior through a limited lesion and yet leave the organism's behavior intact in all other respects.

This description could hardly be called an explanation of behavior. We intended nothing more ambitious than to furnish a few props to the imagination that may help to form an idea of the still incomprehensible complexity of the function of the brain and its relationship to behavior.

(3) *Relevance to Language*

In accordance with our previous argument, language-relevant "engrams" or percepts cannot easily be imagined to have an exclusively horizontal organization within the cortex. It is more in keeping with the findings of the experiments discussed to think of them as consisting of temporally patterned activities with a predominantly vertical orientation (that is, an interchange between cortical and subcortical structures). Credence is lent to this way of thinking through the recent experience with diencephalic surgical lesions and the danger of ensuing speech disorders discussed in Chapter Two.

Furthermore, the ablation experiments reviewed earlier should be a warning to "aphasiologists" not to interpret specific clinical symptoms of aphasic patients as disruption of associations or structural, cortical disconnections. There is no experimental evidence that any associative bonds may be disrupted by discrete cortical lesions. (For an opposite point of view see Geschwind, 1965). Language is not a huge collection of paired associates; a number of considerations dispute such a simple association theory of language.

First, it is not clear what is being associated during language learning; words are not labels of physical objects but of processes of conceptualization (see Chapter Eight). Second, aphasic symptoms give little support for a strict associationist hypothesis; the patient who cannot name objects upon command can recognize the proper word when it is presented to him among many inappropriate ones and may have much less naming difficulty during spontaneous discourse. Third, there is no evidence that any part of the brain stores anything like primitive fragments of behavior (such as exclusively auditory or exclusively visual percepts) that are then amalgamated into tight audio-visual associations; pattern-recognition may be disturbed by a combination of lesions, but these disturbances do not have the appearance of dissociations or fragmentations into disjunct percepts. Fourth, audio-visual associations can hardly be relevant to the capacity for language, since congenitally blind but otherwise healthy children acquire a vocabulary with the same ease as seeing children.

Alexia and agraphia may very well be interferences with pattern formation, caused by lesions in specific locations producing a disorder analogous to those observed by Mishkin (in press), Mishkin and Pribram (1954) and Mishkin (1954). It is important to stress, however, that neither the symptoms nor neurological considerations can induce us to interpret these clinical disorders as a severance of formerly conjugated skills. Since both reading and writing require temporal integration, it is plausible to consider the syndromes as a consequence of disorders in timing mechanisms. The patient experiences a loss of nexus in the course of time.

Our considerations about transcortical integration, about the maturational history of functional localization in the human brain (Chapter Four), and our ignorance about the physiological role of association areas make it clear that we must not explain the origin of human language as the consequence of the species-specific fiber architecture, the topographical relationship between primary projection to association areas, or the connections between cortex and thalamus. Neuroanatomy will not reveal the secret.

(4) *Time, the Most Significant Dimension in Language Physiology*

The essence of language is structure and pattern, not any invariant physical detail that could be studied in isolation. The dimensions of language patterns are entirely of a temporal nature. This seems logical enough, *a priori,* since utterances progress through time; however, it is difficult for our imagination to carry this thought to its logical conclusion. The formation of concepts, for instance, is sometimes represented speculatively as structural changes with spatial dimensions in a horizontal plane (that is, relative to the neuraxis). The demonstrable lack of isomorphism between visual stimulus pattern and cortical excitation pattern, the independence from specific cell-assemblies, and the difficulty to abolish behavior by discrete cortical lesions, clearly militate against such theories. A close study of language and its disturbance illustrates beautifully the all-important role of temporal phenomena.

(*a*) *Aphasic Symptoms as Temporal Disorders.* Almost all of the central nervous system disorders of speech and language may be characterized as disorders of timing mechanisms. Possible exceptions are only those disorders due to paralysis and neurogenic muscular pathology. The disarranged timing is most obvious in the case of errors of order, in rate and rhythm alterations, and in discoordinations when various organs fail to interact at the right time. The more typically aphasic symptoms may also be regarded as disorders of temporal phenomena. In paraphasic symptoms, for example, it is not the muscles or articulatory organs that are disarranged in their temporal order, but higher units such as well-formed speech sounds (resulting in jargon words), common English words (resulting in odd phrases), or even well-formed constituents of sentences (resulting in agrammatisms). The patient is incapable of planning for the order of these units, and so they tumble into the production line uninhibited by higher syntactic principles.

The concepts of inhibition (holding back for a while) and recruiting (making available, at the proper point) are highly relevant to aphasia and are both aspects of timing mechanisms. Compare the composition of discourse to the assembly of a train, where the individual coaches have to be attached while the locomotive keeps moving forward. There is an over-all plan that determines the order of the cars; they are held in readiness, but at a specific time they must be released and hitched on to the moving train. Word-finding difficulties are analogous to a timing failure for the proper car to be made available at the right time. A similar situation exists in the subfluency (sometimes also called motor-speech apraxia); this may be visualized as a failure to make available, at the proper time, perhaps not the car itself, but part of the plan according to which the composition of the train is determined. A superfluency is a loss in the timing of inhibitory mechanisms; the cars are released too early. These illustrations are inappropriate insofar as they still conjure up spatial dimensions, whereas it is necessary to think of language as events that are patterned only in time.

The explanation of receptive disorders in acquired aphasia follows the same line of argument. Since the understanding of an incoming message can only proceed by assigning each element to a place (part or role) in a pattern (remembering that the pattern is entirely of a temporal nature) and then matching the pattern to one that is stored inside,* and since this process has to progress with the same essential time characteristics as an individual's own production of discourse, it can be seen that failure to understand may well be due to certain time-disorders in the hearer. What is difficult to understand is that receptive disorders can occur relatively independent from productive disorders. However, it must be stressed that this is rare (I have never seen an exclusively receptive disorder). As a rule, receptive disorders are accompanied by severe productive disorders (more frequently superfluencies than subfluencies) and apparently in the vast majority of cases by at least some clearly noticeable abnormalities of the production of utterances. Also, we may postulate a lesion that interferes with activities that are predominantly involved in receptive processing. (For experimental research emphasizing the time dimension in language processing and language disturbances see Efron, 1963; Holmes, 1965; McMahon, 1963).

---

* This recognition process has been termed *analysis by synthesis*. For important elaborations and applications to machine recognition of speech see Halle and Stevens (1962).

V. POSTSCRIPT ON INNATE MECHANISMS FOR PERCEPTION AND PRODUCTION

Throughout this monograph innate mechanisms have been postulated implicitly and sometimes explicitly. We may briefly stop to ask whether these notions fit into a biological theory, in general, and into neurological considerations, in particular.

When we throw a cat into the air, the animal's upward displacement is not regarded to be part of the animal's behavior repertoire; but the twisting movements of the righting reflexes are. This illustrates a most important feature of behavior. An animal is not like a transmission channel but like a cocked automaton. The central nervous system always responds in entirely its own ways. The configuration of physical properties of the stimulus is translated into a neural code (probably largely temporal). Chains of neural events are set off, outlasting the stimulus, consisting of a symphony of modulations, activations, and inhibitions in many parts of the brain. None of the observable responses, either within the nervous system or peripheral behavior, bears any clear physical resemblance to the input.

As scientists, we are committed to a mechanistic point of view. What type of machine behaves like this? There are machines that store potential energy and that may be triggered into operation by a stimulus of much less energy than is expended in the machine's response. Therefore, the input energy does not correlate with the output energy; stimuli under a threshold value have no effect and above a ceiling-value they do not increase the response. These devices are necessarily more restricted in their modes of operating and responding than in their methods of being triggered into action. Furthermore, it is clear that *the conditions for triggering and the modes of operation are entirely due to the structure of the machine.* The behavior of the machine is completely determined by its physical constitution. This statement is true regardless of the occasions on which the machine operates, the person who operates it, how often, how long, or for what purpose it is operated.

Animals may be thought of as functioning like machines. Their internal structure is not the result of accidental circumstances. The machine unfolds during development, and the internal structure is programmed into the ontogenetic process. Let us call the internal structure *innate mechanisms* and the modes of operation that are determined by these mechanisms *innate behavior.*

To deny that animals and man have innate behavior as a consequence of innate structure and innate mechanisms is simply to give up the mechanistic point of view. Theoretically, only ghosts and zombies may arbitrarily assume any shape and structure and thereby be capable of unlimited sensibilities and response repertoires.

There is, then, nothing unscientific about the claim that a species-specific behavior pattern, such as language, may well be determined by innate mechanisms. The mechanisms must be ascribed to central rather than peripheral conditions because there are several species whose peripheral sensory organs, the ears and eyes, are sufficiently similar to man's to make the physical perception of language signals possible. (The anatomy of the articulators is of secondary importance; see Chapter Seven).

It would be presumptuous to try to explain the nature of the innate events that control the operation of language. We may, however, assume that mechanisms are involved, such as (1) the modulation of firing characteristics of nerve cells; (2) the triggering of temporal patterns in neuronal chains; (3) the modulation of oscillatory characteristics of endogenous activities; and (4) the production of spreading of disturbances. These are some of the components of the automaton. How these phenomena interact to elaborate language remains a mystery. Considerations of language universals (Chapter Nine), universal strategies for language acquisition (Chapter Seven), and dependencies upon cognitive processes (Chapter Eight) make it necessary to assume that there is just one peculiar mode of neural activity for aural-oral communication in man; if an individual communicates at all, or may be reached by communication, it is by virtue of this basic, unique, unalterable function.

During childhood the neural automata are activated by appropriate input, and the machine becomes operative; the incoming signals are processed through its unique type of operation, and the emission of language responses are likewise generated by the operation of the same basic mechanism.

It is the assumption of a unique, single "machine" that runs its own course like an automaton and can operate in just one essential way, and which serves at the same time as receiver, interpreter, and producer of language messages, that explains such superficially incomprehensible clinical occurrences as a child's acquisition of language-understanding in the presence of organic disability to speak (Chapter Seven). It is also this kind of implicit assumption that underlies the motor theory of speech perception, promulgated by the Haskins laboratories (Liberman et al., 1963) and the "analysis by synthesis theory," advocated by the speech analysis laboratories at M.I.T. (Halle and Stevens, 1962).

VI. CONCLUSION

Some aphasic symptoms bear certain similarities to the common derangements of speech and language seen in individuals in good health under conditions of mental exhaustion or states of drowsiness; but in disease these derangements assume greater and more severe proportions, are often irreversible and may, in many cases, be more specifically confined to the realm of language performance.

Clinically, we may encounter an almost kaleidoscopic combination of idiosyncratic failure or sparing of particular skills which renders precise correlations between pathological anatomy and pathological verbal behavior very difficult. Language may be interfered with by cortical lesions, but the topography of the optimal interference points differs to some extent from cortex to cortex. It is because of these relatively marked individual variations that an inventory of an individual patient's aphasic symptoms does not usually lend itself to exact predictions of the location of the lesion.

Language is never totally and specifically lost except in combination with complete disruption of cognition. All disorders are aspects of interference with physiological processes prerequisite for the normal function of speech and language. Aphasic symptoms give no evidence of a fragmentation of behavior, that is, of dissolution of associatively linked "simpler percepts." Most of the symptomatology may be seen as disorder of temporal integration, of "lack of availability at the right time."

The neurological processes underlying language are not confined to cortical areas. Many parts of the brain take part in the elaboration of speech and language, and interference may be produced not only by cortical but also by subcortical, diencephalic and mesencephalic lesions, although these tend to affect motor-coordination more than language.

In order to reconcile the experimental findings regarding the relationship between the cerebral cortex and behavior in animals, and to relate those findings to our clinical experience with man, it appears reasonable to assume that complex, species-specific behavior patterns, such as language, result partly through subcortical, highly centralized integrating mechanisms, and partly through interaction of activities on the most rostral levels.

It is helpful to think of the neural messages that are relevant to speech and language as time-coded signals. Cortical lesions primarily interfere with temporal integration of a higher order (words or grammatical category), whereas deeper lesions disrupt the necessary convergence of various afferent signals and the intimate coordination and integration for efferent impulses, thus producing disorders of production.

Innate mechanisms are understood as neuronal analogues to automata that may be triggered into action by a variety of stimuli (originating either from outside or from within the individual). A mechanistic view leads us to expect greater limitations in the modes of operation of such mechanisms than in the range of potential stimuli.

REFERENCES

Adams, R. D. (1958), Affections of speech, in *Principles of Internal Medicine,* T. R. Harrison, R. D. Adams, I. L. Bennett, Jr., W. H. Resnik, G. W. Thorn, and M. M. Wintrobe (eds.), pp. 366–376. McGraw-Hill, New York.

Alajouanine, T. and Lhermitte, F. (1964), Non-verbal communication in aphasia, in *Disorders of Language,* A. V. S. de Reuck and M. O'Connor (eds.), Ciba Foundation Symposium. Little, Brown and Co., Boston.

Attardi, D. G. and Sperry, R. W. (1963), Preferential selection of central pathways by regenerating optic fibres, *Exp. Neurol.* **7**:46–64.

Bard, P. (1933), Studies on the cerebral cortex. I. Localized control of placing and hopping reactions in the cat and their normal management by small cortical remnants, *Arch. Neurol. and Psychiat.* **30**:40–74.

Bard, P. and Macht, M. B. (1958), The behaviour of chronically decerebrate cats, in *Neurological Basis of Behaviour.* Ciba Foundation Symposium, pp. 55–71. Little, Brown and Co., Boston.

Békésy, G. v. (1960), *Experiments in Hearing.* McGraw-Hill, New York.

Békésy, G. v. (1965), "Inhibition and the time and spatial patterns of neural activity in sensory perception," *Annals of Otology, Rhinology and Laryngology* **74**:445–463.

Brain, R. (1955), Aphasia, apraxia, and agnosia, in *Neurology,* S. A. K. Wilson (2nd ed.). Williams and Wilkins, Baltimore.

Brain, R. (1961), *Speech Disorders: Aphasia, Apraxia, and Agnosia.* Butterworth, Washington.

Creutzfeldt, O. D. (1961), General physiology of cortical neurons and neuronal information in the visual system, in *Brain and Behavior,* M. A. B. Brazier (ed.), Vol. I, pp. 299–358. Amer. Inst. of Biol. Sci., Washington.

Diamond, I. T., Goldberg, J. M., and Neff, W. D. (1962), Tonal discrimination after ablation of auditory cortex, *J. Neurophysiol.* **25**:223–235.

Downer, J. L. de C. (1959), Changes in visually guided behaviour following midsagittal division of optic chiasm and corpus callosum in monkey (*Macaca mulatta*), *Brain* **82**:251–259.

Efron, R. (1963), Temporal perception, aphasia, and déjà vu, *Brain* **86**:403–424.

Evarts, E. V. (1952), "Effects of ablation of prestriate cortex on auditory-visual association in monkey," *J. Neurophysiol.* **15**:191–200.

Fair, C. M. (1965), The organization of memory functions in the vertebrate nervous system, *Neurosciences Res. Prog. Bull.* **3**(1):27–62.

Fisher, C. M., Karp, H. R., and Adams, R. D. (1958), Cerebrovascular diseases, in *Principles of Internal Medicine,* T. R. Harrison, R. D. Adams, I. L. Bennett, Jr., W. H. Resnik, G. W. Thorn, and M. M. Wintrobe (eds.), pp. 366–376. McGraw-Hill, New York.

Gaze, R. M., Jacobson, M., and Székely, G. (1965), "On the formation of connexions by compound eyes in *Xenopus,*" *J. Physiol.* **176**:409–417.

Geschwind, N. (1965), "Disconnexion syndromes in animals and man," *Brain* **88**:237–294 and 585–644.

Halle, M. and Stevens, K. (1962), Speech recognition: a model and a program for research, *IRE Transactions of the Prof. Group on Info. Theory,* Vol. IT-8, No. 2, pp. 155–159.

Hassler, R. (1961), Motorische und sensible Effekte umschriebener Reizungen und Ausschaltungen im menschlichen Zwischenhirn, *Dtsch. Z. Nervenheilk.* **183**:148–171.

Hassler, R. (1962), New aspects of brain functions revealed by brain diseases, in *Frontiers in Brain Research,* J. D. French (ed.), pp. 242–285. Columbia Univ. Press, New York.

Head, H. (1926), *Aphasia and Kindred Disorders of Speech.* Cambridge Univ. Press, London.

Holmes, H. L. (1965), *Disordered perception of auditory sequential patterns in aphasia.* Unpublished Ph.D. dissertation submitted to the Department of Social Relations, Harvard University, Cambridge, Massachusetts.

Hubel, D. H. and Wiesel, T. N. (1962), Receptive fields, binocular interaction and functional architecture in the cat's visual cortex, *J. Physiol.* **160**:106–154.

Hubel, D. H. and Wiesel, T. N. (1963), "Receptive fields of cells in striate cortex of very young, visually inexperienced kittens," *J. Neurophysiol.* **26**:994–1002.

Hunsperger, R. W. (1956), Role of substantia grisea centralis mesencephali in electrically-induced rage reactions, in *Progress in Neurobiology* (proceedings of the First International Meeting of Neurobiologists), Ariens Kappers (ed.). Elsevier, Amsterdam.

Jasper, H., Ajmone-Marsan, C., and Stoll, J. (1952), Corticofugal projections to the brain stem, *Arch. Neurol. Psychiat.* **67**:155–177.

Jung, R. (1960), Microphysiologie corticaler Neurone: ein Beitrag zur Koordination der Hirnrinde und des visuellen Systems, in *Structure and Function of the Cerebral Cortex* (proceedings of the Second International Meeting of Neurobiologists), pp. 204–232. Elsevier, Amsterdam.

Kainz, F. (1943), *Psychologie der Sprache,* Vol. II. F. Enke, Stuttgart.

Kleist, K. (1962), *Sensory Aphasia and Amusia; the Myeloarchitectonic Basis.* Pergamon, New York.

Leão, A. A. P. (1944), Spreading depression of activity in the cerebral cortex, *J. Neurophysiol.* **7**:359–390.

Le Beau, J., Choppy, M., Gaches, J., and Rosier, M. (1954), *Psychochirurgie et fonctions mentales: techniques, résultats, applications physiologiques.* Masson, Paris.

Liberman, A. M., Cooper, F. S., Harris, K. S., and MacNeilage, P. F. (1963), Motor theory of speech perception, *J. acoust. Soc. Am.* **35**:1114.

Lindsley, D. B. (1961), Electrophysiology of the visual system and its relation to perceptual phenomena, in *Brain and Behavior,* M. A. B. Brazier (ed.), pp. 359–392. Amer. Inst. of Biol. Sci., Washington.

Maturana, H. R., Lettvin, J. Y., Pitts, W. H., and McCulloch, W. S. (1960), Physiology and anatomy of vision in the frog, *J. gen. Physiol.* **43**(Suppl.):129–175.

McMahon, L. E. (1963), *Grammatical analysis as part of understanding a sentence.* Unpublished Ph.D. dissertation, submitted to the Department of Psychology, Harvard University, Cambridge, Massachusetts.

Milner, B. (1962), Les troubles de la mémoire accompagnant des lésions hippocampiques bilatérales, in *Physiologie de l'Hippocampe,* P. Passouant (ed.), Ed. du C. Nat. Rech. Scient., Paris.

Milner, B. and Penfield, W. (1955), "The effect of hippocampal lesions on recent memory," *Trans. Amer. Neurol. Assoc.* **80**:42–48.

Mishkin, M. (1954), Visual discrimination performance following partial ablations of the temporal lobe: II. Ventral surface vs. hippocampus, *J. comp. physiol. Psychol.* **47**:187–193.

Mishkin, M. (in press), Visual mechanisms beyond the striate cortex, in *Frontiers of Physiological Psychology.*

Mishkin, M. and Pribram, K. H. (1954), Visual discrimination performance following partial ablations of the temporal lobe: I. Ventral vs. lateral, *J. comp. physiol. Psychol.* **47**:14–20.

Monrad-Krohn, G. H. (1947), Dysprosody or altered melody of language, *Brain* **70**:405–415.

Myers, R. E. (1956), Function of corpus callosum in interocular transfer, *Brain* **79**:358–363.

Nielsen, J. M. (1946), *Agnosia, Apraxia, Aphasia: Their Value in Cerebral Localization* (2nd ed.). Hoeber, New York.

Overton, D. A. (1964), State-dependent or dissociated learning produced with pentobarbital, *J. comp. physiol. Psychol.* **57**:3–12.

Penfield, W. and Roberts, L. (1959), *Speech and Brain Mechanisms.* Princeton Univ. Press, Princeton, New Jersey.

Reuck, A. V. S. de and O'Connor, M. (eds.), (1964), *Disorders of Language,* Ciba Foundation Symposium. Little, Brown and Co., Boston.

Ross, A. S. C., Clarke, P. R. F., and Haddock, N. L. (1964), "Edition of text from a dysphasic patient," in *Disorders of Language,* A. V. S. de Reuck and M. O'Connor (eds.), Ciba Foundation Symposium. Little, Brown and Co., Boston.

Russell, I. S. and Ochs, S. (1963), Localization of a memory trace in one cortical hemisphere and transfer to the other hemisphere, *Brain* **86**:37–54.

Schuell, H., Jenkins, J. J., and Jimenez-Pabon, E. (1964), *Aphasia in Adults.* Harper and Row, New York.

Sperry, R. W. (1958), Physiological plasticity and brain circuit theory, in *Biological and Biochemical Bases of Behavior,* H. F. Harlow and C. N. Woolsey (eds.), pp. 401–424. Univ. of Wisconsin Press, Madison, Wisconsin.

Sperry, R. W. (1961), Cerebral organization and behavior, *Science* **133:**1749–1757.

Sperry, R. W. (1963), "Chemoaffinity in the orderly growth of nerve fiber patterns and connections," *Proc. Nat. Acad. Sci.* **50(4):**703–710.

Sperry, R. W. and Miner, N. (1955), Pattern perception following insertion of mica plates into visual cortex, *J. comp. physiol. Psychol.* **48:**463–469.

Sperry, R. W., Miner, N., and Myers, R. E. (1955), Visual pattern perception following subpial slicing and tantalum wire implanations in the visual cortex, *J. comp. physiol. Psychol.* **48:**50–58.

Teuber, H.-L. (1961), Neuere Beobachtungen ueber Sehstrahlung und Sehrinde. in *The Visual System: Neurophysiology and Psychophysics,* R. Jung and H. Kornhuber (eds.). Springer, Berlin.

Teuber, H.-L., Battersby, W. S., and Bender, M. B. (1952), "Effects of cerebral lesions on intellectual functioning in man," *Fed. Proc. Am. Soc. exp. Biol.* Vol. XI, p. 161.

Thompson, R. (1965) Centrencephalic theory and interhemispheric transfer of visual habits, *Psychol. Rev.* **72:**385–398.

Trevarthen, C. B. (1960), Simultaneous learning of two conflicting problems by split-brain monkeys, *Am. Psychologist* **15:**485.

Weinstein, S., Teuber, H.-L., Ghent, L., and Semmes, J. (1955), Complex visual task performance after penetrating brain injury in man, *Am. Psychologist* **10:**408.

Weisenburg, T. and McBride, K. E. (1935), *Aphasia: A Clinical and Psychological Study,* New York Commonwealth Fund. Hildred and Co., Brattleboro, Vermont.

Weiskrantz, L. (1961), Encephalisation and the scotoma, in *Current Problems in Animal Behavior,* W. H. Thorpe and O. L. Zangwill (eds.), pp. 30–58. Cambridge Univ. Press, London.

Zangwill, O. L. (1964), Intelligence in aphasia, in *Disorders of Language,* A. V. S. de Reuck and M. O'Connor (eds.), Ciba Foundation Symposium. Little, Brown and Co., Boston.

CHAPTER Six

Language in the light of evolution and genetics

I. LIMITATIONS ON INFERENCES FROM ANIMAL COMPARISON

We tell our children that the cow says "moo," the lamb says "bah," and the rooster says "cock-a-doodle-doo." Most animals around us seem to "say" something, and there is a temptation to assume that they are "communicating"; but how, what, and to whom these animals "speak" are questions to which there are but vague answers. Most vertebrate species emit some kind of acoustic signal, and the sensory receptors of each species are sensitive to the broadcasts of their own kind. The ubiquity of this phenomenon suggests that some biological functions are served by it. However, we do not know whether these functions are the same for all species—in fact, there is good evidence against this. An acoustic broadcast may serve to warn territorial intruders, to call and attract sexual mates, to threaten adversaries, to lure bait, to call the young, to transfer information; it may function to strengthen social cohesion in large groups or to prevent the breaking up of single couples only; it may have the effect of arousing or of lulling; it may be directed at members of other species, at members of the same species, at only certain individuals, or only to the self, as in echo-navigation.

Animal communication does not merely fascinate us as a zoological phenomenon; it also encourages us to believe that appropriate comparative studies will reveal the origin of human communication. The rationale here is approximately this: since Darwin has shown that man is not the product of special creation but that he descended from more primitive animal forms, neither his structure nor his behavior are special

227

creations. His forms of communication must have descended from primitive animal forms of communication, and a study of the latter is likely to disclose that there is indeed a straight line of evolution of this feature. This type of reasoning we shall call the *continuity theory of language development*. I do not agree with it, and the first part of the chapter will be devoted to a critical analysis. I will then propose a *discontinuity theory* and show that this is not only biologically acceptable but, in fact, more in line with present theories in developmental biology than the former type theory (Roe and Simpson, 1958; Simpson, 1949; Haldane, 1949; Rensch, 1954).

(1) *Continuity Theory A: Straight Line Evolution of Language With Only Quantitative Changes*

This type of theory rests on the belief that there is no essential difference between man's language and the communication of lower forms. Man's noises just sound different, and his repertoire of messages is merely much larger than that of animals, presumably due to a quantitative increase in nonspecific intelligence. Theorists of this persuasion might picture the development of communication systems in the animal world as a straight road towards language such as shown in Fig. 6.1, with various animal communication systems as early way-stations. Human language is thought to be much more advanced, perhaps by virtue of some kind of proliferation of elements (more memory units; or more classification devices; or more computing elements).

It can be only this kind of implicit belief that encourages investigators to count the number of words in the language of gibbons, to look for phonemes in the vocalizations of monkeys or songs of birds, or to collect the morphemes in the communication systems of bees and ants. In many other instances no such explicit endeavors are stated, but the underlying faith appears to be the same since much time and effort is spent teaching parrots, dolphins, or chimpanzee infants to speak English. The rather wide-spread belief that many animals have a language of a very primitive and limited kind (or that the animal pupils of English instruction can enter the first stage of language acquisition) is easily refuted by a comparison with man's beginnings in language, discussed in Chapter Seven.

At the root of the idea that human language is merely quantitatively different from animal "language" is the idea that all animals have something that might be called "nonspecific intelligence," but that man has much more of this endowment and that this intellectual potential hap-

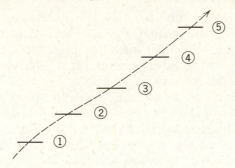

FIG. 6.1. Diagram of a "straight-line" evolution theory; numbers indicate traits of various species thought to be direct antecedents of 5.

pens to be useful in the elaboration of a universal biological need for communication. Animals are thought to be unable to learn to understand English because of an insufficiency of this intellectual capacity. There are grave difficulties with this reasoning.

Intelligence or intellectual capacity are difficult to define in the context of general zoology. Insofar as intelligence is a measurable property within our own species (and there are those who have their doubts about this), we have seen (Chapter Four and Seven) that it correlates poorly with language capacity. Within certain IQ ranges there is virtually no correlation whatever; and in the extreme low range, where there is an apparent correlation, it is rare to find individuals who have not even the capacity to understand simple spoken language. Most idiots and even imbeciles may be given verbal commands and many also acquire, spontaneously, the use of some words or even simple phrases. When the concept of intelligence must be applied to disparate species, the problem of scaling and measurement is enhanced greatly.

Clearly, intelligence is not a physical property that can be measured objectively. It is always tied to specific tasks and to the frame of reference of a given species. When we test different species by requiring animals to solve a certain problem, the similarity in task is seen by us, the human experimenter, but different species are likely to "interpret" an apparently similar task in their own, species-specific manner. Comparing the intelligence of different species is comparable to making *relative* measurements in *different* universes and comparing the results in *absolute* terms. When we say that a cat is more intelligent than a mouse, and a dog more intelligent than a cat, we do not mean that the one can catch the other by superior cunning but that one solves *human* tasks with greater ability than the other. The animal's way of "interpreting" a problem situation becomes more and more similar to that of humans as the experimental animal is phylogenetically closer to man. But from this we cannot infer that language acquisition is just another problem-solving experiment and that phylogenetic proximity to man increases the capacity for language.

In man, the ability to acquire language appears to be relatively independent of his own ability to "solve problems," that is, of his type of "nonspecific intelligence." Why should we, therefore, expect that an animal's ability to solve human problems is relevant to his ability to acquire verbal behavior? In most animals the "cognitive strategy" for solving a given problem is quite different from that used by man (Uexküll, 1921).

It may seem as if the cross-species comparisons of cognitive function and behavior by Harlow (1949 and 1958), Schrier et al. (1965), David D. Smith (1965), and by Rensch (1959, 1964) and their students were contradictions to our assertions. Actually, these findings are not contrary evidence, but they are not relevant to language acquisition, however. Let us picture the various skills that are relevant to communication as overlapping maps such as those shown in Fig. 6.4. There are some common skills as well as specializations. Let us assume that man's language is closely tied to his cognitive structure. We might diagram the cognitive structures of other animals also as overlapping but not coterminous maps so that each has its own peculiar deviation. Suppose that language is in that part of man's cognitive realm which *most* diverges from the "common region." We see that it may take more than overlap to be capable of learning to speak.

(2) Continuity Theory B: Straight-Line Evolution of Complexity by Stepwise Accretion (with Missing Links)

Proponents of theories of this type admit of qualitative differences between human and animal communication, but they also believe that the extant communication behavior of animals has a discernible and continuous history. Language is seen as a complex of more or less independent features, each with its own history. In the course of evolution, more and more features developed and were added to the structure of communication behavior but, because of the various fates of individual species and phylogenetic off-shoots, there are a number of "missing links" or empty cells, so to speak, as diagrammed in Fig. 6.2.

Thus, we find zoologists who are concerned with what they consider to be the biological prerequisites for speech and language, to search for each of these prerequisites independently throughout the animal kingdom. For instance, O. Koehler (1951, 1952, 1954–a, and 1954–b) believes that there are at least nineteen biological prerequisites for language. Due to felicitous circumstances all of these nineteen prerequisites are present in man. Except for one or two, the prerequisites are common zoological characteristics which man has preserved owing to his animal nature. No lower animal is endowed even with all those prerequisites that are not specifically human. A given species may have just a few of them—not enough to learn to understand or to speak—whereas a few species have so many of the prerequisites that they are either able to reach the lowest stage of human language-learning (parrots), or engage in behavior that is an excellent parallel of human language (such as v. Frisch's honey bees).

Koehler proposes that one of the first prerequisites of language is the existence of concepts (*unbenanntes Denken*), that is, un-named thoughts. In a great number of experiments he has shown that many birds and mammals are capable of "counting" at least to three and many up to seven or even eight but none beyond. This suggests to Koehler that a number-concept is present and that this concept is practically universal among higher animals. The language of the bees and the research on bird navigation indicate that spatial concepts are also widespread. Thus all or most animals have *unbenanntes Denken* according to Koehler. Man has a peculiar skill in attaching symbols or names to these concepts which Koehler considers to be the essence of language. But he feels that even in this skill man is not totally alone. Parrots can also name concepts, that is, are supposedly able to learn the meaning of a few words; and rudiments of the same skill are also seen by Koehler in aspects of the bees' communication system.

Speech-motor skills are innate in man, but biologically they are no innovation because some animals can learn to say things. Also the

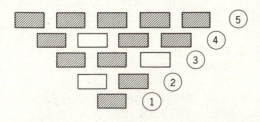

FIG. 6.2. The evolution of "complex behavior" such as language is sometimes explained as accretion of individual traits (shown as boxes); empty boxes are thought to be "missing links"; numbers correspond to communication systems of different species.

ontogenetic development of vocalizations in man has parallels in birds
just as birds go through characteristic song-stages after hatching, human
infants go through characteristic stages of vocalization. Koehler ex
plains the onset of words by an essential law of effect. The infant notices
the results or effects of his crying and babbling and thus begins to make
use of these vocalizations in order to bring about certain consequences
The early history of vocalizations and the beginning of language, he
thinks, are identical with developments in certain birds, and are thereby
evidence for the biological nature of these phenomena. Man and his
language differ from animals and their communication (1) by degree of
certain universal skills, particularly a nonspecific learning ability, and
(2) by accretion of new skills such as man's ability to combine and per-
mute the named concepts, that is, words. So much about Koehler's
views.

I share some of Koehler's beliefs, but not all of them. However
what is important here is that his views necessarily imply that language
is not a unique and integral behavioral development but a conglomera-
tion of skills and abilities each of which has its own, independent phylogenetic history. Except for one aspect of language, verbal behavior is a
continuation and amplification of ubiquitous zoological properties
There is a suggestion here of continuity with only a few recent innovations that lifted an earlier type of communication into the realm of
human language. I reject this type of continuity theory on several
counts.

(1) The prerequisite skills for language can only in a few cases be
shown to have a fully documented phylogenetic history that reaches up
to *Homo sapiens.* Actually, this is the exception. Continuity theories are
bolstered by citing examples from all over the animal kingdom in complete disregard for phylogenetic proximity to man. One parallel comes
from birds; the next from insects; another from fishes; still another from
aquatic mammals. Frequently, only one species within a given genus
or family even possesses the trait, indicating clearly that we are dealing
with species-specificities, probably all of comparatively recent date. The
reason the examples are so disparate is that parallels are rare. This suggests accidental convergence (if, indeed, it is even that) rather than
milestones within one continuous phylogeny.

(2) In addition to being unsatisfactory proof for a continuous
history, the examples customarily cited might even serve as evidence of
discontinuities of skills and behavior patterns because of the sporadic
occurrence on the branches of the phylogenetic tree.

(3) Language is not a loose association of relatively independent abil-

ities. There is no evidence that language comes about by a gradual accretion of skills. If this were so, we should be able to see all but a few of such skills in our closest relatives; further relatives should show a few less, and so on down the line of evolution. Nothing like this seems to be the case.

(4) What is thought to be the beginning of language in parrots, monkeys, or dolphins, is empirically totally different from the beginnings of language in the human infant.* At the most primitive stages of language acquisition, man does not imitate sounds, words, or sentences, but generates novel sound-sequences that are recognized as speech and language because the rules of generation bear certain *formal* similarities to those of the standard language. A healthy child does not ordinarily parrot (or at least no more often than at special occasions). The outstanding characteristics of language are the all-pervasive principles of productivity (see Chapter Eight). These principles are totally lacking from the examples of animal communication.

Another line of thought, different from O. Koehler's in approach but similar in theoretical structure, was contributed by Hockett (1960) and applied to animal communication by Altmann (1966) and other zoologists (see also Marler, 1961). Hockett also begins with an analysis of language in terms of what we shall call for the moment essential attributes, and then examines a great variety of animal communication systems with a view to discovering how many and which of the essential attributes of human language are discernible in the communication of other species. In contrast to Koehler, his attributes are almost entirely of a logical nature (that is, not physiological or psychological). He calls them *design features,* a terminology that expresses well the intent of the investigation: it is a study of the efficiency and effect of the communication system, the result and outcome, so to speak, of behavior rather than the mechanism of the behavior itself.

I believe this approach is an innovation in biological investigations and it is apt to focus attention on many interesting aspects of communication, including the underscoring of parallel but different developments and phenotypic convergences by very different means. For instance, some of the design features that characterize language (Hockett distinguishes thirteen) are also characteristic of the so-called language of the honey bee (broadcast, rapid fading, total feedback, and

---

* It is true that human ontogeny need not be a recapitulation of the evolutionary events that led up to the formation of language capacity. On the other hand, the first stages of language acquisition in the child are the only types of language that we may confidently label as primitive beginnings. We have no other empirical data from which we could infer language-primitivity in a phylogenetic sense.

perhaps specialization and discreteness), but the physical means used for the incorporation of these design features into "bee-language" are quite different from those of human language.

This is an important point. A study of design features may give us insight into some of the biases that enter into the process of natural selection, into the biological usefulness of certain features of animal communication but it is not relevant to the reconstruction of phylogenetic history. For the latter we are only interested in the relation of types of anatomical structure (including molecular structure) and physiological function (including motor coordination and sensory acuity), but we disregard the *usefulness* or *efficiency* of these features to the contemporary form. Thus whatever similarities exist on the surface between dolphins and fishes, shrews and rodents, bats and birds, pandas and bears must be ignored in our attempts to reconstruct the respective phylogenies and, in fact, the more abstract and pragmatic our criteria for comparison are, the less relevant will they be to a reconstruction of phylogenetic history. For instance, among the most abstract pragmatic criteria is *successful adaptation to the environment*; this may be accomplished by an apparent infinity of means. If we could rank-order adaptation in terms of success, it might tell us something about life in general, but it would tell us little about phyletic descent.

The converse of this argument is also true. Suppose we are interested in locomotion. Although it may be quite revealing to study such logical design features as (1) range of speeds, (2) the radius of an individual's movements, (3) endurance, etc., it will be immediately obvious that commonality in any of these criteria does not define phyletic relatedness. Thus we must guard against the application of Hockett's design features—interesting as they are for certain purposes—to any argument concerning the evolution of language.

(3) *Justification for a Discontinuity Theory of Language Evolution*

(*a*) *The Search for True Antecedents.* A discontinuity theory is not the same as a special creation theory. No biological phenomenon is without antecedents. The question is, "How obvious are the antecedents of the human propensity for language?" It is my opinion that they are not in the least obvious. The fact that most vertebrates vocalize is not very informative. There is every indication that different species have adapted this common feature to very different functions, that they have carved out specializations from a common potential. No living animal represents a direct primitive ancestor of our own kind and, therefore, there is no reason to believe that any one of *their* traits is a primitive form of any one of *our* traits. The noise-making aspect of language, at least today, is only one incidental feature of our form of communication (the deaf have language without noise-receiving or making). Clearly, there are other processes involved in language and the history of these is no less important than that of vocalization.

It is, for instance, entirely possible that certain specific principles of categorization and recombination which we encounter again and again in the perception of speech as well as in its production, in phonology, in syntax, and in semantics, are modifications of physiological principles evident in motor coordination. The ability to name may be related to perceptual and modified neurophysiological processes. Certain innate neurophysiological rhythmic activities might have been adapted to sub-serve speech in a highly specialized way (see Chapter Three). These remarks are speculative and merely serve to point out that the range of possible antecedents is vast and that in addition to the abstract and logical aspects of language (most often discussed now in the literature), there are also physiological prerequisites for speech and language.

(*b*) *Phylogenetic Change.* If our time-perspective is deep enough, all species are in a continuous state of change with respect to structure and function. But there is great variation in rates of change. Some species have not changed their structure appreciably for many millions of years while others have undergone relatively rapid change preceded or fol-lowed by periods of relative constancy. Also individual aspects of species may have different rates of evolution. For instance, skeletal structure may very well be less susceptible to modifying influences than behavioral adaptations. But change, that is evolution, is a continuous, ever-present phenomenon in all respects of life.

Evolutionary change is attributed to two general types of principles. First, the relative instability of genetic, replicative processes within cells. This provides the raw materials for potential change; and second, selec-tive biases that operate to allow some variations to remain while others are eliminated. The variations due to imperfections in the replication process need not have any direction though ideal, and perfect random-ness is also very unlikely because the molecular structure of the genic material probably always favors some variations over others (cf. the principle of "canalization" discussed below). However, it is nowadays assumed by most students of the genetic basis of evolution that the variations due to imperfection of replication would be rich enough to have a self-cancelling effect, counteracting one another in such a way that the end-result of evolution would be erosion of all species-specifici-ties and general leveling of all characteristics (death of species, in other words) were it not for the biases of natural selection which tends to preserve some variations but not others.

The source material for reconstruction of the history of changes is primarily fossilization; most aspects including "soft" anatomy, physiological functions, and behavioral traits do not fossilize, and so we have a very imperfect record of evolutionary changes of species in their actual integrated, whole form and function.

The continuity of evolutionary change is not identical with the phenomenon of creation of new species or branching. The latter may be viewed as a possible but not necessary by-product of the former. If the replicative process is sufficiently unstable and selection pressures sufficiently high and specific, the species may undergo rapid alterations, but this does not result in branching out into a radiation of new species unless certain conditions affecting population mechanics are present. The latter are variables which are quite independent of variables controlling mutations or the nature of selection pressures (for details see Mayr, 1963). Branching is merely a phase in the total history of changes and probably in many instances a relatively short-lived one.

If evolutionary change proceeded at a constant rate, then the gaps between extant species would be directly proportional to the age of the branching that separated any two species. Since branching occurs at irregular times, we would expect a great variation in the size of gaps between any two species and the existence of discontinuities should not surprise us in the least. In fact, the rate of evolution varies quite considerably and this enhances the spread in size of discontinuities even further. The phylogenies of taxonomic groups may be reconstructed by ordering the size of the discontinuities. This principle, together with the fossil history, yields a hypothetical history of man such as shown in Fig. 6.3 from which it is apparent that we must expect considerable gaps between many aspects of *Homo* and the other Hominoidea.

According to Dobzhansky (1962) and most primatologists, the present properties of our species are the result of so-called phyletic evolution, that is changes without branching. A look at Fig. 6.3 shows that there was enough time for such changes to occur.

Although it is quite conceivable that behavioral propensities yield more readily to selection pressures and are, perhaps, also more easily affected by genetically conditioned variations, thus changing at a more rapid rate than skeletal structure, for instance, we must still remember that all evolutionary changes affect animals as a whole. Entire patterns of life, so to speak, are altered but at each time-slice there is, necessarily, full integration and mutually adaptive interaction of all of the animal's features; it is the condition for viability and successful continuation of

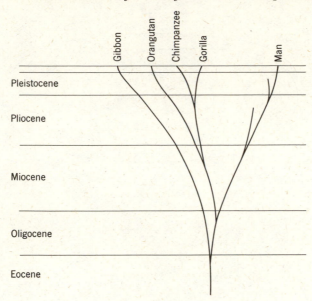

FIG. 6.3. Schema of the evolution of the Hominoidea.

the species. This consideration has an important consequence for reasonable expectations of the phylogenetic history of one specific trait, such as human language. Individual traits of an extant species can never have a continuous history because they do not evolve independently from the rest of the animal. Thus we see that there is every reason to believe that animal communication is a discontinuous affair and that logical commonalities among communication systems are not necessarily indicators of a common biological origin.

(c) *The Sharing of Traits.* These assertions are not contradicted by the wealth of evidence that some sort of symbolic behavior can be demonstrated in a wide variety of animals, that the communication of affect is very common, or that territoriality, protection of the young, or maternal behavior is frequently accompanied by vocalizations. It is true that animals share certain traits; it follows directly from the tree-like relationship between species. Notice, however, that the phylogenetic relationship between species cannot, in most cases, be represented by a single, unique tree-diagram that accounts for absolutely all of the commonalities and all of the specific differences. A tree that characterizes the relationship of skeletal structures of certain species fairly well, may differ in some (usually small) respect from a tree that characterizes the relationship between given protein structures (Goodman, 1963).

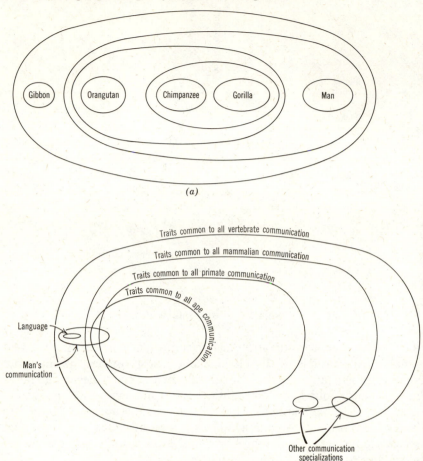

FIG. 6.4. Tree diagrams of descent may be represented as Euler-Venn diagrams. (*a*) is a representation of Fig. 6.3 (Chapter Six). Individual traits of behavior are often distributed over species in such a complex way that tree diagrams cannot be used at all, and set diagrams can only be used at the risk of oversimplification. (*b*) is a hypothetical representation of vertebrate communication systems that could not be shown by a single tree.

This is due to a number of circumstances; for example, certain aspects of life do not allow of as many (or any) variations as others; or there may be only one or very few possible biochemical solutions to a given problem posed by the environment so that a similar condition comes about more than once throughout the animal kingdom; or certain features are lost or added by individual species.

Tree-diagrams may be converted to Euler-Venn diagrams such as shown in Fig. 6.4 where (*a*) is a representation of the tree in Fig. 6.3 and (*b*) is a hypothetical diagram that might show some of the relationships of individual traits, some of them pertinent to human language. Each of the rings may be labelled; the labels tend to become more abstract as we move from center to periphery. The inner circles represent phenomena that can be directly observed on present-day animals. Each encompassing ring is a postulation of a more general form of the contemporary phenomenon. If an outer ring be *vocalizations,* this will not be a homogeneous set of behaviors but a collection of types of behavior each of which is today a highly specialized biological function. Thus we see once more that the sharing of traits does not necessarily reveal the history or nature of any specific development.

II. ARE BIOLOGICAL THEORIES OF LANGUAGE DEVELOPMENT COMPATIBLE WITH CONCEPTS OF GENETICS?

Before we proceed with further speculations about the biological origins of language, we must pause to ask whether present-day concepts of genetics and development are compatible with the facts known about language.

(1) *Genes and Ontogenetic Development*

The first problem is posed by what is known about the specific action of genes. DNA molecules, the biochemical correlates of genes, probably do no more than control the protein synthesis within the cell. The undifferentiated cells of higher animals have, however, a very large repertoire of different "instructions" for different types of synthesis, and these come into play at various stages of development (Beermann, 1963). The puzzle now is: if the inherited genetic information concerns essentially nothing but intracellular events, how could something like the capacity for language have a genetic foundation? The phenomenon is, after all, entirely supracellular or even more general, namely an interrelation of activities of complex assemblies of cells.

This puzzle is, of course, not peculiar to the problems of the genetic basis of language but to the relationship between genic action and the inheritance of traits in general. Although we can only speculate on this point, our speculations with regard to language are no more daring than with regard to most other structural or functional features.

Animals develop as an integrated whole including structure, function and behavioral capacities; the latter two are not secondary installations after embryogenesis. Therefore, it may not be too far-fetched if we say a word about development in general, the assumed role of genes in ontogenetic and phylogenetic development, and how these concepts apply to the development of language.

It is common knowledge that the first cells formed during mammalian ontogenesis have embryological equipotentiality. Up to the stage called gastrulation, the cell aggregate may be divided artificially in two, and each remaining half will develop into a well-shaped individual. But soon some of the cells in the gastrula become specialized, a division of labor has set in among the cells which soon deprives them of the capacity to change their own structure and function back to the original state. A certain spot in the gastrula begins to act on surrounding cells, thus inducing fast cell division, local expansion, folding, invagination, tubular structures, inclusions, etc. We speak of an *organizer* that has developed and which has caused some differentiation in its neighborhood. Organizer after organizer develops. At later stages entire tissues or organs serve as organizers or inducers for other tissues and organs.

The multiple unfolding that takes place is entirely dependent upon temporo-spatial overlapping, a continuous meeting in time and space, a sequence of events that must be precisely synchronized so that one phenomenon may act on another at the right time at the right place. The entire ontogenetic process must be seen as a precision schedule that determines the evolvement of a temporo-spatial pattern of interactions between cells and tissues.

Some geneticists believe that induction comes about through the biochemical alteration of regional, cellular environments (Bonner, 1952). These alterations have the effect of activating specific genes that had been present earlier but had been in some state of dormancy. Gene activation induces a new type of protein-synthesis within the cell, a molecular reconstitution, resulting in cell and tissue differentiation (Markert, 1963). Different internal environments activate different genes. Thus cells are acted upon by their environment which, however, is itself made up of cells and their metabolic products; a very complex chain of events ensues, until a relatively steady state, called maturity, is reached.

As cells become differentiated, various kinds of enzymes are produced by them that serve as catalysts for the biochemical reactions involved in development as well as in general metabolic function of the whole organism. The synthesis and biochemical structure of the enzymes are directly controlled by the molecular structure of genes, and small alterations in the latter (due to mutation) may easily affect the catalyzing efficiency of the enzymes and thereby change the temporal proportions of many far reaching reactions. The untoward temporal irregularities may affect growth rates by failing to initiate or inhibit growth activities, and this may result in irregularities of spatial contiguities and relations, thereby altering the entire spatio-temporal pattern. We see now how genes may be responsible for the inheritance of certain structural characteristics such as the famous Hapsburg lip, or a shortening of the chin, or excessively long legs. In these instances, growth is allowed to continue unhampered for a slightly longer time than is common, or it may be inhibited at a slightly earlier period.

But, as is well known, genes do not merely control the size and shape of structure but skills and capacities as well (Bernstein, 1925; Haecker and Ziehen, 1922, McClearn, 1964). These too may very well be due to spatio-temporal alterations in the ontogenetic schedules. For instance, the differential growth of internal or peripheral organs may clearly be accompanied by differences in capacities; enlarged heart and lung may improve the ability to run; an enlarged liver, the endurance for prolonged intake of alcoholic beverages; a thinning of the fingers, the capacity for assembling electronic equipment. Some skills may be improved through structural alterations that have the effect of lowering sensory thresholds, whereas the ability to dive may be enhanced by a heightening of tolerance for CO_2 concentration in the blood.

More directly related to temporal events during ontogeny may be the prolongation of certain primitive undifferentiated stages. By postponing differentiation, either specific tissues, or perhaps the entire developing individual, may become more susceptible to environmental influences (either the internal or external environment), and this may result in the creation of various types of critical periods, such as have been briefly discussed in Chapter Four. These considerations make it clear that it is not strictly correct to speak of genes for long ears, for auditory acuity, or for the capacity for language. Genes can only affect ontogenesis through varying the cells' repertoire of differentiation, but this, in turn, may have secondary effects upon structure, function, and capacities.

(2) *Relative Growth*

Certain aspects of growth can be quantified and treated mathematically. Let us merely refer to one instance, namely the phenomenon of

FIG. 6.5. Species differ in their rates of growth of specific parts of the body. *Above:* beak growth of *Limosa limosa; below: Vanellus cristatus:* posthatching day 2, 8, and 52; and 3, 21, and 52 respectively. (Rensch, 1954.) Species also differ in maturation rates of physiological function and of behavior.

allometric growth. Different portions of the body and limbs grow at different rates, and, therefore, an animal's proportions are altered throughout development (Fig. 6.5). This is partly due to the existence of growth gradients (J. Huxley, 1932) along various axes of trunk and limbs. It has been found empirically (Reeve and Huxley, 1945) that the relation between the size and weight of two parts of the body (y and x) is that of an exponential function of the form

$$y = ax^b,$$

where a and b are constants. It is convenient to write this formula in its logarithmic form

$$\log y = \log a + b \log x$$

and to plot measurements on double logarithmic paper so that all exponential functions appear as straight lines. If, for instance, we plot the weight of cats' brains against the weight of the same animals' body weights and take measurements at various stages of development, we find that the simple relationship, expressed by the allometric formula, holds fairly well throughout ontogenetic development. The curves indicate differences in growth rate in various parts of the body and show that the proportion between such rates remains constant. The curves do not reflect the actual time it takes the animal to attain any of the values.

There is a wealth of data to which the allometric formula has been successfully applied, including measurements of length, volume, weight, and chemical proportions (Needham, 1964) during development. We are therefore dealing with something that may be fundamental to the growth process itself, and this is not irrelevant to the development of functions and capacities. As tissues grow and differentiate, they serve immediately a physiological function. The functions themselves grow and differentiate to the measure of tissue growth and differentiation, and, therefore, growth laws that hold for tissues may have their parallels with respect to function. Unfortunately, quantification and mathematical treatment is much more difficult in this respect, and we must, therefore, be satisfied with the somewhat vague conclusion that the regularity in the emergence of behavior is related directly or indirectly to the lawfulness of growth and physical development.

It is interesting to note that the allometric formula also describes a number of quantitative relationships between species. Instead of taking pairs of measurements on growing individuals within the same species, pairs of measurements are made on adult individuals of different species. By this method it can be shown that certain relations of magnitudes obey a simple law that is related to the fundamental phenomena of general growth. Thus, the relationship of cerebro-cortical surface in rodents to the weight of their body (Bok, 1959), or the volume of the neocortex to the volume of the brain in all primates (v. Bonin, 1950) can be expressed by simple mathematical formulae. The existence of regularities of this kind should warn us not to attach too great importance to certain structural differences found between species, because they may not necessarily be signs of specific adaptations to a unique condition but simply result from changes in over-all size of the animal. As an example we may cite the extent of folding of man's cerebral cortex or the size of his corpus callosum or certain transcortical fiber connections, or the size and extent of association cortex, which may be the consequence of growth laws expressed by formulae such as the allometric one instead of being a unique specialization for intelligence or language (see also Sholl, 1948). One of these interpretations does not automatically exclude the other but together they point to the complexity of evolutionary events.

The purpose of these excursions was to show that physiological processes are ultimately dependent upon certain structural features of the organism, even though these features may not be obvious upon superficial inspection. This is particularly so in cases where the dependence is upon internal organs or upon the molecular constitution of component tissues and cells. The peculiarities of structure, on the other hand, are entirely a function of developmental growth; and growth is to be described by temporal and directional (spatial) parameters. The great regularity of developmental histories within species indicates that time and direction of growth must be controlled by factors that may be traced back to intracellular activities which are under the control of genes and their influence upon the elaboration of certain enzymes at certain times. The route through which genes affect the over-all patterns of structure and function is their action upon and direction of onto-genesis, especially the prolonging and shortening of growth and differ-entiation periods; genetic variations between species should, therefore, find their immediate and most dramatic expressions in embryological and postnatal developmental histories. Such an idea is not new. It was proposed (sometimes together with far-reaching and even unwarranted conclusions) by Garstang (1922), Sewertzoff (1931), and more recently by Goldschmidt (1938) and (1952).

Considerations of this type show that it is possible to talk about language in connection with genetics without having to make shaky assumptions about "genes for language." It is true that we do not know what the direct relationships are between man's complement of genes and his mode of communication; we merely wish to outline the theo-retical possibilities for relating the two. It is in this vein that the observa-tions on twins and pedigrees, cited below, are to be interpreted (cf. Georgacopoulos, 1954; Grothkopp, 1934; Howie et al., 1961). There is, in fact, one line of evidence that makes the general line of argument used here even more plausible. If gene-variations are the raw materials for speciation (played upon by selection) and this is reflected in inter-species differences in ontogenetic history, then a highly species-specific feature such as the capacity for language might well be involved in some fashion in species-specific developmental peculiarities. Marked inter-specific differences in maturational histories are well-documented and reported upon by Altman and Dittmer (1962), and the material on primates is beautifully reviewed by Schultz (1956).

In Chapter Four we have pointed out that man's history is markedly different from that of other primates. The human neonate is consider-ably more immature at birth than our closest of kin, with a concomitant prolongation of differentiation periods and increased susceptibility for various factors to impinge upon the direction of further development. The acquisition of language plays a definite part in this developmental history, its emergence occupying a fixed position within the array of developmental milestones, and there are definite indications that its development is contingent upon a certain aspect of what might be called (for lack of more accurate knowledge) cerebral plasticity. This is especially obvious in the natural history of the development of cerebral organization with respect to lateralization.

(3) *Transformations of Form and Function*

Closely related to Huxley's method of studying allometric growth is D'Arcy Thompson's (1917) famous method of transformations in which he compares related forms such as shown in Fig. 6.6 by the superimposition of Cartesian coordinates. A rectangular system is drawn over a two-dimensional representation of one form so that the distortions of the coordinates may be studied that result from drawing lines through the homologous points on the second form. This method is purely descriptive and difficult to quantify. But it illustrates the topological relationships between certain forms and how certain differences in structure may be accounted for by a single principle, usually changes in growth gradients during ontogeny. In cases where specific dimensions can be compared allometrically, we would find different values for the parameters a and b (compare Needham, 1964, on allomorphosis), of the allometric formula. In an important discussion of D'Arcy Thompson's transformations, Woodger (1945) pointed out that the phenomenon demonstrated here must be understood in the light of genetics and embryology because no mature form can change, by a process of transformation, into any other.

However, there may be intracellular genetic alterations such that ontogenetic histories are altered resulting in two different mature forms. The situation is diagrammed in Fig. 6.7. There are two molecular structures, Σ_1 and Σ_2, that are at the basis of two developmental histories H_1 and H_2. Σ_1 and Σ_2 are related to one another by the specification of a molecular transformation called T_m. The developmental histories H_1 and H_2, result in mature structures S_1 and S_2. In the case described by D'Arcy Thompson, an apparent transformation relation, T_a, persists that is characterized through the distorted coordinate systems. Notice, however, that the biological connection rests entirely in the molecular and "invisible" transformation T_m and that the apparent transformation T_a is more or less incidental—certainly not essential—for it is obvious that some or even most molecular transformations will alter the developmental histories in such a way that the corresponding two mature structures either lose their isomorphism (as in the isolated case of two-headed monsters or other deformities) or remain the same to the eyes of the unaided observer as in the case of certain inherited diseases such as hemophilia. Thus, D'Arcy Thompson's transforma-

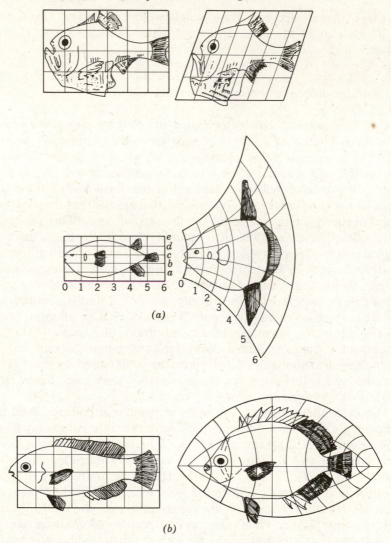

FIG. 6.6. Morphological relations between selected species shown here as geometric transformations. (*a*) *Argyropelecus olfersi* and *Sternoptyx diaphana; middle: Scarus sp.* and *Pomacanthus;* (*b*) *Diodon* and *Orthagoriscus.* (From Thompson, 1917.)

tions are probably special cases of a much more universal phenomenon.

A discussion of these transformations has some unsuspected relevance to the biological study of language, particularly the comparison of human language with animal forms of communication. We have said before that what is true of ontogeny and transformations of molecular structures is also relevant to the biological foundations of behavior because of the dependence of the latter upon the former. Thus, the emergence of a species-specific form of behavior has, essentially, a molecular transformational history. Just as in the case of mature structure, mature forms of behavior are the result of species-specific developmental histories H_1 and H_2, and the biological connections between any two forms of behavior must be sought for on the level of the molecular transformations T_m. What we have said of the apparent transformation T_a, holds *a fortiori* for the comparison of behavior.

Correspondences on this surface level will be special cases; in many more instances, all isomorphism will be lost to our eyes. We would expect mature behavior forms (that is, the homologues to S_1 and S_2) to vary with much greater freedom and into many more directions than gross structure, because the selection biases upon skeletal form are likely to be much more restraining than on behavioral modality, and it is also possible that epigenetic canalization (Waddington, 1956 and 1957) allows of fewer directional alternatives in the case of structural alterations than behavioral ones. Although these are speculations, it is a fact that there is greater variety in behavior among animals than in their types of *Bauplan* or structural pattern. In the light of this, the present thesis on the biological origins of language becomes very clear.

We assume that our potential for language has a biological history

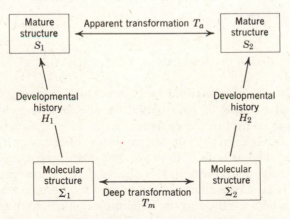

FIG. 6.7. Species are related to each other by transformations in molecular structure of genic material. These transformations affect the developmental histories of the animals in the course of which the original relationship may become obscured; the resulting mature structures may or may not bear resemblance to one another.

that is written in terms and on the level of molecular transformations T_m; but this belief commits us in no way to expect the occurrence of apparent transformations T_a. If human language be S_2, we cannot even be sure, in fact, what may be assumed to be tokens of S_1. Similarly, if a superficial resemblance is pointed out to us between language and some behavioral aspect of another species, we cannot be certain how close or distant the underlying relationship T_m actually is, or for that matter, if there is any such relationship whatever. Because modifications of behavior may be freer and go into many more directions than modifications of structures, molecular transformations T_m may leave in many fewer cases apparent transformations T_a than is the case for skeletal structure and thus there is the danger of being misled by similarities that are in fact not objective but that are entirely due to anthropomorphic interpretation of animals' activities. (Examples of this are not restricted to animal "language" but may be found in statements about animal "play," or animal "families," or animal "pleasures."

The transformational picture leads us to expect that molecular alterations indirectly caused changes in the temporal and spatial dimensions of the species' developmental history and that the resulting alterations in structure and function brought with them prolonged and changed periods during which one function could be influenced by others, thus creating critical periods of special sensitivities and opening up new potentials and capacities. This is just the framework within which we would like to see our thoughts move; it is too vague to be a theory. Let us look at it as the direction for possible explanations that are yet to come.

III. EVIDENCE FOR INHERITANCE OF LANGUAGE POTENTIAL

The inheritance of behavioral traits in man can never be definitively demonstrated because of our inability to do breeding experiments. Also, absolute control of the environment is difficult to achieve. If we are staunch believers in the sole determination of behavior by the social environment, there is no way to prove that in any given case the social environment was held constant. It is always possible to argue that there might have been subtle differences in human relations so that even two individuals who are raised in the same home might have experienced different treatment, invisible to the observer, and that all differences in behavior might be due to these variations. Similar but converse arguments are also possible in the case of identical behavior in apparently different environments.

We recognize these difficulties. If the supposition of inheritance of language potential were based on merely one type of evidence, we could not make a strong case for it. However, we are fortunate in that all types of evidence usually adduced for inheritance in man, also support the thesis that genetic transmission plays a role in our ability to speak.

(1) *Family Histories*

Scientific investigations into genetics of language and its disorders have been carried out since the beginning of the century, (Gutzmann, 1916; Orton, 1930; and many others cited by Luchsinger, 1959). In more recent years the familial occurrence of a variety of speech disorders has been described by Huyck (1940), Mussafia (1960), and Pfaendler (1960). A closely related disorder, congenital dyslexia, a peculiar difficulty with learning to read, also tends to run in families (Drew, 1956, and Hallgren, 1950). On the basis of these studies, a clinical syndrome has been identified called congenital language disability, consisting of a combination of any of the following deficits: markedly delayed onset of speech (in the presence of otherwise normal developmental milestones), poor articulation often persisting into the teens, poorly established hand preference or frank leftism, marked reading difficulties, either complete inability or marked difficulty for acquiring a second language after puberty (Eustis, 1947; Gallagher, 1950). Intelligence is usually not affected.

The familial occurrence of congenital language disability is well documented through a number of published pedigrees (Luchsinger and Arnold, 1959; Arnold, 1961; Brewer, 1963) partly reproduced in Fig. 6.8. After a survey of all published cases we may well agree with Brewer's conclusion that congenital language disability is probably a dominant, sex-influenced trait with at least fair penetrance.

Pedigrees for more specific language and speech disturbances are also available, notably for the occurrence of stuttering (Luchsinger, 1959). Luchsinger (1940) has also studied the familial incidence of the general ease of language-expression. Of particular interest are the extremes of the normal range. Both global language-facilitation and global language-difficulties may be attributed to inherited factors. Transitions from borderline normal to borderline abnormal appear as delayed onset of speech, protracted articulatory difficulties in childhood, congenital expressive disorders, or conversely, hyperfluency resulting in cluttering or pathological talkativeness. In the latter instance, ease of communication and intelligibility may suffer as much as

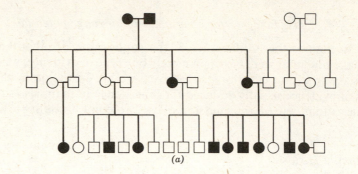

(a)

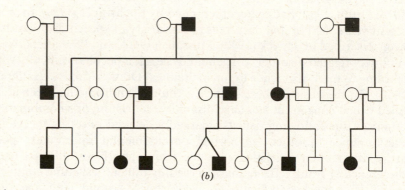

(b)

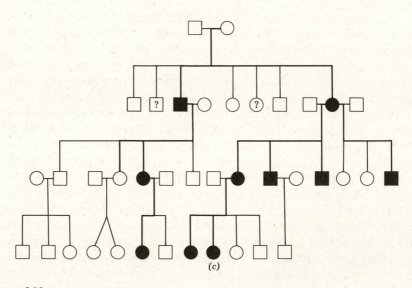

(c)

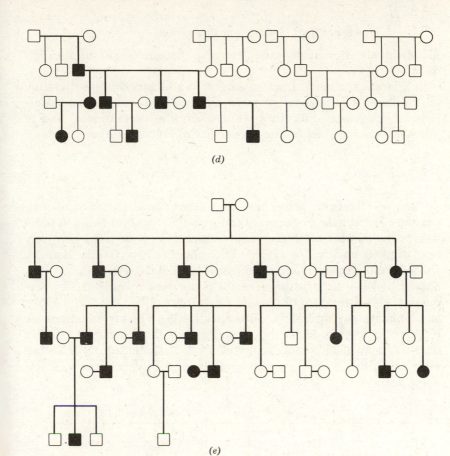

(d)

(e)

☐ Normal male

◯ Normal female

■ Male with language, speech, or reading deficit

● Female with language, speech, or reading deficit

FIG. 6.8. Five pedigrees showing the inheritance of specific language disabilities. [Redrawn (a), (b), and (c) from Arnold, 1961; (d) from Luchsinger, 1959; (e) from Brewer, 1963.]

in individuals who actually suffer from the opposite pole of the disorder-scale.

In a recent summary, Luchsinger (1959) also surveyed the literature on the familial occurrence of word-deafness and speech-sound deafness, of congenital difficulties with acquisition of grammar, and of psychological variables on the heritability of voice qualities.

(2) *Twin Studies*

The role of genetic factors may be further elucidated through comparison of speech development of fraternal and identical twins. A fairly impressive number of studies exists. Aspects of voice in twins have been studied by Schilling (1936), Luchsinger (1944), Gedda, Bianchi, Bianchi, and Neroni (1955), and Gedda, Fiori-Ratti, and Bruno (1960). Speech and language disturbances of twins were investigated by Seemann (1937), Brodnitz (1951), and Luchsinger (1953, 1957, and 1961), and language psychology by Gottschick (1939). The investigations are reported in varying detail and thoroughness which makes pooling of data and statistical computations of level of significance impossible. Only Luchsinger's work includes blood typing of subjects and complete

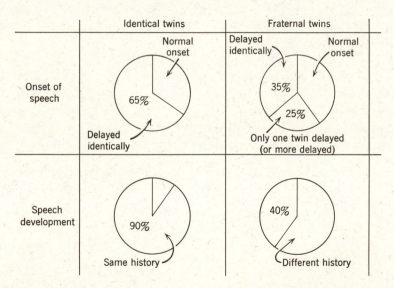

FIG. 6.9. The onset of speech and the subsequent development tend to be much more uniform among identical twins than fraternal twins.

tabulation of all relevant facts. All studies agree that fraternal twins are much more prone to differences in language development than identical twins. The proportions shown in Fig. 6.9 are essentially based on Luchsinger's publications but have been rounded off by comparing his findings with those of Seemann (1937). The diagrams are merely intended to show the trends in rough figures.

The developmental history of identical twins tends to be much more synchronous than that of fraternal twins. Among the former, motor milestones, menarche, change of voice, and growth rate are more likely to occur at the same time than among the latter. The same is reflected in the onset of speech (that is, the age at which the first few words appear, words are joined into phrases, and grammatical mistakes become minimal). It is only among the fraternal twins that difference in onset occurs, whereas identical twins seem to progress simultaneously. It is the general consensus of the investigators that these divergences cannot be simply explained on the grounds of imitation or differential treatment by parents.

If the developmental history as a whole is compared, that is the occurrence of milestones and/or the occurrence and nature of speech and language abnormalities, the difference between identical and fraternal twins is even greater. In this case, however, it is more difficult to refute the hypothesis that fraternal twins who tend to look different will not react to one another as easily as identical ones. But it is also not possible to prove this hypothesis and to disprove also the assumption of genetic differences.

(3) *Miscellaneous Evidence*

There are some further tantalizing indications for a direct and profound dependence of language capacity on genetic constitution. Unfortunately, the evidence is still too scanty to base any elaborate theory upon it. Let us merely refer to these matters for the sake of completion and in the hope that further research will clarify these points. First, there is a report from Moorhead, Mellman, and Wenar (1961) on a chromosome study in a family in which a mother and four of her five children had low intelligence and disproportionately poor speech. The father and a fifth child had normal behavior. The behaviorally aberrant individuals also had a chromosome abnormality which was absent from the karyotype of the normal members of the family. The interpretation of these findings will have to wait further discoveries of speech defects associated with the same chromosomal defect.

Second, there is an inherited error of metabolism producing a disease called histidinemia which particularly affects the development of speech. The few cases that have been described in the medical literature (Auerbach et al., 1962; Ghadimi et al., 1961 and 1962; La Du et al., 1963) do not yet allow any safe inferences about the significance of this association between behavioral and metabolic disorders. If the association should eventually be shown to be statistically interesting, it will lay the foundation for some further and perhaps very revealing research into the developmental history of the capacity for language. For the time being it may be wiser to reserve judgment.

(4) *The Darlington-Brosnahan Hypothesis*

Darlington (1947) proposed that the sound complement of a natural language is an expression of its speakers' vocal preference which, in turn, is controlled by genes. He suggested that there might be slight structural differences in the vocal tracts of various speaker-communities and that the present phonetic inventory of a living language is ultimately due to the speakers' desire to minimize their vocal efforts. Brosnahan (1961) enlarged on the original suggestion and collected a great deal of material which, he believed, supported Darlington's hypothesis. Perhaps the most impressive support is derived from the geographic distribution of certain sounds, especially the intradental spirant /th/ in European languages. Today this sound is confined to peripheral countries of Europe (Scandinavian countries, British Isles, Iberic peninsula and the Balkan). Thus, it is found among three unrelated language families: Finno-Ugric, Indo-European, and Basque; but historically it covered most of central Europe. The authors of the hypothesis believe that the /th/ is disappearing in Europe through gradual anatomical changes in the vocal tract of speakers in the central European area and that this change is due to genes which are slowly diffusing through the mating groups in an East-to-West direction. Brosnahan has made an admirable effort to defend this hypothesis against a number of objections but I believe it is fair to say that the hypothesis still lacks cogency. The anatomical evidence for European speakers is not sufficient (Roberts, 1962) and is totally lacking for speakers of other continents where speech sounds also diffuse geographically and regardless of language-family boundaries. Nor is it possible to demonstrate that minimization of effort is indeed responsible for sound shifts (Lenneberg, 1962). Arguments based upon principles of least effort are always dangerous.

IV. LIMITATIONS ON THE RECONSTRUCTION AND "DATING" OF THE HISTORY OF LANGUAGE

There were days when learned treatises on the origin of language were based on nothing more than imagination. The absence of ascertainable facts rendered these essays disreputable early during the rise of empirical sciences. For some time the topic became taboo in respectable scientific circles. But recently it seems to have acquired new probity by adumbration of the speculations with empirical data. Let us test the soundness of the various types of arguments by examining the corroborative evidence in terms of relevance to the problem of the phylogenetic history of language.

(1) *Arguments Based upon the History of the Brain and Skull*

In contrast to the first section of this chapter, in which attempts were discussed to derive the biological origin of language from a comparison of animal communication, we shall now deal with efforts to reconstruct language history through a reconstruction of brain history.

The brain does not fossilize. Therefore, its history is based on secondary indications; either by a comparison of the brains of present-day animals, or by a study of the bony enclosure of the brains of extinct forms. We must examine these two sources individually.

(*a*) *Comparison with Brains of Contemporary Animals.* From earlier discussions in this chapter it is obvious that we need not compare the brains of any other species but those of primates, because the hope of encountering behavioral mechanisms that are directly related to human language fades with phylogenetic distance to man. There is fair agreement on the relationship between species within the order so that we may confine ourselves to the family most closely related to us, namely the great apes (Pongidae). Unfortunately there are still vast gaps in our knowledge of the comparative neuro-anatomy of these forms. The literature on cerebral cortex (von Bonin and Bailey, 1961), basal ganglia (Feremutsch, 1961), thalamus (Feremutsch, 1963), and autonomic nervous system (Wrete, 1962) has recently been reviewed and the general phylogenetic trends are discussed there (see also Connolly, 1950 and Starck, 1965). However, the history of the human brain is far from clear.

Many aspects, and perhaps the most important ones for an understanding of language, remain completely unexplored from a comparative point of view; for instance, the connectivity between cells and cell aggregates. Furthermore, not all details of the brains examined fall into a linear order of evolution because we are not dealing with primitive, primordial but contemporary and adapted brains. Some of the peculiarities of the human brain are predictable on the basis of allometry and may therefore be attributed simply to general growth factors instead of to behavioral specializations. The greatest problem in this connection arises from the uncertainty about neurological correlates of language. This has been pointed out in detail in Chapters Two and Five. It is not at all clear that the capacity for language depends on any grossly observable structural peculiarity of the brain—not even the central region of the left cerebral cortex because if this part of the brain is removed surgically early enough in life, language may develop without impairment through specialization of other areas. Thus it is perhaps only molecular structure which affects function, especially relative speeds of conduction in various parts of fiber-systems, that is relevant to brain-history of language capacity. At the present time nothing is known about this.

There are some very general, methodological questions regarding the usefulness of comparative neuro-anatomy for an elucidation of the phylogenetic emergence of behavior. In a sense species make different "use" of particular brain structures in the elaboration of their species-specific behavior. The anatomy of the visual system of mammals differs quantitatively rather than qualitatively. However, the destruction of large parts of the area striata appears to have different consequences for chimpanzee than for cats; and the peculiarities of pattern perception and the recognition of similarities characteristic for a given species can never be explained through neuro-anatomy. This type of phenomenon makes it difficult to say that "language could only have come about after a certain type of fiber-connection had developed or a given cortical area had expanded." Language *is* the end-product of many interacting processes depending upon a variety of cerebral mechanisms. But the now-existing associations of language with central-nervous-system peculiarities do not mean an evolutionary inevitable and necessary relationship. Similar behavior might have come about in different combinations of ways.

Earlier forms of communication might have implicated other brain characteristics. It is an *ad hominem* argument to say that language is "due" to a given brain development, just as it would be inaccurate to say that man is a poor swimmer *because* of his lack of fins, scales, and fish brains. This is not the reason (many animals live in water without these attributes). There is no other *reason* but that the phylogenetic history of man did not adapt him for aquatic life. We may say that today the capacity for language is dependent upon a human brain; but we cannot write a causal history of this relationship (see also Overhage, 1959).

In short, the evolutionary history of man's cerebral capacity for language cannot be easily elucidated by examining the brains of other living species. Probably man was separated from other primates long before his brain began to evolve in the direction of the language-prerequisites.

(*b*) *Relevance of the History of the Skull.* Could the palaeontological history of the human skull give us clues about the emergence of language? Critical evaluation of the evidence speaks against this. Instead of brains from fossil men, we have only an array of skull fragments. From these fragments, endocasts are made, that is, plaster-casts of the concavities. Unfortunately, the patterns of cortical sulci are not well-delineated on the calvarium. The main landmarks inside the extant bones are the meningeal vessels which, in modern man, do not bear a constant relationship to fissures and sulci of the sub-pial cortical surface. Thus, endocasts give no language-relevant information. They tell us something about the brain's approximate size and shape, but nothing about cortical fields, subcortical connections, or other internal structure.

If a group of experts were handed fragments of the cranium (or the entire exenterated skull, for that matter) of modern man, say an individual who died three years before under unknown circumstances, and were asked to say whether or not that person had acquired language, they could only give an answer in terms of statistical probabilities, namely the incidence of persons who do and who do not have language in the presence of normal bone formation. Their judgment would be based entirely on their knowledge of conditions prevailing today among the population at large. The bones themselves could give them no clue as to the language capacities of the deceased. He might have been a normocephalic retardate or a great orator, or, if the skull is subnormally small, it might have belonged to an African pygmy or a birdheaded dwarf—in either case in possession of language—or it might have been a microcephalic individual with no more than a few words at his command. If one cannot make unfailing deductions from recent bones, one can hardly presume that inferences are possible about fossil men who lived under almost totally unknown circumstances.

The extraordinary size of modern man's brain and the cause of its relatively rapid phylogenetic development have captured the imagination of virtually every student of human descent. This evolutionary event has been generally linked to our capacity for language. Although

I tend to be skeptical about this relationship, based on the evidence mentioned elsewhere, I admit that there can be no proof for the historical independence of brain size and language.

The oldest fossil which some authorities are willing to regard as the first human ancestor is *Australopithecus* who lived one to two million years ago (there is considerable uncertainty about the age). His brain was about as large as that of a modern gorilla, but he was slighter in build than the modern ape, so that he might have had a relatively large brain. If we are right in classifying him into a family distinct from the Pongidae (chimpanzee, gorilla, orangutang), we must also accord him some peculiar brain functions. If the modern apes do not talk, this is no evidence against the possibility that *Australopithecus* had some potential for a primitive form of speech-like communication. A study of his skull cannot decide the question. Later, more distinctly hominid fossils, such as Java man and Peking man, had successively larger cranial capacities. Toward the end of the third glacial, fairly suddenly, a new race appeared with brains as large as ours: Neanderthal man. It appears to be the consensus today that this form was a racial specialization that became extinct without affecting the ancestorial line from which we have come. Our direct forebears, the Cro-Magnon race, emerged about fifty thousand years ago. Their brains had the same size as Neanderthal's; in fact, on the average, the cranial capacity was slightly larger than that of modern man. Cro-Magnon's skull had one characteristic in which it differed from all other types of human fossils: its shape. The skull was shorter but higher, and there was a forward shift of its center of gravity; it was balanced differently on the spinal column.

Haldane (1949) and Mayr (1963) have pointed out that the rise of modern man, particularly the increase in cranial capacity, has occurred within a spectacularly short period. Although evolutionary changes are often measured in terms of millions of years and a time-span of a hundred million years for some given change is quite common, the most significant hominid feature, the increase of the brain, took place within a mere few hundred thousand years. We may wish to speculate on the target of the selection pressures at work. What was so advantageous about a large brain and skull?

It is tempting to relate the size of the brain to man's two most outstanding characteristics: his capacity for language and his general cognitive capacities. Intuitively, this relation may be reasonable. But it is important to remember that it rests on no more than just that: intuition. There is no way of demonstrating that cognitive or language capacities either required or resulted from a rapid increase in the number of brain cells.

One common line of argument in favor of relating brain size to intelligence and language is based on observations of feeble-minded individuals. In this case, it is not uncommon that abnormally small brains are correlated with a lowering of intellect, and language learning ability may be affected also. However, feeble-minded patients are not replicas of primitive human races; they are not a viable subspecies. Their constitution and growth patterns are deeply abnormal; their brain functions have not developed properly, and little is known about the quantitative aspects of their brain-cell populations. These deviants can tell us nothing about evolutionary history of the brain.

Furthermore, there are abnormally small human brains (namely of nanocephalic dwarfs) that are capable of learning language, and the surgical removal of up to one-third of the cerebral mass early in childhood does not restrict the capacity for language acquisition. Dart (1956) cites further anthropological data which show that individuals with much smaller brains than those normally seen in Europe, America, and Asia can learn language, and Schultz (1962) describes the skull of a gorilla that had a 752 cc capacity, that is, within the range in which several microcephalic humans have an appreciable degree of linguistic facility. There is, then, little that compels us to think of language or communication in general as the prime selection target responsible for the present size of our brain (for a well-argued opposite point of view see Hockett and Ascher, 1964). To postulate a given brain size as the Rubicon for the capacity to speak (Keith, 1948) does not appear to be justified.

There is, however, another line of argument that induces many scholars to suspect a close relationship between brain size and intelligence. It is based on purely logical considerations; in fact, the reasoning underlying it is by analogy. The capacities of an electronic computer or desk calculator are directly related to the number of its constituent elements. This engenders the belief that an increase in the number of units in the brain has a similar consequence. However, evidence for this is surprisingly poor. Perhaps Lashley's early observations might be cited in support of this contention, namely that the *quantity* of cerebro-cortical destruction is inversely related to the complexity of task and pattern perception an animal is capable of. But it is not clear how these studies relate to human intelligence. For instance, Teuber (1959) and Ghent, Mishkin, and Teuber (1962) have compared intelligence test scores of war veterans at the time of their recruitment with scores on the same test several years later and after extensive brain injuries; there was no significant difference between before and after cortical destructions. Nor did short term memory change as a consequence of frontal-lobe tissue destruction.

If the increase in neuronal elements did bring about an increase in capacity (and this remains a reasonable assumption), we are still incapable of defining *capacity*. There is no clear indication whether it is related to storage, to simultaneous processing, to internal efficiency of processing, to more advantageous utilization of input, or to speeding up of processing time, etc. We do not know how any of these purely theoretical aspects of *capacity* are related to particular quantitative dimensions such as brain weight, cell counts, and neurodensity. It is not good enough to say, "there is nothing else that a large brain could be good for *than* to bring about greater intelligence and language!" This is merely a reflection of our ignorance on the causes of particular evolutionary changes.

Since this point is of no small consequence for our image of man, his capacities, and his place in the primate order, one last consideration on the nature of cognition may be in order. Suppose we explore cognitive capacities of animals and man by systematic measurements of a great number of aspects of psychological activities. Let it include various types of memory, of pattern recognition, of associative capacities, of generalization, and propensity for inference. Each type of measurement constitutes a dimension with which we can construct a multidimensional, mathematical space; let us call it the *generalized cognition-space*. The total capacities that characterize a given species, that is, its species-specific cognition, becomes now a locus in the cognition-space. Cognitive evolution could be expressed, in such a space, as vectors; the locus of an earlier form is thus connected with that of a later form. The directionality and length of the vector represent the peculiar changes that took place in the course of evolution to bring about the species-specific cognition of a given animal. In terms of this conceptualization, could we expect all evolutionary cognitive changes to be vectors that have the same direction? Such a supposition seems absurd. On the other hand, the enlargement of the brain is a widespread and recurring phenomenon. It appears to be contrary to our empirical findings that an increase in size changes cognitive capacity into a specific direction. Thus, man's peculiar type of intelligence is not the "logical or necessary" outcome of the enormous growth of his brain, and his capacities today could not have been predicted simply from a knowledge of the evolutionary trend of the change of brain-volume.

In short, we do not know why the brain increased so rapidly in size.

Since man is distinct from other hominidae in many ways, we cannot reconstruct which feature added most to selection pressures and which came about through pleiotropic effects (Caspari, 1958). Although it is entirely possible that the emergence of language and intelligence are historically related to the increase in size of the brain, the case is certainly not yet irrefutably proven, and the various arguments adduced for one or the other position are too weak to allow us to date the onset of language from fossil remains.

(2) *Arguments Based on Other Skeletal Features*

Most relevant here are the shape of the jaws and oral cavity, the suspension of the tongue, and the shape and mechanisms of pharynx and larynx. Unfortunately, with the exception of the first two items, these structures are not preserved in the fossils, and the reconstructions are so speculative that they need not be considered here. The mandible, with its absence or presence of a chin and the shape of the denture surely has an influence on the acoustic production of sounds. But all we may deduce from this evidence is that the vocalizations of fossil men did not bear any close acoustic resemblance to the speech sounds of any modern tongue. But we may not dismiss the possibility that the early vocalizations might already have had ethological or biological characteristics that foreshadowed modern languages in some way. None of the language aspects discussed throughout this book can be reconstructed from the palaeontological findings.

(3) *Racial Diversification and the Emergence of Language*

All races appear to have the same biological potential for the development of culture and the acquisition of language. Thus we must assume that the evolutionary events favoring culture and language go back to the common ancestor of all modern races. This would mean that the age of language is no less than say 30,000 to 50,000 years. Credence is lent to this hypothesis not only on the grounds of racial evidence; the cultures associated with the fossils of this period give evidence of the development of a symbolic medium other than language; graphic representation. The cave drawings of that time are extremely skillful and, what is more important, they are highly stylized and, in a sense, abstract. Thus it is likely that the cognitive processes of Cro-Magnon had a number of characteristics in common with modern man.

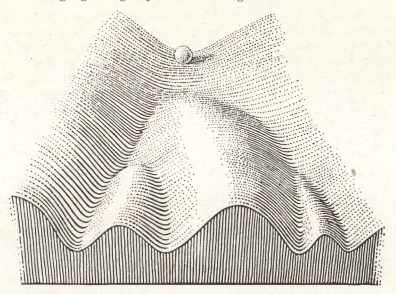

FIG. 6.10. An "epigenetic landscape." A representation of a developmental system as a surface (sloping toward the observer) on which there are valleys along which the processes of differentiation tend to run. Evolutionary changes would alter the landscape in such a way that the ball now runs down a different valley from its former course. (From Waddington, 1956.)

The possibility that language is of much older age is not precluded. One authority (Coon, 1962), has advanced the hypothesis that the races have individual ancestries that go back as far as *Australopithecus*. Mayr (1962) has pointed out that this thesis is far from substantiated but also not entirely impossible. If this were so, language or its prerequisites could have been present as long as half a million years ago. Another theoretical possibility is that the biological matrix for language is of great age but that earliest fossil-man did not yet "utilize" it fully. This brings to mind Waddington's epigenetic landscape (Fig. 6.10) representing the notion of canalization. The evolutionary trend might have entered a particular groove which canalized the subsequent developments and thus made language the necessary outcome, owing to a peculiar evolutionary antecedent.

We see that consideration of modern races sets a time at which we might reasonably assume language to have been in existence. But it does not enable us to carry the dating of its emergence any further.

(4) *Cultural Status as Evidence for Language*

Do the cultural remains of prehistoric man furnish clues for the dating of the development of language? If one could be certain that language is the necessary concomitant of either *tool-making,* or *social organization,* or *cultural complexity,* one could make fairly precise statements about the time of the birth of language. Unfortunately, such certainty does not exist for the first two phenomena and even the third gives but vague indications.

The use of objects as instrumentalities for behavior is not reserved to man among the primate order (Miyadi, 1964; Goodall, 1963; Birch, 1945; W. Köhler, 1927). Apparently a primitive capacity for the *use of tools* is common to several primate species and is therefore not necessarily tied to the human form of communication. However, even the earliest forms of *Homo* must have made a very different and much more extensive use of tools than any subhuman primate today. Miller (1964) has proposed that the use of tools and the use of language demand very similar, biologically given capacities. I consider this to be a fruitful way of looking at language but, at the same time, it must be stressed that it does not compel us to assume simultaneous emergence of the two skills. One may have been present before the other and there is no way to decide which might have had the lead. Nor does the nature of the tools or the state of primitivity allow us to postulate concomitant levels of primitivity for a form of communication. (Miller suggested no such correlation.)

Degree of social organization must be related to efficiency of intra-species communication. This is almost a truism. But the communication may, and does, take on an infinite variety of forms. Our speculations about the beginnings of language are seriously handicapped by two unknown factors. First, we can only make the vaguest of assumptions about the social structure and organization of prehistoric men and second, their forms of communication might have been highly developed but very different in nature and principle from our present form. Therefore, Dart's (1959) postulate that evidence of hunting and fishing technology makes the possession of language a reasonable assumption cannot be accepted uncritically. Perhaps a certain activity calls for good communication, but whether this was a direct, primitive antecedent of what we now call language is uncertain.

The most difficult evaluation of evidence for the existence of language is *cultural complexity.* At one time our phylogenetic ancestors must have had a truly primitive form of culture. On the other hand, the neolithic cultures of fifty thousand years ago may not have been any less complex than the most primitive living cultures today, for example, say in Central Brazil or New Guinea. When did "complexity of culture" arise? Can we be certain that the prehistoric cultures were as primitive as their physical remains today would indicate? The older the culture, the more tenuous must be our guesses. Even the notion of "complexity" is itself a source of inaccuracy. We cannot measure degrees of complexity of culture. There is a further difficulty in using culture as an indication for language.

Today we may study cultures that are essentially neolithic in their state of development, as well as cultures advanced enough to split the atom and explore interplanetary space. Surprisingly, the natural languages spoken throughout this range of cultures appear to be based on similar principles. It is an empirical fact that today neither the tools commonly occurring in a given culture nor the social structure associated with that culture can give us clues about the complexity of structure of the language now spoken by the individuals of that culture. Natural languages cannot be ordered in terms of complexity. A complex task should be more difficult to learn than a simple one and therefore take more time and effort. But all natural languages are learned with the same ease by children of a certain age, which seems to confirm the "equal complexity" hypothesis.

It is reasonable to assume (though not absolutely necessary) that Cro-Magnon man, whose material culture might not have been too far removed from the most primitive present-day cultures, and who had all the physical characteristics of modern man, was in possession of language as we know it today. There is nothing that requires us to think of his language as substantially more primitive than ours, or to postulate any "uk-uk-theory." * It is likely that Cro-Magnon and Neanderthal men were speaking creatures. We have no means of deciding whether earlier races had a form of communication that was in any way similar to that of Cro-Magnon. Attempts at dating the origin of modern types of language development seem unwarranted.

V. SUMMARY

The biological history of language is "covert"; its evolution is hidden in the series of transformations, structural and functional, that took

---

* By "uk-uk-theory" is meant all of those accounts in which the beginning of language is characterized as the discovery that the original animal evocations (such as a supposed "uk-uk") could be used for transmitting information to other individuals.

place in the course of the formation of modern man. It is tied to the history of physiological adaptations, cognitive specializations, and sensory specifications.

The evolutionary process underlying language is analogous to the geometric transformations of form, described by D'Arcy Thompson, or perhaps comparable to the changes in allometric tendencies in different species. Some earlier functions seem to have been transformed to subserve communication.

Our present capacity for language may well go back to species-specific alterations in genetic material (intracellular changes) which, however, affected certain rates and directions of growth during ontogeny (temporo-spatial gradients), producing a peculiar ontogenetic phase of an optimal confluence of various abilities; thus a critical period for language acquisition might have come about. This is not just a matter of protracted infancy; during a given period various types of facilitations and inhibitions are at an optimum constellation (including something we might call, for lack of a better term, perhaps, cerebral plasticity). Therefore, the artificial retardation of a chimpanzee's development could not bring about language capacity because it would simply slow down, that is, change the time scale of chimpanzee ontogeny but would not introduce the peculiar and necessary overlaps that we may assume to play a role in language acquisition.

Pedigrees and twin studies suggest that genetic transmission is relevant to language facilitation. However, there is no need to assume "genes for language."

The biological history of language cannot be revealed through a random comparison with animal communication; this is particularly so if the basis of comparison is pragmatic or "logical" and without regard to the animals' phylogenetic relation to man. Comparison of language with animal communication beyond the order of primates is dangerous because of the phenomenon of *convergence*.

Reconstruction of the origin of language is impossible except for some very simple determinations. This is because of the following limitations: (1) the size and shape of the brain furnish no secure clue about the capacity for language; (2) given morphological peculiarities of the central nervous system do not bear a fixed relationship to behavior; the same cerebral feature may promote somewhat different aspects of behavior in different species, and vice versa; the relation of behavior to certain aspects of the brain may have undergone several changes during the course of evolution of modern man; (3) even if we had direct knowledge of social structure or cultural complexity of the societies of various fossil men, we could not draw conclusions about language as we know it today. Different types of communication might have pre-vailed at those times.

The identical capacity for language among all races suggests that this phenomenon must have existed before racial diversification.

There is nothing unbiological about recognizing language as unique behavior in the animal kingdom; such uniqueness is to be expected from the evolutionary process as well as from genetic mechanisms.

REFERENCES

Altman, P. L. and Dittmer, D. S. (eds.) (1962), *Growth: Including Reproduction and Morphological Development.* Federation of American Societies for Experimental Biology, Washington, D. C.

Altmann, S. A. (ed.) (1966), *Social Communication among Primates.* Univ. of Chicago Press, Chicago.

Arnold, G. E. (1961), The genetic background of developmental language disorders, *Folia phoniatrica* **13**:246–254.

Auerbach, V. H., Di George, A. M., Baldridge, R. C., Tourtellotte, C. D., and Brigham, M. P. (1962), Histidinemia: A deficiency in histidase resulting in the urinary excretion of histidine and of imidazolepyruvic acid, *J. Pediatr.* **60**:487–497.

Beermann, W. (1963), Cytological aspects of information transfer in cellular differentiation, *Am. Zoologist* **3**:23–32.

Bernstein, F. (1925), Beitraege zur mendelistischen Anthropologie. Quant. Rassenanalyse auf Grund von statistischen Beobachtungen ueber den Klangcharakter der Singstimme, *Sitzungsberichte d. Preuss. Akad. d. wissenschftl. math. physikal. Kl,* pp. 61–82.

Birch, H. G. (1945), The relation of previous experience to insightful problem-solving, *J. comp. Psychol.* **38**:367–383.

Bonin, G. v. (1950), *Essay on the Cerebral Cortex.* C. Thomas, Springfield, Illinois.

Bonin, G. v. (1963), *The Evolution of the Human Brain.* Univ. of Chicago Press, Chicago.

Bonin, G. v. and Bailey, P. (1961), Pattern of the cerebral isocortex, in *Primatologia: Handbook of Primatology,* H. Hofer, A. H. Schultz and D. Starck (eds.), Vol. II, part 2, fasc. 10. Karger, Basel.

Bonner, J. T. (1952), *Morphogenesis: an Essay on Development.* Princeton Univ. Press, Princeton, New Jersey.

Brewer, W. F. (1963), *Specific Language Disability: Review of the Literature and a Family Study.* Honors thesis, Harvard University.

Brodnitz, F. S. (1951), Stuttering of different types in identical twins, *J. speech hearing Dis.* **16**:334–336.

Brosnahan, L. F. (1961), *The Sounds of Language: an Inquiry into the Role of Genetic Factors in the Development of Sound Systems.* Heffer, Cambridge.

Caspari, E. (1958), Genetic basis of behavior, in *Behavior and Evolution,* A. Roe and G. G. Simpson (eds.). Yale Univ. Press, New Haven.

Connolly, C. J. (1950), *External Morphology of the Primate Brain.* C. Thomas, Springfield, Illinois.

Coon, C. S. (1962), *The Origin of Races,* Knopf, New York.

Darlington, C. D. (1947), The genetic component of language, *Heredity* 1:269–286.

Dart, R. A. (1956), The relationships of brain size and brain pattern to human status, *S. Afr. J. Med. Sci.* 21:23–45.

Dart, R. A. (1959), On the evolution of language and articulate speech, *Homo* 10:154–165.

Dobzhansky, T. (1962), *Mankind Evolving.* Yale Univ. Press, New Haven.

Drew, A. L. (1956), A neurological appraisal of familial congenital word-blindness, *Brain* 79:440–460.

Eustis, R. S. (1947), The primary etiology of the specific language disabilities, *J. Pediatr.* 31:448–455.

Feremutsch, K. (1961), Basalganglien, in *Primatologia: Handbook of Primatology,* H. Hofer, A. H. Schultz, and D. Starck (eds.), Vol. II, part 2, fasc. 8. Karger, Basel.

Feremutsch, K. (1963), Thalamus, in *Primatologia: Handbook of Primatology,* H. Hofer, A. H. Schultz, and D. Starck (eds.), Vol. II, part 2, fasc. 6. Karger, Basel.

Gallagher, J. R. (1950), Specific language disability: A cause of scholastic failure, *New Engl. J. Med.* 242:436–440.

Garstang, W. (1922), The theory of recapitulation: a critical restatement of the biogenetic law, *J. Linn. Soc. London* 35:81–101.

Gedda, L., Bianchi, L., Bianchi, A., and Neroni, L. (1955), La voce dei gemelli, *Acta genet. med. Gemellologiae* 2:121.

Gedda, L., Fiori-Ratti, L., and Bruno, G. (1960), La voix chez les jumeaux monozygotiques, *Folia phoniatrica* 12:81–94.

Georgacopoulos, A. (1954), A propos de deux cas de macroglossie congénitale, *Rev. Laryng.* 75:34–38.

Ghadimi, H., Partington, M. W., and Hunter, A. (1961), A familial disturbance of histidine metabolism, *New Engl. J. Med.* 265:221–224.

Ghadimi, H., Partington, M. W., and Hunter, A. (1962), Inborn error of histidine metabolism, *Pediatrics* 29:714–728.

Ghent, L., Mishkin, M., and Teuber, H.-L. (1962), Short-term memory after frontal-lobe injury in man, *J. comp. physiol. Psychol.* 55:705–709.

Goldschmidt, R. B. (1938), *Physiological Genetics.* McGraw-Hill, New York.

Goldschmidt, R. B. (1952), Evolution as viewed by one geneticist, *Amer. Scientist* 40:84–135.

Goodall, J. (1963), My life among wild chimpanzees, *Natl. Geogr.* 124 (2): pp. 278–308.

Goodman, M. (1963), Man's place in the phylogeny of the primates as reflected in serum proteins, in *Classification and Human Evolution,* S. L. Washburn (ed.). Aldine Publ., Chicago.

Gottschick, J. (1939), Sprachpsychologische Zwillingsuntersuchungen, *Arch. ges. Psychol.* 103:1–70.

Grothkopp, H. (1934), Erblichkeit bei Lippen- und Gaumenspalten, *Vox* **20**: 43–54.

Gutzmann, sen., H. (1916), *Die Vererbung der Sprachstoerungen*. Thieme, Leipzig.

Haecker, V. and Ziehen, H. (1922), *Zur Vererbung und Entwicklung der musikalischen Begabung*. Ambros. Barth, Leipzig.

Haldane, J. B. S. (1949), Suggestions as to quantitative measurement of rates of evolution, *Evolution* **3**:51–56.

Hallgren, B. (1950), Specific dyslexia (congenital word-blindness), *Acta psychiatr. neurol. scand.,* Suppl. 65.

Harlow, H. F. (1949), The formation of learning sets, *Psychol. Rev.* **56**:51–65.

Harlow, H. F. (1958), The evolution of learning, in *Behavior and Evolution,* A. Roe and G. G. Simpson. Yale Univ. Press, New Haven.

Hockett, C. F. (1960), Logical considerations in the study of animal communication, in *Animal Communication,* W. E. Lanyon and W. N. Tavolga (eds.), pp. 392–430. Am. Inst. of Biol. Sci., Washington, D. C.

Hockett, C. F. (1960), The origin of speech, *Scientific American* **203**:89–96.

Hockett, C. F. and Ascher, R. (1964), The human revolution, *Current Anthrop.* **5**:135–168.

Howie, T. O., Ladefoged, P., and Starck, R. E. (1961), Congenital sub-glottic bars found in 3 generations of one family, *Folia phoniatrica* **13**:56–61.

Huxley, J. S. (1932), *Problems of Relative Growth.* The Dial Press, New York.

Huyck, E. M. (1940), The hereditary factor in speech, *J. speech hearing Dis.* **5**:295.

Keith, A. (1948), *A New Theory of Human Evolution.* Watts, London.

Koehler, O. (1951), Der Vogelgesang als Vorstufe von Musik und Sprache, *J. f. Ornithol.* **93**:1–20.

Koehler, O. (1952), Vom unbenannten Denken, *Verh. Dtsch. Zool. Gesell.* in Freiburg, pp. 202–211.

Koehler, O. (1954*a*), Vom Erbgut der Sprache, *Homo* **5**:97–104.

Koehler, O. (1954*b*), Vorbedingungen und Vorstufen unserer Sprache bei Tieren, *Verhandlungen d. Dtsch. Zool. Gesell. i. Tübingen,* pp. 327–341.

Köhler, W. (1927), *The Mentality of Apes* (2nd ed.). Harcourt, Brace, and World, New York.

La Du, B. N., Howell, R. R., Jacoby, G. A., Seegmiller, J. E., Sober, E. K., Zannoni, V. G., and Canby, J. P. and Ziegler, L. K. (1963), Clinical and biochemical studies on two cases of histidinemia, *Pediatrics* **32**:216–227.

Lenneberg, E. H. (1962), Review of L. Brosnahan, The sounds of language *Contemp. Psychol.* **7**:230–231.

Luchsinger, R. (1940), Die Sprache und Stimme von ein- und zweieiigen Zwillingen in Beziehung zur Motorik und zum Erbcharakter, *Arch. Klaus-Stift Vererb. Forsch.* **15**:459.

Luchsinger, R. (1944), Erbbiologische Untersuchungen an ein- und zweieiiger Zwillingen in Beziehung zur Grösse und Form des Kehlkopfes, *Arch. Klaus Stift. Vererb. Forsch.* **19**:393–441.

Luchsinger, R. (1953), Die Sprachentwicklung von ein- und zweieiigen Zwillinger und die Vererbung von Sprachstoerungen. *Acta Genet. med.* (Roma) **2**:31–48.

Luchsinger, R. (1957), Agrammatismus und Dyslalie bei eineiigen Zwillingen, *Acta genet.* **6**:247–254.

Luchsinger, R. (1959), Die Vererbung von Sprach- und Stimmstoerungen, *Folia phoniatrica* **11**:7–64.

Luchsinger, R. (1961), Die Sprachentwicklung von ein- und zweieiigen Zwillingen und die Vererbung von Sprachstoerungen in den ersten drei Lebensjahren, *Folia phoniatrica* **13**:66–76.

Luchsinger, R. and Arnold, G. E. (1959), *Lehrbuch der Stimm- und Sprachheilkunde* (2nd ed.). Springer, Wien.

Markert, C. L. (1963), Epigenetic control of specific protein synthesis in differentiating cells, in *Cytodifferentiation and Macromolecular Synthesis,* Michael Locke (ed.), pp. 65–84. Academic Press, New York.

Marler, P. (1961), The logical analysis of animal communication, *J. Theoret. Biol.* **1**:295–317.

Mayr, E. (1958), Behavior and Systematics, in *Behavior and Evolution,* A. Roe and G. G. Simpson. Yale Univ. Press, New Haven.

Mayr, E. (1962), Origin of the human races (book review of Coon's *The Origin of Races*), *Science* **138**:420–422.

Mayr, E. (1963), *Animal Species and Evolution.* Belknap Press of Harvard University, Cambridge, Massachusetts.

McClearn, G. E. (1964), Genetics and behavior development, in *Review of Child Development Research,* M. L. Hoffman and L. W. Hoffman (eds.), Vol. I, pp. 433–480. Russell Sage Foundation, New York.

Miller, G. A. (1964), Communication and the structure of behavior, in *Disorders of Communication,* D. McK. Rioch and E. A. Weinstein (eds.), *Ass. Res. Nerv. Ment. Dis.* **42**:29–40.

Miyadi, D. (1964), Social life of Japanese monkeys, *Science* **143**:783–786.

Moorhead, P. S., Mellman, W. J., and Wenar, C. (1961), A familial chromosome translocation associated with speech and mental retardation, *Am. J. hum. Genet.* **13**:32–46.

Mussafia, M. (1960), Le rôle de l'hérédité dans les troubles du langage, *Folia phoniatrica* **12**:94–100.

Mussafia, M. (1961), Retard "simple" du langage chez des triplés, *Folia phoniatrica* **13**:62–65.

Needham, A. E. (1964), *The Growth Process in Animals.* Van Nostrand, Princeton, New Jersey.

Orton, S. T. (1930), Familial occurrence of disorders in acquisition of language, *Eugenics* **3, 4**:140–147.

Overhage, P. (1959), Das Problem der Anthropogenese, in *Das stammesgeschichtliche Werden der Organismen und des Menschen,* A. Haas, Vol. 1. Herder, Basel.

Pfaendler, U. (1960), Les vices de la parole dans l'optique du généticien, *Akt. Probl. der Phoniatr. und Logopaed.* **1**:35–40.

Reeve, E. C. R. and Huxley, J. S. (1945), Some problems in the study of allometric growth, in *Essays on Growth and Form,* W. E. Le Gros Clark and P. B. Medawar. Clarendon, Oxford.

Rensch, B. (1954), *Neuere Probleme der Abstammungslehre* (2nd ed.). F. Enke, Stuttgart.

Rensch, B. (1959), Trends towards progress of brains and sense organs, *Cold. Spr. Harb. Symp. quant. Biol.* **24**:291–303.

Rensch, B. (1964), Memory and concepts of higher animals, *Proc. Zool. Soc. Calcutta* **17**:207–221.

Roberts, D. F. (1962), Review of Brosnahan, L. F., The sounds of language, *Heredity* **17**:290–292.

Roe, A. and Simpson, G. G. (1958), *Behavior and Evolution.* Yale Univ. Press, New Haven.

Schilling, R. (1936), Ueber die Stimme erbgleicher Zwillinge, *Klin. Wochenschr.* **15**:756–757.

Schrier, A. M., Harlow, H. F., and Stollnitz, F. (eds.) (1965), Behavior of Nonhuman Primates. Academic Press, New York.

Schultz, A. H. (1956), Postembryonic age changes, in *Primatologia: Handbook of Primatology,* H. Hofer, A. H. Schultz and D. Starck (eds.), Vol. I. Karger, Basel.

Schultz, A. H. (1962), Die Schädelkapazität männlicher Gorillas und ihr Höchstwert, *Anthrop. Anz.* **25**:197–203.

Seemann, M. (1937), Die Bedeutung der Zwillingspathologie für die Erforschung von Sprachleiden, *Arch. Sprach-Stimmheilk.* **1**:88.

Sewertzoff, A. N. (1931), *Morphologische Gesetzmässigkeit der Evolution.* G. Fischer, Jena.

Sholl, D. A. (1948), The quantitative investigation of the vertebrate brain and the applicability of allometric formulae to its study, *Proc. Roy. Soc. B.,* **135**:243–258.

Simpson, G. G. (1949), *The Meaning of Evolution.* Yale Univ. Press, New Haven.

Smith, D. D. (1965), *Mammalian Learning and Behavior.* Saunders, Philadelphia.

Starck, D. (1965), Die Neencephalisation, in *Menschliche Abstammungslehre,* G. Heberer (ed.). Fischer, Stuttgart.

Teuber, H.-L. (1959), Some alterations in behavior after cerebral lesions in man, *Evolution of Nervous Control.* A.A.A.S., Washington, D. C.

Uexküll, J. v. (1921), *Umwelt und Innenwelt der Tiere.* Berlin.

Waddington, C. H. (1956), *Principles of Embryology.* MacMillan, London.

Waddington, C. H. (1957), *The Strategy of Genes: a Discussion of Some Aspects of Theoretical Biology.* George Allen and Unwin, London.

Woodger, J. H. (1945), On biological transformations, in *Essays on Growth and Form, presented to D'Arcy W. Thompson,* W. E. Le Gros Clark and P. B. Medawar (eds.). Clarendon, Oxford.

Wrete, M. (1962), Autonomes Nervensystem, in *Primatologia: Handbook of Primatology,* H. Hofer, A. H. Schultz, and D. Starck (eds.), Vol. II, part 2, fasc. 11. Karger, Basel.

CHAPTER Seven

Primitive stages in language development

I. THE PROBLEM

In an earlier chapter we have discussed language development with respect to age and onset. Now we must search for regularities within stages of development as well as regularities in the strategy of language acquisition regardless of the age at which this happens.

Our language is such an intimate aspect of our thoughts and behavior that it is difficult for us to obtain an objective appreciation of its mechanisms. The common description of its structure is a woeful over-simplification:

"Language consists of elemental, invariant units, that is, speech-sounds; these are joined together into morphemes or words; and words are put together into sentences. Speech-sounds have no meaning, but words do. They acquire meanings by an associative process in which the visual image of an object is linked to the sound of a word."

The attractive simplicity of statements such as these has prevented many students of human behavior from recognizing the deep problems posed by the true structure of language and by the infant's amazing ability to acquire these skills within two years time. A few examples may help to show some of the hidden problems.

Let us look first at phonological aspects. Suppose we could build a typewriter that could print out (for instance, in international phonetic alphabet) anything that is spoken into it, hopefully in any language. What are the tasks of this machine? In order for it to be successful it would have to be capable of a highly peculiar form of pattern recognition. For instance, it is not enough that it can recognize isolated examples of English speech sounds. The acoustic peculiarities of a given phoneme are never twice the same, and there are instances in which two acoustically very different sounds represent the same phoneme. Interpretation of a sound as one or another phoneme often depends on the acoustic context. Furthermore, phonemes are not simply linked as in a chain during production, but they affect each other, and the influence may work both ways: a later phoneme may be influenced by an earlier one or, because of anticipation, an earlier phoneme may be influenced by a later one. Acoustic analysis also shows that speech sounds, instead of neatly following one another, may actually overlap either partly or wholly; by giving a vowel /o/ an /R/ coloring, or nasalizing it, or palatalizing it, an R-, ŋ-, or y-quality is produced together with the vowel, but it may be interpreted, under certain conditions, as if it were following it. In addition, every speaker influences his utterances by idiosyncrasies due to the peculiar shape of his vocal tract and the peculiarities of his own motor-skills; this means that every utterance he produces undergoes acoustic transformations.

A machine that prints a graphic symbol for every acoustic feature heard in the sounds of *any* language would produce very unreadable records. Speech-recognition of a natural language involves focusing attention on specific types of phonetic relations or contrasts, and on ignoring many other acoustic phenomena as irrelevant for transmission of information in a particular language. Every natural language selects its own set of contrasts, and recognition of the sound patterns of one language is governed by its own peculiar set of rules. (Although all such sets of rules have common formal properties; see Chapter Nine and Chomsky's Appendix A.) In order to be useful, the typewriter would have to be able to select the right set of rules for every input, in other words, it would have to be able to recognize one of several natural languages and then behave in accordance with this selection. Clearly, pattern-recognition of an acoustically operated typewriter is dependent upon rules which must take into consideration many factors and which must operate on much longer sound configurations than single or short speech sound segments. The relational patterns, even on the level of speech sounds, are very intricate. The reason why the many attempts to build such a typewriter have not been successful (except for very limited input) is probably not entirely due to technical limitations; it may be because of our ignorance of the proper rules that regulate speech perception.

Suppose we had solved all of these problems and had succeeded in constructing a typewriter that at least transcribes English. The device could not be considered a model of an infant who is developing speech. The problems to be solved by the infant whose task it is to "crack" the society's communication code are much more complicated; he is biologically constituted to learn to recognize any type of natural language, and the acoustic input is usually not limited to one narrow topic.

When the intricacies of patterns and relations in the structure of language are discussed abstractly, it is often interjected that the child's task might be simplified because he does not learn an abstract or formal system but is learning meanings at the same time, and this might facilitate the situation. Let us look into this matter more closely.

First, it is necessary to make a distinction between reference and meaning. Reference deals with the relationship between an individual word and some aspect or object of the physical environment. The problems of reference need not be considered here as they constitute the subject matter of Chapter Eight. Meaning deals with the semantic interpretation of utterances (or written material), and these come invariably in the form of sentences in various states of completion or degrees of imperfection; this includes the special case of one-word sentences which we shall discuss presently. Because discourse is not encountered in anything but the essential form of sentences, and sentences can be interpreted only through grammatical analysis, meaning cannot be divorced from grammatical structure (Chomsky, 1957; Chomsky and Miller, 1963; Miller and Chomsky, 1963).

Grammatical structure can not be understood as a phenomenon of transitional probability of specific lexical items or parts of speech. Something more intricate must be involved as may be seen from the following examples, suggested mostly by Chomsky. Consider the following strings of words:

(1) colorless green ideas sleep furiously
(2) furiously sleep ideas green colorless

Of these two strings (1) sounds more like a sentence than (2). Thus, we may say that (1) is grammatical but (2) is not. Although neither (1) nor (2) says anything about the physical world, it may be conceded that (1) is more likely to have meaning, say to a modern poet, than (2). There is, then, a certain affinity between meaning and grammatical structure. However, it is also clear from these examples that meaning could not be used as a criterion for grammaticality, for (1) may have no meaning to a prosaic person, but he would nevertheless be perfectly capable of deciding which of the two strings sounds more like a sentence in English than the other.

How does an adult speaker of English decide on the matter of grammatical structure? Certainly not by estimating the probability of occurrence of the sentence as a whole, because sentence (1) as well as sentence (2) had a zero probability of occurrence before Chomsky made them famous. Thus the difference between (1) and (2), which is fairly obvious to most speakers of English, can not be due to a difference in transitional probabilities of individual words (see also Miller, Galanter and Pribram, 1960). Jenkins and Palermo (1964)* sought to account for the interpretative difference between the two sentences by postulating transitional probabilities between parts of speech. If this were so, speakers of English would always perceive a chain consisting of adjective, noun, verb, and adverb as grammatical, whereas the reverse order should result in the perception of grammatical chaos. But take the sentences

(3) occasionally call warfare useless

and

(4) useless warfare call occasionally

String (3) might occur in an instruction booklet on pacifistic rhetoric; it is judged to be grammatical, and it is susceptible to semantic interpretation. None of this is true of (4). But the order of parts of speech of (3) is that of the ungrammatical string (2), whereas the grammatical string (1) has the order of (4). Clearly, the transitional probability of parts of speech is irrelevant either to our understanding of grammar or to semantic interpretation of a sentence. Nor is it possible to assume that the order of morphemes *-less, -s, -ly* determines grammaticalness because the sentence

(5) Friendly young dogs seem harmless.

orders these morphemes as in (2), not (1).

One of the many problems that an infant who is learning to speak must face is the fact that the meaning of individual words can not ordinarily give a clue to the meaning of a sentence. This is easily seen by citing such sentences as

(6) The fox chases the dog.

and

(7) The dog chases the fox.

The complexities involved in understanding sentences may be further illustrated by the sentence

(8) The dog is chased by the fox

which is understood as having the same meaning as (6) even though the order of subject and object is that of (7).

Once more it is tempting to explain our understanding of the grammar of these sentences by postulating a simple chain of uni-directional

---

* From personal communication with these authors I know that they have since abandoned this point of view.

associations between elements. For instance, take a sentence in which the first noun-phrase is the subject; here we learn to expect this noun-phrase to be followed by another noun-phrase that serves as object, except if the first noun-phrase is followed by an *is,* the verb by an *-ed* and the verb-phrase by the word *by*; when these morphemes appear, they would signal the reversal of subject and object. Again, the source for our interpretation of the meaning of a sentence must be due to a deeper understanding of grammatical structure than these rules would indicate. The sentence

(9) The fox is interested by virtue of his nature in chasing the dog

may not be elegant and even contrary to fact; but it is a grammatical string, and its meaning is associated more closely to (6) than to (7), showing that morphemes do not have the same function in a sentence as, for example, a verbal stimulus in a word-association task. Word association seems to be irrelevant to that process of grammatical analysis which must be performed by every speaker and language-acquiring infant.

If phonology and syntax pose many unsolved problems, the association between words and things is by no means less difficult to understand. A great number of different words occur in physical and temporal contiguity with *one* phenomenon (say a dog); some examples are: "wow-wow," bark, naughty, dog, big, up on the . . ., careful, etc. On the other hand, *one and the same word,* for instance, "bye-bye" (or up, or good, or truck), may occur in the presence of constantly *changing* physical stimulus configurations. Why is the child not confused by this?

We cannot help but wonder how an infant at little over one year of age can ever learn to understand and produce this behavior. The number of articles and books that deal with the development of language goes up into the thousands. But only few authors have seen that there is a formidable and totally unsolved problem here. How does the child develop language? To say vaguely that it must be discrimination learning, secondary reinforcement, or stimulus generalization does not bring us any closer to a solution, because it is not at all clear *what* has to be discriminated or *what* is generalized from or to, nor is it clear *what* is being reinforced, when and how. Oversimplifications, and even representations that are blatantly contrary to observable facts regarding the nature of language, have often led to explanations for language learning that rest on nothing but fiction.

The problems involved in language development cannot be understood in the absence of an analysis of the structure of language; and it is quite possible that the proper understanding of language structure is dependent upon empirical investigations into the acquisition process.

II. PRELANGUAGE DEVELOPMENT

(1) *Articulation*

Sounds emitted by very young infants have recently been investigated by Ringel and Kluppel (1964), Bosma and Lind (1962), and Fisichelli et al., (1961), each using a different set of instruments. The difficulties and pitfalls of sound analysis of the prelanguage child have been discussed by Lane and Sheppard (1965) who have contributed a computer-based technique to this line of investigation. Although the purely naturalistic approach to the problem is clearly unsatisfactory, instrumental analysis still leaves much to be desired. A warning is particularly pertinent with regard to the uncritical use of the commercially available sound spectrograph (the "sonagraph" manufactured by Kay electric). This instrument does not perform well when the fundamental frequency of the speaker's voice approaches 300 cps, which is the case in children under five years, particularly in the neonates. There are, nevertheless, certain generalizations that may be made safely from this kind of analysis.

Naturalistic observations as well as acoustic studies indicate that there are two distinct types of vocalization and that each has its own developmental history. The first type includes all sounds related to crying. It is present at birth (and potentially present even before the end of normal gestation). It undergoes modifications during childhood and then persists throughout life. These sounds as well as other sounds more immediately related to vegetative functions seem to be quite divorced from the developmental history of the second type of vocalization, namely all of those sounds which eventually merge into the acoustic productions of speech.

This second type of sound emerges only after about the sixth to eighth week. It begins with brief, little cooing sounds that fairly regularly follow the smiling response. It has the characteristics of a reflex that may be elicited by a specific stimulus, namely a nodding object resembling a face in the visual field of the baby (Spitz and Wolf, 1946), (Lenneberg, Rebelsky, and Nichols, 1965). Cooing sounds are obtained most easily and indiscriminately, however, between the tenth and thirteenth week; after this age, the visual and social stimuli become more and more differentiated. Soon it is necessary that the face be a familiar one in order to elicit smiling and cooing.

The spectrograms of crying noises illustrate the absence of any articulation, apart from opening or closing the mouth. In essence, the infant simply blows his horn without operating the keys. What little modulation is present, is achieved primarily by laryngeal changes and variations in subglottal pressure. The control of voicing mechanisms is not yet well-developed in the two-week old, causing the fundamental frequency to waver irregularly over periods of 20 to 50 msec. This creates the variation in the density of the vertical stria, seen in Fig. 7.1.

The cooing sounds that begin to appear toward the end of the second month are acoustically fairly distinct from crying sounds. Their duration is characteristically about half a second, and energy is distributed over the frequency spectrum in a way that soon reminds us of vowel formants. This impression is reinforced because cooing contrasts with crying in that it shows resonance modulation almost at once in addition to fundamental frequency modulation. In other words, during cooing some articulatory organs are moving (mostly tongue), whereas during crying they tend to be held relatively still.

Although cooing sounds are "vowel-like," we must guard against describing them in terms of specific speech sounds of English, for example. They are neither acoustically, nor motorically, nor functionally *speech sounds*. For instance, their acoustic onset differs from the more common vocalic onset in Germanic languages by having either no glottal stop at the beginning or an overaspirated glottal stop such as never occurs in standard English. Early vocalizations seem to be different motorically from adult speech sounds, because the articulating organs move somewhat erratically and discoordinately.

By about six months the cooing sounds become more differentiated into vocalic and consonantal components. New articulatory modulations appear.

There are varying degrees of sound attenuation; they still occur

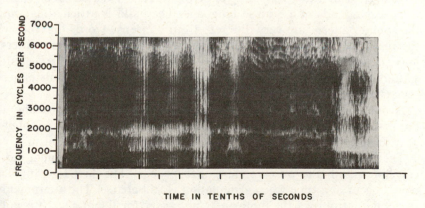

FIG. 7.1. Spectrogram of a two-week-old boy crying vigorously.

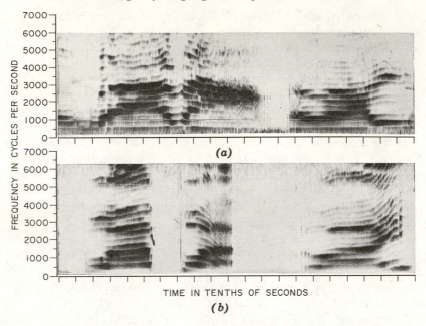

FIG. 7.2. (*a*) Spectrogram of a three-months-old boy cooing; (*b*) mother imitating her child after listening many times to a tape-loop on which the baby's noises are recorded.

somewhat randomly. This produces spectrographic patterns that show a general configuration not unlike that of connected speech; but it is important to stress once more that the analysis of these sounds makes it quite clear that they may not yet be regarded as isolated occurrences of speech sounds of a natural language. The child is articulating, but the sound patterns are very different from nonsense words that follow the phonological rules of English. Figure 7.2 demonstrates the differences between the sound productions of the prelanguage child and adult sound production. A mother who is imitating the cooing sounds of her own child makes very different noises from her baby.

Acoustic analysis of most vocalizations (except crying) throughout the first year continues to show evidence of poorly coordinated interplay among respiratory, laryngeal, and oropharyngeal mechanisms.

The articulatory signs of immaturity are, interestingly enough, not correlated with the onset of language proper. The first identifiable words occur at a time when articulation is still coarse. The attainment of good control over the motor acts necessary for fluent speech is not the milestone at which language has its first beginnings.

III. EVOLVEMENT OF LANGUAGE IN THE HEALTHY CHILD

(1) *Phonology*

The first feature of natural language to be discernible in a child's babbling is contour of intonation. Short sound sequences are produced that may have neither any determinable meaning nor definable phoneme structure, but they can be proffered with recognizable intonation such as occurs in questions, exclamations, or affirmations. The linguistic development of utterances does not seem to begin by a composition of individual, independently movable items but as a whole tonal pattern. With further development, this whole becomes differentiated into component parts; primitive phonemes appear which consist of very large classes of sounds that contrast with each other. R. Jakobson (1942) was the first to point this out clearly.

Such development seems reasonable enough if we consider the mechanisms of sound-making in man. The vocal tract is an instrument in which a dozen or more (the number is somewhat arbitrary) different adjustments may be made. A given speech sound results from selecting just one set of adjustments. During the prelanguage stage, movements are made erratically, and thus the ever-changing quality of the sounds is like the flux of patterns in a kaleidoscope. Gradually the child gains control over the fine execution of these movements, apparently over the laryngeal adjustments first, although there seems to be considerable individual variation in the order of these developmental events.

Perceptually, the child reacts also to whole patterns rather than to small segments, and so the intonation pattern of a sentence is the more immediate input rather than individual phonemes. Order is introduced into the uncontrolled variation of sound-producing movements by a succession of refinements in skills in making various adjustments and combinations of adjustments. The mass of random sounds begin to be lined up into some fundamental classes that contrast with one another in terms of articulatory mechanisms, roughly corresponding to some of the distinctive features described by Jakobson, Fant and Halle (1963). If the baby has control over glottal and labial adjustments, he might go through a stage of four primitive phonemes as illustrated in Table 7.1.

There is little regularity from child to child in the order of emergence of specific functional phoneme-units. The example of Table 7.1 is quite academic; in fact, it is doubtful whether the distinction between voiced and unvoiced labials is actually ever made at the first stage. The two

TABLE 7.1. *Example of a Primitive Phoneme Repertoire*

	Voice	
	Present	Absent
Lips moved rhythmically	/b/-type sounds	/p/-type sounds
Lips held steady	Vowel sounds	—

cells to the right may, at first, be merged or, conversely, some tongue movements may add a third dimension right from the beginning of the development of language-like phonology. The important point is that the first words are not composed of acoustically invariant speech sounds. Instead there are equivalence classes of sounds, and each class functions as a primitive phoneme. The actual sound that is uttered at a specific instant is merely one of many possible sounds out of its given class.

The structure of contrasting sound-classes becomes more and more complex, and the differentiation takes place along articulatory dimensions until the complete distinctive feature matrix is established. Although it is true that the development is one of gradual phoneme-differentiation, it does not follow that the child *only* learns the distinctions that are phonemic in the language surrounding him. There are many phonetic niceties, styles, or mannerisms that are also acquired and that are irrelevant to the phonemic structure. Interestingly enough, these are usually late developments and may still be in a process of formation at eight or ten years of age.

(2) *Primitive one-word utterances*

Between the twelfth and eighteenth months the toddler is heard to utter unmistakable single words. There is evidence that at first these words serve quite a different function from that of mature speech. The difference is on all levels: phonological, syntactic, and semantic. The acoustic shape is merely a crude replica of the adult word, and it is only by means of our capacity to see pattern similarities that we can recognize the child's word. This is common enough knowledge. But perhaps it has not been stressed sufficiently that it is not merely the adult who must be able to equate the child's utterance to an English word; the child must have similar skills in pattern recognition and equation.

For almost a whole year children are satisfied with general pattern similarity and dispense, so to speak, with segment by segment phonetic identity. Surely this has to do with their initial clumsiness and thus with maturational factors.

If this were not so, we might expect that many children would choose a different strategy toward language acquisition, namely, first to perfect their phonetic skills and only when they can reproduce a word with phonetic perfection, go on with syntax and semantics. This is what parrots do and, in fact, it is the usual strategy of teachers who want to train nonspeaking children (the retarded or the deaf) or animals to speak. It is also the strategy that most adults adopt in learning or teaching a second language. Therefore, the infant's initial lack of concern for phonetic accuracy is by no means a trivial or logically necessary phenomenon. It points to a fundamental principle in language acquisition: what is acquired are patterns and structure, not constituent elements.

There are also dramatic deviations in the realm of semantics during the first stage of single words. This is true of reference as well as of meaning. At the beginning, a word such as *daddy* covers a different and wider range of objects than later. There is overgeneralization. However, at no time does the multitude of reference relationships and the multilevel overlap of synonymy, homonymy, metonymy or the names of particulars as against the names of generalities, of aspects, qualities or objects to which the language-learning child is exposed from the beginning cause a chaotic use of words. The reference classes of objects in the beginner's language are merely less differentiated than in adult language, but from the start there is something which we might call an "understandable logic" to the word-object relationship. It is as if the child did *in principle* the same as adults do, only on a more general level.

It has already been pointed out that meaning is intimately related to syntax, because the meaning of the sentence is never equivalent to an unordered summation of the reference of words contained in the sentence.

A short elaboration on a certain aspect of the grammatical structure of adult utterances is necessary here. Is it correct to say that the unit of discourse is the *sentence?* Two objections are often raised in this connection. First, in adult speech we frequently hear single words uttered; in what respect are these sentences? Second, the transcripts of conversations always show drastic infringements upon grammar; can we call these distortions "sentences?"

Take the first point. Someone may hold out an opened pack of cigarettes and ask, *"Smoke?"* or a person may answer the question

"Do you smoke?" by means of the one-word utterance *"Yes!"* or the question "Which one of these boys was seen to smoke?" by *"Johnnie!"* and so on. Countless other examples are possible. In every instance, we are clearly dealing with ellipsis. The single word utterances are only interpretable by virtue of the listener's ability to supplement the omitted parts of the sentence. The first instance is interpreted as the sentence, "Do you smoke?", the second as "I smoke" (or, "I do smoke; hence "Yes, I do smoke."); and the third as "Johnnie has been seen to smoke." There may, in some instances, be ambiguity because not enough context is given to enable the listener to place the single word into the intended sentence. But generally it is correct to say that the meaning of words is uninterpretable in social commerce, unless we have enough clues with which to construct a sentence for that word.

The second point is factually correct: utterances heard in colloquial English (or any language, for that matter) do not conform to what we know to be correct grammar. We must make here a distinction. There are indeed utterances that are totally "ungrammatical," but they are also uninterpretable—we do not know what the speaker was trying to say. On the other hand, much more often we do know what the speaker wanted to say even though his utterances are clearly ungrammatical. This may be because he omitted part of the sentence or because a sentence is begun as if it were to end in one way but is actually concluded by using the second half of a different type of construction. (Several variations of this are possible.) Our capacity to understand such semi-sentences can only be due to a facility to supplement the omitted part of incomplete sentences. Thus, the interpretation of semisentences is not simpler than the understanding of grammatical sentences but actually requires a special ability: to supplement the missing parts of a partially concealed pattern (analogous to pattern-completion in visual perception). If a sentence is remodeled under certain circumstances [Osgood (1957) cites the example, "Garlic I taste!"], this is not necessarily a sign that syntax may be abandoned at will but rather of the existence of possible rules of correspondence that do not ordinarily enter into the writing of normative grammars. The rule of correspondence in this case relates the form of the "Garlic" sentence to the form of such sentences as "I taste garlic!" The example cited is not necessarily an instance of agrammatism but merely that of an admissible rule. That the types of such rules are limited (or that the rules have a psychological reality) is seen in the fact that the words in this sentence cannot be permutated in *all* possible ways.

In the light of this discussion, how do we explain the onset of language development where it is a universal finding that children begin with one-word utterances? Does this mean that the observations on adult language are false? or that they are irrelevant? I do not believe that either is the case. To the contrary, if we assume that the child's first single word utterances are, in fact, very primitive, undifferentiated forms of sentences, and that these utterances actually incorporate the germs of grammar, a number of phenomena may be explained.

There is a period at which an infant may have a repertoire of up to 50 words including such items as *daddy, here, milk, up, baby,* etc. He will utter any one of these words in isolation and they may mean: Daddy, come here; Daddy went by-by; I want to be picked up; thanks, no milk; more milk, please; etc. But even though the child's memory is sufficient to know all of the 50 words, and even though he hears such phrases as *here is your milk, shall daddy take you by-by,* etc., he will neither join together any two words he knows nor can he be induced to do so upon request. This cannot be explained by assuming that he makes himself better understood this way, or that the reference of the words (that is, the association with the object) is still too narrow and fixed; or that he has no need for putting words together; or that he cannot vocalize for that long a period of time; or that this is due to poorly developed general memory. All of these assumptions are refutable by observations. Nor would any of these assumptions make it clear why the child suddenly and spontaneously *does* begin to join words into two-element phrases.

The assumption that the early single word utterances are primitive syntactic units—in a sense primitive sentences—finds support in the following considerations. Semantically, and in terms of communication, the single words seem to function in the same way that sentences come to function later on: they cover a complete proposition; for instance, they may stand for a statement such as, *Daddy is coming down the street.* Phonologically they may be operated upon by a given rule, much the way a whole string of symbols is operated upon later on; for example, one of a variety of intonation patterns influences the utterance— such as declarative, interrogative, or hortative pitch-contours. It is reasonable to assume that the formal processes that regulate the perception and production of sounds are essentially the same as those that enter into syntax and that the one-word stage is simply a transitional stage during which the rules are extended from the interaction of articulatory movements to the interaction of larger language units, namely morphemes and words, and that the eventual acquisition and mastery of grammar has its origin right at the beginning of language development; otherwise we would have to assume that some day the child "discovers" grammar and makes an effort to learn this phenomenon, which seems farfetched.

(3) *Theoretical Considerations*

(*a*) *Understanding-Speaking*. It is easier to construct a theory that explains why adults understand sentences the way they do, than a theory that explains why or how a given sequence of words is produced by a specific person at a specific time. This is not to say that understanding language is based on a separate mechanism from producing language. Both are based on the same apparatus of principles. But if we test an individual's understanding of sentences, we are more exclusively exploring this apparatus than when we survey the utterances that he produces. In order to say something at a certain occasion it takes more than a knowledge of the language. There must be certain motor capacities, memory, motivation, a specific train of thoughts, given social conditions and other factors.

It is easier to study general capacities for behavior than the specific forms that behavior will take at any one time, and it is easier to predict the capacity for understanding than the capacity for speaking, because there are fewer factors affecting the former than the latter. A similar point, but with further refinement, is made by Chomsky, Appendix A, under the headings of *competence* and *performance*.

The distinction made here is relevant to many types of behavioral studies. Suppose we wanted to make a psychobiological study of chess playing. For instance, we wanted to know, "What are the mental characteristics necessary for this game?" or, "Can a chimpanzee learn to play it?" The empirical questions that would be asked in this research are: can a given subject learn the various moves? Can he develop a strategy? Does he see the implications of his adversary's moves? and so on. We would want to know whether he can comprehend the game. If we had nothing but a catalogue of his moves without a report of what his opponent was doing (that is, how he understood his opponent's game), we should have an imperfect idea of his competence as a chess player.

That the understanding of language is more relevant to an estimation of language capacities may also be seen from the following: we can learn to understand a language without ability to speak it. This is true of primary language acquisition, as well as the acquisition of a second language. In these cases, the underlying principles of the language are acquired, but the development of the skills for production are lagging.

There is an interesting situation here which would be a paradox unless we were willing to make assumptions on the nature of the learner: as investigators of the nature of language, it is preferable to concentrate on understanding; the objects that are to be understood are sentences; the sentences that are actually heard are frequently "degraded specimens" from a grammatical point of view—they are semisentences at best; on the other hand, the understanding of semisentences is apparently more difficult than proper sentences. We first seem to learn the rules and principles underlying grammatically correct sentences, and only by virtue of having acquired these can we begin to understand semisentences. (This becomes particularly evident in the acquisition of a second language by an adult person; we understand correct sentences, for instance, uttered by a good lecturer or presented in print, long before we can understand a conversation which is heavily loaded with semisentences). The paradox is this: if the child's task is to abstract principles that generate correct sentences, but is presented indiscriminately with semi- and proper-sentences, how can the correct principles be established, and why or how does his understanding of sentences become fairly explainable in terms of a grammatical theory? The assumption that we have to be willing to make here concerns the cognitive machinery that we must suppose to be developing in the child.

If the most promising source-material for a theory on syntactic mechanisms is understanding, what data should we use to construct a theory on the development of syntax in children? Preferably, the child's *development of understanding.* His actual utterances may, in certain cases at least, be irrelevant to his development of syntactic mechanisms (for instance, in children with severe psychiatric disease who may not choose to speak, or who prefer to make animal noises, or in children whose noises cannot be understood). By and large it is true that young children can understand more than they can say.*

Children between 18 and 36 months seem to have a tendency to run constantly through their repertoire of capacities. This is also reflected in their verbal behavior in that during this period the gap between their understanding and speaking capacity normally remains fairly constant and predictable. This may be tested by asking them on the one hand to execute certain verbal commands or to point to pictures that are being described to them in more or less complex sentences, and on the other hand to require them to repeat accurately sentences that are given them.

Since a sentence contains so much detail we cannot repeat it cor-

* But Roger Brown (personal communication), in his extensive investigations of the first steps toward language acquisition, has found that this is not always and necessarily true. For example, there were instances in his sample in which plural inflections were used productively at a time when experiments on the child's semantic progress indicated that he did not yet know what this particular suffix signals. Similar observations were described by Fraser et al. (1963).

rectly upon a single presentation unless we can apply grammatical principles to it by means of which the mass of information can at once be recoded and thus processed in much simplified form (Mehler and Miller, 1964). The utterances of a child who is just beginning to speak (normally not much later than 30 months) may thus reflect the stages that his development of language capacities, particularly understanding, have traversed, even though one may actually have taken place some 2 months before the other. By about 30 months, however, production soon becomes as unreliable an indicator of language capacities as is the case in the adult. Unfortunately, no studies have yet been published that have undertaken systematic research on the development of grammatical understanding of the child at this age and older. Even the best studies have relied too heavily on production.

(b) *How Mature Speakers Understand Sentences.* Some insight into this problem is provided by asking ourselves why a sentence such as

They are boring students

has two meanings. Here the explanation is quite simple; we may choose to link the word *boring* to the word *are* as in Fig. 7.3*a,* or to the word *students,* as in Fig. 7.3*b.* (This is what is meant by "bracketing" in Chomsky's Appendix A). Each of the circles may be characterized by

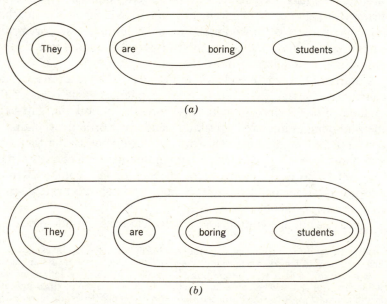

FIG. 7.3. Alternative ways of relating words.

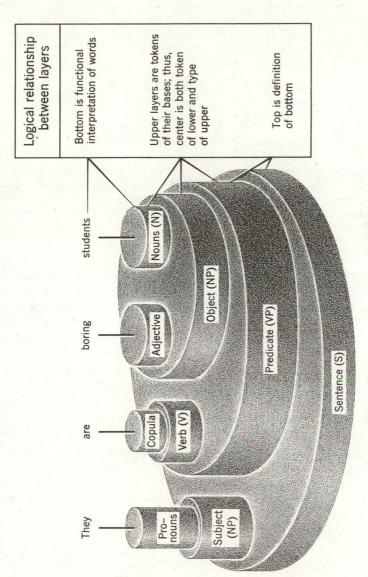

Logical relationship between layers

Bottom is functional interpretation of words

Upper layers are tokens of their bases; thus, center is both token of lower and type of upper

Top is definition of bottom

students

Nouns (N)

boring

Adjective

are

Copula

Verb (V)

They

Pro-nouns

Subject (NP)

Object (NP)

Predicate (VP)

Sentence (S)

FIG. 7.4. The labels of the circles of Fig. 7.3 (*b*).

TABLE 7.2. *Definitions of Labels of Fig. 7.4**

Sentence (s)	is a combination of words interpreted as containing a subject and a predicate. The former belongs to the syntactic category (*NP*) which stands for noun-phrase; the latter (*VP*) which stands for verb-phrase.
Subject (NP)	is a word or a combination of words interpreted as having an actor-function in the sentence. It may consist of a pronoun, or a noun, or a noun modified by some other element.
Predicate (VP)	is a word or a combination of words interpreted as saying something about the action of a sentence. It may consist of some verbal form (*V*) or a (*V*) and an object which has the same shape and syntactic function as any (*NP*) defined above.

* Oversimplification is unavoidable in these definitions. Consider this table merely as an example of one form of analysis.

an abstract name such as shown in Fig. 7.4. Instead of writing the names on cylinders or circles we might set up a list of definitions such as shown in Table 7.2. Similar information as that shown in Fig. 7.4 as a cylinder-diagram and in Table 7.2 as a list of definitions is represented by Chomsky in the form of a tree diagram which he calls phrase-marker. The grammatical principles illustrated in Figs. 7.3 and 7.4 may be diagrammed by phrase-markers as in Fig. 7.5.

A phrase-marker, then, is simply a graphic representation of how a speaker of English understands a sentence. Another way of saying the same thing is this: a person who knows a given language interprets a string of words by fitting a phrase-marker to it; he understands the sentence in terms of a phrase-marker. In the case of certain ambiguities, more than one phrase-marker (or interpretation) may be fitted, the selection of one or the other depending upon the context of the sentence. Notice that a phrase-marker, or tree diagram, is not a "recipe for how to make a sentence." It is an explanation of how a string of words is understood or structured in perception.

Although these considerations belong to simple high school grammar, certain implications that are of particular importance for a theory of language acquisition are frequently ignored. The ambiguity of the sentence quoted is in this case directly due to the fact that the word *boring* is once functioning as an inflected verb-form and once as an adjective, modifying the noun *students*. In Indo-European languages (and probably in most others as well), the words that are most critical for the conveyance of meaning of a sentence are not rigidly tagged as

either adjectives, *or* nouns, *or* verbs, but there is considerable freedom
of syntactic categorization. In English, most one-syllable nouns may
function as verbs; the gerund of most verbs may function as an adjective or noun; most nouns may enter compounds in which they come to
function as a modifier of another noun (for example, table-tennis); and
there are constructions in which nouns assume adverbial roles (for
example, Go Navy).

If we go back to Fig. 7.4 and move from level of abstraction to level
of abstraction, that is, from parts of speech to the constituents of the
sentence, we find similar freedom. A pronoun may appear in the subject
or in the object, and the same is true of adjectives and nouns; nor is
the left to right order constant (although it is regulated by rules) as
shown earlier in this chapter. The freedom becomes broader as the
syntactic categories become more comprehensive. In highly inflected
languages the inflectional morphemes may mark a word unmistakably
as belonging to one or the other syntactic category but the problem is
basically no different, because even there most word roots may appear
in all three syntactic categories (verb, adjective, noun), and the selection

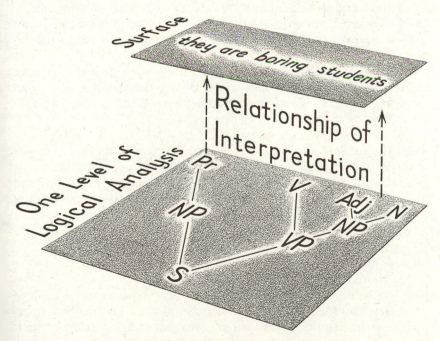

FIG. 7.5. Phrase-markers represent structural interpretations of strings of words.

and coordination of inflectional morphemes is possible only after the speaker has already assigned the root to a given category.

It is clear then that the major information-bearing words are not intrinsically stamped with respect to their syntactic function. Because of this and the various possibilities of arrangement of higher-order categories, it should be impossible to learn to understand the meaning of sentences (that is, to acquire the sentence structures to which a string may be fitted) by having no other knowledge than the symbol-referent relationship that holds between word and object (which in itself is so complicated that we cannot yet explain just how this is accomplished). The simple sequence or physical contiguity cannot give any clues as was shown in the introduction. With these considerations, we have also ruled out the possibility that a word acquires "verbness" or "noun-ness" by having appeared many times in the speaker's experience in a slot of a fixed sentence frame. (If I introduce a nonsense word *shlock,* it may be used by any speaker of English as a verb, adjective, or noun.) Thus there can be no doubt that it is the psychological reality of the phrase-marker that imposes meaning upon a sentence; it is the tool of grammatical analysis which turns words into syntactic categories, whereas the words, in their phonetic reality, could never constitute the elements for the building up of grammar. Words can only become syntactically functional in the presence of grammatical mechanisms, but the grammatical mechanisms cannot be built up through the simple accumulation of words.

Grammatical understanding cannot always be explained simply by looking at the immediately underlying phrase-markers. In most cases, there are much more intricate relationships. Chomsky has demonstrated this by the ambiguous phrase

the shooting of the hunters,

where the ambiguity cannot be explained through an option of analysis in terms of either of two possible, but different phrase-markers, but two semantic interpretations are possible in the presence of one and the same phrase-marker. There is, then, something even more abstract which differentiates the meanings of this phrase. One interpretation is related to the sentence

Hunters shoot,

whereas the other has a grammatical affinity to

Hunters are shot.

Each of these latter sentences has a distinct phrase-marker. Each of these sentences (that is, one that has either of these grammatical structures) may be cast into a different grammatical form, namely a gerundial phrase. More succinctly stated: the reason the first phrase "the shooting of the hunters," may be interpreted in either of two ways is that speakers of the language see grammatical relatedness to two semantically very different sentences. The fact that all speakers imme- diately see these relationships clearly indicates that this must be based on some underlying grammatical principle by which one grammatical structure, that is, one type of phrase-marker, may be related to another. We have illustrated a universal principle of grammatical knowledge or understanding: there must be lawful ways in which certain types of structure may be related to other types of structure. The grammatical

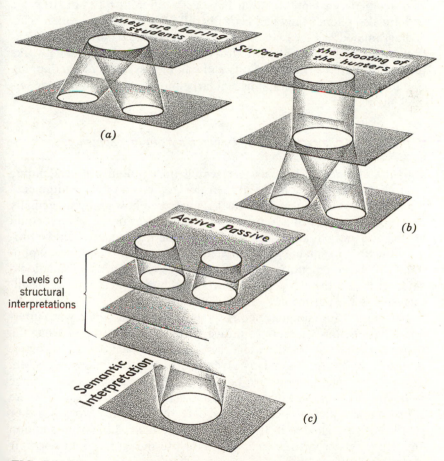

FIG. 7.6. Structural interpretations have varying levels of depth. Semantic inter- pretation is another level. (The diagram is not meant to convey any depth-ordering between semantic and structural interpretations.)

laws that control these relations have come to be called *transformations*.

Transformations are statements of grammatical as well as semantic and phonological connections.

In Fig. 7.6 are diagrammed varying levels of ambiguity. In Fig. 7.6a the ambiguity may be resolved by direct reference to immediate phrase-markers that may underly the sentence, whereas in Fig. 7.6b there is only one phrase-marker-interpretation possible, and therefore there is a still deeper level on which the ambiguity must be resolved.

Another prominent feature in the understanding of sentences is the ubiquitous possibility of seeing relationships and various types of affinities between sentences that have very different types of structure and are also phonetically and lexically different from one another. This is diagrammed in Fig. 7.6c, and an example is the passive transformation. Apparently, grammatical structures constitute intricate networks of transformational interrelations and complex systems of overlapping syntactic categories containing similarly functioning elements or sets of elements.

(4) *Structural Characteristics of Children's Primitive Sentences*

In the absence of systematic research on children's understanding of adult sentences, and hence of their developing "analytic equipment" for syntax, we can only make educated guesses at how grammar actually develops. The study of adult syntax makes it clear that discourse could not be understood, and that no interpretable utterances could be produced, without syntactic development *pari passu* with lexical and phonological development. Syntax is the calculus, so to speak, of functional categories, and the categories are arranged hierarchically from the all-inclusive to the particular.

The child whose language consists of nothing but single word utterances has obviously a more primitive syntactic understructure than the mature speaker. Syntactic categorization is the speaker's act of superimposing structure; he assigns given lexical items to parts of speech. The child's syntax is primitive because all of his words have the same syntactic function: they may be used as a self-sufficient utterance. There is just one undifferentiated syntactic category, and any word heard or produced is assigned to it. If we wish to introduce Chomskian notation already at this primitive stage, we might use the equation or *rewriting instruction* as he calls it,

$$S \rightarrow W$$

which reads in this grammar a sentence S is formed by the use of any word that belongs to the class *W,* and all of the child's words do belong to it.

Notice that it would make no sense to ask whether the child, at this stage, knows more adjectives than nouns or whether he has any verbs. Strictly speaking, *adjectives, nouns, verbs* are modes of functioning, given a complex syntax. But since the syntactic conditions for such functioning are not yet present, we cannot ask whether the infant has verbs. We do not ask whether a fertilized human egg thinks or what the social order among chicks is before they have hatched.

The joining of two words in a single utterance is a sign that the initial global category, labeled *W,* is splitting up into two functionally distinct categories. The following examples, collected from Braine (1963), Brown and Fraser (1963), Brown and Bellugi (1964), and Ervin (1964), show that the two words are not random concatenations but that a functional distinction is emerging.

"find it"	"here sock"	"more milk"
"fix it"	"here allgone"	"more nut"
"drink it"	"here is"	"more up"
etc.	etc.	etc.

A paradigm is clearly being formed.

One of the two words has a higher frequency of occurrence and seems to be a grammatical functor, whereas the other word appears to come from a large pool of lexical items with a great variety of meanings. Braine (1963) has called the functor words the *pivot* of these two-word sentences. The entire utterance seems to "turn around them."

It is not always easy to recognize the pivot of the two-word utterances, and we cannot always be sure how to characterize the sentences formally. For instance, "mommy sandwich," "baby highchair," "throw daddy," "pick glove" are all quite typical productions. At present, there are no reliable procedures to demonstrate that the two elements of these sentences belong to two different syntactic categories, although such an assumption is not unreasonable. We may have the primitive subject-predicate distinction.

The structure of these second-stage sentences might be characterized formally by diagrams such as these:

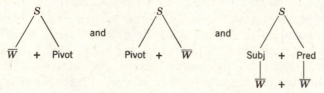

By the time he uses three-word sentences, further differentiations of categories have taken place. We now find utterances such as these:

"fix a Lassie"   "my horsie stuck"
"here two sock"   "poor Kitty there"
"more nice milk"   "that little one"

At this stage, many types of utterances are heard, and it becomes increasingly difficult to describe the child's syntactic skills by an exhaustive catalogue of phrase-markers. Instead we endeavor to discover the principles by which these structures are recognized and produced.

The last examples cited illustrate, however, the progressive differentiation of syntactic categories. The structure of these sentences may be characterized by postulating a splitting of the earlier category W into two, namely a modifier m and a noun N. A tree diagram might look like the following:

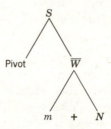

(5) *General Comments on the Genesis of Phrase-structure, Nested Dependencies, and Recursiveness*

So far we have described how sentences (primitive or mature) are understood, that is, what the relationships are between the component elements. We have studied phrase-structure. The diagram that characterizes any particular structure is the phrase-marker. The ontogenetic development of "phrase-structuring" is a differentiation process of grammatical categories. Notice that a similar differentiation process takes place in other aspects of language: in the child's semantic development, any motor vehicle may at first be labeled by the single term *car* until the referents are subdivided, perhaps into cars and trucks, with each word still being applied to a wider range than is customary. Gradually more and more distinct semantic groups emerge until the full vocabulary is established. In phonology, we have pointed out a similar procedure. Global sound-patterns become differentiated further and further until the phonemic inventory of a natural language is present.

This differentiation process is not confined to language. In fact, it is the hallmark of *all* development. In the visual sphere, we have already mentioned how the three-months old tends to smile to a wide variety of facelike objects. Soon a painted mask is no longer reacted to in the same way as a human face. Psychologists speak here of discrimination procedures, which, in this context, is synonymous with visual differentiation. As this process advances, specific faces become differentiated into distinct visually perceived structures.

We also have parallels in motor development. The movement of the embryo of lower vertebrates consists of gross, undifferentiated movements involving the whole trunk (Carmichael, 1954). Gradually a global flexion may give way to undulation and parts of the body begin to gain some autonomy. Similarly, in the human neonate we see both arms move synchronously at first, whereas independent control comes only at a later stage of differentiation of motor coordination. Thus, the differentiation process is quite universal, and the building-up of phrase structuration by differentiation of categories may be seen as a natural consequence of maturation in the field of language.

The process of differentiation, seen during ontogeny, becomes a process of specification or elaboration in the mature speaker. The string

> That man thinks.

is a complete and mature sentence. We can specify or elaborate on the main elements of this sentence, a process which is formally similar to the differentiation process of categories during ontogeny. We may elaborate on *man* by saying

> That old man thinks.

This expansion comes about by "applying an elaboration principle." We may apply this principle as often as we wish. For instance, we may say

> That old old man thinks.

The repetitive application of the identical principle is called *recursiveness*. Obviously, the sentence may be expanded in many ways not only by reapplying the same principle just introduced, but also by applying other, similar but not identical principles of elaboration or specification. Thus we may produce a sentence

> That old, old, hoary man who is well known by all who were folk-music lovers as far back as the early twenties thinks he is the great Italian opera singer Caruso.

In this sentence, elements were being differentiated progressively and/ or repeatedly. As a consequence of these differentiations, the elements *man* and *thinks* have become physically separated although they continue to be related or dependent upon one another, and the same is true of other elements interposed between these two words, for instance, the words *known* and *lovers.* This phenomenon of splitting up elements by introducing other elements, which in turn may be split up, is called *nested dependencies.* Both recursiveness and nested dependencies are simply consequences of differentiation or specification.

Again there are parallels in vision, although we are dealing here with the receptive side (that is, with the understanding of structure). From tachistoscopic studies we know that it takes considerable time to "understand" a picture. The more complex the picture, the more time it takes. This can be explained by assuming that we take in only certain details or aspects at a time, say a 30 msec period; as our eyes move across the stimulus, further and further details are sent up for processing. In fact, the perception of figures may not be simply a piecing together of various fragments of the picture as a whole, but various aspects such as color, contours, contrasts, etc., take different amounts of time for perception and integration. These elements "mean nothing" in isolation. They are temporally integrated, and an interpretation is fitted to them, so to speak. This is not that there is a template stored for a specific figure, but a peculiar mode for processing the details must be presupposed. A picture that has many details is a good analogue to the complex sentence. The over-all schema is expanded and elaborated upon; as we keep gazing at the picture, there is further and further differentiation, without, however, interrupting the relational dependencies of the main structure or main elements.

We are discovering a basic process that is reflected in language as well as in many other aspects of behavior. It consists of first grasping a whole that is subsequently further differentiated, each of the specifics arriving at a different time and being subordinated to the whole by a process of temporal integration. In productive behavior a plan for the whole is differentiated into components, and the temporal integration results in ordering of movements (or thoughts). Organization of phrase-structure with the resulting phenomenon of recursiveness and nested dependencies appears as a "natural phenomenon" once we assume that a ubiquitous process is influencing a specific behavior. Nevertheless, the execution of this behavior seems to necessitate specific cognitive and thus biological adaptations.

(6) *General Comments on the Genesis of Transformations*

Transformations have come to play a major role in the interpretation of grammar. It may be well to outline the basic ideas and to show that

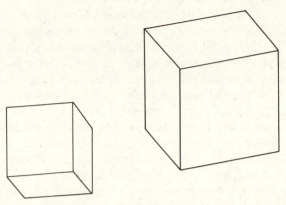

FIG. 7.7. Two physically different patterns, recognized as similar due to rules of geometrical transformations.

we are dealing also here with a very general phenomenon. Since a technical account is available in the Appendix, we may approach the problem in this chapter from a very different angle.

Let us disregard words and sentences for a moment and concentrate on visual phenomena again. In Fig. 7.7 we have two patterns that are physically very different from each other, but by the application of certain rules (in this case rules of perception and transformational rules of geometry coincide), we immediately see a marked similarity between them. Conversely, Fig. 7.8 constitutes a single graphic pattern, but as we stare at it, we begin to see it representing one pattern and then another. The ambiguity of the figure is due to an alternative application of either of two available rules (again perceptual and geometric) that we have stored within ourselves: one rule imposes one interpretation; the other imposes another interpretation.

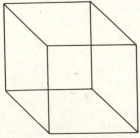

FIG. 7.8. The Necker cube illusion which is due to alternative transformations to either of the two patterns of Fig. 7.7.

Let us now look more generally at the phenomenon of similarity. All animals have the ability to group together stimulus configurations which may be physically totally different from each other; however, the animal makes an identical response to certain ones and thus treats them as if they were similar in some respect; we cannot escape the conclusion that for the animal, some similarity exists among such stimuli. Man is no different from other animals. From a wealth of ethological studies we know that species differ considerably in the specific perceptions of similarities and correspondences. For instance, a child needs no special training to see the similarity between a black-and-white photograph of a birthday cake and the physical object. Cats and dogs do not have the capacity to see that similarity or to relate this one type of stimulus configuration to this other one. It is a matter of empirical investigation to trace out the extent and the rules that allow a specific animal to relate any two stimulus configurations to each other.

So far, we do not know exactly how similarities are recognized between patterns which do not have any topological invariant qualities. For instance, why can any child recognize the similarities between the two patterns shown in Fig. 7.9? In Chapter Eight it is shown that semantic labeling has nothing to do with this. All we can say is that each of the patterns in Fig. 7.9 is a member of a large and abstract category and that any member of this category has a common denominator. Since it is not necessary that there be any one common physical attribute, we may conclude that the common denominator is an *abstract schema.* This type of reasoning is familiar from philosophy since ancient time. We can see similarities whenever we can transform two or more physically given patterns into the same, common abstract schema. In this terminology, similarities are due to transformations from the

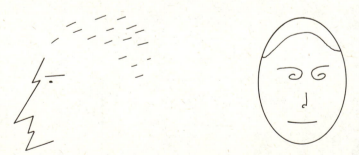

FIG. 7.9.   The patterns that are recognized as similar in some respects, although no point to point correspondence exists between them. (There is similarity only in deep, but none in surface structure.)

physically given (surface) to abstract (deep) schemata. Thus all similarities involve transformational processes. The similarities of Fig. 7.7 are special cases because we need not assume the transformational bridge through the abstract schema; instead we might argue that the similarity is due to the geometric correspondences. However, in most instances of similarities it is necessary to assume the transformational route via the abstract schema (because of the absence of tangible invariance), and therefore it is more economical to assume that the similarity of Fig. 7.7 is merely a special case of the general phenomenon of seeing similarities.

The necessity for assuming transformations from the physically given to abstract representations or schemata is best seen in discussions of perceived similarities. The need for such an assumption is a universal one, relevant to all fields of pattern recognition, and it is not confined to theories on human perception.

It is not surprising, therefore, that when we discuss the perception of sentences, it is also necessary that we have to assume the existence of specialized transformational capacities, for instance, to account for the perceived similarities among sentences:

$$\text{The dog chases the fox.} \begin{cases} \text{The fox is chased by the dog.} \\ \text{Why does the dog chase the fox?} \\ \text{The chasing of the dog.} \\ \text{etc.} \end{cases}$$

It is interesting to note that the similarity among these sentences is in some sense a special case much the way the similarity between the cubes of Fig. 7.7 were. The transformations involved in these cases have fairly easily discernible rules; they may be called concrete rules of correspondence (between one phrase-marked structure and another).

The necessity for assuming transformational procedures that mediate between the concretely given and the deep or abstract schemata goes much beyond the type of perceived similarities demonstrated in these sentences. At age four a child understands most types of sentences, and most of his utterances are interpretable in terms of syntactic structures. That is, he can recognize the structure of a given sentence which by itself is totally novel to him. If you say to him, "Did you know that the piffles fly to the curda every night?" he is liable to ask back, "Who is flying to the curda every night?" or "What are piffles and why do they fly?" or some such question, indicating his comprehension of the syntactic structure of your statement, even though the significance or meaning of the sentence is not clear to him. Thus, there is evidence that a child can recognize structural similarities in a string of words that compose a sentence even if he has never seen or heard the sentence before. Applying now the same argument used previously, we begin to see that structural similarity between two strings of words implies the transformation of the physically given sound-patterns into an abstract schema (such as a phrase-marker) or, in other words, grammatical structure is the name of that class of abstract schemata by means of which we recognize structural similarity between physically different sentences. The question of whether the string, *Colorless green ideas sleep furiously,* is or is not a sentence is decided upon by searching for a structural similarity between this string and classes of other strings which belong to the set of grammatical sentences. Thus we discover that Chomsky's sentence is similar to any one of the infinite set of sentences patterned after the structural schema

subject predicate

or more specifically

> subject (consisting of a noun modified by an adjective that is modified by an adverb) predicate (consisting of an intransitive verb modified by an adverb).

This is the abstract schema to which sentences such as

> Colorless green ideas sleep furiously.
> Very interesting movies run longer.
> Friendly little dogs bark loudly.
> etc.

are transformed in the course of perceiving and understanding them. We do not have to assume, however, that the child knows the grammar consciously. A tennis player or bicycle rider responds to and behaves in accordance with laws of physics without being able to formulate them or to work out consciously any of the computations that his nervous system is doing for him.

Reference to Chomsky's Appendix and the technical literature cited there will introduce the reader to the fine intricacies of the many types of transformational processes that must be assumed to underlie our power of structuration of verbal material. Not only are there various types of transformations and various levels of abstraction (depths, according to Chomsky's terminology) but an intricate net of perceived similarities between types of structures may be accounted for in terms of transformations, ambiguities may be resolved and explained, and subtle perceived differences between strings having similar surface structure are explicated by reference to transformational procedures.

We may once more ask, when and how these transformational operations come about? This is as difficult to answer as the question of when and how the perception of visual similarities comes about. This is the general type of phenomenon we are dealing with. It is true that both are empirical questions, but because they are inquiries into the modes of processing input data (which in the case of language happen to be identical with the mode of processing neural events underlying a specific output: discourse), they require verification techniques that are not well-developed as yet. This is an obstacle that will be overcome sooner or later.

As soon as we have appropriate techniques we will be able to answer these questions more specifically. However, we can never expect to find that the basis for perceiving similarities, or processing data transformationally, is a skill that is suddenly acquired. The perception of similarities must be a deeply ingrained process; it is the very nature of perceptual and even more generally, behavioral, organization. In Lashley's example, for instance, he states that most of us learn to write with our right hand. Nevertheless, it is possible to take a pencil into the left hand (or between the teeth), close our eyes, and write our name upside-down. It is possible to produce something quite legible at first try. Lashley argued that in this case, where entirely different sets of muscles in a different part of the body are being activated and the direction of movements is opposite to the one we are used to, we must assume the existence of a central (*abstract*) schema for a motor pattern by means of which we are capable of transferring the skill from right to left (or to the muscles that guide the head movements). Thus the peripheral motor patterns are transformed into a schema, and the schema again is applied to different peripheral structures; the two motor patterns are related *transformationally.*

The ontogenetic history of transformational development is also one of gradual differentiation and elaboration. The essence of transformations must go back to neonate days and may well be discernible at even more immature stages. Gradually, various types of transformations emerge—those that organize visual input, those that organize motor output, and, eventually, those that organize verbal input and output. The perception of specific types of similarities may presuppose a given degree of organization and so emerge only at a later stage and as a clear-cut milestone of development. Certain types of grammatical transformations may be beyond the language-learner's capacity; he does not understand the sentence; he cannot organize the material, nor can he produce any utterance containing specific transformational relationships between the component parts. But apart from this gradual differentiation of various transformational relationships, it can hardly be expected that transformation as a general type of process for organization is "suddenly learned."

If phrase-structure and transformations are simply special applications of general modes of organization, modes that are common to the organization of the behavior of all higher animals, why is language species-specific? There is only one possible answer. In order to achieve such special adaptation, cognitive processes must be highly adapted biologically. The slightest alterations in the peculiarities of data-acceptance, data-storage, and temporal integration apparently interferes with the proper reception and production of the peculiar patterns called sentences.

(7) *The Development of Some Specific Syntactic Mechanisms*

(*a*) *Questions and Negations.* In English, the construction of these forms is built around the auxiliary verb, a peculiarity of our language that introduces a certain amount of complexity, comparable in degree to the intricate system of inflections encountered in the so-called polysynthetic languages. For a technical treatment of these constructions in English see Katz and Postal (1964), Klima (1964), Chomsky (1965). Although the growing child hears correct sentences of this type in abundance, he will, at first, produce utterances such as the following:

> No Mommy eat
> No a boy bad
> I ride train?
> What cowboy doing?
> Where my milk go?   (Bellugi, 1966)

Even when he is asked to repeat a correctly formed sentence such as "Dogs don't like it!" or "Are you coming?" or "Where did he go?" the child will repeat "Dog no like it (no dog like it)," "You coming?" or "Where he go?" This cannot be attributed to a general inability to produce utterances of no more than four words. Even longer utterances occur spontaneously and the uncommon, primitive forms also occur when the model sentence has only three words: "Are you coming?" Bellugi (1966) has carried out the most sophisticated and careful analysis of the development of questions. Her findings may be summarized as follows: at first a string of words may turn into a question by casting it into a specific intonation pattern (a gradual rise in pitch), and negatives are simply expressed by prefixing a *no* to the string. Bellugi found that at this time the child gives no evidence of understanding the construction of certain types of questions. At a second stage, it becomes apparent that such complex constructions are understood (the child begins to give proper answers to respective questions), but in the child's own productions the only interrogative markers are still either a rise in intonation (for questions that demand a yes/no answer) or the initial occurrence of a question word (what, where, how, etc.). The third stage, occurring some ten months after the child has begun to form two-word utterances, is characterized by a further change: auxiliary verbs become functional and at the same time well-formed questions and negative sentences make their appearance. In one of Bellugi's subjects, the third stage was foreshadowed by the introduction of a stereotyped 'preverb' "Do-you-want," which was simply placed before the common type of utterance, forming such strings as

> Do you want me get it?
> Do (you) want he walk like this?

The most impressive aspect of these investigations was that all three children followed by Bellugi and Roger Brown's group * acquired the auxiliary system relatively late in their language development. When it was finally acquired, it was soon applied to most sentences in which it was appropriate, quickly superseding the more primitive constructions. Furthermore, Bellugi noted that at the beginning of the third stage there seemed to be a limited number of transformational operations that the child could perform on a single given string. Thus, if a negative plus a question was to be compounded in a single utterance, only one *or* the other aspect was well-formed. Thus, one of the children asked properly, "Can't it be a bigger truck?" but failed to make the proper inversion in the question, "Why the kitty can't stand up?"

(*b*) *Inflectional endings.* In school grammar the study of inflection is called *morphology* and is treated separately from syntax, which is thought to be primarily the study of word order. However, modern theory of grammar has made it clear that there is no essential difference among the so-called morphological and syntactic phenomena. Good observations have been made on the various steps toward normalization of inflectional endings which deserve a quick review.

The first occurrence of past tense is not signaled by a verb plus the suffix –*ed* (or its phonetic correlates) but various past-tense forms of the so-called strong verbs (or irregular verbs), particularly *went, was,* and *were,* but also an occasional *took, gave,* etc. At a later stage the past tense morpheme /ed/ appears but now is generalized also to those forms where it does not occur in the adult grammar; this may now result in forms such as *goed,* as well as *wented, gived, gaved,* etc. Such

* Including C. Frazer, J. Berko-Gleason, D. McNeill, and D. Slobin.

errors persist for a very long time and may often extend into the first grades of school. Deviations of this kind are most informative. Apparently, *pastness* is first learned as a semantic phenomenon, and it is most saliently labeled in the case of the linguistically ancient suppletive forms in which the word for the past is phonetically totally different from the present. Once the semantic past is linked to the *-ed* form, a rule is generated and then applied universally. This process of overgeneralization was studied experimentally by Berko (1958) who induced children of four years and older to change spontaneously nonsense words into plural, past tense, third person singular, and possessive forms. By this age the basic inflectional mechanisms appear to be very well-established, although some age-grading exists in the use of correct phonetic variants (allomorphs).

R. Brown and Bellugi (personal communication), Leopold (1953–1954), and several others have noted that it takes a relatively long time until the plural *s* is established, although this is usually accomplished by the third birthday. This is difficult to explain. Grammatical agreement within a sentence is accounted for by supposing that the elements in the subject of a sentence fall into two distinct subclasses—singular and plural. Chomsky has shown that grammatical agreement is possible if we suppose that there is an obligatory ordering of rules for the expansion of elements. In fact, all rules of generative grammar have an order of application. The child's difficulty with pluralization cannot be due simply to lack of attention or insufficient phonetic salience in the adult language, because pluralizations do occur for a long period of time, but they are not in agreement with other parts of the sentence.

IV. FURTHER ELUCIDATION OF LANGUAGE ACQUISITION THROUGH THE STUDY OF DEFECTIVE CHILDREN

The study of the biological basis of behavior in man is severely handicapped by the impossibility of doing crucial experiments that systematically interfere with physiology, growth of structure, and development. We must, therefore, take recourse to pathological deviations. These, of course, are never controlled situations and therefore introduce inaccuracies, but since we have nothing more exact to study in its place, the "experimental" shortcomings must be taken into account and accepted as inevitable. Simply to ignore or overlook these phenomena is inexcusable as it may result in theories that are flatly contradicted by pertinent facts in pathology.

It is often said that it is difficult enough to understand the development of behavior in the healthy individual and that we should, therefore, not complicate our task by trying to understand at the same time behavioral development in the presence of disease. Such a statement is based on the false assumption that disease results in more complicated behavior. However, we may consider it axiomatic that disease processes *do not usually add to the complexity of structure* of behavior. Disease may distort or modify some aspects of behavior; or it may block inhibitions or eliminate balancing components of the behavioral structure, throwing development or performance into disequilibrium, such that one component becomes much more prominent than another; or it may eliminate certain superstructures, thus bringing more primitive layers of behavior into prominence. But disease will not ordinarily produce behavior that goes beyond the level of complexity which is the norm. It might often be dangerous to study merely one disease process and then make generalizations based on this one type of pathology. However, if we view a given behavior pattern in the light of a whole spectrum of pathological modifications, we may be able to attain some insight into aspects of that behavior not ordinarily seen.

(1) *Language Acquisition in the Absence of Speech Production*

Most psychological theories on language acquisition assume that the *conditio sine qua non* for this development is the presence of an appropriate response system (most recently emphasized by Premack and Schwartz, 1966), namely random babbling, that may be shaped into words, phrases, and complete and mature utterances. It is a fundamental assumption here that responding is prior, in a sense, to understanding. However, there is a type of childhood abnormality that contradicts this assumption. These are children with an inborn disability to coordinate their muscles of the vocal tract sufficiently to produce intelligible speech. The disturbance is seen in varying degree ranging from mild impediment to congenital anarthria.

I have had an opportunity to study one such case in great detail over a five-year period. This was a child who was nine years old when seen last. He has never been able to babble or, with advancing age, to say anything at all, but there can be no question that he has complete understanding of English. Over the years much material was collected about this case including detailed medical prenatal and postnatal histories, neurological examinations, family and social histories, laboratory and psychological test results (repeated at various intervals), X-rays and electroencephalography, observations during free play in the child's home and in my office; records were kept during attempts to train him in speech (unsuccessfully), and a report is available on daily private tutoring throughout one summer. This was conducted as a demonstration project to teach this totally inarticulate child the elements of reading. The latter was relatively successful. * The technique used is of considerable interest; the child demonstrated his ability to read by learning to match pictures to words and simple sentences. Absence of articulation should not be automatically regarded as a hindrance to instructing inarticulate children in the three R's.

The technical details and background for this case are reported in Lenneberg (1962) and a discussion of the etiology of this condition may be found in Lenneberg (1964). Some details of the patient's communication behavior may be worth reporting here.

His crying and laughter had sounded normal since birth. He was able to make other noises, for instance, short, coughlike grunts, accompanying his pantomimed communications. While playing alone, he would readily make noises that sounded somewhat like Swiss yodeling (though he had never had any experience with these sounds) and which do not resemble any kind of vocalization heard among normal American children. When I first saw him, he appeared to have some difficulty in bringing his voicing mechanism under voluntary control. For instance, he was unable to make the pointer of the VU meter in an Ampex tape recorder jump by emitting grunts into a microphone even though he was fully aware of the logical connection between sound and deflection of the pointer and was fascinated by it. He would hold on to the microphone and move his head and lips toward it as if to prompt himself for the action; after a few futile attempts and with signs of rising frustration, he would, in desperation, gesture to the examiner's mouth, inviting him to make the needle jump, or else simply resort to clapping his hands and accomplish his end this way. With advancing age he learned to control his vocal apparatus to a greater extent. At the time he was last seen, he could repeat—with a considerable show of strain— a few words, but the words were barely intelligible and were never produced without support from the speech correctionist or the mother. They had to say the words simultaneously with him.

Some of the spontaneous sounds emitted by the patient at four years were analyzed spectrographically. The spectrograms are grossly abnormal for a child of this age and resemble those of a neonate in a number of respects, such as the unsteadiness in the formant pattern, the intermittent bursts of nonharmonic overtones, and the almost

---

* Carried out in cooperation with the Harvard School of Education; special thanks are due to Dr. Helen Popp and Mr. Joel Weinberg.

random change in resonance distribution over the spectrum (Lenneberg, 1962). The spectrograms may be interpreted either as grossly immature or as evidence of a fixed central nervous system abnormality implicating the basic mechanisms for speech synergism.

From the patient's first visit to the clinic it had been obvious that he had a normal and adequate understanding of spoken language. He has been seen more than twenty times since then, and his full comprehension has been confirmed by neurologists, psychologists, speech therapists, medical residents, and teachers. A number of tape recordings have been made of interviews, including a visit to the patient's home. Most of the examinations were done without the presence of his mother. At one time, a short series of instructions were tape recorded and transmitted to the patient through earphones. He followed the instructions without being able to see the examiner.

At the age of eight his capacity to comprehend was fully documented in a 16-millimeter sound film which is publicly available.* The film was not rehearsed and the interviewer had been known to the patient by sight only. The demonstration includes the following items: ability to chew, swallow, and suck; sounds emitted while playing at age four; tape recordings of mother's "conversation" with subject, recorded during a home visit; following commands and answering questions by nodding; a short story is told followed by questions on it which are couched in complex grammatical constructions.

It is tempting to explain the patient's responses to verbal instructions by extralinguistic means. Perhaps he is merely responding to visual cues given by the examiner and has, in fact, not learned to understand English! Could children with his type of abnormality develop perceptual skills such as were observed in von Osten's famous horse, *der kluge Hans,* who supposedly could stamp his hoof in response to questions posed to him in German, but who, upon close examination by the psychologist Pfungst, had merely learned to observe the questioner, picking up minute motor cues related to posture and respiratory patterns which signaled to him whether to stop or to continue to stamp his hoof? There is direct evidence against this hypothesis. The child described can react to tape-recorded instructions in the absence of any observer. Further, his responses do not consist merely of nodding but also of doing things which could not easily be conveyed by inadvertent motor cues. In the film which documents the case, it is clear that the child frequently follows commands without looking at the examiner.

* *The Acquisition of Language in a Speechless Child,* 16-millimeter sound film. Running time is 18 minutes, distributed by Psychological Cinema Register, Pennsylvania State University.

TABLE 7.3. *Number of Subject's Correct, Indecisive, and Incorrect Responses*

	Classification of Subject's Response						
	Correct		Indecisive		Incorrect		
Type of Response Required	No Cue Possible	Cue Possible or Certain	No Cue Possible	Cue Possible or Certain	No Cue Possible	Cue Possible or Certain	Total
Action	19	5	0	0	2	2	28
Yes-No nodding	2	11	0	3	0	1	17
Total	21	16	0	3	2	3	45

Only three times (out of the 45 responses) was there vacillation between correct and incorrect answers, and the last answer in each case is correct. On the other hand, there was no hesitation in the three instances when incorrect answers were given. There is no reason to assume that this child has a horse's ability to respond to visual cues instead of assuming that he has learned what every other child of his age has learned—to understand English. Table 7.3 summarizes the child's performance. It is the result of a panel of three judges who scrutinized the film, viewing each command and its execution individually with as many repetitions as were necessary in order to determine, by unanimous agreement, whether there was any likelihood of extralinguistic cuing.

Might it not be possible that this patient had no understanding of syntactic connections but merely responded to key words in the commands and questions? This possibility is extremely unlikely in the face of his understanding of such sentences as "Take the block and put it on the bottle." "Is it time to eat breakfast now?" "Was the black cat fed by the nice lady?"

Congenital anarthria, as reported here, is a rare condition, but the case is by no means unique, and the discrepancy between speech skills and the capacity for understanding may, indeed, be observed in every child. The theoretical importance of the extreme dissociation between perceptive and productive ability lies in the demonstration that the particular ability which we may properly call *"having knowledge of a language"* is not identical with *speaking*. Since knowledge of a language may be established in the absence of speaking skills, the former must be prior, and, in a sense, simpler than the latter. Speaking appears to require additional capacities, but these are accessory rather than criterial for language development.

(2) *Language Development in Mongoloid Children*

There are several different causes for mental retardation, and each disease has its typical manifestations. Nevertheless, the development of language, insofar as it occurs at all in these patients, follows some general laws of evolvement which may be traced among all of these conditions and which, indeed, are not different in nature from the unfolding of language in healthy children. Among the retarded the entire developmental process is merely slowed down or stretched out during childhood and is regularly arrested during the early teens. This affords the opportunity to study language development in slow motion, and the developmental arrest at puberty produces "frozen" primitive stages which are inalterable at that age by further training.

The study of children with mongolism offers certain advantages for research. The condition may be spotted at birth. Victims have a relatively good chance for reaching middle age. The condition is common. The patient population is relatively homogeneous, and a large number of patients are taken care of at home, and grow up in a normal social environment.

It is thought that mongoloid stigmata are manifestations of slowed or incomplete embryological development, apparently due to a chromosomal, intracellular disorder. In the process of postnatal maturation some but not all of the signs of immaturity gradually disappear. With increasing age, structure, physiology, and behavior tend toward the norm, but all developmental facets progress at markedly slowed rates. In some areas, development is arrested at a level corresponding to three or four-year-old children in the normal population, whereas in other areas development continues to stages comparable to adolescence.

A large proportion of mongoloids pass their motor milestones with only mild delay, and menarche and secondary sexual characteristics appear in the midteens. Yet these individuals may never learn to make any social discriminations, write more than a few words, or to change money. The order in which developmental tasks are mastered is disarranged by differential slowing; those tasks which depend on common sense seem to suffer most.

Lenneberg, Nichols, and Rosenberger (1964) studied, over a three-year period, sixty-one mongoloid children who were all raised by their

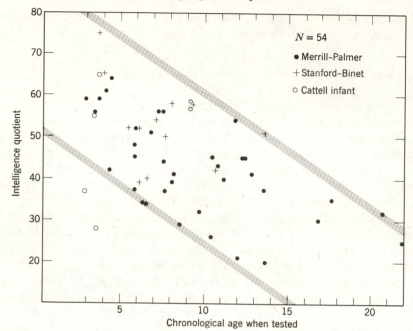

FIG. 7.10. Relationship between chronological age and IQ in 54 mongoloid children.

own parents and were living at home. The children were examined periodically, the frequency of the visits differing in accordance with the patient's stage of development. Data consisted of medical history, neurological examination, psychological testing, tape recording of spontaneous utterances made while playing, performance on an articulation test and a sentence-repetition test; and assessments of vocabulary, understanding of commands, and nature of vocalization.

An interesting question concerns the role of intelligence in the acquisition of language. Is mastery of this, in a sense, highly abstract behavior dependent upon measurable intelligence? The problem is complicated (1) by the definition of intelligence and (2) by the changing intelligence quotients with chronological age among the feeble-minded. An individual whose cognitive status remains constant on a level comparable to that of the normal three-year-old appears to have a steadily falling IQ throughout childhood due to the peculiar way in which this figure is computed. The situation is well-illustrated in the scattergram of Fig. 7.10. (Compare also Zeaman and House, 1962.) The study of the mongoloid population, as well as that of additional cases of mental retardation, indicates that there is a certain "IQ threshold value" that varies with age and that must be attained for language to be acquired. Individuals below this threshold have varying degrees of language primitivity, as illustrated in Fig. 4.3 (Chapter Four). It is noteworthy that this threshold is relatively low. If we take a population whose IQ is at or just above threshold, which is the case of mongoloids, intelligence figures correlate quite poorly with language development. Only if we confine our observations to the low grades of feeblemindedness can a relationship between intelligence and language learning be established.

Among the mongoloids, whose prognosis for mental development is not the worst, chronological age is a much better predictor for language development than computed IQ's.

The relationship between physical maturation and language development has been treated in Chapter Four. Relevant to the same topic is Table 7.4.

TABLE 7.4. *Relationship Between Stages of Language Development and Various Aspects of Motor Skill* *

	Language Development		
	Mostly Babble	Language Developing	Total
Motor skill			
Walk and run	14	39	53
Toddle or less	7	1	8
Total	21	40	61
	$\chi^2 = 8.94$	$P < 0.01$	
Dress self	4	27	31
Need help dressing	17	13	30
Total	21	40	61
	$\chi^2 = 12.93$	$P < 0.001$	
Feed self well	11	35	46
Feed self poorly	10	5	15
Total	21	40	61
	$\chi^2 = 7.36$	$P < 0.01$	
Are right-handed	6	23	29
Are left-handed	3	3	6
Are ambidextrous	3	3	6
Have no determined handedness	9	11	20
Total	21	40	61

* Entries are number of subjects. Yate's correction was used.

TABLE 7.5. *Correlation Matrix of Language Variables**

	Extent of Naming	Size of Vocabulary	Quality of Under standing	Articulation	Stage of Language Development
Extent of naming	–	0.94	0.92	0.60	0.95
Size of vocabulary		–	0.94	0.23	0.95
Quality of under-standing			–	0.30	0.95
Articulation				–	0.41
Stage of language development					–

* Entries are tetrachoric coefficients of correlation based on two-by-two charts such as shown in Tables 7.6 and 7.7; for levels of significance compare the chi-square values in the tables.

(The criteria for "language developing" was the predominance of words and phrases in all utterances and absence or at most a modicum of random babbling.) The relationship between development of gait and of language appears to be roughly similar to that of normal children; there is greater likelihood for language acquisition after gait is established than before. The development of hand preference is particularly interesting. Right-handedness emerges at the time that language unfolds, even though this occurs at a considerably later time than in normal children.

Mongoloid children are known for their simple but affectionate and pleasant personalities. They are eager to please those surrounding them and, of course, are more dependent on parental care than the ordinary child. They have a tendency toward clowning, and they love to imitate. (Such generalizations are possible because they are remarkably alike in their disposition!) Because of their retardation both their state of dependency and their babbling phase are protracted often years beyond the normal duration of these periods. Considering these data, we may well wonder how the development of language differs in these children from that of the rest of the population. If dependence upon adults, extensive babbling, and propensity for imitation were sufficient factors for language development, these children should develop better language than others. Naturally, their mentation must be deemed insufficient for rapid language progress. On the other hand, some *do* eventually develop all the essentials of language, and, in these cases, we can hardly suppose that they eventually improve their mentation. Once more we are brought to believe that there is an immanent schedule of evolvement in which apparently one set of events sets the stage for a subsequent set, and so on. However, in the case of the mongoloids, where the entire developmental sequence deviates from the normal, where worried parents make often desperate efforts to teach their child to speak, where bodily imitation is frequently specifically rewarded by those tending to the child's needs, we might expect that the children differ among themselves and from other children in "their strategies" for language acquisition. Would it not be possible, theoretically, that one child first tried to perfect his articulation before trying to increase his vocabulary; another might always try to make sentences out of the ten words he knows; or still another might have all his needs taken care of by his family and therefore content himself with learning to understand language without making an effort to speak himself.

Our investigations have shown that this is not so. In all the patients

TABLE 7.6. *Contingencies Between Stages of Language Development and Naming, Vocabulary and Understanding**

	Language Development		
	Mostly Babble	Language Developing	Total
Naming			
Names everyone	1	36	37
Names few	20	4	24
Total	21	40	61
	$\chi^2 = 38.43$ $P < 0.001$		
Vocabulary			
More than 50 words	2	40	42
50 words or less	18	0	18
Total	20	40	60
	$\chi^2 = 47.23$ $P < 0.001$		
Understanding			
Good	5	39	44
Limited	16	1	17
Total	21	40	61
	$\chi^2 = 33.62$ $P < 0.001$		

* Entries are number of subjects. Yate's correction was used.

TABLE 7.7. *Relationship Between Articulation and Understanding, Vocabulary and Stage of Language Development**

	Articulation		
	50% or Less Comprehensible	More Than 50% Comprehensible	Total
Understanding			
Good	33	10	43
Limited	15	2	17
Total	48	12	60
		$\chi^2 = 0.42$ not significant	
Vocabulary			
More than 50 words	31	10	41
50 words or less	16	2	18
Total	47	12	59
		χ^2 0.67 not significant	
Language development			
Language developing	29	10	39
Mostly babble	19	2	21
Total	48	12	60
		χ^2 1.32 not significant	

* Entries are number of subjects. Yate's correction was used.

studied, the sequence of learning phases and the synchrony of emergence of different language aspects remained undisturbed by the disease. The correlation matrix of Table 7.5 shows that progress in one field of language learning is well correlated with progress in all other fields, except for articulation.

The variables of the matrix are all dichotomized and qualitative; the data for the correlations are shown in the six contingencies shown in Tables 7.6 and 7.7.

The simultaneous unfolding of language, "across the board," is of great importance for language theories. There is no *a priori* reason why a child who has stopped babbling and whose utterances are always attempts at saying words or phrases, should also have a vocabulary of 50 words or more (he might be content to say the same five words again and again; or he might still be babbling randomly at times while already in possession of some hundred different words); nor is it immediately obvious why the postbabbler should have adequate understanding of spoken commands (he might have learned to imitate like a parrot); or that he should have the same facility in naming people as in naming classes of objects. The one exception to the rule of simultaneous unfolding of language skills is the children's articulation. This lag is not due to structural abnormalities of fauces or tongue (see complete report, Lenneberg et al., 1964).

It is exactly the opposite of what we might expect from at least one theoretical point of view. If the development of speech were the consequence of the child's hearing, his own utterances, and noticing the similarities between his own and his parent's sounds, and if the pleasure in speaking derived from his ability to reproduce, for example, his mother's sounds, then his first "aim" should be to replicate as accurately as possible the mature sounds he hears. The mental defect should be no obstacle here, or perhaps even an advantage much the way talking birds say sentences without the benefit of a human mentality.

The poor articulation of the mongoloid child may actually be related to a lack of motivation. Usually these children *can* articulate better than they do, but apparently exact acoustic rendering of utterances is not important to them. The children in our mongoloid sample were given an articulation test consisting of simple words in which the most common phonemes of English were embedded in vocalic or consonantal surroundings for consonants and vowels respectively. The child was asked to repeat one word at a time. The performance of a selected sample of children ($N = 25$) on this articulation test was compared with their articulation of spontaneously produced words and phrases. The analysis was performed by two linguists.* In all cases studied, performance on the test was considerably better than during spontaneous speech, thus demonstrating that the child is organically capable of accurate articulation.

An expedient way for testing understanding is to have subjects repeat sentences. Most of us have attempted at one time or another to repeat something in a totally foreign language. In the absence of understanding, even the reproduction of a single word may be difficult, whereas short sentences are an impossibility.

Consider the following transcribed attempts at sentence repetition. This is a twelve-year-old mongoloid girl whose language development is comparable to that of a normal two-and-a-half year old.

---

* Jacqueline Wei Mintz and Peter Rosenbaum. Throughout the observation period the child wore a condenser microphone in a bib around his chest. Recording equipment was of high fidelity. The examination room was soundproofed.

Model Sentence	Mongoloid Child's Repetition
(1) Johnny is a good boy.	Johnny is good boy.
(2) Johnny is a good boy.	Johnny is a boy.
(3) He has two dogs.	He has two dogs.
(4) He takes them for a walk.	He take them to the walk.
(5) He takes them for a walk.	He takes them to a walk.
(6) Lassie does not like the water.	He no like the water.
(7) Lassie does not like the water.	Lassie doesn like water.
(8) Does Johnny want a cat?	Johnny wants a cat? (question marked by intonation pattern)
(9) "Pretend you are asking your mother" Does Johnny want a cat?	Johnny want to have a cat, mother?
(10) The cat is chased by the dog.	Chased by the dog.
(11) The cat is chased by the dog.	Cat chasing the dog.
(12) The dog is fed by Johhny.	Fed by Johnny.
(13) "Tell me, who is fed by Johnny?"	The dog.
(14) "Very good; now say: The dog is fed by Johnny.	Fed the dog by Johnny.

The first nine sentences seem to have been essentially understood, but in all sentences except three the repeated sentence is slightly different from the model sentence. The alterations in several instances are not grammatical English, so that the child could not have heard them before. This patient is still deficient in some of the more refined rules of English, but the basic sentence type is present. The "do-constructions" are understood but the rules do not function well enough yet to enable this patient to apply them to sentences. Consequently, sentences (6), (8), and (9) are changed back into grammatically simpler but incorrect forms. Sentence (7) is the only attempt, only partially successful, to use the "does-not-form." The passive construction in sentences (10) to (14) is not well understood, although question (13) is answered correctly. However, all attempts at repetition of the sentences are failures.

In sentences (10) and (12) repetition is attempted by apparently taking recourse to a different strategy. Instead of trying to understand the meaning of the sentence and to reproduce the sentence in its essentials, the meaning of the sentence is ignored entirely and repetition is attempted as in a rote memory task. When we are asked to repeat a string of random digits, we are only able to repeat the last ones, and the number of digits remembered is a function of memory span. When grammatical connections between words is not understood, the subject behaves as if a string of randomly concatenated words had been presented. This blind repetition may be called *parroting*.

In our study of language-understanding among the mongoloid, we were interested to know at what stage of development a child would take recourse to parroting. A child was said to be simply parroting if he only repeated the last word or words of the sentence spoken to him instead of picking out some functionally important words such as the subject-noun and the verb. We classified the responses of a selected group of children ($N = 25$) into: (1) correct repetitions of the original sentence; (2) sentences that are grammatically correct but different from the original; (3) recognizable sentences that are grammatically incorrect; (4) two-word phrases that are not parroting; and (5) parroting. This subsample of our patients was divided into five groups according to their grammatical ability. Figure 7.11 shows the result.

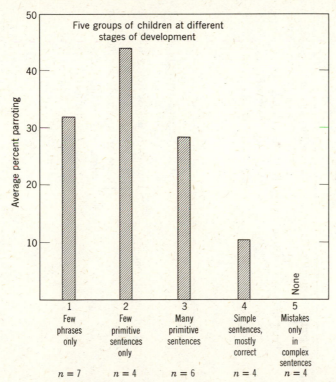

FIG. 7.11. Distribution of "parroting responses" with respect to stages of development in 25 mongoloid children.

TABLE 7.8 *Transformational Relations between Conjunctional Constructions and their Underlying Sentences*

Underlying Sentences	Perform the Following Operation	Resulting in:	
		Preliminary Form	Final Form
Peter likes small cookies	Add conjunction *and* to this sentence	Peter likes small cookies and	
Peter likes red lollipops	Delete those words of this sentence that are repetitions of the first one	- red lollipops	
	Add the preliminary forms		Peter likes small cookies and red lollipops.*
Peter wants one	Add the conjunctional phrase *and so*	Peter wants one and so	
Johnny wants one	Transform this sentence to its emphatic form	Johnny does want one	
	Delete those words of the second Preliminary form that are repetitions of the first preliminary form	Johnny does	
	Transpose the subject and what remains of the predicate	does Johnny	
	Add the last preliminary form to the first one		Peter wants one and so does Johnny.

*It has recently been shown that this type of sentence may be accounted for in simpler ways which further strengthens the point of structural differences between the two examples.

318

Parroting does not seem to be the way to begin language. This was also clearly brought out in a recent study by Ervin (1964). Parroting is resorted to when the grammar of the original sentence is simply not understood. It is comparable to a panic-response elicited by the pressure of the examiner to get the subject to "try his best."

The reality of grammatical structure is well-illustrated by the following two sentences taken from the sentence repetition test:

(1) Peter likes small cookies and red lollipops.
(2) Peter wants one, and so does Johnny.

These sentences have seven words each and all the words have a common occurrence in the discourse of children. Yet sentence (1) was found to be much easier for our subjects than sentence (2). Even though mistakes are often made in the repetition of sentence (1), the nature of the mistakes clearly shows that the child has understood the original sentence in its basic structure and semantic content. Following are two typical attempts at repeating this sentence:
"Peter like red cookies and red lollipops."
"Peter like cookies and he like lollipops."
When sentence (2) was attempted, three times as many parroting responses (for example, "Johnny", "So does Johnny") occurred than for sentence (1), and the mistakes showed a lack of insight into the grammatical structure and meaning of the sentence; examples are:
"Peter want—uh—Johnny."
"Peter does no want one too and so but Jimmy."

The best explanation for the difference in ease of repeating these two sentences may be found in an analysis of their grammatical structure.

Table 7.8 is a rough sketch (with a number of simplifications) of the grammatical structure of these sentences. It is obvious that they differ enormously in their degrees of complexity and this is clearly the cause of the children's difficulty with the second one. Familiarity or frequency of occurrence can hardly be used as explanatory factors because the children can repeat sentences they have never heard before, and which are therefore totally unfamiliar, as long as the underlying structure is clear to them. This grammatical explanation appears to be further corroborated by the types of mistakes made on sentence (2) by those children who are in possession of the basic elements of grammar (but with some "higher-order rules" still missing). For instance, one child, after a moment's reflection, repeated sentence (2) as "Johnny wants one and Peter wants one" which conforms verbatim to our analysis here.

When very young children (24 to about 30 months) are compared with the mongoloids in terms of their respective performance on the sentence repetition test, we are impressed with the similarity. Unfortunately, there is no reliable method available at present to quantify this impression, but the inaccuracies, mistakes, and occasional forays into parroting-strategies appear to be strikingly alike. Thus, the intellectual limitation does not produce bizarre language behavior; it merely results in arrest at primitive, but "normal," stages of development.

(3) *Language Acquisition in the Congenitally Deaf**

The last type of handicap to be considered in this chapter is congenital, profound deafness. The following observations apply only to peripheral nerve deafness in children who are otherwise well, particularly from a neuropsychiatric viewpoint.

Language development in these children is of great interest for a language theory, because it can be shown that despite this devastating handicap, it is entirely possible to develop good language skills (though, unfortunately, only a few achieve complete perfection). In order to appreciate fully the magnitude of this achievement, we must realize to what extent the deaf child is quantitatively and qualitatively deprived of language input.

In America it is not until the child is four or five that intensive language training is begun, and during the first year the training is merely preparatory, that is, readiness for the instruction in articulation, lip reading, and reading and writing. When instruction proper begins there is, in many schools, a decided unwillingness to put too much reliance on the graphic medium. Although words and sentences are written on the blackboard and the child himself also learns to write, the emphasis is usually on the production of sounds and lip reading. If communication between pupil and teacher fails, the child is often not allowed either to gesture or to make use of his newly acquired writing skills, and the teachers also hesitate to facilitate their communications by writing (except for specific classroom instruction) in order to foster what is known as an "oralist attitude" among their

---

* Following comments are based on several years of observation in schools for the deaf throughout the country. I would like to thank the principals and teachers for their cooperation, assistance, and hospitality, and to express my admiration for their devoted and patient efforts to help these children, so underpriviledged by nature. If the following remarks are critical (as they are meant to be), they are not intended to belittle the thought, experience, and good will that is the background of present-day education of the deaf. My remarks, despite their sketchiness, are offered here as a possible contribution—not a deprecation.

charges. Many schools also instruct the parents not to take recourse to writing for communication in the home, for the same reason, and we have had many a teacher of the deaf tell us that it is not desirable for deaf children to make reading for fun a hobby while they are still in school.

Thus there can be no doubt that the deaf come in contact with language at an age when other children have fully mastered this skill and when, perhaps, the most important formative period for language establishment is already on the decline; furthermore, their contact with language samples, even at this late age, is dramatically reduced in amount in comparison with the amount of language to which a hearing child is exposed; and finally, these children have to process visually what other children receive aurally. The latter point is of no small consequence because there are indications that the eye is slower in its temporal integration than the ear, and, therefore, even if perfection could be attained in lip reading (the most proficient lip readers cannot identify more than 40 to 50% of articulated phonemes (Eggermont, 1964), ordinary discourse would be so fast that only small parts could be followed adequately.

Language proficiency varies a great deal among pupils in the schools. This is primarily due to such factors as the profoundness of the handicap, its cause, the age at which hearing was lost, and the adaptability of the child to the school environment. Below is a sample of quite average language proficiency of a congenitally deaf boy, aged sixteen (eleven years of schooling).

A Boy Liked a Cigar*

A boy was named Robert Kennedy. His age was twelve years old.

When his father went shopping, he had a nothing to do except to eat something. He remembered his father told him promised to his father not to eat somethings. Later he had a big idea. He went to library room. He walked over his father's new sofa. The sofa was dirty. He opened the box of cigar. He picked one. And he think and remember his father told him to do. He putted back it. He leave library room. And one of tiny devil told him disobey his father. He said, "OKay!" He went to back to the library room. He got it. He lighted it. He smoked for one hour. Later his father came to home. He slept and felt very sick. His father called him. But he did not called. His father thought he ran away. He ran and looked many rooms. The last room he found. He brother him. His father told him what happen to you. He said, "Nothing!" His father smelled smoke.

* This is a written composition about a picture shown to the class.

His father asked him, "Did you smoked my cigar?" He said, "Yes".
His father scold him. And a tiny angle was fight with a tiny devil.

It is clear that this boy has achieved an amazing amount of competence in English, considering the obstacles. Nevertheless, there are many mistakes of grammar and style. In the course of my work with the deaf, I have received a sizeable collection of letters from young deaf parents and also older individuals. Among all of these correspondents, there are some individuals who have been profoundly deaf all their lives but whose letters are perfect in grammar. The vast majority, however, make grammatical mistakes of varying degree of severity, and about half have the proficiency exemplified in the previous sample.

I am inclined to believe that the failures in proficiency are primarily due to shortcomings in instruction and training, and not due to inherent learning incapacities of the deaf. My clinical experience with congenital anarthria suggests that language competence in the deaf could be vastly improved if they were given much more graphically presented language material and at a much earlier age. It is my impression that their language difficulties (in writing) are due to an acute input deficiency—they have just not been given enough examples (raw data to foster their own language synthesis) during the critical early years. This impression is corroborated by those deaf adults who write good grammar, because they are invariably the most avid readers, and have been so for many years. Although peripheral deafness is injurious to oral speech performance, there is no reason why the basic capacity to acquire knowledge of language ought to be implicated as well. The argument that early acquaintance with and recourse to reading and writing is detrimental to these children's skills in oral communication and lip reading lacks evidence. In fact, we might assume that if these children had better knowledge of language, both of these other skills might be facilitated considerably.

Present-day language instruction of deaf children is of theoretical interest for yet another reason. In contrast to the hearing child, who is simply surrounded by a sea of sentences, well-formed and poorly formed and who builds up his sentence-making skill without knowing how, the deaf child is usually immediately introduced to theoretical grammar. In the course of his first year of language instruction, he is told that he must speak in *sentences* and that a proper sentence is made up of *nouns* and *verbs,* that nouns must have *articles,* and so on. These theoretical terms are written on the blackboard and also appear in some of the books that are used in the lower grades. Thus we have a situation in which the children are on the one hand quantitatively deprived of a large body of examples, and on the other hand are immediately given a meta-language, a language about the language which they do not yet have. Their own spontaneity of putting out the type of primitive sentences which, as we have seen, are apparently the necessary developmental stage that must precede the complete unfolding of grammar in hearing children, is restricted by teachers who do not tolerate answers in "incomplete sentences." The child's flow of communication is constantly stopped by the teacher's instructions "to complete the sentence," which is accompanied by a theoretical discussion of how to do this ("verb is missing," "the article is not correct," etc.).

This mode of instruction raises an important question. Is it possible to instruct somebody how language works by giving him rules—particularly when he has little language as yet? The invariable emergence of written intelligible language (oral speech of at least half of the profoundly and congenitally deaf remains difficult to understand throughout their lives) is a testimony to man's enormous capacity to develop language competence even under conditions of severe deprivation.

Following are a few illustrations of language development under these circumstances: (each composition is the complete, written description of a picture).

Language sample of a child after one year of instruction:

A boy is stoling candy. He is on the chair. He is a light. He is a short. He ate candy. His mother nuaght. He is crying.

Sample of a child's language after two years of instruction:

The boy went to the school. We buy a Card Valentine her mother. the dog a dirty feet the rain because he was shoe dirty because she was saw the boy came home

Sample of a child's language after three years of instruction:

Edd and Brownie got mud on his house. He make a flower for his mother. He forget to closte the door. Outside is rain. He was dope because he was little boy know nothing about it. His mother will angry with him because he was careless boy. His mother didn't want to clean the house because she will tried of it. He will help dog get a bath because he take dog for a walk.

Sample of a child's language after five years of instruction:

One day he lived in England. His named Jim. He went to the television and put on there. He sat on the floor and watched television. Then he was quietly and he climbed up the chair. He was stolen many candy on the shelf and he ate it mote and more. The candy was gone. He was enough. He was ill. Then his mother saw him. What did you tell his mother? His mother know about him. She scolded him. Jim cried. His mother told him that he went to bed at 4 hours. Jim wanted going outdoors.

From these examples it is clear that the construction of proper sentences is not facilitated by telling a child how to do it. It must be admitted that no one knows how it *is* done. The new approach to grammatical theory, generative grammar, is no more useful in this respect than the grammars that were handed down to us from antiquity. In fact, the new grammars are, substantively, not so different from the old ones, except for greater accuracies, special attention to peculiarities in given grammars of natural languages, more rigorous formulations, and, in certain other ways, they constitute a more objective approach, as may be gathered from the Appendix and its bibliography. No grammar, old or new, furnishes us with a recipe of how to speak grammatically. There is no grammatical system available that could be used to help an essentially language-deficient person to put words together to form good sentences. So far, grammars merely specify the underlying structure of sentences and explain how sentences of different structure are related to each other.

It is true that the sentences of the deaf gradually improve as they advance in school. It is also true that this is due to instruction, but it is probably not so much due to *grammatical* instruction as to the child's increasing contact with language examples from which he begins to abstract structural commonalities that help him to synthesize his own sentences. He knows as little about how he does this as we who are capable of speaking or writing in grammatically correct (or at least *understandable*) sentences.

Because of examples such as those quoted here we are led to the conclusion that language instruction of the deaf would profit from (1) greater access to written material at an earlier age, (2) greater freedom in written expression, (3) greater acceptance (on the part of teachers and parents) of primitive language productions and grammatical deviations, and (4) a ban of grammatical meta-language until a basic proficiency in language is fully established.

V. SUMMARY AND CONCLUSION

The study of grammar in the adult and in the child leads to the following hypothesis. In the mechanisms of language we find a natural extension of very general principles of organization of behavior which are biologically adapted to a highly specific ethological function. With maturation, the neonate begins to organize the perceptually available stimuli surrounding him and also to organize the movements of his muscles. Sensory data become grouped into as yet undifferentiated, global classes of gross patterns, and these, subsequently, become differentiated into more specific patterns. Similarly, movements which at first involve the entire body become differentiated into finer motor patterns. Both the perceived patterns and the self-produced patterns of movements become organized or grouped in functional categories, and hierarchies of categories. Members of a particular category are functionally equivalent because they either elicit an identical response or they serve one and the same function within the over-all structure of a particular behavior pattern. It is these general principles of differentiation and categorization that appear in specialized form in verbal behavior. They influence the organization of perceived material as well as the organization of the motor output.

Thus the characteristics of phrase-structure (as described by phrase-markers) appear as the natural outcome of an application of the differentiation principle to the acoustic patterns, called language. Also, the transformational principle in language appears to be virtually identical with the cognitive principles that underly the ability to categorize both the patterns of the environment and the patterns produced by our own movements. Whenever grouping occurs in terms of a common denominator (in other words, categorization that is in some empirically determinable way natural to the categorizer, be it animal or man), an essentially "transformational" process is involved. This is most clearly seen where the constituents of a single category lack any common physical dimension and where the commonality is thus an abstracted pattern or structure. In these cases, the physically given, sensory "reality" is *transformed* into abstracted structure, and similarity between the two physically different patterns is established through the possibility of transforming the abstracted structures back to either of the physically given patterns. All perceptions of similarities and relations depend upon the organism's capacities for transformations; but this capacity is limited biologically. There are only certain ranges of transformations that a given species can handle. The range is always quite narrow and may be discovered by empirical investigations (just as sensory thresholds may be determined); but within the established limits there is still an infinity of possible transformations. Some such transformations may be possible but difficult for a given species to handle, and the animal may require much experience before it can make the transformation.

The transformations of grammar are biologically specialized transformations, applicable to acoustic patterns that have in man the function of communication. This type of transformational capacity is clearly biologically given, but the specific transformations as they occur in one or another language are just some of the infinitely possible ones.

A superficial survey of language development in defective children revealed the following points: an individual's *knowledge* of language, as determinable by testing his comprehension, may be established in the complete absence of capacities for language- or speech-specific *responses,* that is, the ability of the learner himself to speak. This emphasizes the importance of Chomsky's competence-performance distinction and makes those language theories doubtful that are primarily based upon a response-shaping hypothesis.

A comparison of language in retarded children with language development of normal children indicates that there is a "natural language-learning strategy" that cannot be altered by training programs. Language unfolds lawfully and in regular stages. Language progress in the retarded appears to be primarily controlled by their biological maturation and their development of organizational principles rather than intelligent insight. The pathologically lowered IQ of the retarded does not result in bizarre use of language but merely in "frozen" but normal primitive language stages.

A remarkable degree of language competence is achieved by the congenitally deaf, despite apparently overwhelming handicaps. Thus, language may still develop under very abnormal conditions. The specific teaching of grammatical rules (no matter whether they are old-fashioned ones or modern) does not appear to help the children substantially in their language development. There is no reason to doubt that their language proficiency would develop in the same manner as it develops in the hearing who are simply given a great number of grammatical (and often semigrammatical) sentences from which they abstract the structural principles by which they themselves begin then to form new sentences. Deaf children could hardly differ in the capacity for doing this from hearing children, provided they were given enough examples and are allowed to go through a natural order of grammatical development. We do not know how hearing children develop their ability to abstract structural principles, and we do not know how deaf children might do it. But this is no reason to try to instill language habits by means (teaching of grammatical rules) which have never been shown to be of any use for any other language-learning child.

REFERENCES

Bellugi, Ursula (1966), Development of Negative and Interrogative Structures in the Speech of Children, in T. Bever and W. Weksel (eds.), *Studies in Psycholinguistics.* Holt, Rinehart and Winston, New York (forthcoming).

Berko, J. (1958), The child's learning of English morphology, *Word* **14**:150–177.

Bosma, J. and Lind, J. (1962), Upper respiratory mechanisms of newborn infants, *Acta Paediat.* Suppl. **135**:32–44.

Braine, M. D. S. (1963), The ontogeny of English phrase structure: the first phase, *Language* **39**:1–13.

Brown, R. and Bellugi, U. (1964), Three processes in the child's acquisition of syntax, in E. Lenneberg (ed.), *New Directions in the Study of Language.* M.I.T. Press, Cambridge, Massachusetts.

Brown, R. and Fraser, C. (1963), The acquisition of syntax, in *Verbal Behavior and Learning,* C. N. Cofer and B. S. Musgrave (eds.), McGraw-Hill, New York.

Carmichael, L. (1954), *Handbook of Child Psychology* (2nd ed.), John Wiley and Sons, New York.

Chomsky, N. (1957), *Syntactic Structures,* Mouton and Co., The Hague.

Chomsky, N. (1965), *Aspects of the Theory of Syntax.* M.I.T. Press, Cambridge, Massachusetts.

Chomsky, N. and Miller, G. A. (1963), Introduction to the formal analysis of natural languages, in R. D. Luce, R. Bush, and E. Galanter (eds.), *Handbook of Mathematical Psychology,* Vol. II. John Wiley and Sons, New York.

Eggermont, J. P. M. (1964), *Taalverwerving bij een groep dove kinderen.* Wolters, Groningen.

Ervin, Susan M. (1964), Imitation and structural change in children's language, in E. Lenneberg (ed.), *New Directions in the Study of Language.* M.I.T. Press, Cambridge, Massachusetts.

Fisichelli, V. R., Karelitz, S., Eichbauer, J., and Rosenfeld, L. S. (1961), Volume-unit graphs: their production and applicability in studies of infants' cries, *J. Psychol.* **52**:423–427.

Fraser, C., Bellugi, Ursula, and Brown, R. (1963), Control of grammar in imitation, comprehension, and production. *J. verb. Learn. verb. Behav.* **2**:121–135.

Jakobson, R. (1942), Kindersprache, Aphasie und allgemeine Lautgesetze, *Uppsala Universitets Aarsskrift.*

Jakobson, R., Fant, C. G., and Halle, M. (1963), *Preliminaries to Speech Analysis; the distinctive features and their correlates* (2nd ed.). M.I.T. Press, Cambridge, Massachusetts.

Jenkins, J. J., and Palermo, D. S. (1964), Mediation processes and the acquisition of linguistic structure, in U. Bellugi and R. Brown (eds.), *The Acquisition of Language,* monograph of the Society for Research in Child Development, Serial No. 92, Vol. 29, No. 1.

Katz, J. J. and Postal, P. M. (1964), *An integrated theory of linguistic descriptions.* Research Monograph No. 26. M.I.T. Press, Cambridge, Massachusetts.

Klima, E. S. (1964), Negation in English, in J. A. Fodor and J. J. Katz (eds.), *The Structure of Language: Readings in the Philosophy of Language.* Prentice-Hall, Englewood Cliffs, New Jersey.

Lane, H. and Sheppard, W. C. (1965, in press), Presentation at Conference on Language Development in Ann Arbor, 1965.

Lenneberg, E. H. (1962), A laboratory for speech research at the Children's Hospital Medical Center, *N. E. J. Med.* **266**:385–392.

Lenneberg, E. H. (1962), Understanding language without ability to speak, *J. abnorm. soc. Psychol.* **65**:419–425.

Lenneberg, E. H. (1964), Language disorders in childhood, *Harvard Educational Review* **34**: No. 2, 152–177.

Lenneberg, E. H., Nichols, I. A., and Rosenberger, E. F. (1964), Primitive stages of language development in mongolism, in *Disorders of Communication,* Vol. XLII: Research Publications, A.R.N.M.D., pp. 119–137.

Lenneberg, E. H., Rebelsky, F. G., and Nichols, I. A. (1965), The vocalizations of infants born to deaf and to hearing parents, *Vita Humana (Human Development)* **8**:23–37.

Leopold, W. F. (1953–1954), Patterning in children's language learning, *Language Learning* **5**:1–14.

Mehler, J. and Miller, G. A. (1964), Retroactive interference in the recall of simple sentences, *Brit. J. Psychol.* **55**:295–301.

Miller, G. A. and Chomsky, N. (1963), Finitary models of language users, in R. D. Luce, R. Bush, and E. Galanter (eds.), *Handbook of Mathematical Psychology,* Vol. II. John Wiley and Sons, New York.

Miller, G. A., Galanter, E., and Pribram, K. H. (1960), *Plans and the Structure of Behavior.* Holt, Rinehart and Winston, New York.

Osgood, C. E. (1957), Motivational dynamics of language behavior, in *Nebraska Symposium on Motivation,* M. R. Jones (ed.). Univ. of Nebraska Press, Lincoln, Nebraska.

Premack, D. and Schwartz, A. (1966), Preparations for discussing behaviorism with chimpanzee, in *The Genesis of Language: in Children and Animals.* M.I.T. Press, Cambridge, Massachusetts.

Ringel, R. L. and Kluppel, D. D. (1964), Neonatal crying: a normative study, *Folia phoniatrica* **16**:1–9.

Spitz, R. A. and Wolf, K. M. (1946), The smiling response; a contribution to the ontogenesis of social relations, *Genet. Psychol. Monogr.* **34**:57–125.

Zeaman, D. and House, B. J. (1962), Mongoloid MA is proportional to log CA, *Child Development* **33**:481–488.

CHAPTER Eight

Language and cognition

I. THE PROBLEM

The general problem to be considered in this chapter may be called the problem of *reference;* that is, the relationship between words and things, and the role that our capacity for naming may play in man's organization of cognition.

That the capacity for naming has a biological dimension may be seen from the difficulties that animals experience in this respect. For instance, it is possible to train a hunting dog to "point," and it may be quite possible to teach him to point to a specific set of objects in a specific environment upon appropriate command in a natural language. But it does not appear to be possible to teach a dog to do the "name-specific stimulus generalization" that every child does automatically. The hound who has learned to "point to the tree, the gate, the house" in the trainer's yard will perform quite erratically when given the same command with respect to similar but physically different objects, in an unfamiliar environment. The correctness of the animal's responses may even vary with such extralinguistic cues as the geographical position, posture, and bodily movements of his master, the time of day, or the clothes that people are wearing while he is being exercised. There is no convincing evidence that any animal below man has ever learned to relate any given word to the same range of stimuli that is covered by that word in common language-usage. So-called proof to the contrary always lacks proper controls on interpretation. For instance, there is a report on a parrot who could say good-by (in German) and who supposedly knew what this word meant or when it is properly used. Once the bird was also heard to say good-by upon the arrival of some friends of the family; the proud owner judged this to be a sign that his pet did not merely know the meaning of the word but was even using it to produce a desired effect: to send the just-arrived friends away, presumably because he had taken a dislike to them.

It may be well to stress once more that our concern is with the capacity for (natural, human) language which, ordinarily, leads to the understanding of a definably structured type of utterance; or, in other words, with *knowing* a language. The infant who has a repertoire of three tricks (wave by-by, show me your tongue, show me how tall you are) which he can perform upon the appropriate commands but who can understand no other sentence of the same grammatical, structural type has not yet begun to acquire language. The essence of language is its productivity; in the realm of perception and understanding of sentences, it is the capacity to recognize structural similarities between familiar and entirely novel word patterns. Thus our criterion for knowing language is not dependent upon demonstrations that an individual can talk or that he goes through some stereotyped performance upon hearing certain words, but upon evidence that he can analyze novel utterances through the application of structural principles. It is the purpose of this chapter to show that the understanding of the word-object relationship, the learning and acquisition of reference, is also dependent upon certain cognitive, analytic skills, much the way understanding sentences is. The problem of reference cannot be discussed without simultaneous considerations of the relationship between language and cognition.

Evidence for understanding language may be supplied by different kinds of response. It is not necessary that the subject has the anatomical and physiological prerequisites for actual speech production. In the case of man, we may cite children who have learned to understand language but who cannot speak; compare this to children who have the anatomical equipment for speech production but whose cognitive apparatus is so poorly developed that only the primordia for language are detectable but not fullfledged comprehension. In the case of animals, we have birds who can talk but who give no evidence of language understanding and we have the famous case of Clever Hans, the horse, who had a nonacoustic response repertoire (stamping of hoofs) that, unfortunately, gave the erroneous impression of a coding system for the German language. Had the horse actually had the cognitive capacity for acquiring a natural language, his motor response limitations would have been no obstacle to his giving evidence for language comprehension. A similar argument could be made for the physical nature of the input data. Language acquisition is not dependent in man upon processing of acoustic patterns. There are many instances today of deaf-and-blind people who have built up language capacities on tactually perceived stimulus configurations.

II. TOWARD A BIOLOGICAL CONCEPTION OF SEMANTICS

The activity of *naming* or, in general, of using words may be seen as the human peculiarity to make explicit a process that is quite universal among higher animals, namely, the organization of sensory data. All vertebrates are equipped to superimpose categories of functional equivalence upon stimulus configurations, to classify objects in such a way that a single type of response is given to any one member of a particular stimulus category. The criteria or nature of categorization have to be determined empirically for each species. Frogs may jump to a great variety of flies and also to a specific range of dummy-stimuli, provided the stimuli preserve specifiable characteristics of the "real thing."

Furthermore, most higher animals have a certain capacity for discrimination. They may learn or spontaneously begin to differentiate certain aspects within the first global category, perhaps by having their attention directed to certain details or by sharpening their power of observation. In this differentiation process initial categories may become subdivided and become mutually exclusive, or a number of coexisting general and specific categories or partially overlapping categories may result. Again, the extent of a species' *differentiation capacity* is biologically given and must be ascertained empirically for each species. Rats cannot make the same range of distinctions that dogs can make, and the latter are different in this respect from monkeys. The interspecific differences cannot merely be explained by differences in peripheral sensory thresholds. Apparently, a function of higher, central processes is involved that has to do with cognitive organization.

Most primates and probably many species in other mammalian orders have the capacity to relate various categories to one another and thus to respond to *relations* between things rather than to things themselves; an example is "to respond to the largest of any collection of things." Once more, it is a matter of empirical research to discover the limits of relations that a species is capable of responding to.

In summary, most animals organize the sensory world by a process of *categorization,* and from this basic mode of organization two further processes derive: *differentiation* or discrimination, and interrelating of categories or the perception of and tolerance for *transformations* (Chapter Seven). In man these organizational activities are usually called concept-formation; but it is clear that there is no formal difference between man's concept-formation and animal's propensity for responding to categories of stimuli. There is, however, a substantive difference. The total possibilities for categorization are clearly not identical across species.

(1) *Words as Labels for Categorization Process*

The words that constitute the dictionary of a natural language are a sample of labels of categories natural to our species; they are not tags of specific objects. When names have unique referents, such as Michelangelo, Matterhorn, Waterloo, they may be incorporated into discourse but are not considered part of the lexicon. Thus most words may be said to label realms of concepts rather than physical things. This must be true for otherwise we should have great difficulty in explaining why words refer to *open* classes. We cannot define the category labeled *house* by enumerating all objects that are given that name. Any new object that satisfies certain criteria (and there is an infinity of such objects) may be assigned that label. It is easier to say what such criteria are *not* than to say what they are. They are not a finite set of objectively measurable variables such as physical dimensions, texture, color, acidity, etc. (except for a few words, which constitute a special case; these will be discussed under the heading "The Language of Experience"). We cannot predict accurately which object might be named *house* and which not by looking only at the physical measurements of those objects. Therefore, categorization and the possibility of word-assignment must usually be founded on something more abstract.

The infant who is given a word and has the task of finding the category labeled by this word does not seem to start with a working hypothesis that a specific, concrete object (his father) uniquely bears the name *daddy;* instead, initially the word appears to be used as the label of a general and open category, roughly corresponding to the adult category *people* or *men.* Thus categorization by a principle, or the formation of an (abstract) concept is apparently prior to and more primitive than the association of a sound pattern with a specific sensory experience. The same thing may be expressed in different words; stimulus generalization is prior to stimulus discrimination.

Let us consider more closely the process of categorization that underlies semantics. Is it possible to characterize this cognitive activity any further? For instance, if the classification criteria are not usually physical dimensions, what are they? The most outstanding feature of the "criteriality" is its great flexibility. Sometimes the criterion is primarily one of "use that man makes of the objects"; sometimes it is a given aspect; sometimes a certain emotional state that all objects in that class may elicit in the viewer. Any one category is not definable by only one, consistently applied criterion. For instance, the word *house* is usually applicable to structures that serve as shelter for men, animals, or objects. But the criterion for categorizing is frequently changed by metaphorical or quasi-metaphorical extensions, as in House of Lords, house of cards, house of God, the house of David, etc. The ease with which the criterion for categorization may be changed and the naturalness with which we understand such extensions point to the fact that categorization is a creative process of cognitive organization rather than an arbitrary convention. It is precisely due to the absence of rigidly adhered to classification criteria that not only the physical world can be grouped and the groups named, but the classification criteria may be bent, stretched, and altered to include virtual figments, that is, physically nonexisting entities, resulting in words without reference (or obvious referents), but which label a concept (for example, the word *ghost*). The procedure also makes possible the development of the meaning of the word *times* in the phrase four *times* five.

The abstractness underlying meanings in general, which has been the focus of so much philosophizing since antiquity, may best be understood by considering concept-formation the primary cognitive process, and naming (as well as acquiring a name) the secondary cognitive process. Concepts are superimpositions upon the physically given; they are modes of ordering or dealing with sensory data. They are not so much the *product* of man's cognition, but conceptualization is the *cognitive process itself.* Although this process is not peculiar to man (because it essentially results from the mode of operation of a mechanism that can only respond in limited ways to a wide variety of inputs), man has developed the behavioral peculiarity of attaching words to certain types of concept formation. The words (which persist through time because they may be repeated) make the underlying conceptualization process look much more static than it actually is, as we shall demonstrate presently. Cognition must be the psychological manifestation of a physiological process. It does not appear to be a mosaic of static concepts, or a storehouse of thoughts, or an archive of memorized sense-impressions. The task of cognitive organization never comes to an end and is never completed "in order to be used later." Words are not the labels of concepts completed earlier and stored away; they are the labels of a *categorization process or family of such processes.* Because of the dynamic nature of the underlying process, the referents of words can so easily change, meanings can be extended, and categories are always open. *Words tag the processes by which the species deals cognitively with its environment.*

This theoretical position also elucidates the problem of translation or the equation of meanings across natural languages. If words label modes of cognizing, we would expect that all semantic systems have certain formal commonalities. For instance, if we hear a given word used in connection with a given object or phenomenon, we are able to intuit the general usage of that word—it does not have to be paired with 200 similar objects or phenomena before we can make predictions whether the name applies to a new object. Man's cognition functions within biologically given limits. On the other hand, there is also freedom within these limits. Thus every individual may have highly idiosyncratic thoughts or conceptualize in a peculiar way or, in fact, may choose somewhat different modes of cognitive organization at different times faced with identical sensory stimuli. His vocabulary, which is much more limited and unchangeable than his capacity for conceptualizing, can be made to cover the novel conceptual processes, and other men, by virtue of having essentially the same cognitive capacities, can understand the semantics of his utterances, even though the words cover new or slightly different conceptualizations. Given this degree of freedom, it becomes reasonable to assume that natural languages always have universally understandable types of semantics, but may easily have different extensions of meanings, and that, therefore, specific semantic categories are not coterminous across languages.

It does not follow from this that differences in semantics are signs of obligatory differences in thought processes, as assumed by Whorf (1956) and many others. The modes of conceptualization that happen to be tagged by a given natural language need not, and apparently do not, exert restrictions upon an individual's freedom of conceptualizing. This will be discussed subsequently.

(2) *Differentiation of Categories*

Since there is freedom, within limits, to categorize, there must also be freedom to substructure a category. Not only can the infant adjust his initial broad category *doggy* from all quadrupeds to the species *Canis familiaris,* but child and man alike are free to superimpose further classifications upon inclusive categories, and the criteria for the formation of these narrower categories or for the process of substructuring in general are as variegated as those for the initial categories.

Thus differentiation may result from labeling the direction of attention to one aspect of the object (high, wet, bulging) or from differentiating some relationship that exists between the speaker and the object (*this* noun, *that* noun). Instances of this type of differentiation process make it obvious that words cannot be attachment to things, but only acoustic markers of cognitive processes—signals of how the individual deals with the task of organizing input. Since languages may differ in the peculiar cognitive process that is being tagged lexically, the semantics of a language reflect merely one of many possible ways of dealing with the cognitive organization task.

Differentiation may result in peculiar hierarchies of inclusiveness-exclusiveness of categories or in contrasting categories as in antonyms, partially overlapping categories as synonyms, etc. The manifold structures produced by the basic freedom of differentiation points, once more, to the underlying dynamics of the semantic process. A lexicon is like a photograph that freezes motion. Differentiation is part of the organization processes, and it goes on continuously and in many ways. A natural language captures some of those ways, but it is not as fixed or as rigid a system as it may appear; in fact, it does reflect the ongoing creative or productive process if analyzed with care. Naming is a method and a process more than it is a rigidly established relationship. The speaker who must communicate a peculiar form of substructuring a category will immediately take recourse to novel ways of naming, as we shall see from the empirical experiments described below.

(3) *Interrelating of Categories (Transformations)*

The transformational process of syntax discussed in Chapter Seven has its counterpart in semantics also. Just as certain structural principles underlying given sentence-types bear relations to one another, so do the similarity-principles that are the basis for the formation of categories. For instance, there are objects called knife, fork, and spoon. We may extract some common denominator from these and choose to give the abstraction a label, say *flatware*. Other objects, such as cork-screw, ladle, and rolling pin may be subsumed under the categorical label *utensils*. There are certain relationships between the two categories that are completely constant. For instance, certain similarity-relationships hold for any object that is part of *flatware* and any object that is part of *utensils*. The cognitive calculus with categories is easily reflected in naming habits. This goes so far as to enable us to write semantic rules that have the same formal structure as syntactic rules and that predict what kinds of words may be interchanged in sentence frames without changing the grammaticality of the sentence. For further details see Fodor and Katz (1963).

Categories may also be related to one another such that the relationship itself is labeled by morphemes or words (for example, *by, –ing, for, $-s_{pl}$, is,* etc.). The semantics of these relational elements perhaps illustrates best how words do not refer to real things but to cognitive processes. It is in connection with the cognitive process of relating abstract concepts (name categories or structural sentence-types) that the intimate relationship between semantics and syntax is most clearly revealed.

(4) *Preliminary Conclusions*

The basic cognitive mechanisms underlying semantics appear to be similar to those of syntax, namely processes of categorization, differentiation, and interrelation (transformation). Indeed, the latter two are merely aspects of the categorization process itself. This argument may also be extended to include the cognitive processes underlying phonology. Although categorization is a universal phenomenon in the animal kingdom, the categorizations peculiar to language operate through the application of highly species-specific principles.

Naming is a process, not a catalogue of rigid conventions. There are two types of constraints that determine naming-behavior: the biological constraint upon the physiological processes that determine the species' cognitive capacities, particularly the conditions under which similarities are recognized; and the constraint necessitated by the communicative function subserved by naming. Notice, however, that the naming process may go on in the absence of communication. Neologisms are created and assigned meanings by the schizophrenic patient or the genius creating words for his highly idiosyncratic concepts, regardless of whether they will actually transfer information from one individual to another.

It is a matter of social dynamics, roles, values, or group-mechanisms whether anybody will take the trouble to discover what conceptualization process was being tagged by such neologisms. Communication is a social phenomenon, whereas naming is an intrapersonal one; the intrapersonal process may become a social one by virtue of enormous similarities between the cognitive functioning of all individuals and an apparent specific motivation in humans to interact socially. Again, group cohesiveness is a widespread phenomenon in the animal kingdom, but the mechanisms vary greatly from species to species. In man, the prime vehicle of this interaction is the mutual adjustment of concept formation, tagged by words.

III. THE EMPIRICAL STUDY OF NAMING: THE LANGUAGE OF EXPERIENCE

In section II I have proposed that words tag conceptualization processes, not things directly. But since the input to at least some conceptualization processes is the sensory perception of things, there is, of course, also a relationship between words and objects. This relationship may be studied empirically, under laboratory conditions. For this purpose, it is desirable to choose words that have simple referents, in the sense that they can be exhaustively described by objective measurement of *all* of their physical properties. This condition is fulfilled in only a small class of words, namely those that describe the sensation of certain physical properties themselves. Let us refer to these words collectively as the *language of experience;* examples are words for temperature, taste, hearing, or vision.

(1) *Description of the Referents*

The language of experience is particularly well-suited for research because its referents have four advantages over the referents of most other types of words: first, they may be ordered by objective, logical criteria (for example, the centigrade scale for temperatures; the frequency scale of pure tones of equal intensity, etc.), whereas furniture, relatives, or most other concrete referents have no such logical and unique orders.) Second, the referents have continuity in nature (for example, within certain limits any degree of temperature may be encountered or any sound frequency heard, whereas the domain of chairs do not grade into the domain of, say, benches, nor do uncles grade into aunts. Third, words in the language of experience refer to *closed classes;* our sensory thresholds set limits to perception and thus there is a bound to the range of phenomena that may be called hot, loud, green, etc. Fourth, the referents are simple in the sense that each instant may be completely specified by a fixed and very small number of measurements. Temperature is specified by just one measurement; pure tones by two —intensity and frequency; colors by three—for example, the Munsell scales of hue, brightness, and saturation.

(2) *Referent Spaces*

If it is possible to describe phenomena completely and accurately in terms of certain dimensions, it is also possible to construct coordinate systems in which every point corresponds to one specific phenomenon. Every point on a thermometric scale corresponds to one specific temperature; every point within a pitch-intensity coordinate system corresponds to one specific pure tone. Sometimes such coordinate systems are called *spaces.* The coordinate systems mentioned so far are unidimensional and two-dimensional spaces; for the specification of color we need a three-dimensional space, and since these *spaces* are merely abstract, mathematical concepts, one can also have four-, five-, and *n*-dimensional spaces. The three-dimensional color space is most easily visualized. Figure 8.1 shows the arrangement of the coordinates, and Fig. 8.2 shows an actual model of a color space. The choice of a polar coordinate system is arbitrary. It offers some conveniences, but the three dimensions might have been arranged differently.

With the introduction of the notion of a color space we might review once more why we wish to arrange physical phenomena in this way. Our aim is to study how words relate to objects. But we cannot study the behavior of *words* unless we keep some control over the objects.

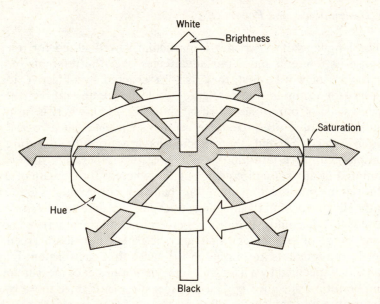

FIG. 8.1. Schematic diagram showing relations between hue, brightness, saturation in the Munsell Color System.

FIG. 8.2. Psychological color solid. *Left:* for colors perceived under good visual color matching conditions such as those of a textile color matcher; *right:* for colors perceived under supraliminal conditions, as when using a good instrument. (From Nickerson and Newhall, 1943.)

We must do everything we can so as to bring some order into physical "reality." We have chosen phenomena that can be measured and ordered with respect to each other. The color space is simply an ordering device that allows us to assign every possible color a specific position or point. The entire world of color is encompassed in the color space. Our next step now is to discover how the color words of a given language, say English or Navaho, fit into this space. Where are the colors in our space that answer to the name *red?* Obtaining replies to this type of question will be called *mapping color terms into the color space.* Naturally, every language is likely to have somewhat different maps; but the color space, which merely describes the psychophysical properties of colors, is constant for all of mankind.

(3) *Names Mapped into Referent Spaces*

Let us now consider how the words of the language of experience apply to the referents as we have ordered them into spaces. Much work has been done on color terminology and its relationship to the color space. Our task is twofold: we might start with a collection of color words in use by English speakers (for instance, by asking a sample of speakers to write down all the words for colors they can think of) and then try to assign each word a region in the color space; or we might sample the color space itself by selecting two hundred colors, evenly distributed throughout the space, and then show each color to a representative sample of speakers of English and ask them to write down the English word or words that best describe that color. Let us call the first procedure *Approach A* and the second *Approach B*.

When *Approach A* is used, we obtain a name-map that reflects the meaning of certain words in the lexicon of a natural language. This type of information must be distinguished from the actual use that speakers make of these words. It does not completely reveal the mechanism of naming. This becomes most obvious from the fact that *Approach A* leaves certain parts of the color space unmapped. There will be certain colors to which none of the words collected earlier (in the absence of color samples) properly refers. The operations that lead to such results are quite simple. Subjects are presented with comprehensive color charts (Brown and Lenneberg, 1954, used the Munsell book of colors) and are asked to point to all the colors that might be called *x* (*brown, lavender, orange,* etc.). There will be some words which some subjects cannot locate at all (say, heliotrope); he may not know what the word means, or there may be wide disagreement between subjects what the proper location of a word is (say, magenta). After having given all the words in our compilation to all our subjects we will discover that there is a residue of physical colors to which no one assigned any of the names —the "innominate regions."

Now, when *Approach B* is used the "innominate regions" of the color space all but disappear. Although one or another subject may say "I don't know what one calls that color," there will be others who quite readily assign some descriptive phrase to any color shown. *Approach B* reflects much better the versatility or basic productivity inherent in the act of naming, while it provides at the same time some statistic on the actual usage in a given language.

Since subjects will differ among themselves in their precise naming-habit and since there will be colors that are ambiguous with respect to common names in English, colors will differ in their probability of being called *x*. In fact, many colors will be called by more than one name, each name having a different probability of being assigned to a given color.

Figure 8.3 shows how name maps are associated with a *gradient of probability*. This renders the structure of name maps always more complex than the structure of the referent space. The shape of the probability gradient itself can vary considerably as may be gathered from

Fig. 8.3, and this is a variable that plays a definite role in the learning of names and in the ease of communication. I have shown experimentally (Lenneberg, 1957) that speakers of English do not only distribute their words—in this case for colors—in a characteristic and language-specific way over the stimulus continuum, but that one can also elicit from subjects correct estimates of probability that a given stimulus will be given a specific name.

If we take the color space and ask how does the word *red* fit into this continuum, it will appear that a certain circumscribed region of points

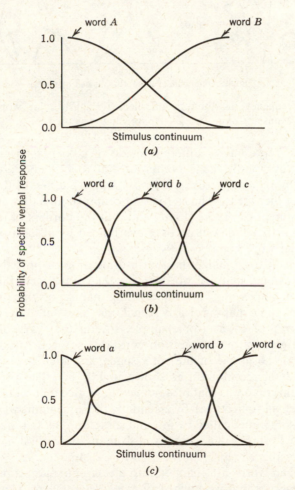

FIG. 8.3. Hypothetic probability gradients for three types of vocabularies; (*a*), (*b*), and (*c*).

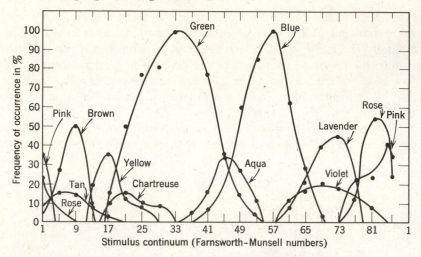

FIG. 8.4. Frequency distributions of selected English color words over the Farnsworth-Munsell Colors. $N = 27$. Approach *B* was used.

(each point represents a different shade of color) is covered by this word. However, only some points are felt to be "good *reds;*" other points are more *orangy reds* or *brownish reds*. That means that the map or region of the word *red* has a focus or center (points that are the most typical examples of the word *red*) and that the borders of the map are never sharp; they fade out and are overlapped by at least one, usually several other word maps.

It is difficult to visualize the fourth dimension of probability in the three-dimensional maps of words inside the color space. But the overlapping, encompassing, and subdividing nature of the probabilistic gradients of name maps is clearly seen if one takes out of the color space a linear array of colors (for example, stimuli that vary only in hue, holding brightness and saturation constant) so as to produce a unidimensional subsample of the color-space, and then maps the vocabulary on to this continuum as shown in Fig. 8.4. The procedure for obtaining this map was that of *Approach B*. Notice that there are certain colors which all subjects call by essentially the same name whereas other colors are sometimes called by this and sometimes by that name. Colors Nos. 4 and 13 in Fig. 8.4 were given so many individual names that it was not possible to represent them all by a distinct curve.

Thus, when words are mapped into a referent space, a probabilistic variable emerges that we might call *name-determinacy*. The loci in the referent space vary with regard to the name-determinacy. The determinacy is greatest in the center of the foci and decreases centrifugally from these points; it is lowest at the intercept of name-maps. The region which appeared to be "innominate" under *Approach A* is one of great and widespread name-indeterminacy. Name-determinacy is, of course, a social phenomenon.

The procedures outlined here are a convenient way of demonstrating some of the semantic differences between languages. For instance, color name maps have been worked out for Žuni (Lenneberg and Roberts, 1956) and partially for Navaho (Landar et al., 1960) and Conklin (1955) adopted the Lenneberg-Roberts technique for the study of Hanunoo color categories.

This type of empirical research on semantic relationships in various languages can only be carried out within a very small part of the total vocabulary of a language, namely only on the language of experience. Therefore, it is not possible to verify empirically the far-reaching claims that have been made about the "total incomparability of semantics" among unrelated languages. The languages investigated all have names for colors and apart from finding mergers of two of our English color maps into one, or the substructuring of one of our maps, or shifts in border lines nothing particularly astonishing has been discovered. We gather that man, everywhere, can make reference to colors and communicate about color fairly efficiently.

(4) *Contextual Determinants in Common Naming*

The insight gained through the application of *Approach B* still gives an inaccurate picture of how the naming of phenomena proceeds. The structure of the name-maps might induce us to believe that the English word *red* can only be used for a very few colors (the focus of the region "red"); and that as we move away from the focus the word would always have to be qualified as for instance *yellowish-red, dirty red,* etc. However, when one refers to the color of hair, or the color of a cow, or the skin color of the American Indian the word *red* is used without qualifiers. Conversely, the physical color which is named *brownish-orange* when it appears in the Munsell *Book of Colors,* and *red* when it is the color of a cow, may be called *ochre* when it appears on the walls of a Roman Villa.

Quite clearly the choice of a name depends on the context, on the number of distinctions that must be made in a particular situation, and on many other factors that have little to do with the semantic structure of a given language *per se*; for example, the speaker's intent, the type of person he is addressing himself to, or the nature of the social occasion may easily affect the choice of a name.

Only proper names are relatively immune from these extra-linguistic determining factors. But although the attachment of the name Albert Einstein to one particular person remains completely constant, it implies that in instances such as these the most characteristic aspect of language is eliminated, namely the creative versatility—the dynamics— and it may well be due to this reduction that proper names are not "felt" to be part of a natural language. Once more we see that there are usually no direct associative bonds between words and physical objects.

It is also possible to study empirically the naming behavior that is specific to a given physical context. This was first done by Lantz and Stefflre (1964), who used a procedure which we may call *Approach C.* In this method subjects are instructed to communicate with each other about specific referents. There are several variants for a laboratory set-up. The easiest is as follows: two subjects are each given an identical collection of loose color chips. The subjects may talk to each other but cannot see each other. Subject *A* chooses one color at a time and describes it in such a way that subject *B* can identify the color chip. For instance, subject *A* picks one color and describes it as "the color of burned pea soup." Subject *B* inspects his sample and makes a guess which color the other subject might have picked; the experimenter records the identification number of both colors and measures the magnitude of the mistake (if any) in terms of the physical distance between the colors. * If this procedure is done on a sufficiently large number of subject-pairs one may statistically reduce individual competence factors and come up with a measure, called *communication accuracy,* that indicates how well each of the colors in the particular context presented may be identified in the course of naming behavior.

Note that *Approach C,* leading to the estimation of communication accuracy, no longer indicates exclusively the nature of the relationship between particular words and objects and is thus somewhat marginal to the problem of reference. For instance, a given color chip, say a gray with a blue-green tinge, may obtain a very low communication accuracy score if it is presented together with fifty other grays, greens, blues and intermediate shades, but a very high score if it is presented with fifty shades all of them in the lavender, pink, red, orange, and yellow range. Although this approach emphasizes the creative element of naming, it probably does not distinguish between the peculiar semantic properties of one natural language over another. The difference between the three approaches is summarized in Table 8.1.

---

* This is possible if we choose a linear stimulus array with perceptually equidistant stimuli as, for instance, described by Lenneberg, 1957.

	Yields a Variable Called	Gives Information on	Assuming that The Stimulus Array Is	Has Following Unrealistic Elements	Cannot Predict
Approach A	(No name)	The common reference of specific words found in the lexicon of a natural language	A large sample of points homogeneously distributed through the color space	Assumes dictionary meanings to be a set of rigid word-thing associations, ignoring that naming is a process that changes with situation	What name a person actually will use in any instant
Approach B	Codability. (originally this word referred to a combination of highly correlated variables); for simplicity we are equating codability here with what is called in the text name-determinacy	The probability of various words that might be used by a language community with respect to a given stimulus	A small sample of points distributed through the color space in a predetermined way	Essentially same assumption as above	What name a person actually will use in any condition *other* than a particular stimulus array and under specific experimental conditions
Approach C	Communication accuracy	How efficiently a community may identify one stimulus in a collection of others, using words	No assumptions about nature of sample; however, results vary with every sample and therefore communication accuracy is not a quality imposed invariantly upon a stimulus by a natural language	Does not reveal semantic peculiarities of any one natural language; does not distinguish clearly between commonality among subjects due to culture as against due to language	How efficiently a color may be identified in an unspecified or unknown context

IV. NAMING AND COGNITIVE PROCESSES

(1) *General Strategies*

How certain can we be that naming is actually the consequence of categorization, as claimed in the introduction, instead of its cause? If there is freedom (within limits) to categorize and recategorize, could the semantic structure of a natural language restrict the biological freedom? Is our cognitive structure influenced by the reference relationships of certain words? What would cognition be like in the absence of language?

Questions of this sort may be partially answered by following either of two strategies. We may use various features of natural languages as the independent variable and study how these affect certain features of cognitive processes; or we may use the relative presence or absence of primary language as the independent variable and see to what extent the development of cognition is dependent on language acquisition. Congenitally deaf children are the most interesting subjects if the latter approach is used. The former approach harbors a few hidden difficulties that are worth mentioning here.

Superficially it may appear as if the most direct procedure in language and cognition studies were the comparison of the performance of say Navaho and English speakers on some cognitive task. If their language background is irrelevant to their test performance the two groups should have equal scores. Unfortunately, it does not follow that if their test scores are different, such differences must be due to their native languages. When we compare groups of different native speakers, we usually compare at the same time individuals of different cultural background. In most instances, it is very difficult to work with two perfectly matched groups, differing in nothing but their native language. But even if these conditions were met, the logic underlying this experimental procedure would still leave much to be desired. It is a rather weak hypothesis that predicts nothing more specific than a general difference in cognitive processes due to a general difference in language background. The argument would not become convincing unless we could specify the semantic or structural peculiarity of a given language that we expect to affect one or another cognitive process.

In other words, we ought to make more specific predictions on the nature of the difference in performance between the two groups of speakers. But this requirement conjures up new difficulties. Suppose the structural peculiarity were the presence of inflection in one language vs. its absence in the other. First, it is difficult to intuit what type of cognitive process might be affected by this structural feature. Second, we would not know whether, among the multiplicity of other structural and semantic features of either of the languages, there might not be other aspects that fully compensate, cognitively, for the structural difference noted. Thus one language may introduce redundancy by inflections while the other language has an equal degree of redundancy which is introduced through the obligatory use of function words and word order. Even if we could match speakers for their nonlinguistic variables, we cannot match language structures and peculiarities in such a way that the two languages differ in only one respect. Since languages are highly integrated patterns, one can do little more than rank-order the global degree of difference between given languages (English has greater affinity with Dutch than with Arabic), but it is very tricky and usually quite meaningless, to single out specific features and compare these in disregard of the total structural complexities (cf. Lenneberg and Roberts, 1956).

These considerations should induce us to shy away from experimental designs that call for the comparison of speakers of different languages. Instead it seems more promising to follow what I have called (1953) the *intralinguistic approach*. Here the language variable is some peculiarity within one and the same natural language, for instance, some feature of its lexicon. Suppose a language has in its dictionary words that refer to one set of physical phenomena, say different types of snow, but not to another set of phenomena, say different types of clouds; can we make predictions about the speaker's perception of or memory for those things? In this approach we need not match groups of speakers nor different languages. We could simply compare different responses (to snow and clouds respectively) of individual native speakers, so that every subject is in effect his own control. This is the basic strategy followed in most of the experiments described below.

There is, however, a further problem that must be dealt with. It is necessary that the relationship between individual words and natural phenomena can be studied empirically so that we have an objective measure of how well or how poorly the language actually deals with one or the other phenomenon. In the previous section we have discussed this matter in detail and have given reasons why the best types of words to be used in this kind of study are those that refer to sensation, in short the language of experience.

Colors have been the favorite stimulus material because their physical nature can be described relatively easily, standard stimulus material is readily available, the relative frequency of occurrence in the environment is not too likely to affect subjects' reactions in an experiment, and perceptual qualities may also be controlled relatively easily.

(2) *Acuity of Discrimination*

There is a collection of colors, known as the Farnsworth-Munsell Test (Farnsworth, 1949), consisting of 86 chips of equal brightness and saturation but differing in hue. These colors were chosen by the authors of the test so as to constitute an instrument for the testing of hue discrimination. Subjects are presented with two chips, say one green and one blue, and are asked to put a disarranged collection of shades between these two colors into the proper order so that an array results with all chips finely graded from green to blue. Similar tasks are required with shades between blue and purple, purple and red, and red and green. When the test is administered to a noncolor-blind standard population of young American adults, a certain average number of sorting mistakes occur, but the mistakes occur with equal likelihood anywhere in the spectrum (and the mistakes for any one color chip have a frequency distribution that is the same for all colors.)

The question now arises whether the construction and standardization of the test might have been biased by the language habits of its authors who were English speaking individuals. Since the color vocabulary superimposes a classification upon the physical color continuum might it not have predisposed us to pay more attention to the borderline cases, thus sharpening our acuity across wordclass boundary, and to pay relatively less attention to the clear-cut cases, thus dulling our acuity within the word classes?

Lenneberg and J. Bastian (unpublished data) administered the Farnsworth-Munsell Hue Discrimination Test to a group of Zuni and Navaho Indians whose color vocabulary had been mapped into the stimulus continuum by Lenneberg and Roberts (1956) and Landar et al. (1960) respectively. The different locations of the Zuni and Navaho color-name boundaries did not predict in either case systematic difference in discriminatory acuity between the Indians and a control group of Anglo-American farmers living in the same region. Thus there is little ground to assume that the peculiarities of English color words have affected the construction of the Farnsworth-Munsell Test in any basic way.

There is, however, some other type of evidence that may cause us to reconsider our conclusions. Beare (1963) elicited English color words for a series of monochromatic lights. Her stimulus material had the advantage of being perfectly controlled in its physical properties and each color could be specified in terms of wavelength. She required subjects to name every stimulus presented as red, orange, yellow, green, blue, violet and to make the response as fast as possible. After an appropriate decision had been made the subject was allowed to qualify the name given by further adjectives. If a stimulus fell within a name map the response was made relatively quickly and few or no qualifiers were used. A stimulus that fell between maps had a longer response latency and elicited a greater number of qualifiers. Thus, she used *Approach B* to map words into the particular referent space represented by her stimuli.

The same stimulus material had been used earlier for another experiment (Judd, 1932) designed to discover acuity of hue-discrimination. In that experiment it was found that the differential limen was not constant for the visible spectrum. In some spectral areas our eye was shown to discover smaller hue differences than in other spectral areas. In Fig. 8.5 Judd's hue discrimination curve is shown; low points indi-

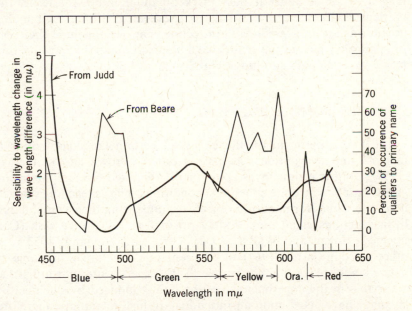

FIG. 8.5. Relationship between Judd's (1932) data on sensibility to wavelength change and Beare's data (1963) on English speakers' likelihood of using qualifiers in their color names. Judd's curve shows that acuity of color discrimination varies with wavelength. It is sharpest (minima in curve) in those areas of the spectrum where our color categories overlap. (Data redrawn to scale.)

cate relatively high acuity. The other curve plotted in Fig. 8.5 is based on Beare's naming data; it is the frequency of occurrence of name-qualifiers. This frequency is high when a stimulus is ambiguous with respect to its word-class assignment. The curve reflects what we have called name-indeterminacy. Figure 8.5 suggests that there is a relationship between the two variables. Within the large, clear-cut word classes acuity seems to be slightly less sharp than in the areas of relatively large name-indeterminacy. These findings are merely suggestive, but not conclusive.

Beare used a slightly different procedure to compare her naming data with Judd's acuity data, but she was generally skeptical about a causal relationship between the two. In her own words: ". . . what fit there is between the two functions is tenuous, and it is possible that the configuration of the naming curve will change (if a different stimulus array is used), or with changes in instructions with regard to categories of judgment." Even if Beare shall eventually be proved to have been too modest in her conclusions, we can still not be certain whether the name boundaries of the English words are entirely arbitrary; only if other languages can be shown to have markedly different boundaries for this particular stimulus array and if the speakers distribute their loci of greatest acuity in a predictable direction may we conclude that non-physiological factors have affected hue-discrimination. For the time being, we must withhold judgment.

(3) *Memory and Recognition*

The first experiment on the effects of certain language habits on memory and recognition was carried out by Brown and Lenneberg (1954). Until that time investigators had attempted to manipulate language variables by quite ephemeral conditions such as teaching subjects nonsense names for nonsense objects or influencing their verbal habits by instructions given immediately prior to the cognitive task (Carmichael, Hogan and Walter, 1932; Kurtz and Hovland, 1953; and others cited in Carroll, 1964), but the semantic structure of the subjects' native language was neither known to the experimenter nor utilized as a variable in the experiment. Yet the habits induced by one's native language have acted upon an individual all his life and are, therefore, much more relevant to the basic problems that concerns us here than the verbal habits that can be established during a single experimental session. Thus, experiments that build upon the properties of a natural language are in a sense more crucial than the other type.

The Brown and Lenneberg experiment need not be reported here in any great detail. Subjects were screened for color-blindness and had to be native born American-English speakers. Their task consisted of correctly recognizing certain colors. They were shown one color (or in some experimental conditions four colors) at a time for a short period; these were the *stimulus colors*.

After a timed interval they viewed a large color chart (to which we shall refer as the *color context*) from which they chose the colors they had been shown before. The colors were identified by pointing so that no descriptive words were used either by the experimenter or the subject.

In earlier investigations the foci and borders of English name maps had been determined through *Approach A;* basing ourselves on this information we selected a small sample of colors (the stimulus colors) consisting of all foci and an example of each border. A few additional colors were added (only the region of high saturation was included). This yielded a sample of 24 colors. Next we used *Approach B* in order to obtain lists of words and descriptive phrases actually used by English speakers in order to refer to the colors in our particular sample and context. *Approaches A* and *B* together provided us with background knowledge of the language habits that English-speaking subjects might bring to bear upon the task of color recognition in our experiment. We hypothesized that there would be a relationship between the two.

The measure of name-determinacy, obtained through *Approach B,* was found to be highly correlated with response latency and shortness of response (as confirmed by Beare, 1963) and was called by Brown and Lenneberg *codability*. Codability is essentially a measure of how well people agree in giving a name to a stimulus, in our case a color. Good agreement (that is, high codability) may be due to two independent factors: the language of the speakers may provide, through its vocabulary, a highly characteristic, unique, and unambiguous word for a highly specific stimulus (for example, the physical color of blood); or the stimulus may in fact be quite nondescript in the language, but it is given special salience in a physical context (for instance, red hair). Codability does not distinguish these two factors.

We found that codability of a color did not predict its recognizability when the recognition task was easy (one color to be identified after a seven second waiting period); however, as the task was made more difficult codability began to correlate with recognizability and the relationship was most clearly seen in the most difficult of the tasks (four colors had to be recognized after a three minute waiting period during which subjects were given irrelevant tasks to perform).

At first these results looked like experimental proof that under certain conditions a person's native language may facilitate or handicap a memory-function. However, it became apparent later that the role of physical context needed to be studied further (see also Krauss and Weinheimer, 1965). Burnham and Clark (1955) conducted a color recognition experiment employing essentially the same procedure as Brown and Lenneberg but using a different sample of colors (namely the Farnsworth-Munsell Test Colors instead of the high saturation colors from the Munsell *Book of Colors*). They found that colors differed in their recognizability as shown in Fig. 8.6 with mistakes occurring in specific directions, clearly pointing to some systematic bias in the subjects' performance. Lenneberg (1957) obtained naming data on the same stimulus material and a comparison of these data with those of Burnham and Clark (Fig. 8.4) seemed to show that the bias may be related to the semantic structure "built into" the subjects by virtue of their native English. The only difficulty with this interpretation is this. In the Brown and Lenneberg experiment a positive correlation was found between codability and recognizability, whereas the recognizability of the Burnham and Clark colors was negatively correlated with their codability. This divergence is not due to experimental artifact. Lantz (unpublished data) repeated the Burnham and Clark experiment twice with different groups of adults in different parts of the country and Lantz and Stefflre (1964) replicated the Brown and Lenneberg experiment, all with similar results.

There are strong reasons to attribute the difference in outcome of the two experiments to the peculiarities of the stimulus arrays and the physical context of the individual colors.

Burnham and Clark had hoped to eliminate endpoints by using a circular stimulus array. But *S*s' naming habits restructured the material so as to furnish certain anchoring points: namely, the boundaries between name maps. Thus, a few colors acquired a distinctive feature, whereas most of the colors, all that fell within a name region, tended to be assimilated in memory. To remember the word "green" in this task was of no help since there were so many greens; but to remember that the color was on the border of "green" and "not-green" enabled the subject to localize the stimulus color with great accuracy in the color context.

The Brown and Lenneberg study did not provide subjects with any two or three outstanding landmarks for recognition. Since there was no more than one color within individual name categories, the possibility of assimilating colors (or of grouping colors into classes of stimulus equivalence) was drastically reduced if not eliminated. On

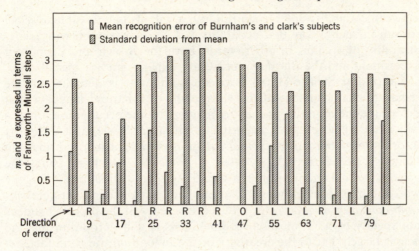

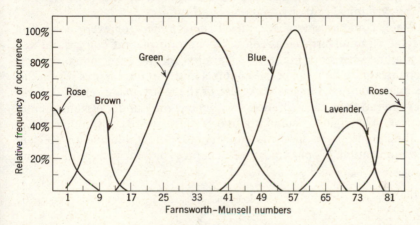

FIG. 8.6. Distribution of errors in color recognition as reported by Burnham and Clark (1955). *Below:* frequency distribution of the most common English color names over the Farnsworth-Munsell color series. Approach *B* was used.

the other hand, so many colors marked boundaries, that *betwixtness* as such was no longer a distinctive feature.

These two experiments suggest that semantic structure influences recognition only under certain experimental circumstances, namely when the task is difficult and the stimuli are chosen in a certain way. If it is possible to obtain a positive as well as a negative correlation between codability and recognizability, it will also be possible to select stimuli in such a way that codability has zero correlation with recognizability of a color. In other words, both the Brown and Lenneberg experiment and the Burnham and Clark experiment are special cases.

Lantz and Steffire (1964) have shown that it is actually not the semantic characteristics of the vocabulary of a natural language that determine the cognitive process *recognition* but the peculiar use subjects will make of language in a particular situation. Instead of using the information from either *Approach A* or *B* (which primarily brings out language peculiarities), they used *Approach C* which measures the accuracy of communication in a specific setting, without evaluating the words that subjects choose to use; their independent variable was *communication accuracy* which reflects efficiency of the process but does not specify by what means it is done. This is quite proper in that the *how* is largely left to the creativity of the individual; he is, in fact, *not* bound by the semantics of his natural language; there is little evidence of the tyrannical grip of words on cognition.

When communication accuracy is determined for every color in a specific stimulus array it predicts recognition of that color quite well as may be seen from Fig. 8.7. Codability, on the other hand, predicts recognizability only in special contexts and stimulus arrays. From this we may infer that subjects make use of the ready-made reference facilities offered them through their vocabulary, only under certain circumstances. The rigid or standard use of these words, without creative qualifications, is in many circumstances not conducive to efficient communication. Communication accuracy or efficiency will depend

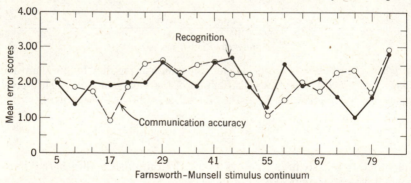

FIG. 8.7. When communication accuracy is determined for every color in a specific stimulus array, it predicts recognizability of that color in that setting well. (Data for this graph and for those of figs 8.9 and 8.10 based on an as yet unpublished article by DeLee Lantz and E. H. Lenneberg.)

frequently on individual ingenuity rather than on the language spoken by the communicator.

The Lantz and Stefflre experiment points to an interesting circumstance. The variable, communication accuracy, is a distinctly social phenomenon. But recognition of colors is an entirely intrapersonal process. Lantz and Stefflre suggest that there are situations in which the individual communicates with himself over time. This is a fruitful way of looking at the experimental results and one that also has important implications regarding human communication in more general terms. It stresses, once again, the probability that human communication is made possible by the identity of cognitive processing within each individual. The social aspect of communication seems to reflect an internal cognitive process. We are tempted to ask now, "What is prior —the social or the internal process?" At present, there is no clear answer to this, but the cognitive functioning of congenitally deaf children, before they have learned to read, write, or lip-read (in short, before they have language) appears to be, by and large, similar enough to their hearing contemporaries to lead me to believe that the internal process is the condition for the social process, although certain influences of the social environment upon intrapersonal cognitive development cannot be denied.

What preliminary conclusions may we draw then from these empirical investigations? Four major facts emerge. First, the semantic structure of a given language only has a mildly biasing effect upon recognition under special circumstances; limitations of vocabulary may be largely overcome by the creative use of descriptive words. Second, a study of the efficiency of communication in a social setting (of healthy individuals) may give clues to intrapersonal processes. Third, efficiency of communication is mostly dependent upon such extra-semantic factors as the number of and perceptual distance between discriminanda. Fourth, the social communication measures become more predictive of the intrapersonal processes as the difficulty of the individual's task increases either by taxing memory or by reduction of cues (cf. also Frijda and Van de Geer, 1961; Van de Geer, 1960; Glanzer and Clark, 1962; Krauss and Weinheimer, 1965).

(4) *Concept Formation*

Concept formation is considered to be synonymous with categorization. A natural language was already said to tag certain types of conceptual processes by means of words. We may ask now whether the existence of such a word (say in the speaker's language knowledge) is responsible for making a given concept particularly salient and easy to attain.

A survey of reports of such tests (Carroll, 1964) does, indeed, give that impression; in most instances concepts that may be named, or where the principle may be formulated easily in the native language of the subjects, are felt to be easier to attain in experiments than when this is not the case. However, these findings do not necessarily indicate that natural language is a biasing factor in the formation of concepts in general. The concepts tagged by the vocabulary of natural languages are not completely arbitrary as may be seen from the large degree of semantic correspondences between languages. It is true that translation always brings out some absence of correspondence between two languages. However, the experience of the physical environment finds expression in all languages. It is mostly the aspect or mode of reference and the metaphorical extensions that vary. Comparative studies in the language of experience indicate that those phenomena that have perceptual or cognitive salience in the environment (for our species) always are particularly amenable to reference, regardless of the natural language. Therefore, if nameability tends to be coupled with cognitive salience, it is not certain whether results in concept formation experiments are due to subjects' naming habits or whether both the naming *and* the concept attainment are due to a more basic factor such as biologically given cognitive organization.

Certain other considerations should make us doubtful about any strong claim upon the "constraint" of words upon its speaker's cognitive capacities. A wide range of human activities is based upon concept formation that must have taken place in the absence of naturally occurring words. Examples are the development of mathematics (where a language is simply created *ad hoc* as the concepts are developed), or of music, or of the visual arts or of science in general. Peoples in underdeveloped countries, who are suddenly introduced to a new technology for which there is no terminology in their language can learn the new concepts by simply introducing foreign words into their vernacular or by making new use of old words. Once more, this may be explained by seeing naming as a creative process, not a rigid convention.

The most dramatic semantic difference between languages may be found in the realm of feelings and attitudes. Here, indeed, translation is often a total impossibility. Are we able to demonstrate that our awareness of personal feelings is selectively enhanced by words handed down to us through semantic traditions? Empirical demonstrations would be difficult and I am, frankly, dubious about its promise.

Consider the difficulty to describe accurately the nature of feelings, for instance during a psychiatric interview; or our awareness of how coarse and nondescript some of the words for feelings and attitudes are, for example, honor, love, pride, etc. In many instances, our emotions appear to be more subtle than can be indicated by the use of these threadbare terms.

(5) *Cognition in Deaf Children*

Until the age of six, deaf children have usually little more than a repertoire of ten to fifty intelligible words and have no skill as yet in understanding language through lip-reading or common reading. Thus, it is fair to say that they have no language as yet. A comparison of their cognitive capacities with those of hearing children ought to be revealing. We must, however, be aware that deprivations of this sort do more to the children than merely render them incommunicado. Because of their handicap their opportunity for asking questions, for developing certain learning sets, for becoming acquainted with social traditions and recorded histories, and for adjustment to adult attitudes (particularly the knowledge that adults are a potential source of information) is dramatically reduced. This general impoverishment of input is very likely to have produced different learning histories for this group than for hearing children. Our investigations, therefore, may not merely indicate whether cognitive processes *can* be carried on in the absence of language, but cognitive differences discovered by certain procedures are in danger of confounding basic cognitive capacities of the child with the presence or absence of previously acquired knowledge.

This is just one of four major reasons why at present the published reports on the cognitive status of deaf children is so contradictory. *

A second reason is the great diversity in aims, methods, and questions underlying the many reports that makes direct comparison between the various studies impossible.

A third source for differences between results is due to the difficult control and exclusion of language from the experimental situation. Even if the task itself does not require a verbal response, high perform-

---

* Deaf children's performance on cognitive tasks are reported to be essentially the same as that of hearing control groups in the following articles: Emmerig (1953), Furth (1961), Glowatsky (1953), Larr (1955), Lowell and Metfessel (1961), Oléron (1953, 1957, 1962), Rosenstein (1960, 1961), The Clark School for the Deaf (1940); whereas cognitive differences were found by Blair (1957), Borelli (1951), Farrant (1962), Gozova (1960), Larr (1956), Oléron (1949, 1951, 1952), Reich (1952), Stafford (1962), Templin (1950), Varva (1956), Wright (1955). This is just a small sample of a very extensive literature.

ance may depend on understanding of complicated instructions and on the ability to ask questions about the purpose of the investigation and the spirit in which it is conducted.

Finally, there is a great deal of difference in statistical sophistication of the various studies published. In some studies we find sweeping statements on the equality of the two or the inferiority of one of the groups of children, based on statistical inferences involving dubious procedures. The most common pitfall here is to discuss "the deaf" as if they were a homogeneous population, whereas in fact the children in the schools for the deaf constitute a very mixed group with many

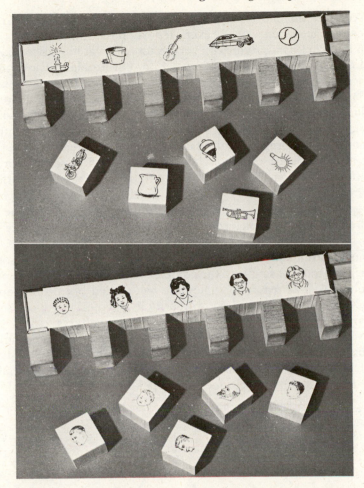

FIG. 8.8. Four examples of concept—formation tasks from the Leiter International Performance Test. (Reproduced by permission of C. H. Stoelting Co.)

different etiologies. In some cases deafness is attributable to diffuse central nervous system lesions while in others it is a purely peripheral loss; there are many more children with psychiatric problems among the deaf than among the hearing; furthermore, the children differ considerably in language proficiency. This great heterogeneity brings with it a difficulty in controlling for untoward variables, and a likelihood that measurements of many relevant variables are not distributed normally. Add to these difficulties the occasional practice of pooling test-scores of the entire sample of the deaf and it becomes clear that one cannot accept uncritically every report on the subject.

On the other hand, studies on very young and carefully selected deaf children may give valuable information for our problem. The cognitive experiments conducted by Oléron (1957), Furth (1961), Rosenstein (1961), and others fall into this category and seem to indicate, on the whole, that there is no general deficiency in the fundamental cognitive skills of congenitally deaf and severely language-handicapped children as compared to normally hearing and speaking children.

In my experience with preschool deaf children (screened for psychiatric and nervous disorders), I have found the individual performances on the Leiter scale (1936–1955), which is a largely language-free concept formation test, to differ in no respect from those of hearing children. In this test, pictures have to be sorted in accordance with given criteria (Fig. 8.8). Toys with toys, musical instruments with musical instruments, four symbols with four symbols. The sorting criteria go from the simple to the complex and require both conceptualization as well as reasoning. They are age-graded but do not, apparently, test knowledge acquired ordinarily in a typical American school system because the test may be used in different cultures.

My colleagues who have used this test on many deaf and hearing children (I am particularly indebted for this information to Dr. Miriam Fiedler) have found that successful performance even of older children than those tested by myself does not depend on the demonstrable lan-

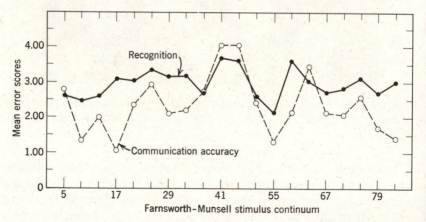

FIG. 8.9. Deaf adult color recognition and its relationship to the communication accuracy scores obtained from that group (responses were made in writing). For the deaf, communication behavior is not as highly correlated with recognition accuracy than for the hearing population.

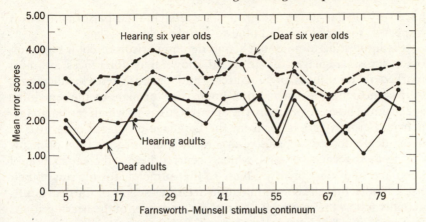

FIG. 8.10. Accuracy for color recognition in four groups of subjects. When the two adult curves are compared with each other or those of the two groups of children, the curves do not fit very well. However, when the deaf children are compared with the deaf adult or the hearing children with the hearing adult there is much better agreement.

guage skills of the individual. Scores depend on maturation or on the presence of psychiatric or neurological disturbance.

Further suggestions concerning the relationship between aspects of cognition and language habits are afforded through the duplication of the color-recognition experiments on congenitally deaf adults and children. Lantz and Lenneberg (unpublished data) have collected communication accuracy scores among deaf adults for the Farnsworth Munsell Colors and have then tested similar groups of deaf adult subjects (Fig. 8.9) and also groups of six-year-old deaf children for color recognition. * This material was compared with results obtained from hearing adults and children. The comparison of the recognition error scores, shown in Fig. 8.10, is rather revealing. Except for the blue-green range of the spectrum, there is fair similarity in performance among the four groups even though each one differs from the other in their grossly observable language proficiency or the number of years during which they have used language. The hearing adults differ from the three remaining groups in their recognition performance in the purple range (the colors were most frequently called *lavender* by this group); both deaf groups differ from both hearing groups in their recognition of blue-green colors, but the deaf and hearing each, among themselves,

---

* The cooperation of the Beverly School for the Deaf, the Horace Mann School, the American School for the Deaf, the Lexington School for the Deaf, and the Kendall School for the Deaf is gratefully acknowledged.

have very similar curves. All groups are alike in their performance with respect to rose-to-green and blue-to-purple colors.

It is interesting to note that semantic comparison of color terminologies across languages of the world shows that differences are most marked in the modes of blue-green and purplish-red classifications. Fair coincidence of demarcation lines exist throughout the remaining spectrum. These are precisely the spectral areas in which the language-deficient groups here differ from the language-proficient ones. It is as if the deaf adopted a cognitive-organizational categorization principle during their formative years, which occurred before the acquisition of language, and subsequently adhere to that principle for the rest of their lives. Notice that the communication accuracy scores of the deaf adults actually follow the communication accuracy scores of the hearing adults (shown in Fig. 8.7) but not the recognition scores of the hearing population. Thus, in contrast to the hearing, the observable language behavior of the deaf does not completely account for their recognition behavior; the latter goes its own way, so to speak. When the deaf communicate with each other in writing, gesture, or lip-reading they avail themselves of the language vehicle as it is provided for in use among the hearing; their social behavior is not different in this respect. But the intrapersonal categorization task which apparently determines the recognition task is, in certain regions of the spectrum, quite independent from their communication habits.

These experiments show that the semantic structure of a language may influence cognitive structuration where our physiological equipment allows for a range of alternative solutions. But there is no indication that the basic organizational capacities are crippled through a crippling of language proficiency. It is probably only in the areas of education proper (as opposed to the biologically given organization of the environment) that language deficits become a serious obstacle for intellectual development.

Relevant to this discussion are also two further types of observation. The first concerns the spontaneous play activities of the deaf preschool child. Unless there is also generalized neurological or psychiatric disturbance, the almost complete absence of language in these children is no hindrance to the most imaginative and intelligent play appropriate for the age. They love make-believe games; they can build fantastic structures with blocks or out of boxes; they may set up electric trains and develop the necessary logic for setting switches and anticipating the behavior of the moving train around curves and over bridges. They love to look at pictures, and no degree of stylizing renders the pictorial representation incomprehensible for them, and their own drawings leave nothing to be desired when compared with those produced by their hearing contemporaries. Thus, cognitive development as revealed through play seems to be no different from that which occurs in the presence of language development. On the other hand, and this is the second type of observation, mentally deficient children may have a much greater degree of language development at age five than the peripherally deaf, but here the language advantage does not help the level of sophistication for play.

(6) *Recent Experiments in Psycholinguistics*

There is a new development in psycholinguistic experiments whose impetus is due largely to George A. Miller (1962, 1964). The aim of these investigations is to show that the theoretically derived structure of a natural language is a psychological reality. It is possible to set up conditions in which latency of response (McMahon, 1963), recall (Savin and Perchonock, in press; Mehler, 1963; Mehler and Miller, 1964), or perception (Miller and Isard, 1963) are predictable from grammatical analysis of the verbal material that is used for stimulation in these experiments. In all cases where the stimulus material consists of strings of words that are sentences in the subjects' native language, performance is governed by rules of grammar that are applied by the subject to the material in order to organize the task. This entire research has recently been summarized by McNeill and Miller (forthcoming) and need therefore not be reviewed here.

V. POSTSCRIPT TO SO-CALLED LANGUAGE RELATIVITY

The term language relativity is due to B. L. Whorf, although similar notions had been expressed before by many others (Basilius, 1952). In his studies of American Indian languages, Whorf was impressed with the general difficulties encountered in translating American Indian languages into European languages. To him there seemed to be little or no isomorphism between his native English and languages such as Hopi or Nootka. He posed the question, as many had done before him, of whether the divergences encountered reflected a comparable divergence of thought on the part of the speakers. He left the final answer open, subject to further research, but it appears from the tenor of his articles that he believed that this was so, that differences in language are expressions of differences in thought. It has been pointed out since (Black, 1959; Feuer, 1953; but see also Fishman, 1960) that there is actually little *a priori* basis for such beliefs.

The empirical research discussed in previous sections (partly stimulated by Whorf's own imaginative ideas) indicate that the cognitive processes studied so far are largely independent from peculiarities of any natural language and, in fact, that cognition can develop to a certain extent even in the absence of knowledge of any language. The reverse does not hold true; the growth and development of language does appear to require a certain minimum state of maturity and specificity of cognition. Could it be that some languages require "less mature cognition" than others, perhaps because they are still more primitive? In recent years this notion has been thoroughly discredited by virtually all students of language. It is obvious that on the surface every language has its own peculiarities but it is possible, in fact assumed throughout this monograph, that languages are different patterns produced by identical basic principles (much the way sentences are different patterns —infinitely so—produced by identical principles). The crucial question, therefore, is whether we are dealing with a universal and unique process that generates a unique *type* of pattern. From the discussions of Chapter Seven we may assume that this is so, and Chomsky, in the Appendix, also argues eloquently to this effect. In syntax we seem to be dealing always with the same formal *type* of rule and in the realm of semantics we have proposed that the *type* of relationship between word and object is quite invariant across all users of words. It is due to this uniformity that any human may learn any natural language within certain age limits.

When language learning is at its biological optimum, namely in childhood, the degree of relatedness between first and second language is quite irrelevant to the ease of learning that second language. Apparently, the differences in surface structure are ignored and the similarity of the generative principles is maximally explored at this age. Until rigorous proof is submitted to the contrary, it is more reasonable to assume that all natural languages are of equal complexity and versatility and the choice of this assumption detracts much from the so-called relativity theory.

Since the use of words is a creative process, the static reference relationships, such as are apparent through *Approach A* or as they are recorded in a dictionary, are of no great consequence for the actual use of words. However, the differences between languages that impressed Whorf so much are entirely restricted to these static aspects and have little effect upon the creative process itself. The diagram of Fig. 8.11 may illustrate the point. Common to all mankind are the general biological characteristics of the species (outer circle) among which is a peculiar mode and capacity for conceptualization or cate-

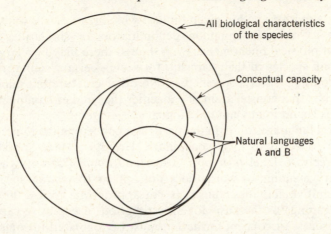

FIG. 8.11. The relationship of natural languages to the human capacity for conceptualization.

gorization. Languages tag some selective cognitive modes but they differ in the selection. This selectivity does not cripple or bind the speaker because he can make his language, or his vocabulary, or his power of word-creation, or his freedom in idiosyncratic usages of words do any duty that he chooses, and he may do this to a large extent without danger of rendering himself unintelligible because his fellow men have similar capacities and freedoms which also extend to understanding.

VI. SUMMARY

Words are not labels attached to objects by conditioning; strictly associative bonds between a visual stimulus and an auditory stimulus are difficult to demonstrate in language. It is usually through the relative inhibition in the formation of such bonds that the labeling of open, abstract categories can take place, which is the hall-mark of the human semantic system. The meaning-bearing elements of language do not, generally, stand for specific objects (proper names are a special case), and strictly speaking, not even for invariant classes of objects. Apparently they stand for a cognitive process, that is, the *act* of categorization or the *formation* of concepts. Operationally, such a process may be characterized as the ability to make a similar response to different stimulus situations within given limits,* which rests on the individual's capacity to recognize common denominators or similarities among ranges of physical phenomena. Even though there may be a large overlap among species in their capacity for seeing certain similarities, one also encounters species-specificities. No other creature but man seems to have just that constellation of capacities that makes naming possible such as is found in any natural language.

Natural languages differ in the particular conceptualization processes that are reflected in their vocabulary. However, since speakers use words freely to label *their own conceptualization processes,* the static dictionary meaning of words does not appear to restrict speakers in their cognitive activities; thus it is not appropriate to use the vocabulary meanings as the basis for an estimation of cognitive capacities.

The process of concept formation must be regulated to some extent by biological determinants; therefore, naming in all languages should have fairly similar formal properties. The basis for metaphorizing in all languages is usually transparent to everyone; it never seems totally arbitrary or unnatural. Also, we have excellent intuitions about what might be namable in a foreign language once one knows something about that community's culture, technology, or religion. Even the demarcation lines of semantic classes are more frequently "obvious" to a foreign speaker than a matter of complete surprise. When we learn new words in a foreign language we do not have to determine laboriously the extent of the naming class for every word we learn; there will be only a few instances where demarcations are not obvious. The incongruences between languages become marked only in certain types of grammatical classifications such as animate-inanimate, male-female, plural-singular, to'ness-from'ness, etc. But, curiously enough, on this level of abstraction, where the semantics of the form-classes often does take on an entirely arbitrary character, cognitive processes seem least affected. There is no evidence that gender in German or the declinational systems of Russian, or the noun-classification systems in the Bantu languages affect thought processes differentially.

Because of methodological obstacles, the relationship between language and cognition cannot be investigated experimentally except for a very restricted realm of the lexicon, namely the words for sensory experience. Three approaches were described that reveal (1) the dictionary meaning of sensory words; (2) the use speakers make of the dictionary meanings in a given situation; (3) the efficiency of com-

---

* I recognize that this formulation leaves the problems of synonymity and homonymity unsolved; but I am not aware of a satisfactory solution through any other formulation.

munication in a given situation, granted complete freedom of expression. The first approach is the most faithful representation of the reference relationships that are peculiar to a given natural language, and the other two approaches are progressively less so; the third approach is the most faithful representation of the communicative freedom enjoyed by speakers of any language, whereas the other two approaches fail to reflect this aspect.

Semantic aspects of words may aid memory functions under certain special conditions, but the bias thus introduced by properties of a natural language are slight and they are minimized or eliminated by other, more potent factors (that have nothing to do with the semantic structure of a language) in most situations. The development of basic cognitive functions gives no evidence of impairment in congenitally deaf children at the time they begin instruction in school and before they have acquired a natural language.

REFERENCES

Basilius, H. (1952), Neo-Humboldtian ethnolinguistics, *Word* **8**:95–105.

Beare, A. C. (1963), Color-name as a function of wave-length, *Am. J. Psychol.* **76**:248–256.

Black, M. (1959), Linguistic relativity: the views of Benjamin Lee Whorf, *Philosoph. Rev.* **68**:228–238.

Blair, F. X. (1957), A study of the visual memory of deaf and hearing children, *Am. Ann. Deaf* **102**:254–263.

Borelli, M. (1951), The birth of logical operations in the deafmute, *Enfance* **4**:222–238.

Brown, R. W. and Lenneberg, E. H. (1954), A study in language and cognition, *J. abnorm. soc. Psychol.* **49**:454–462.

Burnham, R. W. and Clark, J. R. (1955), A test of hue memory, *J. appl. Psychol.* **39**:164–172.

Carmichael, L., Hogan, H. P., and Walter, A. A. (1932), An experimental study of the effect of language on the reproduction of visually perceived form, *J. exp. Psychol.* **15**:73–86.

Carroll, J. B. (1964), *Language and Thought*. Prentice-Hall, Englewood Cliffs, New Jersey.

Chapanis, A. (1965), Color names for color space, *Am. Scientist* **53**:327–346.

The Clark School for the Deaf, Psychological Division, C. W. Barron Research Department, 1940. Studies in the psychology of the deaf, *Psychol. Monographs* Vol. 52, No. 1, Whole No. 232.

Conklin, H. C. (1955), Hanunoo color categories, *Southwestern J. Anthrop.* **11** (4):339–344.

Emmerig, E. (1953), Gesture in the life of a deaf-mute, *N. Bl. Taubstummenbildung* **7**:139–142.

Farnsworth, D. (1949), *The Farnsworth-Munsell 100 Hue Test for the Examination of Color Discrimination; Manual.* Munsell Color Co., Baltimore.

Farrant, R. H. (1962), A factor analytic study of the intellective abilities of deaf and hard of hearing children compared with normal hearing children, *Dissertation Abstracts* **22**(8):2870–2871.

Feuer, L. S. (1953), Sociological aspects of the relation between language and psychology, *Philosoph. Sci.* **20**:85–100.

Fishman, J. A. (1960), A systematization of the Whorfian hypothesis, *Behavioral Sci.* **5**:323–339.

Fodor, J. A. and Katz, J. J. (1963), *Readings in the Philosophy of Language.* Chapters 19 and 20. Prentice-Hall, Englewood Cliffs, New Jersey.

Furth, H. G. (1961), The influence of language on the development of concept formation in deaf children, *J. abnorm. soc. Psychol.* **63**(2):386–389.

Frijda, N. H. and Van de Geer, J. P. (1961), Codability and recognition: an experiment with facial expressions, *Acta Psychol.* **18**:360–367.

Glanzer, M. and Clark, W. H. (1962), Accuracy of perceptual recall: an analysis of organization, *J. verb. Learn. verb. Behav.* **1**:289–299.

Glowatsky, E. (1953), The verbal element in the intelligence scores of congenitally deaf and hard of hearing children, *Am. Ann. Deaf* **98**:328–335.

Gozova, A. P. (1960), Problems of visual-pictorial thinking of deaf-and-dumb pupils, *Dokl. Akad. Pedag. Nauk RSFSR* No. 2, 125–128.

Judd, D. B. (1932), Chromaticity sensibility to stimulus differences, *J. opt. Soc. Am.* **22**:72–108.

Krauss, R. M. and Weinheimer, S. (1965), The effect of referent array and communication mode on verbal encoding (unpublished).

Kurtz, K. H. and Hovland, C. I. (1953), The effect of verbalization during observation of stimulus objects upon accuracy of recognition and recall, *J. exp. Psychol.* **45**:157–164.

Landar, H. J., Ervin, S. M., and Horowitz, A. E. (1960), Navaho color categories, *Language* **36**:368–382.

Lantz, DeL. and Stefflre, V. (1964), Language and cognition revisited, *J. abnorm. soc. Psychol.* **69**:472–481.

Larr, A. L. (1955), An experimental investigation of the perceptual and conceptual abilities of children in residential schools for the deaf, *Dissertation Abstracts* **15**:2482.

Larr, A. L. (1956), Perceptual and conceptual abilities of residential school deaf children, *Except. Child.* **23**:63–66; 88.

Leiter, R. G. (1936–1955), *Leiter International Performance Scale.* C. H. Stoelting Co., Chicago, Illinois.

Lenneberg, E. H. (1953), Cognition in ethnolinguistics, *Language* **29**:463–471.

Lenneberg, E. H. (1955), A note on Cassirer's philosophy of language, *Philosophy and Phenomenological Research* **15**:512–522.

Lenneberg, E. H. (1957), A probabilistic approach to language learning, *Behavioral Sci.* **2**:1–13.

Lenneberg, E. H. (1961), Color naming, color recognition, color discrimination: a re-appraisal, *Perceptual and Motor Skills* **12**:375–382.

Lenneberg, E. H. and Roberts, J. M. (1956), *The Language of Experience: a Study in Methodology,* Memoir 13, Indiana University Publications in Anthropology and Linguistics.

Lowell, E. L. (1962), in *National Symposium on the Deaf—Driving and Employability.* U. S. Dep't. Health Education and Welfare; Vocational Rehabilitation Administration.

Lowell, E. L. and Metfessel, N. S. (1961), Experimental concept formation test for preschool deaf, *J. speech hearing Dis.* **26**:225–229.

McMahon, L. E. (1963), Grammatical analysis as part of understanding a sentence. Unpublished Ph.D. dissertation, submitted to Dep't. of Psychology, Harvard University, Cambridge, Mass.

Mehler, J. (1963), Some effects of grammatical transformations on the recall of English sentences, *J. verb. Learn. verb. Behav.* **2**:346–351.

Mehler, J. and Miller, G. A. (1964), Retroactive interference in the recall of simple sentences, *Brit. J. Psychol.* **55**:295–301.

Miller, G. A. (1962), Some psychological studies of grammar, *Am. Psychol.* **17**:748–762.

Miller, G. A. (1964), The psycholinguists, *Encounter* **23**:29–37.

Miller, G. A. and Isard, S. (1963), Some perceptual consequences of linguistic rules, *J. verb. Learn. verb. Behav.* **2**:217–228.

Nickerson, D. and Newhall, S. M. (1943), A psychological color solid, *J. opt. Soc. Am.* **33**:419–422.

Oléron, P. (1949), A study of the intelligence of the deaf, *Am. Ann. Deaf.* **95**:179–195.

Oléron, P. (1951), The conceptual thought and language performance of deaf-mutes and those that can hear compared in multiple classification tests, *Année psychol.* **51**:89–120.

Oléron, P. (1952), The role of language in mental development; a contribution drawn from the psychology of the deaf-mute child, *Enfance* **5**:120–137.

Oléron, P. (1953), Conceptual thinking of the deaf, *Am. Ann. Deaf* **98**:304–310.

Oléron, P. (1957), *Studies of the Mental Development of Deaf-Mutes.* Monograph of the Centre National de la Recherche Scientifique, 134 p.

Oléron, P. (1962), The development of responses of the identity-dissimilarity relation with relation to language, *Psychol. Franc.* **7**:4–16.

Pertschonok, D. (1959), The language of feeling: a study in the categorization of emotional expression. Harvard University, unpublished doctoral dissertation.

Reich, E. C. (1952), Development of the mathematical sense in deaf children, *Am. Ann. Deaf.* **97**:427–437.

Rosenstein, J. (1960), Cognitive abilities of deaf children, *J. speech hearing Res.* **3**:108–119.

Rosenstein, J. (1961), Perception, cognition and language in deaf children (a critical analysis and review of the literature), *Except. Children* **27**:276–284.

Savin, H. B. and Perchonock, E., Grammatical structure and the immediate recall of English sentences, *J. verb. Learn. verb. Behav.* (in press).

Stafford, K. (1962), Problem-solving ability of deaf and hearing children, *J. speech hearing Res.* **5**(2):169–172.

Templin, M. C. (1950), *The Development of Reasoning in Children with Normal and Defective Hearing.* Univ. of Minnesota Press, Minneapolis.

Van de Geer, J. P. (1960), *Studies in codability: I. Identification and recognition of colors.* Report No. E001–60, 1960, State Univ. of Leyden, Psychol. Institute, The Netherlands.

Varva, F. I. (1956), An investigation of the effect of auditory deficiency upon performance with special reference to concrete and abstract tasks. *Dissertation Abstracts* **16**:2532.

Whorf, B. L. (1956), *Language, Thought and Reality,* J. B. Carroll (ed.). Technology Press of M.I.T., Cambridge, Massachusetts and John Wiley and Sons, New York.

Wright, R. H. (1955), The abstract reasoning of deaf college students, *Dissertation Abstracts* **15**:1911.

CHAPTER Nine

Toward a biological theory of language development (General summary)

We have discussed language from many different aspects, have drawn various conclusions and offered a variety of explanations. If we now stand back and survey the entire panorama, will this synopsis suggest an integrated theory? I believe it will.

I. FIVE GENERAL PREMISES

The language theory to be proposed here is based upon the following five empirically verifiable, general biological premises.

(i) *Cognitive function is species-specific.* Taxonomies suggest themselves for virtually all aspects of life. Formally, these taxonomies are always type-token hierarchies, and on every level of the hierarchy we may discern differences among tokens and, at the same time, there are commonalities that assign the tokens logically to a type. The commonalities are not necessarily more and more abstract theoretical concepts but are suggested by physiological and structural invariances. An anatomical example of such an invariance is cell-constituency—it is common to all organisms. In the realm of sensory perception there are physiological properties that result in commonalities for entire classes of animals, so that every species has very similar pure stimulus thresholds. When we compare behavior across species, we also find certain invariances, for instance, the general effects of reward and punishment. But in each of these examples there are also species differences. Cells combine into a species-specific form; sensations combine to produce species-specific pattern-recognition; and behavioral parameters enter into the elaboration of species-specific action patterns.

Let us focus on the species-specificities of behavior. There are certain cerebral functions that mediate between sensory input and motor output which we shall call generically *cognitive function*. The neurophysiology of cognitive function is largely unknown but its behavioral correlates are the propensity for categorizing in specific ways (extraction of similarity), capacity for problem solving, the formation of learning sets, the tendency to generalize in certain directions, or the facility for memorizing some but not other conditions. The interaction or integrated patterns of all of these different potentialities produces the cognitive specificities that have induced von Uexkuell, the forerunner of modern ethology, to propose that every species has its own world-view. The phenomenological implications of his formulaion may sound old-fashioned today, but students of animal behavior cannot ignore the fact that the differences in cognitive processes (1) are empirically demonstrable and (2) are the correlates of species-specific behavior.

(ii) *Specific properties of cognitive function are replicated in every member of the species.* Although there are individual differences among all creatures, the members of one species resemble each other very closely. In every individual a highly invariable *type* of both form and function is replicated. Individual differences of most characteristics tend to have a normal (Gaussian) frequency distribution and the differences within species are smaller than between species. (We are disregarding special taxonomic problems in species identification.)

The application of these notions to (i) makes it clear that also the cognitive processes and potentialities that are characteristics of a species are replicated in every individual. Notice that we must distinguish between what an individual actually does and what he is capable of doing. The intraspecific similarity holds for the latter, not the former, and the similarity in capacity becomes striking only if we concentrate on the general type and manner of activity and disregard such variables as how fast or how accurately a given performance is carried out.

(iii) *Cognitive processes and capacities are differentiated spontaneously with maturation.* This statement must not be confused with the question of how much the environment contributes to development. It is obvious that all development requires an appropriate substrate and availability of certain forms of energy. However, in most cases environments are not specific to just one form of life and development. A forest pond may be an appropriate environment for hundreds of different forms of life. It may support the fertilized egg of a frog or a minnow, and each of the eggs will respond to just those types and forms of energy that are appropriate to it. The frog's egg will develop into a frog and the minnow's egg into a minnow. The pond just makes the building stones available, but the organismic architecture unfolds through conditions that are created within the maturing individual.

Cognition is regarded as the behavioral manifestation of physiological processes. Form and function are not arbitrarily superimposed upon the embryo from the outside but gradually develop through a process of differentiation. The basic plan is based on information contained in the developing tissues. Some functions need an extra organismic stimulus for the initiation of operation—something that triggers the cocked mechanisms; the onset of air-breathing in mammals is an example. These extra-organismic stimuli do not shape the ensuing function. A species' peculiar mode of processing visual input, as evidenced in pattern recognition, may develop only in individuals who have had a minimum of exposure to properly illuminated objects in the environment during their formative years. But the environment clearly does not shape the mode of input processing, because the environment might have been the background to the visual development of a vast number of other types of pattern-recognition.

(iv) *At birth, man is relatively immature; certain aspects of his behavior and cognitive function emerge only during infancy.* Man's postnatal state of maturity (brain and behavior) is less advanced than that of other primates. This is a statement of fact and not a return to the fetalization and neotony theories of old (details in Chapter Four).

(v) *Certain social phenomena among animals come about by spontaneous adaptation of the behavior of the growing individual to the behavior of other individuals around him. Adequate environment* does not merely include nutritive and physical conditions; many animals require specific social conditions for proper development. The survival of the species frequently depends on the development of mechanisms for social cohesion or social cooperation. The development of typical social behavior in a growing individual requires, for many species, exposure to specific stimuli such as the presence of certain action patterns in the mother, a sexual partner, a group leader, etc. Sometimes mere exposure to social behavior of other individuals is a sufficient stimulus. For some species the correct stimulation must occur during a narrow formative period in infancy; failing this, further development may become seriously and irreversibly distorted. In all types of developing social behavior, the growing individual begins to engage in behavior as if by resonance; he is maturationally ready but will not begin to perform unless properly stimulated. If exposed to the stimuli, he becomes socially "excited" as a resonator may become excited when exposed to a given range of sound frequencies. Some social behavior consists of intricate patterns, the development of which is the result of subtle adjustments to and interactions with similar behavior patterns (for example, the songs of certain bird species). An impoverished social input may entail permanently impoverished behavior patterns.

Even though the development of social behavior may require an environmental trigger for proper development and function, the triggering stimulus must not be mistaken for the cause that *shapes* the behavior. Prerequisite social triggering mechanisms do not shape the social behavior in the way Emily Post may shape the manners of a debutante.

II. A CONCISE STATEMENT OF THE THEORY

(1) Language is the manifestation of species-specific cognitive propensities. It is the consequence of the biological peculiarities that make a human type of cognition possible.* The dependence of language upon human cognition is merely one instance of the general phenomenon characterized by premise (i) above. There is evidence (Chapter Seven and Eight) that cognitive function is a more basic and primary process than language, and that the dependence-relationship of language upon cognition is incomparably stronger than vice versa.

(2) The cognitive function underlying language consists of an adaptation of a ubiquitous process (among vertebrates) of categorization and extraction of similarities. The perception and production of language may be reduced on all levels to categorization processes, including the subsuming of narrow categories under more comprehensive ones and the subdivision of comprehensive categories into more specific ones. The extraction of similarities does not only operate upon physical stimuli but also upon categories of underlying structural schemata. Words label categorization processes (Chapter Seven and Eight).

(3) Certain specializations in peripheral anatomy and physiology account for some of the universal features of natural languages, but the

---

* It is true that this statement introduces some profound problems in the theory of evolution, but our preoccupation with language should not oblige us to solve, at the same time, the general problems that affect all evolutionary phenomena. The emergence of celestial navigation in birds or the diving abilities of whales are no less mysterious than the emergence of a language-enabling cognition.

description of these human peculiarities does not constitute an explanation for the phylogenetic development of language. During the evolutionary history of the species form, function and behavior have interacted adaptively, but none of these aspects may be regarded as the "cause" of the other. Today, mastery of language by an individual may be accomplished despite severe peripheral anomalies, indicating that cerebral function is now the determining factor for language behavior as we know it in contemporary man. This, however, does not necessarily reflect the evolutionary sequence of developmental events.

(4) The biological properties of the human form of cognition set strict limits to the range of possibilities for variations in natural languages. The forms and modes of categorization, the capacity for extracting similarities from physical stimulus configuration or from classes of deeper structural schemata, and the operating characteristics of the data-processing machinery of the brain (for example, time-limitations on the rate of input, resolution-power for the analysis of intertwined patterns such as nested dependencies, limits of storage capacities for data that must be processed simultaneously, etc.) are powerful factors that determine a peculiar type of form for language. Within the limits set, however, there are infinitely many variations possible. Thus the outer form of languages may vary with relatively great freedom, whereas the underlying type remains constant.

(5) The implication of (1) and (2) is that the existence of our cognitive processes entails a potential for language. It is a capacity for a communication system that must necessarily be of one specific type. This basic capacity develops ontogenetically in the course of physical maturation; however, certain environmental conditions also must be present to make it possible for language to unfold. Maturation brings cognitive processes to a state that we may call *language-readiness*. The organism now requires certain raw materials from which it can shape building blocks for his own language development. The situation is somewhat analogous to the relationship between nourishment and growth. The food that the growing individual takes in as architectural raw material must be chemically broken down and reconstituted before it may enter the synthesis that produces tissues and organs. The information on how the organs are to be structured does not come in the food but is latent in the individual's own cellular components. The raw material for the individual's language synthesis is the language spoken by the adults surrounding the child. The presence of the raw material seems to function like a releaser for the developmental language synthesizing process. The course of language-unfolding is quite strictly prescribed through the unique maturational path traversed by cognition, and thus we may

say that language-readiness is a state of *latent language structure*. The unfolding of language is a process of *actualization* in which latent structure is transformed into *realized structure*. The actualization of latent structure to realized structure is to give the underlying cognitively determined type a concrete form.*

(6) The actualization process is not the same as "beginning to say things." In fact, it may be independent from certain restraints that are attending upon the capacity for making given responses. Actualization may take place even if responses are peripherally blocked; in this case actualization is demonstrable only through signs of understanding language. In cases where the proper raw material for language synthesis cannot be made available to the growing child (as in the deaf), the latent structure fails to become actualized either temporarily or permanently.

(7) The maturation of cognitive processes comes about through progressive differentiation. Physiological (and, therefore, cognitive) functions assume characteristics and specificities much the way cells and tissues do during ontogeny. Organs do not suddenly begin to function out of a state of silence, but every function in the mature individual is a derivative of embryologically earlier types of function. Although the primitive functions may often be different from the mature ones, we cannot say just when a later or derived process had its beginning. If language is an aspect of a fundamental, biologically determined process, it is not scientifically profitable to look for a *cause* of language development in the growing child just as we do not look for a *cause* for the development of his ears. It might be more fruitful to think of maturation, including growth and the development of behavior such as language, as the traversing of highly unstable states; the disequilibrium of one leads to rearrangements that bring about new disequilibria, producing further rearrangements, and so on until relative stability, known as *maturity,* is reached. Language-readiness is an example of such a state of disequilibrium during which the mind creates a place into which the building blocks of language may fit.

(8) The disequilibrium state called language-readiness is of limited duration. It begins around two and declines with cerebral maturation in the early teens. At this time, apparently a steady state is reached, and the cognitive processes are firmly structured, the capacity for pri-

---

* This formulation might be regarded as the biological counterpart to what grammarians have for centuries called *universal* and *particular* grammar. Latent structure is responsible for the general type of all features of universal grammar; realized structure is responsible both for the peculiarities of any given statement as well as those aspects that are unique to the grammar of a given natural language.

mary language synthesis is lost, and cerebral reorganization of functions is no longer possible.

(9) The language potential and the *latent structure* may be assumed to be replicated in every healthy human being because they are a consequence of human-specific cognitive processes and a human-specific course of maturation. In other words, universal grammar is of a unique type, common to all men, and it is entirely the by-product of peculiar modes of cognition based upon the biological constitution of the individual. This notion of replication, which is a cornerstone of the present theory, also leads us to assume that the actualization process from latent to realized structure is universal because of replicated sequences of similar states of disequilibrium, and there is evidence for this assumption in the regularity of language-acquisition strategies discussed in Chapters Four and Seven.

(10) Because latent structure is replicated in every child and because all languages must have an inner form of identical type (though an infinity of variations is possible), every child may learn any language with equal ease. The realized structure or outer form of the language that surrounds the growing child serves as a mold upon which the form of the child's own realized structure is modeled. This maneuver is possible only because all languages are so constructed as to conform to the stringent requirements imposed upon them by cerebral language-data processing mechanisms. Insistence upon universal, underlying identity of type in all languages may be difficult to understand in the face of differences in rules of syntax and semantic divergences. This puzzle is solved by considering the remarkable freedom allowed individual speakers to make creative and novel use of word-meanings, to reclassify words into various syntactic categories, and to take creative freedoms with rules of syntax. All aspects of outer form or realized structure are in a state of fluidity (of relatively high viscosity) indicating that it is our "mode of calculating with categories" that is universal, but the categories themselves are not fixed nor the particular choice of the many possible operations.

(11) The raw material from which the individual synthesizes building blocks for his own language development cannot be the cause of the developing structure as evidenced by the autochthonous beginnings in the infant's language acquisition. Primitive stages of language are simply too different from adult language to be regarded as a direct mirroring of the input. Nor is there any evidence that the adults surrounding the child are the causative or shaping agents that determine language onset or his course of development (see discussion of *need* as explanation in Chapter Four and of language teaching in Chapter

Seven). Purposiveness cannot, logically, be the mainspring for language development.

(12) Social settings may be required as a trigger that sets off a reaction. Perhaps a better metaphor still is the concept of resonance. In a given state of maturation, exposure to adult language behavior has an excitatory effect upon the actualization process much the way a certain frequency may have an excitatory effect upon a specific resonator; the object begins to vibrate in the presence of the sound. In the case of language onset, the energy required for the resonance is, in a sense, supplied by the individual himself; if the trigger-analogy is preferred, we might say that he unwinds himself. The resonance analogy, on the other hand, illustrates more vividly how slight variations in the frequencies that impinge on the resonator may affect the quality or nature of the resonance; it is comparable to the child's hearing of French resulting in his speaking of French, each natural language being a selected frequency band from the limited possible frequency range that is capable of eliciting resonance. Once the critical period during which resonance may occur is outgrown, one language is firmly established, and exposure to new and different natural languages is no longer resonated to.

Thus the propagation and maintenance of language behavior in the species are not comparable to cultural tradition which is handed down from generation to generation. The individual does not serve as a passive vehicle or channel through which information is transmitted; instead, he is an autonomous unit constituted in very much the same way as other units around him, ready to behave in the same fashion as they do. His behavior is activated by social contact, and there is some superficial adaptation to the structure of their behavior, but it may be well to remember that he can only function if he can synthesize (recreate might be another word) the entire language mechanism out of the raw material available to him. The raw material is of no use unless it can be broken down as food proteins are broken down into amino-acids and built up again into the pattern of his in-dwelling latent structure. Thus, the individual is seen as functioning by virtue of his own power supply, so to speak; he constructs language by himself (provided he has the raw material to do it with), and the natural history of his development provides for mechanisms by which he will harmonize his function with that of other equally autonomously functioning individuals around him; the outer form of his language will have the outer form of the language of his native community.

(13) Even though biological constitution of the individual is an essential replica of its progenitors, there are, naturally, individual variations.

In fact, there are two distinct levels that are relevant to language: in the formation of the latent structure and in the actualization process from latent to realized structure. The former may be due to variations in the operation of cognitive processes or due to variations in the maturational course; the latter is primarily due to variations in peripheral function and structures such as the vocal tract or the ears. Variations on these two levels explain the main facts about language constancies, language change, and language universals.

III. EXPLANATORY POWER OF THE THEORY

These are the essentials of the theory. Most of its tenets are merely special instances of the general premises (i) through (v) cited at the beginning of the chapter and may, therefore, be considered as fairly common biological phenomena. A few of the tenets, however, may seem novel introductions into the armamentarium of explanations for behavior. But within the wider horizon of biological theory they should not at all look like theoretical innovations or logically illegitimate freedoms. The natural history of species-specific behavior is proposed here to partake of most of the characteristics and peculiarities encountered in the history of differentiated anatomical structures or physiological functions. Sections (5) and (12) particularly make no stronger assumptions than those made by the theory of morphogenesis or general physical development. It is true that the most crucial questions surrounding embryology have yet to be answered, and the same is true of the molecular mechanisms that would underly the phenomena proposed here. Just as the present state of embryological theory, my theory of language development is essentially an interpretive commentary on observable facts.

The observable facts are the absence of any need for teaching of language as well as the relative ineffectiveness of programmed training upon the rate of language acquisition; the resonance phenomenon is most beautifully seen in the language development of twins who influence each other in the actualization process, sometimes resulting in peculiar deviations in their realized structure or outer form when compared to the model form of the language surrounding them. The regularity of language-onset as a milestone that fits into an ordered and fairly constant sequence of other maturational milestones is another observable fact and so is the apparent similarity in language acquisition strategies, the universal similarity of primitive stages, and the difference in outer form between primitive stages and adult language. Other observable facts are the differences between children and adults in their recovery from acquired aphasia. Furthermore, nothing short of statement (5) can account for the perfect ease with which blind children learn meanings, and even blind-and-deaf children may acquire the fundamentals of language although they may have to recode input and output.

Sometimes it is said that the general claim of species-specificity of behavior or the postulation of innate factors that determine such behavior is a return to the preformist position of eighteenth-century developmental theory. Nothing could be farther from the truth. Modern ethology is as epigenetic as embryology itself is today. The preformist believed that the ovum contained a miniature specimen of the adult individual, whereas the epigenetic doctrine teaches that the adult form is the result of gradual formation of structure through a continuing process of reconstitution of molecules, and that every individual is, therefore, created anew, so to speak. It is obvious, however, that the laws of formation must be duplicated in every growing individual and that these laws follow from information or guidelines that are encoded in the genic material of the first cell. Environmental conditions such as gravity, temperature, availability of oxygen, space to expand in, etc., are, in many cases, necessary factors for proper development, but they are never sufficient to determine the formation of the structural plan peculiar to a given species of complex animals. Clearly, our proposal of how language develops in the individual is in no way counter to an epigenetic view.

IV. BIOLOGICAL FOUNDATIONS OF HISTORY AND DISTRIBUTION OF NATURAL LANGUAGES

(1) *Theoretical Foundations*

Most of the general phenomena of natural languages, especially the reasons for change and relative constancy follow logically from the theory postulated here, particularly from propositions (5), (12) and (13), that is, the concepts of latent and realized structure, of resonance, and of individual variations.

The types of changes encountered in the recorded history of languages are too well-known to require further comment here. The relative constancies are also fairly obvious though they are more frequently ignored in discussions of language. Features that remain constant throughout recorded language history are identical with language universals encountered in modern languages. Thus, we find changing inventories of phonemes but complete constancy in the basic phonematic mode of signaling. (All languages are and have been phoneme-languages throughout the documented past. Sound analogy or sound imitation is never encountered un-phonematized.) Although lexica, form-class assignment, and syntactically marked groupings of words may differ through history and place, all languages are concerned with essentially similar aspects of the environment. (There is no language in which we cannot give directions, tell about a past event, describe other persons' behavior, etc.).

The syntax of all languages is of the same basic type: utterances consist of concatenated morphemes and the concatenation is never random. Words and morphemes are always assignable to functional categories; sentences in all languages may be judged as grammatically acceptable or unacceptable by criteria of underlying structure. We see that the superficial structure of languages undergoes noticeable changes in history and thus results in diversification of languages over the face of the earth, whereas there are powerful indications that the underlying structure preserves its essential type over very long periods of time and among all speech communities. Our theory attempts to relate these two levels of language structure to what we have called latent and realized structure, terms that refer to the structure of behavior instead of the structure of the behavioral product.

(*a*) *Source, inhibitors, and determinants of change.* The system of biological replication does not work with ideal precision; random variations occur which, over the long run, would have a totally self-cancelling and, therefore, leveling and difference-eroding effect unless some factors of bias were operating selectively upon this bounty of variations. This is true of life, in general, and of all aspects of organisms. Thus the source for change is in the self-replication mechanism itself, and our problem therefore is not why a given characteristic of the species (in our case aspects of communication behavior) *changes* but what *inhibits* the change.

There must be at least two types of inhibitors: an extremely powerful one that holds the capacity for latent structure relatively constant over a time span of probably no less than 50,000 years, and a very weak one that permits changes in outer form and realized structure to occur within just a few generations. Given the source of variation and inhibiting factors that permit either only very slow or quite rapid changes, what might the nature of the factors be that determines the direction of change? Since there are two types of inhibitors, it is reasonable to assume that the direction-giving determinants are also of two different

TABLE 9.1. *Individual Variations in Biological Propensity for Language*

Degree of Deviation from Population Means	Type of Variation	
	Latent Structure (Relevant to evolutionary changes.)	Actualization or Formation of Realized Structure (Relevant to short-history changes and to language diversification.)
Slight (Occur frequently and constitute the raw material for all changes.)	Competence is affected. Individual's chance for language acquisition and efficiency in communication are inversely proportional to the degree of deviation from the mean.	Language competence is not affected but performance is. Deviations are irrelevant to efficiency of communication.
Marked If they occur rarely these variations will leave no trace upon long or short term histories.	Individual's language is markedly deviant, resulting in a state of isolation. Furthermore, the rarity of occurrence and the fundamental alterations in language function or organization prevent other individuals from resonating to this speech.	Performance is severely affected. If due to faulty response skills, congenital inarticulation with good understanding may result. Peripheral auditory handicaps may inhibit the actualization process so that latent structure becomes a permanent unrealized state (as in poorly educated deaf). Speech tends to be unique making resonance to it unlikely.

382

kinds. The slow changes in the capacity for latent structure are undoubtedly given direction by those factors that are generally held to be
responsible for directionality in evolution (see Chapter Six). They combine to build up selection pressure that is either directly or indirectly
responsible for the shaping of the species. The second type of determinants are probably a combination of social factors (cultural invasion,
diffusion, and prestige factors), internal restructuring of the language
pattern as a whole (for instance, the substitution of word order for
inflection, the introduction of new words due to loss of semantic specificity of older words, or the development of new phonemic contrasts
due to fusion of older contrasts), and perhaps uncontrolled exercise of
freedom for random variations. In the following pages we shall not be
concerned with the factors that determine direction of change but
primarily with the nature of the inhibitors.

(*b*) *Variance in capacity for latent and realized structure.* Table 9.1
presents a rough classification of the most important types of possible
variations. The table is self-explanatory. Alterations of latent structure
may be due to cognitive deviations or due to variations of the maturational course. Here the biological capacity for making use of the language input, that is, breaking down of elements and resynthesizing
them to form a realized structure, is fundamentally affected and thus
the propensity for language or Chomsky's competence is altered. On
the other hand, in alterations in the capacity for actualization, competence remains close to the population mean, whereas aspects of
performance are affected, primarily due to peripheral or generally
incidental reasons. Peculiarities in the individual geometry of the vocal
tract, or auditory peculiarities, or idiosyncracies of general motor
behavior, or other similar factors, will leave their imprint upon an
individual's language output, resulting in different styles of normal
speech.

(*c*) *Tolerance for variance; the mechanism of all changes.* A characterization of the variance is not sufficient to account for the evolutionary
and historical behavior of languages. For this we must introduce the
concept of tolerance. Consider deviations from the population mean
in capacity for latent structure. If the deviations are marked, the individual is either incapable of building up language behavior and thus
can neither understand nor speak, or it is at least theoretically possible
that there is latent structure of an altered type so that the language
that is built up is patterned upon a freak type of underlying structure,
unique in its operation, resulting in the generation of types of rules
that are incomprehensible to the rest of the community. In either case,
this type of language cannot propagate through the biological com-

munity because there would be no individual or not enough individuals whose latent structure is similarly deformed to allow them to resonate efficiently to such deviant behavior. On the other hand, it might be postulated that the deviation is due to a genetically transmitted trait, so that deviant children could resonate to their deviant parents. In fact, language deficient families do exist, although it is not yet certain that the mechanism is necessarily the one postulated here. However, there is another reason why marked deviations of latent structure have a low chance for dissemination.

The role of language is so important for social integration that such abnormality reduces the opportunity for finding a partner, and if the deviation is marked enough, the individual will become virtually in-communicado with great probability of exclusion from the gene-pool. Furthermore, genetically based alterations of a given trait are likely to be accompanied by other deviations, and thus there is a greater proportion of multiply abnormal individuals among the group of people with latent structure alterations than among a random sample of the population. This is corroborated by the fact that children seen in clinics with complaints of severely defective language abilities have a greater incidence of associated abnormalities than children admitted with infectious diseases. Such confluence of abnormalities in the latent structure deficient group raises the barriers to mixing in the general gene-pool and reduces the chances for perpetration of the trait. Thus, only small deviations from the norm are tolerated by the population owing to a potent process of selecting out the deviants. The variance is thereby continuously and actively kept small, resulting automatically in a frequency distribution curve with steep slopes and a narrow base.

Compare this now to variations in actualization. Here, the latent structure or competence is not affected, and, therefore, resonance to this behavior is much more likely to occur, and social communication has a much lower risk of being seriously impaired. Thus, much greater variations in actualization and superficial or manifest structure are tolerated within the mechanisms of social cohesion. Deviations in performance may quite easily be compensated for (compare the con-genitally deaf) so that all but the most extreme cases have a chance to integrate in the group and thus disseminate their idiosyncracies. This markedly greater degree of tolerance results in frequency distribution curves of deviations with much more gradual slopes and a much wider base than in the instances above. Superficial variance tends to be pre-served in contrast to the variance in latent structure. A graphic repre-sentation of theoretical, cumulative frequency distribution of variation in latent structure and actualization or realized form is shown in Fig.

9.1. The norm is arbitrarily defined as consisting of all individuals above the 16th and below the 84th percentile; extreme deviants are defined as those individuals who fall below the sixth or above the 94th percentile, whereas the tolerated abnormal ones occupy the regions between. The graph shows how the two frequency distributions differ in terms of absolute variations encountered in the respective populations. As we look now at Fig. 9.1, the twice 10% of tolerable variations in the properties of the realized structure comprise a wider range of absolute variations than the comparable twice 10% of individuals with variations of latent structure. That is, the raw material for potential change in the superficial structure of languages is richer in tolerated absolute variations than the raw material on the level of underlying structure. Therefore, changes that may be brought about by selection

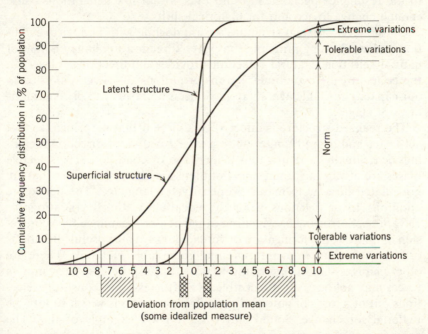

FIG. 9.1. Cumulative frequency distributions of latent and superficial structure traits. (Assume that in every individual, traits are measurable in terms of a common, objective standard.) Reasons as to why the frequency distribution of latent structure properties must have a much narrower base than those of superficial structure were given in the text. The graph shows that if tolerance levels for variation are the same for the two curves and both curves are normal, superficial structure has a wider range of tolerated variations (hatched) than latent structure (cross-hatched).

biases are of a much narrower range for deeper than for superficial structure. In the history of the species, changes of underlying structure should, therefore, occur at a much slower rate than changes of superficial structure. To bring about a change of a given magnitude by very small steps should take much longer than by large steps.

Here we have the core of our explanations: the deep and fundamental capacity for language can only be altered by very small steps, because there is not much variability to select from; the extreme deviants were eliminated before they could interact with the population and those that remain cannot be resonated to. The superficial structure of language can change rapidly and into many different directions because individuals are allowed to enter the group processes despite many kinds of deviations of varying magnitude; these variations can spread owing to the resonance phenomenon and thus within few generations cause enough change to account for historical shifts.

On the level of latent structure we are dealing with biological evolution and the biasing principle that gives direction to change is that of natural selection. Natural selection provides unidirectional biases. In the course of the evolutionary transformations that eventually led to our capacity for language, there have been no returns to or repetitions of prior stages.

The realized structure is affected by different biasing principles that act faster and cause changes with greater freedom of direction including, occasionally, a return to a prior stage or condition. The selective biases are of varying origin; most of them are due to capacities that are not related directly to man's propensity for language. The deliberate additions to or deletions from the vocabulary, the degradations or elevations, narrowing or widening of particular meanings, the suppression of dialects, or glorification of vernaculars are purposeful alterations (that is, selections from the potentially available material). There are other changes that have nothing to do with purpose, and their motive forces may not be easily discernible. Nevertheless, they constitute selections out of a mass of potentially available variations which supply the material for change. Sound shifts are a good example of this. The acoustic specifications of a group of speech sounds are altered, and this will sooner or later affect phonemic structure. All biological variations in anatomy of the vocal tract and articulatory motor coordination leave their effect upon the acoustics of an individual's speech sounds. Since there is a great deal of tolerance for these variations they are allowed freely to enter the community and to affect other speakers, either through the phenomenon of resonance or the spreading of the anatomical and physiological peculiarities through genetic mechanism (as proposed by Brosnahan and Darlington).

(2) *Direction and Rate of Historical Changes*

Linguists have repeatedly looked for universal trends in the direction of recent historical changes of natural languages. There seems to be fair consensus that no modern language is in a more primitive stage today than any other; conversely, none may be considered to have arrived at any ultimate, mature, or final stage. All languages have histories, and no language is expected to remain indefinitely in its present outer form. Sapir (1921) and others have proposed a certain cyclicity or universal drift in which languages go from one general type, for instance, a highly inflectional or polysynthetic type to another un-inflected, analytical type, and then from this type back to one that essentially resembles the former. The drift hypothesis has not been accepted by all philologists, and the extent of cyclicity is quite uncertain. In recent years, a painstaking search for universals in historical changes (Cowgill, 1963; Hoenigswald, 1963) revealed very little that the authors were willing to regard as evidence for such universals. It appears that historical changes may take many directions, although certain types of changes occur again and again. This is essentially what the present theory would expect. The outer form, or the realization of what is possible and latent, permits great variability and, *sub specie,* there is no inherent preference for one or the other course. In fact, tolerance for variability on superficial structure follows directly from the nature of the cognitive mechanisms that underly verbal communication.

We have stressed in earlier chapters that the entire language process may be derived from man's peculiar mode of categorization. Strictly speaking, words are not labels of fixed and conventionally agreed upon classes of objects but labels of *modes* of categorization; they characterize a productive, creative process, and the same is true of the categorization of the deeper schemata called phrase-markers. If language functioned by agreement, instead of merely labeling types of processes, utterances would be extremely limited in scope, we could not talk about anything new, and it would take many more years for children to acquire a stock of *what* to say. Common observation on verbal communication clearly shows that this is not so. Because the vocabulary as well as syntactic rules are manifestations of processes, individuals have considerable freedom to apply them in their own way; the fact that other individuals understand the individualistic modes of rule-application (that is, under-

TABLE 9.2. *Variations and Constancies of Natural Languages*

Level	Aspect of Language	Rate of Change is Measurable in Terms of	Nature of the Constraints and Limits to Change	Mechanisms of Change	Nature of Freedoms within Constraints	Consequences of Transgressions of Constraining Limits
Underlying Structure	All universals: formal, general properties of syntax, semantics, phonology and temporal dimensions	Evolutionary changes	Function and, perhaps, molecular structure of the brain	Genetic diversification and natural selection	Diversity of specific modes of categorization and the interrelation of categories	Either an inability to acquire speech or the acquisition of quasi-speech that can not be learned well by others
Superficial Structure	Everything that distinguishes one natural language from another	Generations (if the rate of occurrence of deviations is constant, the rate of language change is also fairly constant)	The processes of social interaction and their proper functioning	Random variations in skill; tolerance for idiosyncracies in performance of speech and language inherent in the phenomenon of resonance	Individual freedom for style, content and phonetic rendering	Social isolation

stand any new utterance that is formed in accordance with rather broad laws) presupposes the degree of tolerance postulated here. Tolerance extends to the coining of words, syntactic reclassification of words, and small acts of violence to common syntactic and phonological rules; this tolerance is the key to historic change. The freedoms that individuals may take do not appear to be regulated by any constant and ever-present forces. Consequently, languages may move through history in any one of a great many possible directions, and certain features may disappear or reappear again and again without any apparent order.

The rate of change is ultimately controlled by the turnover of generations (as also postulated by Hockett, 1950), and this in turn is related to the resonance phenomenon, that is, plasticity during childhood with subsequent consolidation for the rest of an individual's life. Since each individual becomes stabilized by puberty and does not ordinarily change his language habits, language changes cannot be handed down faster than the duration of one generation. The overlapping of and interaction between generations further slows the rate of change. Thus, historical changes do not become obvious during timespans of less than 60 to 100 years. For a summary of the argument see Table 9.2.

(3) *Distribution*

G. B. Shaw's Professor Henry Higgins has made the world aware of dialect geography. Populations that are geographically stationary and not contaminated by language influences from invading or migrating groups or whose language habits do not become equalized through mass media of communication, such as the radio, tend to organize themselves into dialect communities. The geographic extent of each community is fairly well determined by the extent of social, face-to-face interaction of its members. Interacting individuals infect one another with their speech habits due to the resonance phenomenon. Adjacent dialect communities are distinguishable by clear-cut features (isoglosses), and the number of distinguishable features that separate one community from the other increases with geographic distance (that is, with the number of intervening communities). Dialectal differentiation takes place by discrete steps, and the steps are not of equal size; some isoglosses mark whole bundles of distinctions enhancing the difference between adjacent dialects.

Language geography is further complicated by the fact that the territories of peoples speaking languages of entirely different stock abut. Roman Jakobson noted that it is common for entirely different but adjacent languages to be contaminated by each other in terms of certain phonological features. For instance, clicks are found in many African languages which by their grammar and lexicon cannot be considered as cognate. The distribution of the interdental spirant (th) in Europe is not restricted to cognate languages but is apparently the result of diffusion in the recent past across boundaries of languages of different origin. Some American Indian languages along the Pacific and around the Gulf of Mexico have a characteristic sound-cluster, usually transcribed as /tl/, even though the languages are of very different types.

The crazy-quilt pattern of language- and dialect-maps can be accounted for quite well by the resonance theory. The language-acquiring child does not merely resonate to his own family but to the social group at large. This is best seen in immigrant children in America whose parents speak English with a heavy accent but whose own language is standard American. The child's language is patterned after that of the individuals with whom he comes in contact. Face to face contact in human populations is regulated by certain social institutions and mechanisms. There is no true randomization in individual contacts, not even among those individuals who occupy the same territory. This is due to such factors as national and ethnic affiliations and even social class distinctions. Because of these political and social boundaries, language differences do not become gradually more and more accentuated in direct proportion to geographic distance, but instead we find sudden, discontinuous changes; that is isoglosses are sharp boundaries clearly marking dialectal differences. The discontinuities are, of course, much more dramatic in regions where languages from entirely different stock make contact.

The sharing of phonological features across language boundaries may result from children's resonating to large numbers of individuals in their vicinity who speak with the same foreign accent. This may occur, for instance, along language or national borders. The feature can then penetrate into the language territories through further and further resonance.

(4) *A Note on Adaptive Value*

If the fundamentals of language have evolved in response to natural selection pressures, would it be fair to assume that the present nature of language constitutes in some sense an optimal solution? Such claims have been made, particularly in connection with measurements of the redundancy and information-transmission capacity of natural languages. But the explanations are always *post hoc;* languages are optimal, given the nature of man. But if the nature of language *is* partly the nature of man, as is suggested in the present thesis, these assertions become tautological. Is the nature of man, including his language, in any sense optimal? This becomes a question of religion rather than science. Our present era is not the final goal toward which evolution has striven, and we are merely at one stage in the continuity of life. Evolution of man has not stopped, and we cannot say whether the past, present, or future is in any way optimal.

There is a more interesting question, however. What might be the adaptive value of the resonance phenomenon? Resonance is not unique to man as pointed out previously in (v). It is a feature of a specific type of social mechanism out of a collection of many other types in the animal kingdom that are also linked to critical periods of development. Apparently, the combination of mechanisms for cohesion with simultaneous development of a critical period evolved independently many times over. The physiological and behavioral details that make resonance possible need not be the same in different species. Perhaps man is unique only in the particular way in which he has achieved resonance and the peculiar behavior to which it is relevant.

The evolutionary recurrence of resonance leaves little doubt that it must harbor some selective advantages. What could they be? An examination of acoustic signaling systems among mammals gives us some scanty clues. The noises that most other mammals make can develop ontogenetically in the absence of social contact. Even though communicative behavior may not yet be present at birth, it will develop inexorably according to the species' immanent laws of maturation (given an adequate physical and social environment), and the adult animal will have a species-specific signal repertoire available to it. The development of communication in man (as well as in some bird species) has a different ontogeny. Here the *propensity* matures as inexorably, but the *actualization* is linked to an adaptive feature towards environmental circumstances. It is a two-stage developmental course; at the first stage there is little tolerance for replicative variance, but at the second stage there is very high tolerance. It is this splitting of the tolerance levels that may have important consequences for the evolution of behavior.

Tolerance for variance is probably inversely related to the complexity of the communication system and, consequently, to the repertoire of the messages available to the species. If the communication system is very complex but there is no adaptive feature and the whole behavior pattern emerges in the course of a single-stage rigid development, any small biological deviation from the mean is likely to alter the receptive and productive capacities for patterns, thus rendering individuals that are not perfectly replicated incommunicado, and this difficulty in communication might bar them from interacting with the group. Therefore, perfect maintenance of a very complex system demands very low tolerance bringing with it waste due to exclusion of individuals. The waste can only be reduced if tolerance is raised, but since this will admit individuals with lower capacities, the general level or standard of complexity of behavior would be reduced and leveled out until a stage is reached in which communication can be accomplished by any rough approximation to a given sound pattern. Thus, communication systems that mature in a single stage process have their level of complexity balanced against risk of waste and loss of individuals to the reproductive community.

The two-stage development, through introduction of the resonance phenomenon, circumvents the problem to a certain extent. Latent structure is merely a propensity (still lacking form). Language readiness is a primitive stage with final differentiation yet to come. Perhaps accurate replication at this stage is more easily attained because of this primitivity, and, therefore, tolerance for variance, although low, is not yet a critical problem. As the individual matures, the last stages of differentiation approach, and the process of actualization transforms latent to realized structure. But tolerance for variance in this secondary process is very high; through resonance the individual can adapt to a great variety of situations, can shape the realized form after the forms surrounding him. Through this increase of tolerance, the risk of losing individuals is lowered, whereas, at the same time, there are fewer limits to the complexity of the system. A wider range of variance is allowed to remain, and out of this communication systems may evolve with special mechanisms that generate virtually unlimited repertoires of messages to the great advantage of social cohesiveness and organization of the group structure.

Notice that the resonance phenomenon in man is actually an aspect of his peculiar and species-specific ontogenetic history. Resonance is linked to a postnatal state of relative immaturity and a concomitant lengthening of infancy and childhood, so that environmental influences (the molding after patterns available in the environment) can actually enter into the formative processes. In Chapter Four we have pointed out how man is unique is this respect. Here, then, we have a highly suggestive chain of reactions. Genetic alterations may lead to a peculiar developmental history in which the communication readiness becomes separated from the actualization process, so that latent structure comes

to be distinct from realized structure, each with its own level of tolerance for replicative variance. Although the tolerance for the first level
is lowered, that for the second level is heightened, thus opening up new
possibilities for the development of zoologically unprecedented complexities in the system of communication.

V. INNATE MECHANISMS

There was a time when "innateness" was on the index of forbidden
concepts. Much has changed in the official censorship of technical
terms, but there are still many scientists who regard the postulation of
anything innate as a clever parlor trick that alleviates the proponent
from performing "truly scientific" investigations. This position is odd
to say the least. Organisms are links in a chain of reaction called _life_.
All living forms derive from this event and carry within them its principle; life itself is an innate principle of organisms. At present, biology
does no more than to discover how various forms are innately constituted, and this includes descriptions of a creature's reactions to
environmental forces. Research into these reactions does not eventually
free us from the postulation of innate features but merely elucidates
the exact nature of innate constitutions. The discovery and description
of innate mechanisms is a thoroughly empirical procedure and is an
integral part of modern scientific inquiry.

The relevance to language is best seen if we omit from the discussion
the problem of speech and motor production and focus on understanding of language as a special form of pattern recognition. This is a
concrete and tangible problem as has been demonstrated in the recent
efforts to build machines that could answer questions fed into it in the
shape of unedited English.

Recognition of syntactic patterns cannot be accomplished on the
basis of probability statistics (Chomsky and Miller, 1963; Chomsky,
1963; Miller and Chomsky, 1963). The rules that underly syntax (which
are the same for understanding and speaking) are of a very specific
kind, and unless man or mechanical devices do their processing of
incoming sentences in accordance with these rules, the logical, formal
analysis of the input will be deficient, resulting in incorrect or random
responses. When we say rules must have been built into the grammatical
analyzer, we impute the existence of an apparatus with specific structural properties or, in other words, a specific internal organization.

In a certain sense all organisms are self-organizing systems, and,
therefore, the question that faces us is, "What is the degree of freedom

with which the specific organization necessary for language processing comes into being." If the freedom were unlimited, the nature of man would be unlimited in its capacities. This must be rejected for obvious reasons. There is no other organism with unlimited capacities and we no longer believe that man is different from other creatures in such fundamental ways. In fact, there is no possible way in which we could think of a device, natural or artificial, that is freed from all structural limitations. At best we may assume that a certain mechanism has the capacity to organize itself in more than one way (that is, depending on certain conditions of input, it may eventually be operating in any one of a number of possible modes). This formulation makes it clear that in any case we must assume a biological matrix with specifiable characteristics that determines the outcome of any treatment to which the organism is subjected. Thus the search for innate properties is well within the scope of biological inquiry.

With respect to language, we should like to know how narrowly defined the biological matrix is. This is entirely an empirical question, and the objective is not to find out whether the environment is necessary (it clearly is) and not even how much or what it contributes to the development of language (the answers are almost too obvious to deserve much attention); the only thoroughly interesting problem here is to discover the range of possible alternatives to the common modes of internal organization for language processing. At present, we have only indirect clues (language universals, common age for language onset, and a universal strategy for language acquisition), and these point to great specificity of the underlying matrix.

In the light of these comments we may ask now, "Just what is postulated to be innate in language behavior?" Essentially the modes of categorization as discussed in Chapters Seven and Eight. This is an aspect of the latent structure. Innate also is the general mode of the actualization process but no particular aspect of the realized structure. Thus, no features that are characteristic of only certain natural languages, either particulars of syntax, or phonology, or semantics, are assumed here to be innate. However, there are many reasons to believe that the *processes* by which the realized, outer structure of a natural language comes about are deeply-rooted, species-specific, innate properties of man's biological nature.

REFERENCES

Chomsky, N. (1963), Formal properties of grammars, in *Handbook of Mathematical Psychology,* R. D. Luce, R. R. Bush, and E. Galanter (eds.), Vol. II, John Wiley and Sons, New York.

Chomsky, N. and Miller, G. A. (1963), Introduction to the formal analysis of natural languages, in *Handbook of Mathematical Psychology,* R. D. Luce, R. R. Bush, and E. Galanter (eds.), Vol. II, John Wiley and Sons, New York.

Cowgill, W. (1963), A search for universals in Indo-European diachronic morphology, in *Universals of Language,* J. H. Greenberg (ed.), M.I.T. Press, Cambridge, Mass.

Hockett, C. F. (1950), Age-grading and linguistic continuity, *Language* **26**:449–457.

Hoenigswald, H. M. (1963), Are there universals of linguistic change? in *Universals of Language,* J. H. Greenberg (ed.), M.I.T. Press, Cambridge, Mass.

Miller, G. A. and Chomsky, N. (1963), Finitary models of language users, in *Handbook of Mathematical Psychology,* R. D. Luce, R. R. Bush, and E. Galanter (eds.), Vol. II, John Wiley and Sons, New York.

Sapir, E. (1921), *Language: an introduction to the study of speech,* Harcourt, Brace and World, New York.

APPENDIX A

The formal nature of language

NOAM CHOMSKY

GENERAL PROPERTIES OF LANGUAGE

Many generations of productive scholarship notwithstanding, the questions to which this Appendix is addressed can receive only quite tentative answers. There are few languages for which descriptions in depth are available, and only selected aspects of language have been studied with sufficient care and success to provide support for conclusions of a general nature. Still, it is possible, with some degree of confidence, to outline certain properties and conditions that distinguish human languages among arbitrary systems of symbol manipulation, communication, and self-expression.

COMPETENCE AND PERFORMANCE

At the crudest level of description, we may say that a language associates sound and meaning in a particular way; to have command of a language is to be able, in principle, to understand what is said and to produce a signal with an intended semantic interpretation. But aside from much unclarity, there is also a serious ambiguity in this crude characterization of command of language. It is quite obvious that sentences have an intrinsic meaning determined by linguistic rule and that a person with command of a language has in some way internalized the system of rules that determine both the phonetic shape of the sentence and its intrinsic semantic content—that he has developed what we will refer to as a specific *linguistic competence*. However, it is equally clear that the actual observed use of language—actual *performance*—does not simply reflect the intrinsic sound-meaning connections established by the system of linguistic rules. Performance involves many

397

other factors as well. We do not interpret what is said in our presence simply by application of the *linguistic* principles that determine the phonetic and semantic properties of an utterance. Extralinguistic beliefs concerning the speaker and the situation play a fundamental role in determining how speech is produced, identified, and understood. Linguistic performance is, furthermore, governed by principles of cognitive structure—(for example, by memory restrictions) that are not, properly speaking, aspects of language.

To study a language, then, we must attempt to disassociate a variety of factors that interact with underlying competence to determine actual performance; the technical term "competence" refers to the ability of the idealized speaker-hearer to associate sounds and meanings strictly in accordance with the rules of his language. The grammar of a language, as a model for idealized competence,[1] establishes a certain relation between sound and meaning—between phonetic and semantic representations. We may say that the grammar of the language L generates a set of pairs (s, I), where s is the phonetic representation of a certain signal[2] and I is the semantic interpretation assigned to this signal by the rules of the language. To discover this grammar is the primary goal of the linguistic investigation of a particular language.

The general theory of linguistic structure is concerned with discovering the conditions that any such grammar must meet. This general theory will be concerned with conditions of three kinds: conditions on the class of admissible phonetic representations, the class of admissible semantic representations, and the systems of rules that generate paired phonetic and semantic representations. In all three respects, human languages are subject to stringent limiting conditions. There is no difficulty in constructing systems that do not meet these conditions, and that do not, therefore, qualify as potential human languages despite the fact that they associate sound and meaning in some definite way. Human languages are systems of a highly specific kind. There is no *a priori* necessity for a system relating sound and meaning to be of this kind. As this chapter proceeds, we shall mention some of the highly restrictive conditions that appear to be essential properties of human language.

A grammar generates a certain set of pairs (s, I), where s is a phonetic representation and I its associated semantic interpretation. Similarly, we might think of a performance model as relating sound and meaning in a specific way. A perceptual model, *PM,* for example, might be de-

---

[1] See Notes at end of Appendix.

scribed, as in (1), as a device that accepts a signal as input (along with much else) and assigns various grammatical representations as "output."

(1)

A central problem for psychology is to discover the characteristics of a system *PM* of this sort. Clearly, in understanding a signal, a hearer brings to bear information about the structure of his language. In other words, the model *PM* incorporates the grammar *G* of a language. The study of how sentences are understood—the general problem of speech perception—must, obviously, remain within narrow limits unless it makes use of this basic property of a perceptual model. But it is important to distinguish clearly between the function and properties of the perceptual model *PM* and the competence model *G* that it incorporates. Both *G* and *PM* relate sound and meaning; but *PM* makes use of much information beyond the intrinsic sound-meaning association determined by the grammar *G*, and it operates under constraints of memory, time, and organization of perceptual strategies that are not matters of grammar. Correspondingly, although we may describe the grammar *G* as a system of processes and rules that apply in a certain order to relate sound and meaning, we are not entitled to take this as a description of the successive acts of a performance model such as *PM* —in fact, it would be quite absurd to do so. What we have said regarding perceptual models is equally applicable to production models. The grammatical rules that generate phonetic representations of signals with their semantic interpretations do not constitute a model for the production of sentences, although any such model must incorporate the system of grammatical rules. If these simple distinctions are overlooked, great confusion must result.

In this chapter, attention is focused on competence and the grammars that characterize it; when speaking of semantic and phonetic interpretation of sentences, we refer exclusively to the idealized representations determined by this underlying system. Performance provides data for the study of linguistic competence. Competence, in the sense just described, is one of many factors that interact to determine performance. In general, we would expect that in studying the behavior of a complex organism, it will be necessary to isolate such essentially independent underlying systems as the system of linguistic competence, each with its intrinsic structure, for separate attention.

INITIAL STEPS TOWARD A STUDY OF COMPETENCE

Turning to the study of underlying competence, let us first take note of a few very obvious properties of the grammar of a human language. It is, first of all, quite clear that the set of paired phonetic and semantic representations generated by the grammar will be infinite. There is no human language in which it is possible, in fact or in principle, to specify a certain sentence as the longest sentence meaningful in this language. The grammar of any language contains devices that make it possible to form sentences of arbitrary complexity, each with its intrinsic semantic interpretation. It is important to realize that this is no mere logical nicety. The normal use of language relies in an essential way on this unboundedness, on the fact that language contains devices for generating sentences of arbitrary complexity. Repetition of sentences is a rarity; innovation, in accordance with the grammar of the language, is the rule in ordinary day-by-day performance. The idea that a person has a "verbal repertoire"—a stock of utterances that he produces by "habit" on an appropriate occasion—is a myth, totally at variance with the observed use of language. Nor is it possible to attach any substance to the view that the speaker has a stock of "patterns" in which he inserts words or morphemes. Such conceptions may apply to greetings, a few clichés, and so on, but they completely misrepresent the normal use of language, as the reader can easily convince himself by unprejudiced observation.[3]

To discover the grammar of some language user, we must begin by obtaining information that bears on his interpretation of sentences, on the semantic, grammatical and phonetic structure that he assigns to them. For example, for the study of English, it would be important to discover such facts as the following. Consider the sentence frames (2) and the words "persuaded," "expected," and "happened":

(2) (*a*) John—Bill that he should leave
　　 (*b*) John—Bill to leave
　　 (*c*) John—to leave
　　 (*d*) It is—that Bill will leave

The word "persuaded" can be inserted in (*a*) and (*b*), but not (*c*) or (*d*); "expected" can be inserted in (*b*), (*c*), (*d*), but not (*a*); "happened" can be inserted only in (*c*). Inserting "persuaded" in (*a*), we derive an ambiguous sentence, the interpretation of which depends on the reference of "he"; under one interpretation, the sentence is a near paraphrase of (*b*), with "persuaded" inserted. When "expected" appears in (*b*) and (*c*), the subject-verb relation holds between "Bill" and "leave" in (*b*), but between "John" and "leave" in (*c*). The sentence

"John happened to leave" has roughly the same meaning as "it happened that John left," but "John expected to leave" is not even a remote paraphrase of "it expected that John left." Such facts as these can be stated in many ways, and we might use one or another technique to make sure of their accuracy. These are facts about the competence of the speaker of English. They can be used as a basis for discovering his internalized grammar.

Let us consider the status of such observations with slightly greater care. These observations actually bear directly on the output of a perceptual model such as (1); they relate to the structures assigned to signals by the hearer. Our characterization of the output of (1) is a construct based on evidence of this sort. Then, the perceptual model *PM* itself is a second-order construct. Abstracting further, we can study the grammar that constitutes one fundamental component of (1) as a third-order construct. Thus the evidence cited in the preceding paragraph actually has a bearing on grammar only indirectly. We must, in other words, presuppose the legitimacy of each abstraction. There seems little question of the legitimacy of abstraction in such cases as these, and there is an overwhelming mass of evidence of the sort cited. Once again, we note that idealization of the kind just described is inescapable if a complex organism is to be studied in a serious way.

This process of abstraction can be carried one step further. Consider an acquisition model *AM* that uses linguistic data to discover the grammar of the language to which this data pertains.

(3)

Linguistic data $\longrightarrow$ | *AM* | $\longrightarrow$ Grammar

Just how the device *AM* selects a grammar will be determined by its internal structure, by the methods of analysis available to it, and the initial constraints that it imposes on any possible grammar. If we are given information about the pairing of linguistic data and grammars, we may try to determine the nature of the device *AM*. Although these are not the terms that have been used, linguistics has always been concerned with this question. Thus modern structural linguistics has attempted to develop methods of analysis of a general nature, independent of any particular language, and an older and now largely forgotten tradition attempted to develop a system of universal constraints that any grammar must meet. We might describe both these attempts as concerned with the internal structure of the device *AM*, with the innate conception of "human language" that makes language acquisition possible.[4]

UNIVERSAL GRAMMAR

Let us now turn to the study of underlying competence, and consider the general problem of how a sound-meaning pairing might be established. As a preliminary to this investigation of universal grammar, we must ask how sounds and meanings are to be represented. Since we are interested in human languages in general, such systems of representation must be independent of any particular language. We must, in other words, develop a universal phonetics and a universal semantics that delimit, respectively, the set of possible signals and the set of possible semantic representations for any human language. It will then be possible to speak of a language as a particular pairing of signals with semantic interpretations, and to investigate the rules that establish this pairing. Our review of the general properties of language thus falls naturally into three parts: a discussion of universal phonetics, of universal semantics, and of the overarching system of universal grammar. The first two topics involve the representation of idealized form and semantic content; the theory of universal grammar deals with the mechanisms used in natural languages to determine the form of a sentence and its semantic content.

The importance of developing a universal semantics and universal phonetics, in the sense of the last paragraph, was clearly recognized long before the development of modern linguistics. For example, Bishop Wilkins in his *Essay Towards a Real Character and a Philosophical Language* (1668) attempted to develop a universal phonetic alphabet and a universal catalogue of concepts in terms of which, respectively, the signals and semantic interpretations for any language can be represented. The phonetic alphabet is based on a system of phonetic properties developed in terms of point and manner of articulation. Each phonetic symbol is analyzable as a set of such properties; in modern terms, it is analyzable as a set of *distinctive features*. It is furthermore tacitly assumed that the physical signal is determined, by language-independent principles, from its representation in terms of phonetic symbols. The concepts that are proposed as units of semantic interpretation are also analyzable into fixed properties (semantic features) of some sort, for example, animate-inanimate, relational-absolute, agent-instrument, etc. It is tacitly assumed that the semantic interpretation of a sentence is determined by universal, language-independent principles from the concepts comprised in the utterance and the manner in which they are grammatically related (for example, as subject-predicate).[5] Although the defects in execution in such pioneering studies as that of Wilkins are obvious, the general approach is sound. The theory of universal phonetics has been intensively pursued along the lines just indicated with considerable success; the parallel theory of universal semantics has, in contrast, been very little studied.

UNIVERSAL GRAMMAR: UNIVERSAL PHONETICS

The theory of universal phonetics attempts to establish a universal phonetic alphabet and a system of laws. The alphabet defines the set of possible signals from which the signals of a particular language are drawn. If the theory is correct, each signal of a language can be represented as a sequence of symbols of the phonetic alphabet. Suppose that two physical events are represented as the same sequence. Then in any language they must be repetitions of one another.[6] On the other hand, two physical events might be regarded by speakers of one language as repetitions and by speakers of another language as nonrepetitions. In this case, the universal alphabet must provide the means for distinguishing them. Representation in terms of the universal alphabet should provide whatever information is necessary to determine how the signal may be produced, and it should, at the same time, correspond to a refined level of perceptual representation. We stress once again, however, that actual performance involves other factors beyond ideal phonetic representation.

The symbols of the universal phonetic alphabet are not the "primitive elements" of universal phonetic theory. These primitive elements include rather, what have been called (*phonetic*) *distinctive features,* properties such as voicing, frontness-backness, stress, etc.[7] Each of these features can be thought of as a scale in terms of which two or more values can be distinguished (how many values need be distinguished is an open question, but the number is apparently quite small for each feature). A symbol of the phonetic alphabet is properly to be regarded as a set of features, each with a specified value. A signal, then, is represented as a sequence of such sets.

Three obvious properties of language are reflected in a phonetic theory of this sort. The first is its discreteness—the fact that only a determinable finite number of signals of any given length can be nonrepetitions. The second property is the unboundedness of language—the fact that a signal can be of arbitrary length, so that a language will contain infinitely many semantically interpreted signals. In addition to these formal properties, a phonetic theory of this sort reflects the fact that two segments of a signal, represented by two symbols of the universal alphabet, may be alike in certain respects and distinct in others; and that there are, furthermore, a fixed number of such dimensions of sameness and difference and a fixed number of potentially significant points along these dimensions. Thus, the initial segments of *pin* and *bin*[8] differ with respect to voicing and aspiration but not (significantly) with respect to point of articulation; the two consonants of *cocoa* differ with respect to neither point of articulation nor voicing, but only with respect to aspiration; etc.

It is important to note that the distinctive features postulated in universal phonetic theory are absolute in several senses but relative in others. They are absolute in the sense that they are fixed for all languages. If phonetic representation is to provide sufficient information for identification of a physical signal, then specification of feature values must also be absolute. On the other hand, the features are relative when considered in terms of the notion of repetition-nonrepetition. For example, given three absolute values designated 1, 2, 3 in terms of the feature front-back, we might find that in language L_1 two utterances that differ only in the values 1, 2 of frontness-backness are distinguished as nonrepetitions but utterances differing only in the values 2, 3 are not; whereas in language L_2 the opposite might be the case. Each language would use the feature front-back to distinguish nonrepetitions, but the absolute value 2 that is "front" in one language would be "back" in the other.

In addition to a system of distinctive features, a universal phonetic theory will also attempt to formulate certain laws that govern the permitted sequences and permitted variety of selection in a particular language. For example, Jakobson has observed that no language uses both the feature labialization and the feature velarization for distinguishing nonrepetitions, and he has suggested a more general formulation in terms of which these two features can be regarded as variants of a single, more abstract feature. Generalizations of this sort—particularly when they can be supported by rational argument—can be proposed as laws of universal phonetics.

UNIVERSAL GRAMMAR: UNIVERSAL SEMANTICS

Although universal phonetics is a fairly well-developed subject, the same cannot be said of universal semantics. Here, too, we might hope to establish a universal system of semantic features and laws regarding their interrelations and permitted variety. In fact, the problem of determining such features and such laws has once again become a topic of serious investigation in the past few years,[9] and there is some promise of fruitful development. It can be seen at once that an analysis of concepts in terms of such features as animateness, action, etc. (see p. 402) will hardly be adequate, and that certain features must be still more abstract. It is, for example, a fact of English that the phrase "a good knife" means "a knife which cuts well." Consequently the concept "knife" must be specified in part in terms of features having to do with characteristic functions (not just physical properties), and in terms of an abstract "evaluation feature"[10] that is determined by such modifiers as "good," "terrible," etc. Only by such an analysis can the semantic relationship between "this is a good knife" and "this knife cuts well" be established. In contrast, the irrelevance of "this is a good knife for digging with" to "this knife cuts well" shows that the semantic interpretation of a sentence is determined by grammatical relations of a sort that are by no means transparent.

As in the case of universal phonetics, we might hope to establish general principles regarding the possible systems of concepts that can be represented in a human language and the intrinsic connections that may exist among them. With the discovery of such principles, universal semantics would become a substantive discipline.

UNIVERSAL GRAMMAR: UNIVERSAL SYNTAX

Suppose that a satisfactory theory of universal phonetics and of universal semantics were at hand. We could then define a language as a set of sentences, where a sentence is a particular kind of sound-meaning pair, and go on to study the systems of rules that define human languages. But in fact only the theory of universal phonetics is sufficiently well-established to support this enterprise. Consequently, we must approach the study of language structure in a slightly more indirect way.

Notice that although the notion "semantic representation" is itself far from clear, we can, nevertheless, find innumerable empirical conditions that an explication of this notion must meet. Consider, for example, the following sentence:

(4)   What disturbed John was being disregarded by everyone.

It is clear, first of all, that this expression has two distinct interpretations. Under one interpretation, it means that John was disturbed by the fact that everyone disregarded him; under the second, it means that everyone was disregarding the things that disturb John. Under the first of these interpretations, a certain grammatical relation holds between "disregard" and "John," namely, the same relation that holds between these items in "Everyone disregards John" (the "verb-object" relation). Under the second interpretation neither this nor any other grammatically significant relation holds between "disregard" and "John." On the other hand, if we insert the word "our" between "was" and "being," the sentence is unambiguous, and no grammatical relation holds between "disregard" and "John," although the verb-object relation now holds between "disregard" and "we" (an underlying element of "our").

Examples of this sort can be elaborated indefinitely. They provide conditions of adequacy that the notion "semantic interpretation" must meet (for example, relations of paraphrase and implication and the property of ambiguity must be correctly reflected), and they illustrate clearly some of the ways in which the semantic interpretations of linguistic expressions must be determined from those of their grammatically related parts.

From such considerations, we are led to formulate a more restricted but quite significant immediate goal for the study of linguistic structure. Still taking a language to be a set of sentences, let us consider each abstract "sentence" to be a specific pairing of a phonetic representation with an abstract structure of some sort (let us call it a *deep structure*) that incorporates information relevant to semantic interpretation. We can then study the system of rules that determines this pairing, in a particular language, and the general characteristics of such rules. This enterprise will be significant to the extent that these underlying deep structures do actually provide a way to meet the empirical conditions on semantic interpretation. Semantic theory, as it progresses, will then provide means for enriching deep structures and associating semantic interpretations with them. The empirical significance of a full theory of grammar, comprising a universal phonetics, semantics, and syntax, will depend in part on the extent to which conditions on semantic interpretation can be satisfied by systematic use of the devices and principles that this theory supplies.

Summarizing these remarks, let us establish the following framework for the study of linguistic structure. The *grammar* of a language is a system of rules that determine a certain pairing of sound and meaning. It consists of a *syntactic component,* a *semantic component,* and a *phonological component.* The syntactic component defines a certain (infinite) class of abstract objects (*D, S*), where *D* is a *deep structure* and *S* a *surface structure.* The deep structure contains all information relevant to semantic interpretation; the surface structure, all information relevant to phonetic interpretation. The semantic and phonological components are purely interpretive. The former assigns semantic interpretations to deep structures; the latter assigns phonetic interpretations to surface structures. Thus the grammar as a whole relates semantic and phonetic interpretations, the association being mediated by the rules of the syntactic component that define paired deep and surface structures. The study of the three components will, of course, be highly integrated; each can be investigated to the extent that it is clear what conditions the others impose upon it.

This formulation should be regarded as an informal first approximation. When we develop a precise theory of grammatical structure—for example, the particular version of the theory of transformational grammar sketched below—we will provide a technical meaning for the terms "deep structure" and "surface structure," and in terms of these technical meanings, we can then raise the empirical (not conceptual) question of how deep and surface structures contribute to and determine semantic and phonetic interpretations. In the technical sense that is given to the concepts of deep and surface structure in the theory outlined below, it seems to me that present information suggests that surface structure completely determines phonetic interpretation and that deep structure completely determines certain highly significant aspects of semantic interpretation. But the looseness of the latter term makes a more definite statement impossible. In fact, I think that a reasonable explication of the term "semantic interpretation" would lead to the conclusion that surface structure also contributes in a restricted but important way to semantic interpretation, but I will say no more about this matter here.

Universal grammar might be defined as the study of the conditions that must be met by the grammars of all human languages. Universal semantics and phonetics, in the sense described earlier, will then be a part of universal grammar. So defined, universal grammar is nothing other than the theory of language structure. This seems in accord with traditional usage. However, only certain aspects of universal grammar were studied until quite recently. In particular, the problem of formulating the conditions that must be met by the rules of syntax, phonology, and semantics was not raised in any explicit way in traditional linguistics, although suggestive and nontrivial steps toward the study of this problem are implicit in much traditional work.[11]

A grammar of the sort described previously, which attempts to characterize in an explicit way the intrinsic association of phonetic form and semantic content in a particular language, might be called a *generative grammar*[12] to distinguish it from descriptions that have some different goal (for example, pedagogic grammars). In intention, at least, traditional scholarly grammars are generative grammars, although they fall far short of achieving the goal of determining how sentences are formed or interpreted. A good traditional grammar gives a full exposition of exceptions to rules, but it provides only hints and examples to illustrate regular structures (except for trivial cases—for example, inflectional paradigms). It is tacitly presumed that the intelligent reader will use his "linguistic intuition"—his latent, unconscious knowledge of universal grammar—to determine the regular structures from the presented examples and remarks. The grammar itself does not express the deep-seated regularities of the language. For the purpose of the study of linguistic structure, particular or universal, such grammars are, therefore, of limited value. It is necessary to extend them to full generative grammars if the study of linguistic structure is to be advanced to the point where it deals significantly with regularities and general principles. It is, however, important to be aware of the fact that the concept "generative grammar" itself is no very great innovation. The fact that every language "makes infinite use of finite means" (Wilhelm von Humboldt) has long been understood. Modern work in generative grammar is simply an attempt to give an explicit account of how these finite means are put to infinite use in particular languages and to discover the deeper properties that define "human language," in general (that is, the properties that constitute universal grammar).

We have been concerned thus far only with clarification of concepts and setting of goals. Let us now turn to the problem of formulating hypotheses of universal grammar.

STRUCTURE OF THE PHONOLOGICAL COMPONENT

The syntactic component of a generative grammar defines (generates) an infinite set of pairs (D, S), where D is a deep structure and S is a surface structure; the interpretive components of the grammar assign a semantic representation to D and a phonetic representation to S.

Let us first consider the problem of assigning phonetic representations to surface structures. As in the previous discussion of universal phonetics, we take a phonetic representation to be a sequence of symbols of the universal phonetic alphabet, each symbol being analyzed into distinctive features with specific values. Stating the same idea slightly differently, we may think of a phonetic representation as a matrix in which rows correspond to features of the universal system, columns correspond to successive segments (symbols of the phonetic alphabet), and each entry is an integer that specifies the value of a particular segment with respect to the feature in question. Our problem, then, is to determine what information must be contained in the surface structure, and how the rules of the phonological component of the grammar use this information to specify a phonetic matrix of the sort just described.

Consider once again the example (4) which we repeat in (5) for ease of reference:

(5) What # disturb-ed # John #was # be-ing # dis-regard-ed # by # every-one.

To first approximation,[13] we may think of (5) as a sequence of the *formatives* "what," "disturb," "ed," "John," "was," "be," "ing," "dis," "regard," "ed," "by," "every," "one," with the *junctures* represented by the symbols # and - in the positions indicated in (5). These junctures specify the manner in which formatives are combined; they provide information which is required by the interpretive rules of the phonological component. A juncture must, in fact, be analyzed as a set of features, that is, as a single-column matrix in which the rows correspond to certain features of the junctural system and each entry is one of two values which we may represent as + or −. Similarly, each formative will be analyzed as a matrix in which columns stand for successive segments, rows correspond to certain *categorial features,* and each entry is either + or −. Therefore, the entire sentence (5) can be regarded as a single matrix with the entries + and −.[14]

The categorial features include the universal features of the phonetic system, along with *diacritic* features which essentially indicate exceptions to rules. Thus the matrix corresponding to "what" in the dialect in which the corresponding phonetic representation is [wat], will contain three segments, the first specified as a labial glide, the second as a low back unrounded vowel, the third as an unvoiced dental stop consonant (these specifications given completely in terms of the + and − values of features supplied by the universal phonetic system). The rules of the phonological component, in this case, will convert this specification in terms of + and − values into a more detailed specification in terms of integers, in which the value of each segment with respect to the phonetic features (for example, tongue height, degree of aspiration, etc.) is indicated to whatever degree of accuracy is required by the presupposed theory of universal phonetics, and with whatever range of variation is allowed by the language. In this example, the assigned values will simply refine the bifurcation into + and − values given in the underlying matrix for "what" in (5).

The example just cited is unusually simple, however. In general, the rules of the phonological component will not only give a finer specification of the underlying division into $+$ and $-$ values, but will also change values significantly and, perhaps, insert, delete, or rearrange segments. For example, the formative "by" will be represented with an underlying matrix consisting of two columns, the second of which is specified as a high front-vowel (specification given in terms of values of features). The corresponding phonetic matrix, however, will consist of three columns, the second of which is specified as a low back-vowel and the third as a palatal glide (the specification here being in terms of integral valued entries in a phonetic matrix).[15]

The surface structure of (5), then, is represented as a matrix in which one of two values appears in each entry. The fact that only two values may appear indicates that this underlying matrix really serves a purely classificatory function. Each sentence is classified in such a way as to distinguish it from all other sentences, and in such a way as to determine just how the rules of the phonological component assign specific positional phonetic values. We see, then, that the distinctive features of the universal phonetic system have a *classificatory function* in the underlying matrix constituting a part of the surface structure, and a *phonetic function* in the matrix constituting the phonetic representation of the sentence in question. Only in the former function are the distinctive features uniformly binary; only in the latter do they receive a direct physical interpretation.

The underlying classificatory matrix just described does not exhaust the information required by the interpretive phonological rules. Beyond this, it is necessary to know how the sentence in question is subdivided into phrases of varying size, and what types of phrase these are. In the case of (5), for example, phonological interpretation requires the information that "disturb" and "disregard" are verbs, that "what disturbed John" is a noun phrase, that "John was being" is not a phrase at all, and so on. The relevant information can be indicated by a proper bracketing of the sentence with labeled brackets.[16] The unit contained within paired brackets [$_A$ and]$_A$ will be referred to as a phrase of the category A. For example, the sequence "what # disturb-ed # John" in (5) will be enclosed within the brackets [$_{NP}$,]$_{NP}$, indicating that it is a noun phrase; the formative "disturb" will be enclosed within the brackets [$_V$,]$_V$, indicating that it is a verb; the whole expression (5) will be enclosed within the brackets [$_S$,]$_S$, indicating that it is a sentence; The sequence "John was being" will not be enclosed within paired brackets, since it is no phrase at all. To take an extremely simple example, the sentence, "John saw Bill," might be represented in the following way as a surface structure, where each orthographically represented item is to be regarded as a classificatory matrix:

(6) [s [NP [N John]N]NP [VP [V saw]V [NP [N Bill]N]NP]VP]s

This representation indicates that "John" and "Bill" are nouns (*N*'s) and "saw" a verb (*V*); that "John" and "Bill" are, furthermore, noun phrases (*NP*'s); that "saw Bill" is a verb phrase (*VP*); and that "John saw Bill" is a sentence (*S*). It seems that interpretation of a sentence by the phonological component of the grammar invariably requires information which can be represented in the way just described. We therefore postulate that the surface structure of a sentence is a properly labeled bracketing of a classificatory matrix of formatives and junctures.

The phonological component of a grammar converts a surface structure into a phonetic representation. We have now given a rough specification of the notions "surface structure" and "phonetic representations." It remains to describe the rules of the phonological component and the manner in which they are organized.

The evidence presently available suggests that the rules of the phonological component are linearly ordered in a sequence $R_1, \ldots R_n$, and that this sequence of rules applies in a cyclic fashion to a surface structure in the following way. In the first cycle of application, the rules $R_1, \ldots, R_n$ apply in this order to a maximal continuous part of the surface structure containing no internal brackets. After the last of these rules has applied, innermost brackets are erased and the second cycle of application is initiated. In this cycle, the rules again apply in the given order to a maximal continuous part of the surface structure containing no internal brackets. Innermost brackets are then erased, and the third cycle is initiated. The process continues until the maximal domain of phonological processes (in simple cases, the entire sentence) is reached. Certain of the rules are restricted in application to the level of word-boundary—they apply in the cycle only when the domain of application is a full word. Others are free to iterate at every stage of application. Notice that the principle of cyclic application is highly intuitive. It states, in effect, that there is a fixed system of rules that determines the form of large units from the (ideal) form of their constituent parts.

We can illustrate the principle of cyclic application with some rules of stress assignment in English. It seems to be a fact that although phonetic representations for English must allow five or six different values along the distinctive feature of stress, nevertheless, all segments can be unmarked with respect to stress in surface structures—that is, stress has no categorial function (except highly marginally) as a distinctive feature for English. The complex stress contours of the phonetic representation are determined by such rules as (7) and (8).[17]

(7)   Assign primary stress to the left-most of two primary stressed vowels, in nouns.

(8)   Assign primary stress to the right-most stress-peak, where a vowel V is a stress-peak in a certain domain if this domain contains no vowel more heavily stressed than V.

Rule (7) applies to nouns with two primary stresses; rule (8) applies to a unit of any other kind. The rules apply in the order (7), (8), in the cyclic manner described above. By convention, when primary stress is assigned in a certain position, all other stresses are weakened by one. Notice that if a domain contains no stressed vowel, then rule (8) will assign primary stress to its right-most vowel.

To illustrate these rules, consider first the surface structure (6). In accordance with the general principle of cyclic application, the rules (7) and (8) first apply to the innermost units [$_N$ John]$_N$, [$_V$ saw]$_V$, and [$_N$ Bill]$_N$. Rule (7) is inapplicable; rule (8) applies, assigning primary stress to the single vowel in each case. Innermost brackets are then erased. The next cycle deals with the units [$_{NP}$ John $\overset{1}{}$]$_{NP}$ and [$_{NP}$ Bill $\overset{1}{}$]$_{NP}$ and simply reassigns primary stress to the single vowel, by rule (8). Innermost brackets are then erased, and we have the unit [$_{VP}$ saw $\overset{1}{}$ Bill]$_{VP}$ as the domain of application of the rules. Rule (7) is again inapplicable, since this is not a noun; rule (8) assigns primary stress to the vowel of "Bill," weakening the stress on "saw" to secondary. Innermost brackets are erased, and we have the unit [$_S$ John $\overset{1}{}$ saw $\overset{2}{}$ Bill $\overset{1}{}$]$_S$ as the domain of application. Rule (7) is again inapplicable, and rule (8) assigns primary stress to "Bill," weakening the other stresses and giving "John $\overset{2}{}$ saw $\overset{3}{}$ Bill $\overset{1}{}$," which can be accepted as an ideal representation of the stress contour.

Consider now the slightly more complex example, "John's blackboard eraser." In the first application of the cycle, rules (7) and (8) apply to the innermost bracketed units "John," "black," "board," "erase"; rule (7) is inapplicable, and rule (8) assigns primary stress in each case to the right-most vowel (the only vowel, in the first three). The next cycle involves the units "John's" and "eraser," and is vacuous.[18] The domain of application for the next cycle is [$_N$ black $\overset{1}{}$ board $\overset{1}{}$]$_N$. Being a noun, this unit is subject to rule (7), which assigns primary stress to "black," weakening the stress on "board" to secondary. Inner-

most brackets are erased, and the domain of application for the next
cycle is [$_N$ black board eraser]$_N$. Again rule (7) applies, assigning primary stress to "black" and weakening all other stresses by one. In the final cycle, the domain of application of the rules is [$_{NP}$ John's black board eraser]$_{NP}$. Rule (7) is inapplicable, since this is a full noun-phrase. Rule (8) assigns primary stress to the right-most primary stressed vowel, weakening all the others and giving "John's blackboard eraser." In this way, a complex phonetic representation is determined by independently motivated and very simple rules, applying in accordance with the general principle of the cycle.

This example is characteristic and illustrates several important points. The grammar of English must contain the rule (7) so as to account for the fact that the stress contour is falling in the case of the noun "blackboard," and it must contain rule (8), to account for the rising contour of the phrase "black board" ("board which is black"). The principle of the cycle is not, strictly speaking, part of the grammar of English but is rather a principle of universal grammar that determines the application of the particular rules of English or any other language, whatever these rules may be. In the case illustrated, the general principle of cyclic application assigns a complex stress contour, as indicated. Equipped with the principle of the cycle and the two rules (7) and (8), a person will know[19] the proper stress contour for "John's blackboard eraser" and innumerable other expressions which he may never have heard previously. This is a simple example of a general property of language; *certain universal principles must interrelate with specific rules to determine the form (and meaning) of entirely new linguistic expressions.*

This example also lends support to a somewhat more subtle and far-reaching hypothesis. There is little doubt that such phenomena as stress contours in English are a perceptual reality; trained observers will, for example, reach a high degree of unanimity in recording new utterances in their native language. There is, however, little reason to suppose that these contours represent a *physical* reality. It may very well be the case that stress contours are not represented in the physical signal in anything like the perceived detail. There is no paradox in this. If just two levels of stress are distinguished in the physical signal, then the person who is learning English will have sufficient evidence to construct the rules (7) and (8) (given the contrast "blackboard," "black board," for example). Assuming then that he knows the principle of the cycle, he will be able to perceive the stress contour of "John's black-board eraser" even if it is not a physical property of the signal. The evidence now available strongly suggests that this is an accurate description of how stress is perceived in English.

It is important to see that there is nothing mysterious in this description. There would be no problem in principle in designing an automaton that uses the rules (7) and (8), the rules of English syntax, and the principle of the transformational cycle to assign a multi-leveled stress contour even to an utterance in which stress is not represented at all (for example, a sentence spelled in conventional orthography). The automaton would use the rules of syntax to determine the surface structure of the utterance, and would then apply the rules (7) and (8), in accordance with the principle of the cycle, to determine the multi-leveled contour. Taking such an automaton as a first approximation to a model for speech perception [see (1), p. 399], we might propose that the hearer uses certain selected properties of the physical signal to determine which sentence of the language was produced and to assign to it a deep and surface structure. With careful attention, he will then be able to "hear" the stress contour assigned by the phonological component of his grammar, whether or not it corresponds to any physical property of the presented signal. Such an account of speech perception assumes, putting it loosely, that syntactic interpretation of an utterance may be a prerequisite to "hearing" its phonetic representation in detail; it rejects the assumption that speech perception requires a full analysis of phonetic form followed by a full analysis of syntactic structure followed by semantic interpretation, as well as the assumption that perceived phonetic form is an accurate point-by-point representation of the signal. But it must be kept in mind that there is nothing to suggest that either of the rejected assumptions is correct, nor is there anything at all mysterious in the view just outlined that rejects these assumptions. In fact, the view just outlined is highly plausible, since it can dispense with the claim that some presently undetectable physical properties of utterances are identified with an accuracy that goes beyond anything experimentally demonstrable even under ideal conditions, and it can account for the perception of stress contours of novel utterances[20] on the very simple assumption that rules (7) and (8) and the general principle of cyclic application are available to the perceptual system.

There is a great deal more to be said about the relative merits of various kinds of perceptual model. Instead of pursuing this topic, let us consider further the hypothesis that rules (7) and (8), and the principle of cyclic application, are available to the perceptual system and are used in the manner suggested. It is clear how rules (7) and (8) might be learned from simple examples of rising and falling contour (for example, "black board" contrasted with "blackboard"). But the question then arises: how does a person learn the principle of cyclic application? Before facing this question, it is necessary to settle one that is logically prior to it: why assume that the principle is learned at all? There is much evidence that the principle is used, but from this it does not follow that is has been learned. In fact, it is difficult to imagine how such a principle might be learned, uniformly by all speakers, and it is by no means clear that sufficient evidence is available in the physical signal to justify this principle. Consequently, the most reasonable conclusion seems to be that the principle is not learned at all, but rather that it is simply part of the conceptual equipment that the learner brings to the task of language acquisition. A rather similar argument can be given with respect to other principles of universal grammar.

Notice again that there should be nothing surprising in such a conclusion. There would be no difficulty, in principle, in designing an automaton which incorporates the principles of universal grammar and puts them to use to determine which of the possible languages is the one to which it is exposed. *A priori,* there is no more reason to suppose that these principles are themselves learned than there is to suppose that a person learns to interpret visual stimuli in terms of line, angle, contour, distance, or, for that matter, that he learns to have two arms. It is completely a question of empirical fact; there is no information of any general extralinguistic sort that can be used, at present, to support the assumption that some principle of universal grammar is learned, or that it is innate, or (in some manner) both. If linguistic evidence seems to suggest that some principles are unlearned, there is no reason to find this conclusion paradoxical or surprising.

Returning to the elaboration of principles of universal grammar, it seems that the phonological component of a grammar consists of a sequence of rules that apply in a cyclic manner, as just described, to assign a phonetic representation to a surface structure. The phonetic representation is a matrix of phonetic feature specifications and the surface structure is a properly labeled bracketing of formatives which are, themselves, represented in terms of marking of categorial distinctive features. What evidence is now available supports these assumptions; they provide the basis for explaining many curious features of phonetic fact.

It is important to notice that there is no *a priori* necessity for the phonological component of a grammar to have just these properties. These assumptions about universal grammar restrict the class of possible human languages to a very special subset of the set of imaginable "languages." The evidence available to us suggests that these assumptions pertain to the language acquisition device *AM* of (3), p. 401; that is, that they form one part of the schematism that the child brings to the problem of language learning. That this schematism must be quite elaborate and highly restrictive seems fairly obvious. If it were not, language acquisition, within the empirically known limits of time, access and variability, would be an impenetrable mystery. Considerations of the sort mentioned in the foregoing discussion are directly relevant to the problem of determining the nature of these innate mechanisms, and, therefore, deserve extremely careful study and attention.

STRUCTURE OF THE SEMANTIC COMPONENT

Let us now consider the second interpretive component of a generative grammar, the system of rules that converts a deep structure into a semantic representation that expresses the intrinsic meaning of the sentence in question. Although many aspects of semantic interpretation remain quite obscure, it is still quite possible to undertake a direct investigation of the theory of deep structures and their interpretation, and certain properties of the semantic component seem fairly clear. In particular, as we have noted earlier, many empirical conditions on semantic interpretation can be clearly formulated. For example, we know that sentence (4) on p. 405 must be assigned at least two semantic representations, and that one of these must be essentially the same as the interpretation assigned to both (9) and (10).

(9) Being disregarded by everyone disturbed John.
(10) The fact that everyone disregarded John disturbed him.[21]

Furthermore, it is clear that the semantic representation of a sentence depends on the representation of its parts, as in the parallel case of phonetic interpretation. For example, in the case of (10), it is obvious that the semantic interpretation depends, in part, on the semantic interpretation of "everyone disregarded John"; if the latter were replaced in (10) by "life seemed to pass John by," the interpretation of the whole would be changed in a fixed way. This much is transparent, and it suggests that a principle like the principle of cyclic application in phonology should hold in the semantic component.

A slightly more careful look at the problem shows that semantic interpretation must be significantly more abstract than phonological interpretation with respect to the notion of "constituent part." Thus the interpretation of "everyone disregarded John" underlies not only (10), but also (9) and (4), and in exactly the same way. But neither (4) nor (9) contains "everyone disregarded John" as a constituent part, as does (10). In other words, the deep structures underlying (9) and (10) should both be identical (or very similar) to one of two deep structures underlying (4), despite the wide divergence in surface structure and phonetic form. It follows that we cannot expect deep structure to be very close to surface structure in general.

In the case of a sentence like (6) ("John saw Bill"), there is little difference between deep and surface structure. Semantic interpretation would not be far from the mark, in this case, if it were quite parallel to phonetic interpretation. Thus the interpretation of "saw Bill" can be derived from that of "saw"[22] and that of "Bill," and the interpretation of (6) can be determined from that of "John" and that of "saw Bill." To carry out such interpretation we must know not only the bracketing of (6) into constituents, but also the grammatical relations that are represented; that is, we must know that "Bill" is the *direct-object* of "saw" and that the subject-predicate relation holds between "John" and "saw Bill" in "John saw Bill." Similarly, in the slightly more complex case of "John saw Bill leave," we must know that the subject-predicate relation holds between "John" and "saw Bill leave" and also between "Bill" and "leave."

Notice that at least in such simple cases as (6), we already have a mechanism for representing grammatical relations of just the sort that are required for semantic interpretation. Suppose that we define the relations *subject-of* as the relation holding between a noun phrase and a sentence of which it is an immediate constituent[23] and the relation predicate-of as holding between a verb phrase and a sentence of which it is an immediate constituent. The subject-predicate relation can then be defined as the relation holding between the subject of a sentence and the predicate of this sentence. Thus, in these terms, "John" is the subject and "saw Bill (leave)" the predicate of "John saw Bill (leave)," and the subject-predicate relation holds between the two. In the same way, we can define the relation *direct-object* (in terms of the immediate constituency of verb and noun phrase in verb phrase) and others in a perfectly appropriate and satisfactory way. But returning now to (6), this observation implies that a *labeled bracketing* will serve as the deep structure (just as a labeled bracketing will serve as the surface structure); it contains just the information about constituency and about grammatical relations that is required for semantic interpretation.

We noted that in "John saw Bill leave" the subject-predicate relation holds between "Bill" and "leave," as well as between "John" and "saw

Bill leave." If (6) or something very much like it—see, for example, note 22—is to be taken as the deep structure, with grammatical relations defined as previously, then the deep structure of "John saw Bill leave" will have to be something like (11) (many details omitted):

(11) [s [NP John]NP [VP [V saw]V [S [NP Bill]NP [VP [V leave]V]VP]S]VP]S

The labeled bracketing (11) expresses the subject-predicate relation between "John" and "saw Bill leave" and between "Bill" and "leave," as required.

Moving to a somewhat more complex example, the sentences (9) and (10) (as well as (4) under one interpretation) will each have to contain something like (12) in the deep structure:

(12) [s [NP everyone]NP [VP [V disregards]V [NP John]NP]VP]S.

If this requirement is met, then we will be able to account for the fact that, obviously, the meaning of (4) (= "what disturbed John was being disregarded by everyone") in one interpretation and of (9) (= "being disregarded by everyone disturbed John") is determined in part by the fact that the direct-object relation holds between "disregard" and "John" and the subject-predicate relation between "everyone" and "disregards John," despite the fact that these relations are in no way indicated in the surface structure in (4) or (9).

From many such examples, we are led to the following conception of how the semantic component functions. This interpretive component of the full generative grammar applies to a deep structure and assigns to it a semantic representation, formulated in terms of the still quite obscure notions of universal semantics. The deep structure is a labeled bracketing of minimal "meaning-bearing" elements. The interpretive rules apply cyclically, determining the semantic interpretation of a phrase X of the deep structure from the semantic interpretations of the immediate constituents of X and the grammatical relation represented in this configuration of X and its parts.

Superficially, at least, the two interpretive components of the grammar are rather similar in the way in which they operate, and they apply to objects of essentially the same sort (labeled bracketings). But the deep structure of a sentence will, in nontrivial cases, be quite different from its surface structure.

Notice that if the notions "noun phrase," "verb phrase," "sentence," "verb," can receive a language-independent characterization within universal grammar, then the grammatical relations defined above (similarly, others that we might define in the same way) will also receive a universal characterization. It seems that this may be possible, and certain general lines of approach to such a characterization seem clear (see p. 436). We might then raise the question of whether the semantic component of a grammar contains such particular rules as the rules (7) and (8) of the phonological component of English or whether, alternatively, the principles of semantic interpretation belong essentially to universal grammar. However, we will put aside these and other questions relating to the semantic component, and turn next to the discussion of the one noninterpretive component of the grammar—which we have called its "syntactic component." Notice that as in the case of the phonological component, insofar as principles of interpretation can be assigned to universal rather than particular grammar, there is little reason to suppose that they are learned or that they could in principle be learned.

STRUCTURE OF THE SYNTACTIC COMPONENT

The syntactic component of a grammar must generate (see note 12) pairs (D, S), where D is a deep structure and S an associated surface structure. The surface structure S is a labeled bracketing of a sequence of formatives and junctures. The deep structure D is a labeled bracketing that determines a certain network of grammatical functions and grammatical relations among the elements and groups of elements of which it is composed. Obviously, the syntactic component must have a finite number of rules (or rule schemata), but these must be so organized that an infinite number of pairs (D, S) of deep and surface structures can be generated, one corresponding to each interpreted sentence (phonetically and semantically interpreted, that is,) of the language.[24] In principle, there are various ways in which such a system might be organized. It might, for example, consist of independent rules generating deep and surface structures and certain conditions of compatibility relating them, or of rules generating surface structures combined with rules mapping these into the associated deep structure, or of rules generating deep structures combined with rules mapping these into surface structures.[25] Choice among these alternatives is a matter of fact, not decision. We must ask which of the alternatives makes possible the deepest generalizations and the most far-reaching explanation of linguistic phenomena of various sorts. As with other aspects of universal grammar, we are dealing here with a set of empirical questions; crucial evidence may be difficult to obtain, but we cannot conclude from this that there is, in principle, no right and wrong in the matter.

Of the many alternatives that might be suggested, the linguistic evidence now available seems to point consistently to the conclusion that the syntactic component consists of rules that generate deep structures combined with rules mapping these into associated surface structures. Let us call these two systems of rules the *base* and the *transformational* components of the syntax, respectively. The base system is further subdivided into two parts: the *categorial* system and the *lexicon*. Each of these three subparts of the syntax has a specific function to perform, and there seem to be heavy universal constraints that determine their form and interrelation. The general structure of a grammar would, then, be as depicted in diagram (13):

(13)

$$\xrightarrow{\ B\ } \text{Deep structure} \left\langle \begin{array}{l} \xrightarrow{\ S\ } \text{Semantic representation} \\ \xrightarrow{\ T\ } \text{Surface structure} \xrightarrow{\ P\ } \text{Phonetic representation} \end{array} \right.$$

The mapping S is carried out by the semantic component; T by the transformational component; and P by the phonological component. Generation of deep structures by the base system (by the operation B) is determined by the categorial system and the lexicon.

The lexicon is a set of lexical entries; each lexical entry, in turn, can be regarded as a set of features of various sorts. Among these are the phonological features and the semantic features that we have already mentioned briefly. The phonological features can be thought of as indexed as to position (that is, first, second, etc.); aside from this, each is simply an indication of marking with respect to one of the universal distinctive features (regarded here in their categorial function) or with respect to some diacritic feature (see p. 409), in the case of irregularity. Thus the positionally indexed phonological features constitute a distinctive feature matrix with the entries given as + or − values, as described earlier. The semantic features constitute a "dictionary definition." As noted previously, some of these at least must be quite abstract; there may, furthermore, be intrinsic connections of various sorts among them that are sometimes referred to as "field structure." In addition, the lexical entry contains syntactic features that determine the positions in which the entry in question may appear, and the rules that may apply to structures containing it as these are converted into surface structures. In general, the lexical entry contains all information about the item in question that cannot be accounted for by general rule.

Aside from lexical entries, the lexicon will contain redundancy rules that modify the feature content of a lexical entry in terms of general regularities. For example, the fact that vowels are voiced or that humans are animate requires no specific mention in particular lexical entries. Much of the redundant lexical information can, no doubt, be provided by general conventions (that is, rules of universal grammar) rather than by redundancy rules of the language.

The lexicon is concerned with all properties, idiosyncratic or redundant, of individual lexical items. The categorial component of the base determines all other aspects of deep structure. It seems that the categorial component is what is called a *simple* or *context-free phrase structure grammar*. Just what such a system is can be understood quite easily from a simple example. Suppose that we have the *rules* (14):

(14) S → NP VP
   VP → V NP
   NP → N
   N → Δ
   V → Δ

With these rules we construct the derivation (15) in the following way. First write down the symbol *S* as the first line of the derivation. We interpret the first rule of (14) as permitting *S* to be replaced by NP VP, giving the second line of (15). Interpreting the second rule of (14) in a similar way, we form the third line of the derivation (15) with VP replaced by V NP. We form the fourth line of (15) by applying the rule NP → N of (14), interpreted the same way, to both of the occurrences of NP in the third line. Finally, we form the final two lines of (15) by applying the rules N → Δ and V → Δ.

(15) S
   NP VP
   NP V NP
   N V N
   Δ V Δ
   Δ Δ Δ

Clearly, we can represent what is essential to the derivation (15) by the tree-diagram (16).

(16)

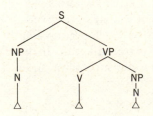

In the diagram (16), each symbol dominates the symbols by which it was replaced in forming (15). In fact, we may think of the rules of (14) as simply describing the way in which a tree diagram such as (16) can be constructed. Evidently, (16) is just another notation for the labeled bracketing (17):

(17) $[_S [_{NP} [_N \Delta]_N]_{NP} [_{VP} [_V \Delta]_V [_{NP} [_N \Delta]_N]_{NP}]_{VP}]_S$.

Domination of some element by a symbol A in (16) (as, for example, V NP is dominated by VP) is indicated in (17) by enclosing this element by the labeled brackets $[_A,]_A$. If we have a lexicon which tells us that "John" and "Bill" can replace the symbol Δ when this symbol is dominated by N (that is, is enclosed by $[_N,]_N$), and that "saw" can replace Δ when it is dominated by V, then we can extend the derivation (15) to derive "John saw Bill," with the associated structure that we have given as (6). In fact, (6) derives from (17) by replacing the first occurrence of Δ by "John," the second by "saw," and the third by "Bill."

Notice that the rules (14) in effect define grammatical relations, where the definitions are given as on p. 417. Thus, the first rule of (14) defines the subject-predicate relation and the second, the verb-object relation. Similarly, other semantically significant grammatical functions and relations can be defined by rules of this form, interpreted in the manner indicated.

Restating these notions in a more formal and general way, the categorial component of the base is a system of rules of the form $A \rightarrow Z$, where A is a category symbol such as S (for "sentence"), NP (for "noun phrase"), N (for "noun"), etc., and Z is a string of one or more symbols which may again be category symbols or which may be *terminal* symbols (that is, symbols which do not appear on the left-hand side of the arrow in any base rule). Given such a system, we can form *derivations*, a derivation being a sequence of lines that meets the following conditions: the first line is simply the symbol S (standing for sentence); the last line contains only terminal symbols; if X, Y are two successive lines, then X must be of the form $\ldots A \ldots$ and Y of the form $\ldots Z \ldots$, where $A \rightarrow Z$ is one of the rules. A derivation imposes a labeled bracketing on its terminal string in the obvious way. Thus given the successive lines $X = \ldots A \ldots$, $Y = \ldots Z \ldots$, where Y was derived from X by the rule $A \rightarrow Z$, we will say that the string derived from Z (or Z itself, if it is terminal) is bracketed by $[_A,]_A$. Equivalently, we can represent the labeled bracketing by a tree diagram in which a node labeled A (in this example) dominates the successive nodes labeled by the successive symbols of Z.

We assume that one of the terminal symbols of the categorial component is the dummy symbol Δ. Among the nonterminal symbols are several that stand for *lexical categories,* in particular N for ("noun"), V (for "verb") ADJ [for "adjective"). A lexical category A can appear on the left-hand side of a rule $A \rightarrow Z$ only if Z is Δ. Lexical entries will then be inserted in derivations in place of Δ by rules of a different sort, extending the derivations provided by the categorial component. Aside from Δ, indicating the position in which an item from the lexicon may appear, the terminal symbols of the categorial component are grammatical elements such as *be, of,* etc. Some of the terminal symbols introduced by categorial rules will have an intrinsic semantic content.

A labeled bracketing generated by base rules (that is, by the phrase structure rules of the categorial component and by the rule of lexical insertion mentioned in the preceding paragraph), will be called a *base phrase-marker.* More generally, we will use the term "phrase-marker" here to refer to any string of elements properly bracketed with labeled brackets.[26] The rules of the transformational component modify phrase-markers in certain fixed ways. These rules are arranged in a sequence $T_1, \ldots, T_m$. This sequence of rules applies to a base phrase-marker in a cyclic fashion. First, it applies to a configuration dominated by S (that is, a configuration [s . . .]s) and containing no other occurrence of S. When the transformational rules have applied to all such configurations, then they next apply to a configuration dominated by S and containing only S-dominated configurations to which the rules have already applied. This process continues until the rules apply to the full phrase-marker dominated by the initial occurrence of S in the base phrase-marker. At this point, we have a surface structure. It may be that the ordering conditions on transformations are looser—that there are certain ordering conditions on the set $\{T_1, \ldots, T_m\}$, and that at a given stage in the cycle, a sequence of transformations can apply if it does not violate these conditions—but I will not go into this matter here.

The properties of the syntactic component can be made quite clear by an example (which, naturally, must be much oversimplified). Consider a subpart of English with the lexicon (18) and the categorial component (19).

(18) *Lexicon: it, fact, John, Bill, boy, future*   (Noun)
         dream, see, persuade, annoy   (Verb)
         sad   (Adjective)
         will   (Modal)
         the   (Determiner)

(19) S → (Q) NP AUX VP
VP → be ADJ
VP → V (NP) (of NP)
NP → (DET) N (that S)
AUX → past
AUX → M
N, V, ADJ, DET, M → Δ

In (19), parentheses are used to indicate an element that may or may not be present in the rule. Thus the first line of (19) is an abbreviation for two rules, one in which *S* is rewritten *Q NP AUX VP*, the other in which *S* is rewritten *NP AUX VP*. Similarly, the third line of (19) is actually an abbreviation for four rules, etc. The last line of (19) stands for five rules, each of which rewrites one of the categorial symbols on the left as the dummy terminal symbol Δ.

This categorial component provides such derivations as the following:

(20) (*a*) S
NP AUX VP
NP AUX be ADJ
N AUX be ADJ
N past be ADJ
Δ past be Δ

(*b*) S
NP AUX VP
NP AUX V NP of NP
DET N AUX V N of DET N that S
DET N M V N of DET N that S
Δ   Δ Δ Δ Δ of Δ   Δ that S
Δ   Δ Δ Δ Δ of Δ   Δ that NP VP
Δ   Δ Δ Δ Δ of Δ   Δ that NP AUX V
Δ   Δ Δ Δ Δ of Δ   Δ that N AUX V
Δ   Δ Δ Δ Δ of Δ   Δ that N past V
Δ   Δ Δ Δ Δ of Δ   Δ that Δ past Δ

These derivations are constructed in the manner just described. They impose labeled bracketings which, for clarity, we will give in the equivalent tree representation:

(21) (*a*) and (*b*)

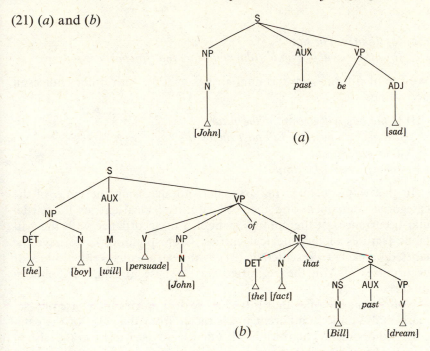

(*a*)

(*b*)

We now use the lexicon to complete the base derivations (20*a*), (20*b*).

Each entry in the lexicon contains syntactic features which identify the occurrences of Δ that it can replace in a derivation. For example, the items of the five rows of (18) can replace occurrences of Δ that are dominated, in the tree representations of (21), by the categorial symbols N, V, ADJ, M, DET, respectively.

But the restrictions are much narrower than this. Thus of the verbs in (18) (line 2), only *persuade* can replace an occurrence of Δ dominated by V when this occurrence of V is followed in the VP by: NP of NP. We can form ". . . *persuade John of the fact*," but not ". . . *dream* (*see, annoy*) *John of the fact*." Similarly, of the nouns in (18) (first line) only *fact* can appear in the context DET—*that* S (that is, "the fact that John left"); only *it* in a NP of the form—*that* S;[27] only *fact, boy,* and *future* in a NP of the form DET—("the fact," "the boy," "the future"), etc. Details aside, the general character of such restrictions is quite clear. Assuming, then, that the lexical entries contain the appropriate lexical features, we can extend the base derivations of (20) to give the terminal strings (22), inserting the items enclosed in brackets in (21).

(22) (*a*) *John past be sad*
    (*b*) *the boy will persuade John of the fact that Bill past dream*

We can also form such terminal strings as (23), with other choices in derivations.

(23) *Q the boy will dream of the future*
    it that John past see Bill past annoy the boy
    John will be sad
    John past see the future

In this way, we form full base derivations, using the rules of the categorial component and then substituting lexical entries for particular occurrences of the dummy symbol Δ in accordance with the syntactic features of these lexical entries. Correspondingly, we have the labeled brackets represented as (21), with lexical entries substituted for occurrences of Δ in the permitted ways. These are the base phrase-markers.

Notice that the rules that introduce lexical entries into base phrase-markers are entirely different in character from the rules of the categorial component. The rules of (19) that were used to form (20) are of a very elementary sort. Each such rule allows a certain symbol A in the string . . . A . . . to be rewritten as a certain string Z, *independently of the context of A and the source of A in the derivation.* But in introducing lexical entries in place of Δ, we must consider selected aspects of the phrase-marker in which Δ appears. For example, an occurrence of Δ can be replaced by "John" if it is dominated in the phrase-marker by N, but not by V. Thus the rules of lexical insertion really apply not to strings of categorial and terminal symbols, as do the rules of the categorial component, but to phrase-markers such as (21). Rules which apply to phrase-markers, modifying them in some specific way, are referred to in current terminology as (*grammatical*) *transformations.* Thus the rules of lexical insertion are transformational rules, whereas the rules of the categorial component are simply rewriting rules.

Let us now return to the examples (22*a*), (22*b*). Consider first (22*a*), with the base phrase-marker (21*a*).[28] We see at once that (21) contains just the information required in the deep structure of the sentence "John was sad." Clearly, the string *past be* is simply a representation of the formative "was," just as *past see* represents "saw," *past persuade* represents "persuaded," etc. With a rule that converts *past be* to the formative "was," we form the surface structure of the sentence, "John was sad." Furthermore, if we define grammatical functions and relations in the manner described earlier (see p. 417), then (21) expresses the fact that the subject-predicate relation holds between *John* and *past be sad,* and it also contains semantic information about the meaning-bearing items *John, past, sad;* we may assume, in fact, that *past* is itself a symbol of a universal terminal alphabet with a fixed semantic interpretation, and the semantic features of the lexical entries of *John* and *sad* can also be assumed to be selected, like the phonological features of these entries, from some universal system of representation of the sort discussed above. In short, (21*a*) contains all information required for semantic interpretation, and we can, therefore, take it to be the deep structure underlying the sentence "John was sad."

What is true of this example is true quite generally. That is, the base phrase-markers generated by the categorial component and the lexicon are the deep structures that determine semantic interpretation. In this simple case, only one rule is needed to convert the deep structure to a surface structure, namely, the rule converting *past be* to the formative *was.* Since this rule is clearly a special case of a rule that applies as well to any string of the form *past* V, it is really a very simple transformational rule (in the terminology of p. 426) rather than an elementary rule of the type that we find in the categorial component. This observation can be generalized. The rules that convert deep structures to surface structures are transformational rules.

Suppose now that instead of the derivation (20*a*) we had formed the very similar derivation (24):

(24) S

  Q NP AUX VP
  Q NP AUX be ADJ
  Q N AUX be ADJ
  Q N M be ADJ
  Q Δ Δ be Δ
  Q John will be sad

with its associated phrase-marker. We intend the symbol Q to be a symbol of the universal terminal alphabet with a fixed semantic interpretation, namely, that the associated sentence is a question. Suppose that the transformational component of the syntax contains rules that convert phrase-markers of the form *Q NP AUX* . . . to corresponding phrase-markers of the form *AUX NP* . . . (that is, the transformation replaces *Q* by *AUX,* leaving the phrase-marker otherwise unchanged). Applied to the phrase-marker corresponding to (24), this rule gives the labeled bracketing of the sentence, "Will John be sad?"; that is, it forms the surface structure for this sentence.

Suppose that in place of (24) we had used the rule rewriting AUX as *past.* The question transformation of the preceding paragraph would give a phrase-marker with the terminal string "past John be sad," just as it gives, "Will John be sad?" in the case of (24). Evidently, we must modify the question transformation so that it inverts not just *past,* in this case, but the string *past be,* so that we derive finally, "Was John sad?" This modification is, in fact, straightforward, when the rules are appropriately formulated.

Whether we select M or *past* in (24), the generated base phrase-marker once again qualifies as a deep structure. The grammatical relation of *John* to *will (past) be sad* is exactly the same in (24) as in (20*a*), with the definitions proposed previously, as required for empirical adequacy. Of course, the surface forms do not express these grammatical relations, directly; as we have seen earlier, significant grammatical relations are rarely expressed directly in the surface structure.

Let us now turn to the more complex example (20*b*)—(21*b*)—(22*b*). Once again, the base phrase-marker (21*b*) of (22*b*) expresses the information required for the semantic interpretation of the sentence "The boy will persuade John of the fact that Bill dreamt," which derives from (22*b*) by a transformational rule that forms "dreamt" from *past dream.* Therefore, (21*b*) can serve as the deep structure underlying this sentence, exactly as (21*a*) can serve for "John was sad," and the phrase-marker corresponding to (24) for "Will John be sad?"

Suppose that in rewriting NP in the third line of (20*b*), we had selected not DET N *that* S but N *that* S [see the fourth line of (19)]. The only lexical item of (18) that can appear in the position of this occurrence of N is *it.* Therefore, instead of (22*b*), we would have derived

(25) *the boy will persuade John of it that Bill past dream,*

with grammatical relations and lexical content otherwise unmodified. Suppose now that the transformational component of the syntax contains rules with the following effect:

(26) (*a*) *it* is deleted before *that* S
     (*b*) *of* is deleted before *that* S

Applying (26*a*) and (26*b*) to (25) in that order, with the rule that converts *past dream* to "dreamt," we derive the surface structure of "The boy will persuade John that Bill dreamt." The base phrase-marker corresponding to (25) serves as the deep structure underlying this sentence.

Notice that the rule (26*a*) is much more general. Thus suppose we select the NP *it that Bill past dream* as the subject of *past annoy John,* as is permitted by the rules of (18), (19). This gives

(27) *it that Bill past dream past annoy John*

Applying the rule (26*a*) (and the rules for forming past tense of verbs), we derive, "That Bill dreamt annoyed John." Alternatively, we might have applied the transformational rule with the effect of (28):

(28) A phrase-marker of the form *it that S X* is restructured as the corresponding phrase-marker of the form *it X that S.*

Applying (28) to (27), we derive, "It annoyed John that Bill dreamt." In this case, (26*a*) is inapplicable. Thus (27) underlies two surface structures, one determined by (28) and the other by (26*a*); having the same deep structure, these are synonymous. In the case of (25), (28) is inapplicable and, therefore, we have only one corresponding surface structure.

We can carry the example (25) further by considering additional transformational rules. Suppose that instead of selecting *Bill* in the embedded sentence of (25), we had selected *John* a second time. There is a very general transformational rule in English and other languages providing for the deletion of repeated items. Applying this rule along with other minor ones of an obvious sort, we derive

(29) *The boy will persuade John to dream.*

from a deep structure that contains, as it must, a subphrase-marker that expresses the fact that *John* is the subject of *dream*. Actually, in this case the deep phrase-marker would be slightly different, in ways that need not concern us here, in this rough expository sketch.

Suppose now that we were to add a transformation that converts a phrase-marker of the form NP AUX V NP into the corresponding passive, in the obvious way.[29] Applying to phrase-markers very much like (21*b*), this rule would provide surface structures for the sentences "John will be persuaded that Bill dreamt (by the boy)" [from (25)] and "John will be persuaded to dream (by the boy)" [from (29)]. In each case, the semantic interpretation will be that of the underlying deep phrase-marker. In certain cases, the significant grammatical relations are entirely obscured in the surface structure. Thus in the case of the sentence "John will be persuaded to dream," the fact that "John" is actually the subject of "dream" is not indicated in the surface structure, although the underlying deep structure, as we have noted, expresses this fact directly.

From these examples we can see how a sequence of transformations can form quite complicated sentences in which significant relations among the parts are not represented in any direct way. In fact, it is only in artificially simple examples that deep and surface structure correspond closely. In the normal sentences of everyday life, the relation is much more complex; long sequences of transformations apply to convert underlying deep structures into the surface form.

The examples that we have been using are stilted and unnatural. With a less rudimentary grammar, quite natural ones can be provided. For example, in place of the sentences formed from (27) by (26) or (28) we could use more acceptable sentences such as "that you should believe this is not surprising," "it is not surprising that you should believe this," etc. Actually, the unnaturalness of the examples we have used illustrates a simple but often neglected point, namely, that the intrinsic meaning of a sentence and its other grammatical properties are determined by rule, not by conditions of use, linguistic context, frequency of parts, etc.[30] Thus the examples of the last few paragraphs may never have been produced in the experience of some speaker (or, for that matter, in the history of the language), but their status as English sentences and their ideal phonetic and semantic interpretations are unaffected by this fact.

Since a sequence of transformations can effect drastic modifications in a phrase-marker, we should not be surprised to discover that a single surface structure[31] may result from two very different deep structures, that is, that certain sentences are ambiguous (for example, sentence (4) on p. 405). Ambiguous sentences provide a particularly clear indication of the inadequacy of surface structure as a representation of deeper relations.[32]

More generally, we can easily find paired sentences with essentially the same surface structure but entirely different grammatical relations. To mention just one such example, compare the sentences of (30):

(30) (*a*) I persuaded the doctor to examine John.
　　 (*b*) I expected the doctor to examine John.

The surface structures are essentially the same. The sentence (30*a*) is of the same form as (29). It derives from a deep structure which is roughly of the form (31):

I past expect it that the doctor AUX examine John

(31)

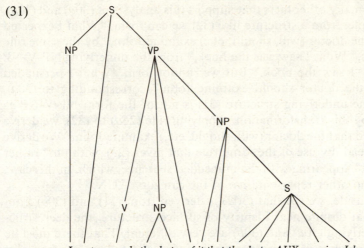

I past persuade the doctor of it that the doctor AUX examine John

I past persuade the doctor of it that the doctor AUX examine John

This deep structure is essentially the same as (21b), and by the transformational process described in connection with (29), we derive from it the sentence (30a). But in the case of (30b), there are no such related structures as "I expected the doctor of the fact that he examined John," ". . . of the necessity (for him) to examine John," etc., as there are in the case of (30a). Correspondingly, there is no justification for an analysis of (30b) as derived from a structure like (31). Rather, the deep structure underlying (30b) will be something like (32) (again omitting details):

(32)

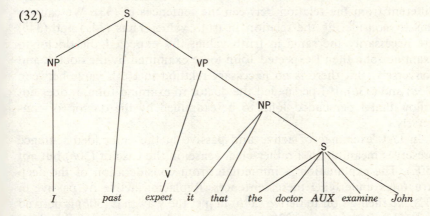

There are many other facts that support this analysis of (30*a*) and (30*b*). For example, from a structure like (32) we can form, "What I expected was that the doctor (will, should, etc.) examine John," by the same rule that forms, "What I saw was the book," from the underlying NP-V-NP structure, "I saw the book." But we cannot form "What I persuaded was that the doctor should examine John," corresponding to (30*a*), because the underlying structure (31) is not of the form NP-V-NP as required by this transformation. Applying rule (26*a*) to (32), we derive "I expected that the doctor (will, should, etc.) examine John." We derive (30*b*), instead, by use of the same rule that gives (29), with "to" rather than "that" appearing with the embedded sentence, which, in this case, contains no other representative of the category AUX.

Details aside, we see that (30*a*) is derived from (31) and (30*b*) from (32), so that despite near identity of surface structure, the deep structures underlying (30*a*) and (30*b*) are very different. That there must be such a divergence in deep structure is not at all obvious.[33] It becomes clear, however, if we consider the effect of replacing "the doctor to examine John" by its passive, "John to be examined by the doctor" in (30*a*) and (30*b*). Thus we have under examination the sentences (33) and (34):

(33) (*a*) I persuaded the doctor to examine John [= (30*a*)].
    (*b*) I persuaded John to be examined by the doctor.
(34) (*a*) I expected the doctor to examine John [= (30*b*)].
    (*b*) I expected John to be examined by the doctor.

The semantic relation between the paired sentences of (34) is entirely different from the relation between the sentences of (33). We can see this by considering the relation in truth value. Thus (34*a*) and (34*b*) are necessarily the same in truth value; if I expected the doctor to examine John then I expected John to be examined by the doctor, and conversely. But there is no necessary relation in truth value between (33*a*) and (33*b*). If I persuaded the doctor to examine John, it does not follow that I persuaded John to be examined by the doctor, or conversely.

In fact, exchange of active and passive in the embedded sentence preserves meaning, in a rather clear sense, in the case of (30*b*) but not (30*a*). The explanation is immediate from consideration of the deep structures underlying these sentences. Replacing active by passive in (32), we then go on to derive (34*b*) in just the way that (30*b*) is derived from (32). But to derive (33*b*), we must not only passivize the embedded sentence in (31), but we must also select "John" instead of "the doctor" as the object of the verb "persuade"; otherwise, the conditions for deletion of the repeated noun phrase, as in the derivation of (29), will not be met. Consequently, the deep structure underlying (33*b*) is quite different from that underlying (33*a*). Not only is the embedded sentence passivized, but the object "the doctor" must be replaced in (31) by "John." The grammatical relations are, consequently, quite different, and the semantic interpretation differs correspondingly. It remains true, in both cases, that passivization does not affect meaning (in the sense of "meaning" relevant here). The change of meaning in (30*a*) when "the doctor to examine John" is replaced by "John to be examined by the doctor" is occasioned by the change of grammatical relations, "John" now being the direct object of the verb phrase in the underlying structure rather than "the doctor." There is no corresponding change in the case of (34*a*), so that the meaning remains unaltered when the embedded sentence is passivized.

The example (30*a*), (30*b*) illustrates, once again, the inadequacy (and, quite generally, irrelevance) of surface structure for the representation of semantically significant grammatical relations. The labeled bracketing that conveys the information required for phonetic interpretation is in general very different from the labeled bracketing that provides the information required for semantic interpretation. The examples (30*a*), (30*b*) also illustrate how difficult it may be to bring one's "linguistic intuition" to consciousness. As we have seen, the grammar of English, as a characterization of competence (see p. 397f.), must, for descriptive adequacy, assign different deep structures to the sentences (30*a*) and (30*b*). The grammar that each speaker has internalized does distinguish these deep structures, as we can see from the fact that any speaker of English is capable of understanding the effect of replacing the embedded sentence by its passive in the two cases of (30). But this fact about his internalized grammatical competence may escape even the careful attention of the native speaker (see note 33).

Perhaps such examples as these suffice to give something of the flavor of the syntactic structure of a language. Summarizing our observations about the syntactic component, we conclude that it contains a base and a transformational part. The base generates deep structures, and the transformational rules convert them to surface structures. The categorial component of the base defines the significant grammatical relations of the language, assigns an ideal order to underlying phrases, and, in various ways, determines which transformations will apply.[34] The lexicon specifies idiosyncratic properties of individual lexical items. Together, these two components of the base seem to provide the information relevant for semantic interpretation in the sense in which we have been using this term, subject to the qualifications mentioned earlier. The transformational rules convert phrase-markers to new phrase-markers, effecting various kinds of reordering and reorganization. The kinds of changes that can be effected are quite limited; we will, however, not go into this matter here. Applying in sequence, the transformations may affect the organization of a base-phrase-marker quite radically, however. Thus the transformations provide a wide variety of surface structures that have no direct or simple relation to the base structures from which they originate and which express their semantic content.

It is a fact of some significance that the mapping of deep to surface structures is not a matter of a single step but is, rather, analyzeable into a sequence of successive transformational steps. The transformations that contribute to this mapping of deep to surface structures can be combined in many different ways, depending on the form of the deep structure to which they apply. Since these transformations apply in sequence, each must produce a structure of the sort to which the next can apply. This condition is met in our formulation, since transformations apply to phrase-markers and convert them into new phrase-markers. But there is very good empirical evidence that the surface structures that determine phonetic form are, in fact, phrase-markers (that is, labeled bracketing of formatives). It follows, then, that the deep structures to which transformations originally apply should themselves be phrase-markers, as in our formulation.

In principle, there are many ways in which a network of grammatical relations might be represented. One of the major reasons for selecting the method of phrase-markers generated by base rules is precisely the fact that transformations must apply in sequence and therefore must apply to objects of the sort that they themselves produce, ultimately, to phrase-markers that have the same formal properties as surface structures.[35]

CONCLUDING OBSERVATIONS

The grammatical theory just presented calls for several comments. We pointed out earlier that the grammar of a language must, for empirical adequacy, allow for infinite use of finite means, and we assigned this recursive property to the syntactic component, which generates an infinite set of paired deep and surface structures. We have now further localized the recursive property of the grammar, assigning it to the categorial component of the base. Certain base rules introduce the initial symbol S that heads derivations, for example, the fourth rule of (19). It may be that introduction of "propositional content" in deep structures by this means is the only recursive device in the grammar apart from the rules involved in forming coordinated constructions, which raise various problems going beyond what we have been discussing here.

It is reasonable to ask why human languages should have a design of this sort—why, in particular, they should use grammatical transformations of the sort described to convert deep structures to surface form. Why should they not make use of deep structures in a more direct way?[36] Two reasons suggest themselves at once. We have already observed that the conditions of lexical insertion are essentially transformational rather than phrase-structural (see p. 426). More generally, we find many nonphrase-structural constraints (for example, those involved in deletion of identical items—see p. 429 and 433) when we study a language carefully. Thus transformations not only convert a deep structure to a surface structure, but they also have a "filtering effect," ruling out certain potential deep structures as not well-formed.[37] Apart from this, we would naturally be inclined to seek an explanation for the use of grammatical transformations in the empirical constraints that linguistic communication must meet. Even the simple fact that sound is unrecoverable imposes conditions on speech that need not, for example, be imposed on a linguistic system designed only for writing (for example, the artificial systems mentioned in note 36). A written system provides an "external memory" that changes the perceptual problem in quite a significant way. We would expect a system designed for the conditions of speech communication to be somehow adapted to the load on memory. In fact, grammatical transformations characteristically reduce the amount of grammatical structure in phrase-markers in a well-defined way, and it may be that one consequence of this is to facilitate the problem of speech perception by a short-term memory of a rather limited sort.[38] This observation suggests some promising directions for further research, but little of substance can be said with any confidence on the basis of what is understood today.

One further point requires some clarification. We noted at the outset that performance and competence must be sharply distinguished if either is to be studied successfully. We have now discussed a certain model of competence. It would be tempting, but quite absurd, to regard it as a model of performance as well. Thus we might propose that to produce a sentence, the speaker goes through the successive steps of constructing a base-derivation, line by line from the initial symbol S, then inserting lexical items and applying grammatical transformations to form a surface structure, and finally applying the phonological rules in their given order, in accordance with the cyclic principle discussed earlier. There is not the slightest justification for any such assumption. In fact, in implying that the speaker selects the general properties of sentence structure before selecting lexical items (before deciding what he is going to talk about), such a proposal seems not only without justification but entirely counter to whatever vague intuitions one may have about the processes that underlie production. A theory of performance (production or perception) will have to incorporate the theory of competence—the generative grammar of a language—as an essential part. But models of performance can be constructed in many different ways, consistently with fixed assumptions about the competence on which they are based. There is much that can be said about this topic, but it goes beyond the bounds of this chapter.

Specifying the properties of the various components and subcomponents of a grammar precisely, along the lines outlined in this discussion, we formulate a highly restrictive hypothesis about the structure of any human language. As we have remarked several times, it is far from necessary, on any a priori grounds, that a language must have a structure of this sort. Furthermore, it seems quite likely that very heavy conditions can be placed on grammars beyond those outlined above. For example, it may be (as, in fact, was traditionally assumed) that base structures can vary only very slightly from language to language; and, by sufficiently restricting the possible range of base structures, it may be possible to arrive at quite general definitions for the categories that function as "nonterminal symbols" in the rules of the categorial component. As observed previously, this would provide language-independent definitions of grammatical relations, and would raise the possibility that there exist deep-seated universal principles of semantic interpretation.

In mentioning such possibilities, we must take note of the widespread view that modern investigations have not only conclusively refuted the principles of traditional universal grammar but have, moreover, shown that the search for such principles was ill-conceived from the start. But it seems to me that such conclusions are based on a serious misunderstanding of traditional universal grammar, and on an erroneous interpretation of the results of modern work. Traditional universal grammar tried to demonstrate, on the basis of what information was then available, that deep structures vary little from language to language. That surface structures might be highly diverse was never doubted. It was also assumed that the categories of syntax, semantics, and phonetics are universal and quite restricted in variety. Actually, modern "anthropological linguistics" has provided little evidence that bears on the assumption of uniformity of deep structures, and insofar as the universality of categories is concerned, conclusions rather like the traditional ones are commonly accepted in practice in descriptive work.[39]

Modern linguistics and anthropological linguistics have concerned themselves only marginally with deep structure, either in theory or practice. A great diversity of surface structures has been revealed in descriptive work, as anticipated in traditional universal grammar. Nevertheless, a good case can be made for the conclusion that the fundamental error of traditional universal grammar was that it was not sufficiently restrictive in the universal conditions it proposed for human languages—that much heavier constraints must be postulated to account for the empirical facts.

Our discussion of the structure of English in the illustrative examples given previously has necessarily been quite superficial and limited to very simple phenomena. But even a discussion of the topics we have touched on requires a fairly intimate knowledge of the language and a reasonably well-articulated theory of generative grammar. Correspondingly, it is only when problems of the sort illustrated are seriously studied that any contribution can be made to the theory of universal grammar. Under these circumstances, it is not too surprising that even today, the hypotheses of universal grammar that can be formulated with any conviction are supported by evidence from a fairly small number of studies of very few of the languages of the world, and that they must therefore be highly tentative. Still, the inadequacy of the evidence should not be overstated. Thus it is surely true—and there is nothing paradoxical in this—that a single language can provide strong evidence for conclusions regarding universal grammar. This becomes quite apparent when we consider again the problem of language acquisition (see p. 401). The child must acquire a generative grammar of his language on the basis of a fairly restricted amount of evidence.[40] To account for this achievement, we must postulate a sufficiently rich internal structure—a sufficiently restricted theory of universal grammar that constitutes his contribution to language acquisition.

For example, it was suggested earlier that in order to account for the perception of stress contours in English, we must suppose that the user of the language is making use of the principle of cyclic application. We also noted that he could hardly have sufficient evidence for this principle. Consequently, it seems reasonable to assume that this principle is simply part of the innate schematism that he uses to interpret the limited and fragmentary evidence available to him. It is, in other words, part of universal grammar. Similarly, it is difficult to imagine what "inductive principles" might lead the child unerringly to the assumptions about deep structure and about organization of grammar that seem to be necessary if we are to account for such facts as those we have mentioned. Nor is a search for such principles particularly well-motivated. It seems reasonable to assume that these properties of English are, in reality, facts of universal grammar. If such properties are available to the child, the task of language-acquisition becomes feasible. The problem for the child is not the apparently insuperable inductive feat of arriving at a transformational generative grammar from restricted data, but rather that of discovering which of the possible languages he is being exposed to. Arguing in this way, we can arrive at conclusions about universal grammar from study of even a single language.

The child is presented with data, and he must inspect hypotheses (grammars) of a fairly restricted class to determine compatibility with this data. Having selected a grammar of the predetermined class, he will then have command of the language generated by this grammar.[41] Thus he will know a great deal about phenomena to which he has never been exposed, and which are not "similar" or "analogous" in any well-defined sense to those to which he has been exposed.[42] He will, for example, know the relations among the sentences (33) and (34), despite their novelty; he will know what stress contours to assign to utterances, despite the novelty and lack of physical basis for these phonetic representations; and so on, for innumerable other similar cases. This disparity between knowledge and experience is perhaps the most striking fact about human language. To account for it is the central problem of linguistic theory.

The basic conclusion that seems to be emerging with increasing clarity from contemporary work in linguistics is that very restrictive initial assumptions about the form of generative grammar must be imposed if explanations are to be forthcoming for the facts of language use and language acquisition. Furthermore, there is, so far, no evidence to suggest that the variety of generative grammars for human languages is very great. The theory of universal grammar suggested by the sketchy description that we have just given will no doubt be proven incorrect in various respects. But it is not unlikely that its fundamental defect will be that it permits far too much latitude for the construction of grammars, and that the kinds of languages that can be acquired by humans in the normal way are actually of a much more limited sort than this theory would suggest. Yet even as the theory of generative grammar stands today, it imposes fairly narrow conditions on the structure of human language. If this general conclusion can be firmly established—and, furthermore, significantly strengthened—this will be a highly suggestive contribution to theoretical psychology. It is hardly open to controversy that today, as in the seventeenth century, the central and critical problem for linguistics is to use empirical evidence from particular languages to refine the principles of universal grammar. I have tried, in this chapter, to suggest some of the principles that seem well-established and to illustrate some of the empirical considerations that bear on such principles.[43]

NOTES

[1] The term "grammar" is often used ambiguously to refer both to the internalized system of rules and to the linguist's description of it.

[2] To be more precise, a certain class of signals that are repetitions of one another, in a sense to which we return subsequently.

[3] Or by some simple calculations of the number of sentences and "patterns" that might be needed, for empirical adequacy, in such repertoires. For some relevant comments, see G. A. Miller, E. Galanter, and K. H. Pribram, *Plans and the Structure of Behavior,* Holt, Rinehart and Winston (1960), pp. 145f.; G. A. Miller and N. Chomsky, "Finitary models of language users," in R. D. Luce, R. Bush, and E. Galanter (eds.), *Handbook of Mathematical Psychology,* Vol. II, John Wiley, New York, 1963, p. 430.

[4] The existence of innate mental structure is, obviously, not a matter of controversy. What we may question is just what it is and to what extent it is specific to language.

[5] This assumption is not explicit in Wilkins, but is developed in other seventeenth and eighteenth century work. See Chomsky, *Cartesian Linguistics,* Harper and Row, New York, 1966, for references and discussion.

[6] In an appropriate sense of repetition. Thus any two physical signals are in some way distinct, but some of the differences are irrelevant in a particular language, and others are irrelevant in any language.

[7] A theory of phonetic distinctive features is developed in R. Jakobson, G. Fant, and M. Halle, *Preliminaries to Speech Analysis,* Cambridge, Mass., 1951 (2nd ed., M.I.T. Press, Cambridge, Mass., 1963). A revised and, we think, improved version will appear in N. Chomsky and M. Halle, *Sound Pattern of English,* Harper and Row, New York (forthcoming).

[8] Observe that although the order of phonetic segments is a significant fact, there is no reason to assume that the physical event represented by a particular sequence of phonetic symbols can be analyzed into successive parts, each associated with a particular symbol.

[9] See J. Katz, *The Philosophy of Language,* Harper and Row, 1965, for a review of some recent work. For another view, see U. Weinreich, Explorations in semantic theory, in T. A. Sebeok (ed.), *Current Trends in Linguistics,* Vol. 3 of *Linguistic Theory,* Mouton and Co., The Hague (1966); and for comments on this and further development, see J. Katz, *Recent Issues in Semantic Theory* (in preparation). There has also been quite a bit of recent work in descriptive semantics, some of which is suggestive with respect to the problems discussed here.

[10] For discussion of this notion, see J. Katz, Semantic theory and the meaning of "good," *J. Philos.,* **LXI,** No. 23 (1964).

[11] See Chomsky, *op. cit.,* for discussion.

[12] See p. 398. In general, a set of rules that recursively define an infinite set of objects may be said to *generate* this set. Thus a set of axioms and rules of inference for arithmetic may be said to generate a set of proofs and a set of theorems of arithmetic (last lines of proofs). Similarly, a (generative) grammar may be said to generate a set of structural

descriptions, each of which, ideally, incorporates a deep structure, a surface structure, a semantic interpretation (of the deep structure) and a phonetic interpretation (of the surface structure).

[13] The analysis that is presented here for purposes of exposition would have to be refined for empirical adequacy.

[14] Notice that every two successive formatives are separated by a juncture, as is necessary if the representation of (5) as a single matrix is to preserve the formative structure. For present purposes, we may think of each segment of a formative as unmarked for all junctural features and each juncture as unmarked for each formative feature.

[15] The reasons for this analysis go beyond the scope of this discussion. For details see Chomsky and Halle, *op. cit.*

[16] In the obvious sense. Thus $[_A \ldots [_B \ldots]_B \ldots [_C \ldots]_C \ldots]_A$ would, for example, be a proper bracketing of the string . . . in terms of the labeled brackets $[_A,]_A, [_B,]_B, [_C,]_C,$ but neither of the following would be proper bracketings:

$$[_A \ldots [_B \ldots]_A; \qquad [_A \ldots [_B \ldots]_A \ldots]_B$$

[17] These are simplified, for expository purposes. See Chomsky and Halle, *op. cit.*, for a more accurate account. In particular, we must assume that if rule (7) is applicable at a particular stage in the cycle, then rule (8) is not applied to the phrase to which rule (7) has applied, at this stage of the cycle. Notice that in this exposition we are using the term "applies" ambiguously, in the sense of "available for application" and also in the sense of "actually modifies the sequence under consideration."

[18] The word "eraser" is, at this stage, bisyllabic.

[19] As earlier, we refer here to "tacit" or "latent knowledge," which can, perhaps, be brought to consciousness with proper attention but is surely not presented to "unguided intuition."

[20] And other aspects. The argument is, in fact, much more general. It must be kept in mind that speech perception is often impaired minimally, or not at all, even by significant distortion of the signal, a fact difficult to reconcile with the view that phonetic analysis in detail is a prerequisite for analysis of the syntactic and semantic structure.

[21] The latter is again ambiguous in an entirely different way from (4), depending on the reference of "him." We will assume, throughout, that it refers to *John.*

[22] But the interpretation of this depends on that of "see" and that of "past tense"; hence, these separate items must be represented in the deep structure, though not, in this case, in the surface structure.

[23] A phrase X is an immediate constituent of the phrase Y containing X if there is no phrase Z which contains X and is contained in Y. Thus, the noun phrase "John" is an immediate constituent of the sentence "John saw Bill," [analyzed as in (6)], but the noun phrase "Bill" is not, being contained in the intervening phrase "saw Bill." "John saw" is not an immediate constituent of the sentence, since it is not a phrase; "John" is not an immediate constituent of "John saw," since the latter is not a phrase.

Notice that the definitions proposed here for grammatical functions and relations make sense only when restricted to deep structures, in general.

[24] In fact, we might think of a grammar as assigning a semantic interpretation to all possible sentences (this being a clear notion, given theories of universal phonetics and semantics), including those that deviate from rules of the language. But this is a matter that we will not go into any further here.

[25] The question of how the syntactic component is organized should not be confused, as it all too often is, with the problem of developing a model of performance (production or perception). In fact, any of the kinds of organization just described (and others) could be used as the basis for a theory of performance of either kind.

[26] It may be that a slightly more general notion of "phrase-marker" is needed, but we will put this question aside here.

[27] This may not seem obvious. We return to the example directly.

[28] We henceforth suppose (21a) and (21b) to be extended to full phrase-markers by insertion of appropriate lexical entries, as indicated.

29 Notice that this transformation would modify the phrase-marker to which it applies in a more radical way than those discussed above. The principles remain the same, however.

30 These factors may affect performance, however. Thus they may affect the physical signal and play a role in determining how a person will interpret sentences. In both producing and understanding sentences, the speaker-hearer makes use of the ideal phonetic and semantic interpretations, but other factors also play a role. The speaker may be simply interested in making himself understood—the hearer, in determining what the speaker intended (which may not be identical with the literal semantic interpretation of the sentence or sentence fragment that he produced). Once again, we must insist on the necessity for distinguishing performance from competence if either is to be studied in a serious way.

31 More accurately, surface structures that are sufficiently close so as to determine the same phonetic representation.

32 Modern linguistics has made occasional use of this property of language as a research tool. The first general discussion of how ambiguity can be used to illustrate the inadequacy of certain conceptions of syntactic structure is in C. F. Hockett's, Two models for grammatical description, *Word* **10**:210–231 (1954), reprinted in M. Joos (ed.), *Readings in Linguistics,* Washington (1957).

33 It seems, in fact, that this phenomenon has escaped the attention of English grammarians, both traditional and modern.

34 It is an open question whether this determination is unique.

35 There are other supporting reasons. For one thing, grammatical relations are not among words or morphemes but among phrases, in general. For another, empirical investigation has uniformly shown that there is an optimal ideal order of phrases in underlying structures, consistent with the assumption that these are generated by a base system of the sort discussed above.

36 It is interesting to observe, in this connection, that the theory of context-free phrase structure grammar (see p. 421) is very close to adequate for "artificial languages" invented for various purposes, for example, for mathematics or logic or as computer languages.

37 And hence, in certain cases, as underlying "semigrammatical sentences" that deviate, in the indicated way, from grammatical rule. This suggests one approach to the problem touched on in Note 24.

38 For some speculations about this matter and discussion of the general problem, see G. A. Miller and N. Chomsky, "Finitary models for the user," in R. D. Luce, E. Galanter, and R. Bush (eds.), *Handbook of Mathematical Psychology,* Vol. II, John Wiley, New York, 1963. The suggestion that transformations may facilitate performance is implicit in V. Yngve, A model and a hypothesis for language structure, *Proc. Am. Philosoph. Soc.,* 444–466 (1960).

39 Traditional theories of universal phonetics have been largely accepted as a basis for modern work, and have been refined and amplified in quite important ways. See the references in Note 7.

40 Furthermore, evidence of a highly degraded sort. For example, the child's conclusions about the rules of sentence formation must be based on evidence that consists, to a large extent, of utterances that break rules, since a good deal of normal speech consists of false starts, disconnected phrases, and other deviations from idealized competence.

The issue here is not one of "normative grammar." The point is that a person's normal speech departs from the rules of his own internalized grammar in innumerable ways, because of the many factors that interact with underlying competence to determine performance. Correspondingly, as a language learner, he acquires a grammar that characterizes much of the evidence on which it was based as deviant and anomalous.

41 We are presenting an "instantaneous model" of language acquisition which is surely false in detail, but can very well be accepted as a reasonable first approximation. This is not to deny that the fine structure of learning deserves study. The question, rather, is what the range of possibilities may be within which experience can cause knowledge and belief to vary. If the range is quite narrow (as, it seems to me, is suggested by considerations of the sort mentioned above), then a first approximation of the sort suggested

will be a prerequisite to any fruitful investigation of learning. Given an instantaneous model that is empirically well-supported, as a first approximation, there are many questions that can immediately be raised: for example, what are the strategies by which hypotheses are sampled, how does the set of hypotheses available at one stage depend on those tested at earlier stages, etc.

[42] Except, tautologically, in the sense that they are accounted for by the same theory.

[43] In addition to works mentioned in earlier notes the following books can be consulted for further development of topics touched on in this chapter: Chomsky, *Syntactic Structures,* Mouton and Co., The Hague (1957); *Current Issues in Linguistic Theory,* Mouton and Co., The Hague (1964); *Aspects of the Theory of Syntax,* M.I.T. Press, Cambridge (1965); Halle, *Sound Pattern of Russian,* Mouton and Co., The Hague (1959); Katz and Postal, *An Integrated Theory of Linguistic Description,* M.I.T. Press, Cambridge (1964). See also many papers in Fodor and Katz (eds.), *Structure of Language: Readings in the Philosophy of Language,* Prentice-Hall, New Jersey (1964). For more information on aspects of English structure touched on here, see also Lees, *Grammar of English Nominalizations,* Mouton and Co., The Hague (1960), and P. Rosenbaum, *Grammar of English Predicate Complement Constructions,* M.I.T. Ph.D. dissertation (1965). For further material see the bibliographies of the works cited.

The history of the biological basis of language*

OTTO MARX

Language has been thought of as being the expression of man's reason, the result of onomatopoeia, invented as a means of communication, considered basic to the formation of society, or simply a gift of God. Each of these definitions of language has been used in the construction of a multitude of language theories [1]. We shall not be concerned with the development of these theories, but limit ourselves to a discussion of the recurrent emergence of the thoughts on the biological basis of language.[1]

The idea that language is one of man's inherent characteristics, like vision or hearing, is found in some myths on the creation of man [2]. In these myths, language is given to man in conjunction with his senses, so that apparently it was considered one of them, and not part of man's cultural or social functions (which are also described as given or taught by the gods). By no means can these assertions of a divine origin be considered antithetical to a natural origin of language; on the contrary, everything natural to man was God's gift to him.[2]

Between the realm of mythology and science stands the experiment of the Egyptian King Psammetichos of the seventh century B.C. and related by Herodotus (fifth century B.C.). Psammetichos supposedly tried to have two children raised by shepherds who never spoke to them in order to see what language they would develop [3]. This experiment is relevant to our discussion in so far as its design implies the belief that children left to themselves will develop language. Psammetichos thought he would be able to demonstrate which language was the old-

* This investigation was supported by a Public Health Service fellowship (IF3MH-16, 590–01A1) from the NIMH.
[1] Notes will be found at the end of this appendix.

est, but apparently did not doubt that even untutored children would speak.

Language first became the subject of discussion by the presocratic philosophers in the latter part of the sixth century B.C. The setting up of antitheses, typical for Greek philosophy, was also applied to the problems which language posed. But discussions of language were limited to a mere consideration of naming and were purely secondary outgrowths of the philosopher's search for general truths. In order to understand the statements on language made by the Greek philosophers, it is essential to give an idea of the context in which they were made and briefly describe the evolution of the meaning of the two ever-recurring terms *nomos* and *physis* in which language was to be discussed. *Nomos* was later replaced by *thesis* and was often wrongly translated as convention, while *physis* has been incorrectly equated with nature.

For Herakleitos (ca. 500 B.C.), *nomos* was the order regulating the life of society and the individual, but he did not see it as a product of society [4]. The *nomos* of society was valid, but not absolute. Similarly names were valid as they reflected some aspect of the object they named. (Apparently, he did not consider them *physis* as had been thought) [5]. *Physis* would have implied that names are an adequate expression of reality or of the true nature of things, an idea to which Herakleitos did not subscribe.

Parmenides, (fifth century B.C.) thought that originally names had been given to things on the basis of "wrong thinking," and that the continued use of the original names perpetuated the errors of men's earlier thinking about the objects around them. To him, and to Anaxagoras and Empedokles, names and concepts were synonymous. Their concern with conventional names and their condemnation of them as *nomos* was related to their critical view of conventional thought. To these philosophers *nomos* and conventional thought had acquired the connotation of incorrectness and inadequacy as opposed to the truth and real nature or *physis* which they were seeking [5].

Pindar (522–433 B.C.) considered all of man's true abilities innate. They cannot be acquired by learning but can only be furthered by training [6]. For him the rules of society which are *nomos* were God-given and, therefore, contained absolute truth. *Nomos* and *physis* were not purely antithetical as it was for Parmenides and his school. It is also well to keep in mind that *nomos* and *physis* had not been antithetical in Greek ethnography. *Nomos* referred to all peculiarities of a people due to custom and not attributable to the influences of climate, country, or food. So Herodotus had ascribed the elongated heads of a tribe, due to their binding of the infant's skull, to *nomos,* but he believed that this would become hereditary (*physis*). In medicine of the fifth century B.C., *physis* came to mean normal[3] [7].

Although we find the *nomos-physis* antithesis in all Greek philosophy and science, the exact meaning of the terms would have to be determined in each case, before we might claim that one of the philosophers made certain pronouncements about language. We have attempted to indicate that none of the presocratic philosophers were concerned with language as such, nor with questions of its origin or development, and in no case could their statements be said to establish language as cultural or natural to man.

In classical philosophy, the relationship of the name to its object continued to be the focal point in discussions on language: naming and language were synonymous. Did the object determine in some way the name by which it was called, just as its shape determined the image we saw of it? In his dialogue, Cratylos, Plato (427–347) attempted a solution of this problem. If the name was determined by the nature of the object to which it referred, then language was *physis,* that is, it could be said to reflect the true nature of things, but if it were *nomos,* then the name could not serve as a source of real knowledge. As Steinthal [8] pointed out, language was taken as given, and the philosophical discussion had not originated from questions about the nature of man or language. Plato's answer could, therefore, have only indirect implications for questions about language origin which were to arise much later. He overcame the antithesis by demonstrating that the name does not represent the object but that it stands for the idea which we have of the object. Furthermore, he declared that the name or the word is only a sound symbol which in itself does not reveal the truth of the idea it represents. Words gain their meaning from their use in communication of ideas [9]. Word language is different from other modes of communication like imitative body movements or noises. The latter are similar to painting in that they are representative but not purely symbolic as is language. The only reference to the origin of language in Cratylos is Socrates' statement that speaking of a divine origin of words is but a contrivance to avoid a scientific examination of the source of names [10].

Aristotle's (384–322 B.C.) interest in language was both philosophical and scientific. In his book on animals the ten paragraphs devoted to language follow immediately after a discussion of the senses. His differentiation of sound, voice, and language is based on his physical concept of sound production. In his opinion, voice was produced in the trachea and language resulted from the modulation of the voice by tongue and lip movements. Language proper is only found in man.

Children babble and stammer because they have not yet gained control over their tongues. Among the animals only the song of birds is similar Language, like the song of the nightingale, is perfected by training [11]. call, "kak kak" in one vicinity and "tri tri" in another and as the song of a bird will differ from that of its parents' if it grows up without them. Language, like the song of the nightingale, is perfected by training [11].

Aristotle had based his differentiation of man's language (logos) from the language of animals (phonē) biologically, for he thought that man's language was produced mainly by movement of the tongue and the sounds of animals by the impact of air on the walls of the trachea. He did not think that human language could have been derived from sounds, noises or the expression of emotions seen in animals and children. "A sound is not yet a word, it only becomes a word when it is used by man as a sign." "The articulated signs (of human language) are not like the expression of emotions of children or animals. Animal noises cannot be combined to form syllables, nor can they be reduced to syllables like human speech" [12]. He rejected an onomatopoeic origin of language and established the primacy of its symbolic function. Because he recognized that the meaning of spoken language was based on agreement, it has been claimed that he thought language to be of cultural origin. In terms of the old antithesis of *physis* versus *nomos,* Aristotle saw both principles operative in language. *Physis* meant to him the law of nature without the virtue of justice which it had contained for Plato, and *Nomos* was replaced by *thesis* and had come to mean man made. Language, as such, he considered *physis,* and the meaning of words he attributed to *thesis* [13].

The question of the origin of language had not been raised in Greek philosophy until Epicurus (341–271 B.C.) asked: "What makes language possible? How does man form words so that he is understood?" [14]. He concluded that neither God nor reason, but Nature was the source of language. To him, language was a biological function like vision and hearing. A different opinion was held by Zeno (333–262 B.C.) the founder of the Stoa, to whom language was an expression of man's mind and derived from his reason. He believed that names had been given without conscious reflection or purpose [15].

Although Epicurus had been the first to contemplate the origin of language, Chrysippos (died about 200 B.C.) a stoic, was the first to consider language in terms broader than names. Before him the ambiguity of some names had been noted but no satisfactory explanation had been found. Chrysippos proclaimed that all names were ambiguous and lost their ambiguity by being placed in context. Thereby he drew attention to the importance of the grouping of words but his belief that language did not follow logic kept his inquiry from proceeding any further [16].

The study of language entered a new phase in the second century B.C. By this time the Greek language had changed so much that the old texts of Homeric times were no longer readily understandable. The task of their interpretation fell to the so-called critics or grammarians who had to evaluate and judge the beauty of the old manuscripts. Formal grammar owes its beginnings and development to their efforts in the succeeding two-hundred years [17].[4]

One group among the grammarians represented by the greatest Alexandrine philologist, Aristarch (220–142 B.C.) and his school, was convinced that the meaning or origin of many old words could be derived by postulating that they had been modified or declined similarly to words with which they were familiar. They therefore contended that language was ruled by analogy. This principle was supposed to rule nature (*physis*) and permit the establishment of natural laws. But because language had not yet acquired any degree of standardization, the claims of the analogists were not as solidly based as we might be led to suppose [18].

The analogists' view was opposed by Krates, a philologist and grammarian, (came to Rome in 169 B.C.) and his school, who saw no lawfulness in language and, therefore, proclaimed its pervasion by anomaly (*nomos*). Anomaly was thought to be characteristic for everything made by man (*nomos* or *thesis*) [19]. Anomaly in language seemed to be confirmed by the observations which had already been made by Democritus (460–352 B.C.), that more than one name could apply to the same thing, that proper names could be changed and that analogy was frequently lacking. The standpoint of the anomalists was, in Steinthal's opinion, the more solidly based in view of the paucity of grammatical rules. Yet at that time the argument could be used that language must be *physis* for otherwise neither blessing nor curse could have any effect [20].[5] But neither the principle of analogy or of anomaly could provide, by itself, the basis for the establishment of a formal grammar which, of necessity, would have to be based on rules but would have to make allowances for exceptions as well.

The establishment of a formal grammar became a pressing need in Roman times. Unlike their Greek predecessors, who had become preoccupied with language studies in their attempt to understand the classics, Roman men of letters required rules in order to write a Latin literature. Moreover, the standardization of Latin usage was of vital importance for the political aims of uniting the Roman Empire. The contributions of the Roman grammarians were primarily of a utilitarian nature and represent the application in practice of some Greek principles of thought. In the field of grammatical theory, Marcus Terentius Varro (116–27 B.C.) resolved the antithesis of anomaly versus analogy by finding a place for both analogy and anomaly in grammar. For him language was a natural ability which had been subjected to cultural development [21].

Lucretius (95–51 B.C.) revived and elaborated the Epicurean ideas when he described language as a physiological function based on an inherent human need to name things [22]. With practical political and social goals as the impetus behind most of the extensive work on language done by the Romans—including the scholarly writings of Caesar and Cicero—the question of the biological basis or origin of language did not enter the discussion [23].

A very serious shortcoming of most Roman writers on language was the limitation of their discussions to Latin and Greek, which Steinthal regarded as the chief factor for their failure to formulate a more general language theory. In the writings of Gaius Plinius Secundus (23–79 A.D.) and of Strabo (63 B.C.–24 A.D.) only Greek and Latin are given serious consideration. One of the few to include other languages as well was the Epicurean Diogenes of Oinoanda (2nd. century A.D.)

Summary: Greece and Rome

Greece

(600–400 B.C.)	1. Presocratic philosophy	The quest for a law of nature. Relationship of name to object.
(400–300 B.C.)	2. Classical philosophy	The quest for truth. Relationship of name to concept.
(300–200 B.C.)	3. Postclassical philosophy	The quest for origins. Physis versus Thesis.
(200 B.C.–0)	4. The grammarians	(*a*) The meaning of words and their conjugation. Anomaly versus Analogy. (*b*) The relationship of words to each other. Techne versus Empeiria.

Rome

	5. Poet-grammarians	The need for rules of the Latin language.
(100 B.C.–200 A.D.)	6. Statesmen and orators	The need for political unity. Standardization of Latin language.

who wrote that men created language everywhere quite naturally; it was not a conscious invention or the result of convention. No single man or god could have created it [24].

The church fathers and Christian thinkers of the first centuries of our era, intent on defining man's relationship to God, were content to establish God's rule over language, and language differences were not of primary concern to them [25]. These differences were to become a problem, once the church had begun to spread the gospel among people with different languages. The study of languages and language theory would receive new impetus whenever a country was to be Christianized.

In the succeeding 1500 years the interpretation of language in terms of revelation and biblical exegesis stood in the foreground of language theory. The natural basis of language was never completely lost to view, and some of the most important theologians included it in their discussions.

The great thinker of the fourth century, St. Augustine (354–430), placed the origin of language in man's reason, as had the stoics, and compared the evolution of language with language development in children [26]. Boethius (480–525), a Roman statesman and philosopher, who translated Aristotle into Latin, emphasized the difference between language and thought. Articulated language is different everywhere, but tears, mourning, and emotional expression are universally understood. The North African, Fabius Claudius Gordianus Fulgentius (480–550) wrote a world history, in which he expressed the belief that language did not come from God but had grown from a "wild root." For the Bishop Isidor of Sevilla (565–636) language was an inseparable characteristic of a people; he believed everyone learned the language of his race without any apparent effort [27].

After an interval of four centuries in which men were absorbed by the problems of the political integration of Europe, the interest in language was revived with the rise of the Schola. Its founder, Anselm of Canterbury (1033–1109), wrote on language in the years after 1060. Language only approximates reality and is not identical with God's creation. It may, therefore, be subjected to analytic study and psychological interpretation. This attitude toward language is also seen in the writings of his student Peter Abelard (1079–1142) who was the most influential language philosopher of his time. He wrote in his "Logia" (ca 1113–1123) that the different designation of the same thing—by different languages—did not imply different meanings; men had only assigned a variety of sounds to the same thing. What people meant was everywhere the same, because meaning was a part of nature. Language was not God's creation; the man of reason is master of his language and never ruled by it. Latin does not provide the basis or limit of human reason; like all knowledge it can be subject to improvement [28].

A few Medieval writers placed even greater emphasis on the natural aspect of language. Petrus Heliae, who taught grammar in Paris after 1140, suggested that there are more systems of grammar as yet unknown and that all languages including the dialects can be systematically described and rationally understood [29]. A contemporary anonymous opusculum of the Bernardine Monastery of Ceteaux expressed the thought that language is the product of a natural law and attempted to substantiate this claim by the law of primacy for the letter *a* in all languages known [30]. But most theories did not go that far. Abelard's student John of Salisbury (ca 1115–1180), wrote in his "Metalogicon" of 1160 that man received his reason and his ability to speak from the *"natura clementissima parens omnium,"* but that names must have been invented by man. (Language was again being considered primarily in terms of names) [31]. This separation between a recognized natural language capacity and man-made languages was maintained by most medieval authors including Petrus Hispanus (ca 1220–1277) who later became Pope John XXI, John de Dacia professor at Paris in 1280 and Thomas Aquinas (1225–1274). Roger Bacon (ca 1214–1294) was to write in 1292 that differences between languages were based on physiological and climatic factors but proposed that language was the result of willful human invention [32].

According to Ricobald of Ferrara, the separation of language capacity and languages was supported by a miracle he observed in 1293. A deaf-mute acquired hearing and speech after praying at the grave of St. Anthony of Padua; he could repeat what was said to him but did not understand the meaning of the words. This proved that the miracle could only establish the God-given physiological language ability but not the knowledge of a particular language which had to be learned [33].

Others believed that there must be a natural language, the direct expression of untutored language ability. Emperor Frederic II (1192/3–1250) was seeking this natural language when he repeated Psammetichos' experiment which failed because the children died. William of Shyreswood (died 1267), an Englishman and professor at the University of Paris, included the "sighs of the sick" and "natural sounds" in his definition of man's language. The Dominican and later Archbishop of Canterbury, Robert Kilwardby (died 1279) proclaimed that grammar should establish rules for language in general. The characteristics of any one language were as irrelevant to a science of grammar as the material of the measuring rod or the physical characteristics of objects were to geometry [34]. The natural origin and basic similarity of all languages was also emphasized by a contemporary anonymous tractate, *"De modis significandi"* and by Thomas of Erfurth at the end of the thirteenth century [35].

The proponents of a "natural scientific" approach had been very few in number, and the majority of the learned had confined their thinking to written language and had framed their opinions in theology.

The beginnings of a separation of language philosophy from theology are found in the writings of Dante Alighieri (1265–1321). In his works on language theory and in the *Divine Comedy,* Dante relegated the contemplation of language origins to language theology. Thereby, he initiated the development of a secular language theory to deal with the diversification and evolution of languages. The multiplicity of languages was no longer regarded as God's punishment for the attempt to build the tower of Babylon, but a natural phenomenon. The primary function of language was human communication and not the search for truth, as Thomas Aquinas had believed [36].

The search for biblical sources was no longer a part of the language philosophy of the Cardinal of Brixen, Nicholas of Cues (1401–1464). In 1440, he attributed language differences to the influences of climate [37].

But the detachment of language history from biblical tradition was only slowly accomplished. Supposedly, King James IV (1473–1513) of Scotland repeated Psammeticho's experiment. His aim was to prove a biblical origin for his country. If the utterings of the children had been in a biblical language, the genealogy of Scotland would extend to the days of the Bible [38].[7]

Language became the subject of an ever-increasing number of writers. The poets who wrote in their native tongue emphasized the creative principle inherent in language, and although some, such as Jacob Boehme (1575–1624) wrote of language as a gift of nature, this was meant in a spiritualistic and mystical sense [39]. Others, for example, the polyhistorian and physician Konrad Gesner (1516–1565), considered language in the wake of the Reformation in terms of religious belief. The Reformators had re-emphasized the bond between language and God when they had translated the Bible [39x].

A more naturalistic approach is evident in the writings of some men very close to the church like Pietro Bembo (1470–1547) a Venetian patrician and secretary to Pope Leo X [40]. The leading Spanish humanist, Juan Luis Vives (1492–1540), a pedagogue and anthropologist who taught at English and French universities, proposed that every language has a natural order which no individual can determine or change. Languages undergo changes with time and his idea that the simpler languages are the oldest was to reappear frequently. He believed in an original perfect "language adamique" but did not equate it with Hebrew. Man's language ability is expressed in the various mother tongues (hence there is no need to search for the natural language) [41].

A sceptic viewpoint was expressed by the French philosopher Michel de Montaigne (1533–1592). Language is not a substance but a sound which just approaches but never accomplishes the definition of things. It is based on a human need and a child growing up alone would have the drive to produce his own language in order to express his concepts [42]. Apparently even the sceptic believed in a natural basis of language.

The philosopher's emphasis on language, as the expression of concepts or of man's reason, undoubtedly was a factor in confining to philosophy the considerations of all language elements. This cannot have been considered a restriction as long as natural science was still a part of philosophy. But the study of nature began to differentiate itself from philosophy in the 17th century. The separation was to some extent influenced by René Descartes (1596–1650). He considered reason and the use of words and signs the two most reliable means of distinguishing man from a human machine. He differentiated language from articulation which man shared with parrots and magpies, and from the expression of emotions which he shared with most animals [43].

Descartes' aim to prove the complete independence of man's soul from his body was to prove fruitful in the development of the scientific study of the body. But because language had been attributed to the soul, the study of a biological basis of language could not develop to the extent to which Descartes' division of man was accepted. Although he had recognized the production of language as inherent in man and believed that children raised alone would develop a language like ours, his concern with language in this connection was the old question of the relationship of language to the true nature of things [44].

Justus Georg Schottel (1612–1676) the best-known German language theoretician of his time wrote, in summarizing his views on language in 1663, that language is not man-made but natural. But the term natural is not to be understood as opposed to cultural, for he considered the characteristics of a society, for instance, natural to it. He believed that the true nature of things was expressed by a natural language which German approximated most closely [45]. The superiority of German, because of its closeness to "language adamique" was also a tenet of Gottfried Wilhelm Leibniz (1646–1716). Language ability was a gift of God, and the form of language was determined by natural instinct, with the exception of Chinese, which could have been invented by a wise man, and some other languages, which may have been the result of selecting words from languages already existent [46]. His view has been interpreted to be a modification of Locke's pure invention theory [47].

John Locke (1632–1704) discussed language because he had found that, "There is so close a connection between ideas and words . . . that it is impossible to speak clearly and distinctly of our knowledge, which all consists of propositions, without considering first, the nature, use, and signification of language" which he did not equate with reason. God had "designed man for a sociable creature, . . . under a necessity to have fellowship with those of his own kind; . . . furnished him also with language . . . the greatest instrument, and common tie of society." To that end man's organs were fashioned "to form articulate sounds" and he was given the ability "to use these sounds as signs of internal conceptions, and to make them stand as marks for the ideas within his own mind. . . ." Reading Locke up to this point, one may have gained the impression that he regarded language and society as creations of God. However, he continues in the next chapter:

"The comfort and advantage of society, not being to be had without communication of thoughts, it was necessary that man should find out some external sensible signs, whereby those invisible ideas . . . might be known to others. For this purpose, nothing was so fit, either for plenty or quickness, as those articulate sounds, which, with so much ease and variety, he found himself able to make." [48]

So that language had been "found" by man in order to benefit from "the comfort and advantages of society" and no longer had he been "designed as a social creature" and simply been "furnished with language." Locke appears to have abandoned the conviction of the importance of the social factor in the origin of language when he later discussed the invention of words by Adam. (According to the Bible Adam was alone when he named the animals) [49]. Locke has been extensively quoted, because the widely held thesis that he saw the origin of language as a free act of invention [50] does not appear acceptable without some reservations.[8]

A defender of Locke's sensualism, the Abbé Etiénne Bonnot de Condillac (1715–1780) thought that man's first language consisted of gestures and inarticulated noises which were "based on the construction of our bodily instruments" [51]. This gesture language already contained artificially chosen and used signs. But Condillac is careful to differentiate *artificially* created from *willfully chosen* signs.[9] Articulated sounds were used initially to emphasize gesture language. Then sounds came to be used in imitation of natural sounds. Gradually, as articulated sounds were increasingly used, gesture language was replaced by articulated language. This transition was favored by the discovery that sounds are suitable for the expression of the physical characteristics of objects. The first names did not contain any truth about the object, for they reflected only peoples' impressions of objects, not the nature of the object itself [52]. The understanding of gesture language, like the comprehension of a picture had required the application of analysis and the use of analogy. Articulated language differed from gesture language only in one respect. Ideas were presented in succession instead of simultaneously [53].[10]

Although Nature gave man "nearly complete freedom to do as he wills" in articulated language, she "guides us by putting the first sounds in our mouths and we discover other sounds by analogy" [54]. Condillac concluded by saying:

"I have said enough . . . to show that languages are the work of nature, that they were formed so to say, without us and that we, as we worked at language, blindly followed our way of seeing and feeling."

Language is for man the result of an inner need, just as it is in children. Once we have begun to speak, we have to drive to enrich our language with new expressions [55]. The inquiry into the basic principles of language would have to consider first that language which we have by virtue of our "bodily organization." Once we shall have discovered the principles according to which we speak, we shall understand the rules for speaking any other language [56]. The organic nature of language or its biological basis was apparently not just a theoretical concept to Condillac, for he saw the need to investigate and apply it to the study of languages.

In the opinion of George Louis Leclerc de Buffon (1707–1788), a specifically active sense of hearing in man plays an important role in language formation. Articulation is considered less important, in view of the belief that apes also have organs for articulation. All people speak naturally, and Buffon is the first to make this the primary difference between man and animal. Man spoke because he had reason. Animals do not have language because they lack man's ability to think and cannot connect concepts [57].

Even for the author of the "Natural History," reason seemed to be the most basic aspect of language. However, in the mid-eighteenth century man's reason was, strictly speaking, not considered a part of nature. A more naturalistic approach is expressed in the "Lectures on the Theory of Language and Universal Grammar," published in 1762 by Joseph Priestley (1733–1804). All social creatures have a God-given way of communication, and languages are like plants, which grow, blossom, and then wilt. The complexity of a language is never the result of design, but is due to accident and the structure of Man's speech organs. Languages are subject to natural law, therefore one should not attempt to fix strict rules for its usage [58].

The president of the Court of Dijon, Charles de Brosses (1709–1777), constructed a language theory in which reason played no basic role. Originally, language had been determined by the properties of the speech organs and by the nature of the objects to be named. Man's speech organs can produce only certain sounds, and the nature of the objects compelled man to designate them with those sounds which depicted their properties. These sounds became names which could arouse the idea of the object in the mind [59]. De Brosses had directly applied the philosophical idea that names are *physis* to a language theory. He concluded that there must have been one organically developed language which all people possessed at some time but which is no longer spoken or known. For natural language was later elaborated by the intellect and utilized to fashion the various languages. The remnants of the original natural language inherent in all languages cannot be easily recognized because of all the multiple fortuitous changes to which languages have been subjected. In this process, the natural relationship between sound and meaning was lost, so that the languages we know are deteriorated languages. The original words and their true meanings can be rediscovered by Etymology [60] (a belief which had also been held by those Greeks who believed that language is *physis*).

De Brosses' ideas have been considered the most typical expression of the spirit of the Enlightenment in the field of language theory. He had attributed language to a biological and a natural basis, but considered contemporary languages predominantly the product of man's reason. The immediate contact with nature had been lost by the intervention of reason. For reason was not a part of nature, and primitive man, a barbarian, did not possess it.

This assumption led Jean Jacques Rousseau (1712–1788) and James Burnet, Lord Monboddo (1714–1799) to believe that man must have fashioned language for himself, after he had become an intelligent being, had formed societies, and developed his arts.[11] The implication was that man had not been originally a social being [61]. Adam Ferguson professor of moral philosophy in Edinburgh (1723–1816) could not accept this belief in his *Essay on the History of Civil Society,* written in 1767. "The earliest and latest accounts . . . represent mankind as assembled in troops and companies . . . [62].

"Man's use of language and articulate sound, like the shape and erect position of his body are to be considered as so many attributes of his nature: they are to be retained in his description, as the wing and the paw are in that of the eagle and the lion . . ." [63].

The exploration of man's mind is not aided by the study of "a wild man caught in the woods," which would "teach us nothing important or new," for the normal development of mental functions is dependent on society. The isolated individual would be defective just "as the anatomy of the eyes which had never received the impressions of light . . . would probably exhibit defects in the very structure . . . arising from their not being applied to their proper functions . . ." [64]. Apparently, Ferguson meant this not just as an analogy. Mental functions depend on the body, "the temper of the heart and the intellectual operations of the mind, are in some measure, dependent on the state of the animal organs."

Moreover:

"Society appears as old as the individual and the use of the tongue is as universal as that of the hand or the foot" [65].

Ferguson's thinking demonstrates that the biological basis of language comes to occupy a central position, once the artificial barriers between mind and body, and man and society have been removed.

But for most thinkers in mid-eighteenth century, language as a function of the mind was a problem for philosophical speculation. Although the natural and inherently biological basis of language had been mentioned, it played no role in the heated argument about the origin of language. The quarrel of whether man had invented language by application of his reason or whether it was God's revelation could assume immense proportions without taking into consideration the biological basis of language. This was only possible because God and man's reason were considered separate and above nature[12] [66].

The argument was resolved by Johann Gottfried Herder's (1744–1803) essay on "The Origin of Language," written in 1770. Herder proposed that language was the product of man's reason and a part of it, but that both language and reason were natural to man[13] [67].

This quarrel and its resolution exemplifies another aspect of language theory. None of the major participants had based their theoretical arguments on work with language, just as most of the proponents of a natural or physiological basis of language had been heretofore satisfied to substantiate their viewpoint philosophically.[14] The concern with language theory had been shared by philosophers, theologians, poets, scientists and thinkers.

This was to change drastically in the nineteenth century, when language theories were to come from men whose work was dedicated to the study of language. In the first part of the century these men were primarily philologists and their efforts were directed at the examination of a particular language as the expression of a particular culture. The biological basis of language received little attention from them. Nevertheless, Franz Bopp (1787–1832) the founder of Indogermanic philology and Rasmus Rask (1787–1832) a student of Icelandic, recognized language as "a natural object, its study resembling natural history" [68].

The biological basis of language became of great interest to quite another group of men; the physicians. To the first among them, the interest in language was not only derived from his encounter with patients who had a language disturbance, but also from his own difficulties with the study of languages as a youth[15] [69].

Franz Joseph Gall (1758–1828) whose importance for the development of neuro-anatomy and neurophysiology has recently been reviewed [70] wanted to put an end to the "highhanded generalizations of the philosophers" who had regarded the functions of the soul without consideration for their biological basis [71]. He thought "to be on firm ground: to say that the language of words in terms of its cause, is not just a product of our faculties as the philosophers claim, but the creation of our internal faculties" [72]. The internal faculties presiding over language were represented in the brain by organs. (As Gall assumed for all "drives, technical abilities, affections, passions, moral and intellectual functions").

Language was common to man and animals. The latter supposedly had sufficient words for their own needs [73]. The two faculties for language were the memory of words, and the sense for spoken language. Man had the natural language of gestures and interjections. The language of words, Gall considered arbitrarily invented signs. Words are not the basis of intelligence, they only aid in its development [74]. Gall's postulation of two simple language centers could not do justice to the complexity of language.

Jean Baptiste Bouillaud (1796–1881) picked up Gall's ideas in connection with cases of aphasia, already in 1825. His thoughts on language were based on his clinical experience, and language was defined in terms of the difficulties his aphasic patients showed in the expression or understanding of single words [75].[16] Most of the subsequent work on aphasia, including the famous papers of Paul Broca (1824–1880), published in the 1860's, and the influential monograph by Carl Wernicke (1848–1905), published in 1874, were predominantly concerned with localization. Language was considered in the simple terms of the reception and emission of single words. This oversimplification undoubtedly contributed to the fact that linguists ignored the implications of the physicians' findings for language science [76]. Earlier we pointed out that the linguists of the first half of the nineteenth century were philologists to whom the biological basis of language was not a central issue, a situation which had been foreseen by Wilhelm von Humboldt in the 1820's. With him we shall now begin our detailed discussion of language scientists in the 19th century.

Wilhelm von Humboldt (1767–1835) had accepted and expanded Herder's original viewpoint which had brought language from the sphere of philosophy into the realm of nature, by including reason in man's natural endowment. Man can understand meaning attributed to sound, or the single word as a concept, only because language as a whole is innately in him. It is therefore inconceivable that language resulted from an accumulation of words. Language has its origin in man's capacity and in his need to speak. Language capacity is an attribute of intellectual man's physiology. The changes which occur in languages with the passage of time, are part of historical development [77].

Language science will have to study both man's language capacity and the history of languages. It will, therefore, have two aims, of which the inquiry into man's language capacity is primary, and the exacting examination of particular language is secondary.

The biological nature of man's language capacity appeared confirmed by the observation that all children acquire language at nearly the same age, although they may be raised under quite different circumstances. It is "characteristic for the unfolding of other biologically given attributes that a certain time is denoted for their development," von Humboldt wrote [78].

No language can be understood in terms of a progressive accumulation of words which later becomes structured. Even the most primitive language requires an understanding of sentence structure [79]. Words cannot be equated with the well-defined symbols of mathematics, for they serve more often to discover unverified truths than to define a truth which has been fully recognized [80]. Languages differ from each other in that each one has a distinctive facility to discover certain truths, so that every language represents a particular view of the world. The similarity of the language structures results from the fact that all languages are the expression of man's inborn language capacity which should be the central point of all language studies. Yet "it is still too early to attempt an over-all theory of human speech . . . or even a general grammar" [81].

Humboldt's discrimination between man's language ability as a biological attribute, and the development of language in terms of language history was well taken. Many of the arguments about the origin and nature of language could have been avoided by adhering to a clear-cut separation of these two basic aspects. For Humboldt understood that they were but two integral components of language and that eventually languages would have to be considered in conjunction with man's language capacity. But the work on languages had not yet progressed to a point where this was feasible.

Humboldt's exposition of the aims of language science had not included a discussion of the appropriate methods. But by mid-century the question as to whether linguistics would belong to the natural or to the social sciences, and this would determine its commitment to a methodology. August Schleicher (1821–1868), linguist and professor at Weimar and Jena, made a decision in favor of natural science. He believed that language had evolved from animal sounds and that its development coincided with the development of the brain and the speech organs. The oldest components of language must have been the same everywhere, namely noises to signify percepts (Anschauungen). Schleicher postulated that the evolution of the human race had progressed through three phases: (1) The development of the physical organism in its most basic aspects. (2) The development of language. (3) Human history. He thought that not all societies had reached this last phase. He was even convinced that the North American Indians had shown themselves unsuited for this phase and would not find a place in history, because of their overly complicated language.

Because language is man's most outstanding characteristic, people should be classified according to their language which is a much more important attribute than their racial characteristics. Language being a "symptom" of cerebral activity, language differences must rest on some slight anatomical difference of the brain [82]. This direct connection between the characteristics of a language and the organ related to language ability was a rash conclusion. Had Schleicher adhered to Humboldt's differentiation (of languages and language ability), his formulations might have proven more fruitful.

Very few linguists concurred with Schleicher's thinking and his commitment to natural science. Surprisingly, Friedrich Max Muller (1823–1900) favored the idea that linguistics was a natural science, for he had rejected Schleicher's opinion that language evolved from natural sounds. This German born, Oxford professor of linguistics and literature popularized linguistics by his lectures and is still quoted today as an authority by nonlinguists. He considered language an irresistible exclusively human instinct. Known languages had developed out of word roots. These roots, the basic components of language, had originally been used in speech. They were composed of phonetic types, the product of a power inherent in human nature. He considered language and thought inseparable, ". . . to think is to speak low, to speak is to think aloud" [83].

The public acclaim which Muller received was not based on his erudition, and this irritated the linguists who recognized his fallacies. In 1892, William Dwight Whitney (1827–1894), professor at Yale, opposed Muller's view on the identity of language and thought, and denied the possibility of a natural science of linguistics. Language was a social product based on a God-given energy. He feared that the inclusion of linguistics in the natural sciences would be used to deny free will which Whitney wanted to preserve at all costs [84].

The view that language was unique to man was not considered contradictory to evolution by Charles Darwin (1809–1882). "The faculty of articulated speech does not in itself offer any insuperable objection to the belief that man has been developed from some lower form" [85]. For Darwin, articulation, association of ideas, and the ability to connect definite ideas with definite sounds, were not unique characteristics of human language. Man differed from animals solely by his infinitely larger power of associating together the most diversified sounds and ideas. Originally, language had evolved out of man's imitation of animal noises. Man had shared with the apes their strong tendency to imitate sound. Now, "man has an instinctive tendency to speak, as we see in the babble of our young children, whilst no child has an instinctive tendency to brew, bake or write. Moreover, no philologist now supposes that any language has been deliberately invented." He found that "The intimate connection between the brain is well shown by these curious cases of brain disease in which speech is specially affected" [86].

The study of aphasia lead John Hughlings Jackson (1834–1911) to formulations on language which went beyond the simple conceptualizations of his predecessors. In his paper written in 1864, he differentiated between intellectual speech used for propositions, and oaths which, like other interjectional expressions, are nonpropositional. Among the workers on aphasia, he was the first to emphasize that "language is not a wordheap" and that meaning is gained by placing words in context [87]. In order to understand the disturbances of language, it would be necessary to have a psychology and a physiology of language. He drew on Herbert Spencer for his psychological formulations and proceeded to construct a very complicated hypothesis to explain the cerebral processes serving language function [88].

He formulated his findings, derived from the observation of cases of aphasia, in terms of cortical function. Learning language would have to be related to the establishment of sensory motor reflexes. For example:

"We learn the word ball, by hearing it and by the consequent articulatory adjustments . . . We learn the object ball, by receiving retinal impressions and by the occurrence of consequent ocular adjustments" [89].[17]

Jackson warned against confusing psychology with physiology and anatomy, but could not always avoid this confusion himself [90]. When he succeeded, it was often by the use of hypothetical constructs. "Internal speech" may serve as an example of this. He had derived it from psychological introspection and attributed to it a physiological motor function of less intensity than uttered speech. An "idea" became physiologically speaking "a nervous process of a highly special movement of the articulatory series" . . . although Jackson had to admit that "no actual movement occurs" [91]. Most of his theoretical elaborations were confined to a consideration of words or images, although he knew that language could not be understood or explained in terms of these elements! The interrelationships of words did not receive the attention which he knew they deserved.

Most physicians were content with the simple mechanistic explanations about single words, but Hughlings Jackson's interest in a language psychology was shared by the most prominent linguist H. Steinthal.[18]

Nearly fifty years after von Humboldt had formulated the aims of linguistics, Heymann Steinthal (1823–1899) undertook the task of providing the discipline with a scientific basis. With the advantage of having voluminous compendiums and detailed grammars at his disposal, Steinthal realized that language could only be fully understood, if it was regarded a part of mind. Its scientific study would have to be based on psychology. Only psychological description would permit the elucidation of man's language capacity and the conditions under which it can develop. "Language appears of necessity . . . when mental development has reached a certain point." It comes about after reflexive body movements had entered man's consciousness, and after the association of perceptions with sounds. Language had not been adequately understood in the past, because it had been regarded solely as a means of communication. It had been incorrectly assumed that man had images, thoughts and the additional ability to express these in terms of sounds. Images and thoughts were themselves based on language.

"We see now . . . how everything man attains at a higher level than animal consciousness and intuitions, is gained by way of language . . . Language is self-awareness, that is, understanding oneself . . . as one is understood by another. One understands oneself: that is the beginning of language" [92].

Steinthal's work had a profound influence on the well-known internist and professor of medicine in Strasbourg, Adolf Kussmaul (1822–1902) who devoted the first fifteen chapters of his book "On the Pathology of Language," to define and describe language as such. "Language may refer to the physical-mental act of the expression of thoughts, or to that which is expressed. To attempt the understanding of language as an act of expression, is the task of physiology and psychology."

His description of the development of language in children is remarkably perceptive: Children are born with a sense of language, an irresistible drive to express themselves. The babbling of infants is a spontaneous reflex activity, as are the uncoordinated movements of their limbs. As the child grows, it begins to listen, to differentiate sounds and to imitate words. This is not a simple process, some words the child understands without imitating them, others it imitates without understanding their meaning. In general terms, language development shows a gradual replacement of "the natural language of the child" (babbling), by the traditional language of the nation. As this is accomplished, language is removed from the spontaneous sphere and comes under the rule of will and habits. Full development of language is equivalent to expression of (conceptualized) thoughts. Once this has occurred, the child has acquired the ability to elaborate the object images connected with words into concepts [93].

Language poses a difficult problem in that it develops "without consciousness or purpose, although (later) we speak consciously and purposefully." This need not surprise us, for most neural and mental activity is predominantly unconscious. Kussmaul thought that it would be premature to discuss language in purely physiological terms, as long as physiology was just beginning to decide on its experimental methods.

It would be just as impossible to ascribe the complex function of language to a simple speech center as to define a simple center of the soul [94].[19] Kussmaul's work is remarkable for its psychological insight and its lucid elaborations on the nature of language and the problem it poses. He judged correctly the precocity of any physiological formulation and the futility of a simple hypothetical speech center where language could be localized.

Most workers on aphasia were content to consider language in terms of the memory and articulation of words, and they constructed complicated diagrams demonstrating the localization of language.[20] Carl Wernicke exemplified the dominating trend of thought in the work on aphasia when he insisted that language must be considered in complete isolation from concept formation and intelligence. The reception and production of language must likewise be considered quite separately. There were undoubtedly many reasons for the reduction to "the simplest hypotheses" in the construction of models for language physiology.[21] Wernicke hints at one of them, when he emphasized the difference between the localization advocated by the phrenologists and his own.[22] [95]. In 1891 *A Critical Study, Towards a Conceptualization of Aphasia* was published by Sigmund Freud (1856–1939). It demonstrated that the difference between Gall's and Wernicke's concept of localization was not a basic one. Just because, "*will* and *intellect* have been recognized as psychological technical terms . . . (one does not) . . . know with greater certainty that simple *sense images* are nothing more than such a technical term." There is no justification for the assumption that the physiological correlate of a simple psychological element is also simple and localizable [96] Freud pointed out.

He had touched the weakest spot of the aphasia theories by demonstrating that the so-called physiology of language was no more than a translation of psychological insights into physiological terms. In their attempt to consider the biological basis of language without becoming involved in psychology, the workers on aphasia had introduced their own psychology in physiological terms.[23]

If nothing else, the basic importance of the brain for language function had been established by the work done on aphasia. Yet neither the brain nor aphasia was even mentioned in one of the most important books on language, published in 1891 by Georg von der Gabelentz (1840–1893). In speaking of the biological basis of man's language capacity, he only mentioned the upright posture and man's unencumbered chest as factors which may have facilitated development of language in the human species. The psychological origin of language was sought in jealousy, boredom, playfulness or other mental and physical needs. Linguistics should not be a natural science, and only man's ability to order his thoughts could be profitably subjected to the method of scientific psychology. The most important function of language, the expression of connected thoughts and concepts, could only be studied by means of logical analysis and metaphysics [97]. Steinthal's hope that language would be considered in a broader frame had not been realized in linguistics.

Herman Paul (1846–1921) devotes only very little space to language capacity in his "Prinzipien der Sprachgeschichte," written in 1880. His formulation is of interest in that he considered language "a product of human culture . . . (but . . . the psychological element is the most important factor in all changes of culture . . . psychology . . . the principal basis of all . . . sciences dealing with culture" [98]. For a psychology he utilized Steinthal's work.

The study of cultures flourished with the development of anthropology. Linguists had advanced beyond the early nineteenth century philologists' preoccupation with grammars and dictionaries, and had directed their attention to spoken language as the expression of a society or culture [99].[24] In this task they had the aid of anthropologists who shared their interest in languages. This development served to reinforce the tendency to consider linguistics as a social science, and concern with the psychological and biological basis of language receded into the background. Linguists may have welcomed this development, for concern with the biological basis of language might have meant a return to the fruitless arguments about language origin which they had just overcome.

That the return to metaphysical arguments would not be essential was demonstrated by Wilhelm Wundt (1832–1900) in his "Grundzeuge der physiologischen Psychologie" published in 1873. He proposed a scientific approach in which "Physiological psychology would examine the internal and external conditions under which language, as the highest form of expression of human life, comes about. Comparative linguistics and Voelkerpsychology would describe the laws of the subsequent development of language, and its influence on the thinking of the individual and of society" [100].

But for some time to come, the psychology which Wundt helped to found was not able to approach the task proposed by him. Physiology was in its beginnings and, as Kussmaul had pointed out, its methods were still uncertain. Freud had shown that most of language physiology had been the translation of introspective psychology into physiological terms. Language capacity was of little interest to linguistics at the end of the nineteenth century. The subsequent development of psychology, physiology, and linguistics belongs to the twentieth century and extends into our own time. With the great progress in all three fields, which has led to new concepts, methods, and findings, the scientific examination of the biological basis of language appears to be a challenging necessity.

NOTES

[1] The history of phonetics has been excluded and the reader is referred to the works of Guilo Panconcelli-Calzia, *Quellenatlas zur Geschichte d. Phonetik.* Hansischer Gilden Verlag, Hamburg, 1940; *Geschichtszahlen d. Phonetik; 3000 Jahre Phonetik.* Hansischer Gilden Verlag, Hamburg, 1941; *3000 Jahre Stimmforschung.* Elwert, Marburg, 1961.

[2] The theory of a divine origin is only remarkable in that it was vehemently defended so much longer than for other human attributes.

[3] For a discussion of *nomos* and *physis* in a special medical field, see M. Michler, Hermes, Vol. 90, No. 4, pp. 385–401 (October 1962).

[4] The Greek word *gamma* referred to the knowledge of language sounds and signs; a grammatikos was originally a schoolmaster who taught reading and writing. A differentiation between a *Kritikos* as literary critic and the *Grammatikos* or Grammarian was made only in Roman times. H. Steinthal, *op. cit.,* pp. 375, 436.

[5] From the discussion it is clear that many of the arguments had arisen from the failure in defining the word *language.* First it had been used synonymously with naming, or it was referred to the Greek language. At other times, man's speaking capacity or the correct use of language were implied when *language* was discussed.

[6] For the Greeks, foreign languages had always been barbaroi-original and unarticulated. See Pauly Wissowa, *Real Encyclopedia,* s.v. "barbaroi."

[7] Borst could find no evidence of the experiment in contemporary sources. A. Borst, *op. cit.,* p. 1010.

[8] Locke's name has been used to lend authority to the invention theory but he may also be quoted to support the idea that language is inherent to man.

[9] *Artificial* meant to Condillac a form of expression which was used purposely and with awareness of the purpose, but without arbitrarily choosing the modes of expression. *Willfulness* implied that the symbols of expression would be arbitrarily made up and used.

[10] Condillac's interesting thoughts on the reciprocal relationship between ideas and language are not presented here, because they have no direct bearing on the subject.

[11] Later on Monboddo suggested a supernatural origin of language. O. Funke, *op. cit.,* p. 82.

[12] Rousseau's invention theory of 1753 had aroused a strong reaction. This was formulated in 1756 by the minister and statistician Johann Peter Suessmilch (1707–1767) who said, that the divine origin of language could not be repudiated without destroying the belief in God.

[13] The essay received the prize in the contest of the Prussian Academy of Sciences, which had asked to prove Rousseau or Suessmilch right. Herder demonstrated that neither viewpoint was adequate. Already in 1774, by which time he held a preacher's position, Herder recanted and wrote that language was Godgiven.

[14] Of those mentioned above, De Brosses and Monboddo are exceptions to this.

[15] For a more detailed description of the physician's views in the nineteenth century, see *Aphasia Studies and Language Theory in the 19th Century* by O. Marx. Bull. Hist. Med. Vol. XL, 1966. pp. 328–349.

[16] The word *aphasia* was coined by Trousseau in 1864. But Bouillaud was the first to differ-

entiate speech defect related to a central lesion, from articulatory defects. See also Bryon
Stookey, *J.A.M.A.* Vol. 184, No. 13, p. 1024 et seq. See also *Aphasia Studies and Language*
by O. Marx, *op. cit.*

[17] What would he have said about bell, a word used by Wernicke in a similar connection?

[18] Jackson was mostly ignored. His use of Herbert Spencer's nomenclature, his own lack
of clarity and consistency may have contributed to this. With an increasing interest
in psychology in the first part of the twentieth century, his papers were republished by
Head (*Brain,* 1915).

[19] Taken out of context, this has been used to imply that he (like Finkelnburg) was against
localization. *Norman Geschwind, Carl Wernicke, The Breslau School,* and *the History
of Aphasia.* Proceedings of Conference on Speech, Language, and Communication.
UCLA Forum in the Med. Sci., 1964.

[20] See also Head's *History of Aphasia* and *Aphasia Studies and Language Theory.*

[21] It was related to the nineteenth century requirements of a natural science and to the
reluctance of the physicians to include psychological considerations. That even Wernicke
was aware of the need for psychology, is evident from the subtitle of his monograph:
A Psychological Study.

[22] Broca had presented his findings and said these might be considered to lend support to
the phrenologists. R. H. Wilkins, *J. Neurosurg.,* Vol. 21, No. 5, pp. 424–431 (May 1964).

[23] A more detailed analysis of Freud's contribution is to be published.

[24] For this formulation as well as many thoughts on linguistics, we owe a great debt of
gratitude to A. Borst.

REFERENCES

1. Révész, Géza, *Ursprung & Vorgeschichte d. Sprache.* Francke, Bern, 1946, p. 103.
2. Panconcelli-Calzia, G., *Quellenatlas zur Geschichte d. Phonetik.* Hansischer Gilden
Verlag, Hamburg, 1940.
    Allen, W. S., Ancient ideas on the origin and development of language, *Transactions
Philol. Soc. London,* 1948, **81,** pp. 35 et seq.
    Borst, Arno, *Der Turmbau von Babel.* Hiersemann, Stuttgart, 1947, p. 439.
3. *The Histories of Herodotus of Halicarnassus.* Translated and edited by Harry Carter.
Oxford University Press, London, 1962, p. 202.
4. Heinimann, Felix, *Nomos und Physis.* Reinhardt, Basel, 1945, p. 59.
5. ———. Pp. 53, 92.
5a. ———. Pp. 50 et seq.
6. ———. Pp. 67, 99.
7. ———. Pp. 15–16, 95–97.
8. Steinthal, Heyman, *Geschichte der Sprachwissenschaft bei Griechen und Roemern.*
Duemmler, Berlin 1863, p. 86.
9. ———. P. 147.
10. *Cratylus in Plato.* Bollingen *LXXI,* E. Hamilton and H. Cairns (eds.), Pantheon, 1961,
pp. 421–474.
11. *Aristoteles Thierkunde,* translated by H. Aubert and F. Wimmer, Engelmann, Leipzig,
1868, pp. 101–111.
12. Steinthal, Heyman, *op. cit.,* pp. 183, 247, 248. *Aristoteles De Anima.* translated by K.
Foster and S. Humphries, Routledge, London, 1951, sec. 477.
13. ———. Pp. 317 et seq.
14. ———. P. 312.
15. Borst, A., *op. cit.,* p. 137.
    Steinthal, H., *op. cit.,* pp. 166, 280.
16. ———. P. 488.
17. ———. Pp. 377, 436.
18. ———. P. 493.

19. Lersch, Laurenz, *Die Sprachphilosophie der Alten.* Koenig, Bonn, 1838, pp. 43 et seq.
    Steinthal, H., *op. cit.,* p. 489.
20. Lersch, L. *op. cit.,* pp. 12, 45.
    Steinthal, H., *op. cit.,* p. 504.
21. Borst, A., *op. cit.,* p. 154.
    Lersch, L., *op. cit.,* pp. 118 et seq., 126, 133 et seq.
    Steinthal, H., *op. cit.,* p. 504 et seq., 677.
22. Titus, Lucretius, *De Rerum Natura,* 1027, 1055, 1086.
    Borst, A., *op. cit.,* p. 156.
    Steinthal, H., *op. cit.,* p. 197.
23. Borst, A., *op. cit.,* p. 156.
    Lersch, L., *op. cit.,* pp. 93, 140, 150, 179.
24. Borst, A., pp. 164, 178.
25. ———. Pp. 237, 356.
26. ———. P. 392.
27. ———. Pp. 424, 426, 450.
28. ———. Pp. 450, 605, 606, 632, 635.
29. ———. Pp. 636–637.
30. ———. P. 638.
31. ———. P. 640.
32. ———. Pp. 797–800, 810 et seq., 901–902.
33. ———. P. 864.
34. ———. Pp. 756, 796, 799.
35. ———. Pp. 798, 895.
36. Apel, Karl O., *Archiv f. Begriffsgeschichte.* Bonn, 1963, Vol. 8, pp. 104–106.
    Borst, A., *op. cit.,* pp. 801, 871 et seq.
37. ———. P. 1027.
38. Panconcelli-Calzia, Guilo, *Sprachformen,* Vol. I. 1955, p. 272. Cited by A. Borst, *op. cit.,*
    p. 1010.
39. Hankamer, Paul, *Die Sprache.* Cohen, Bonn, 1927, p. 123 et seq.
39x. Borst, A., *op. cit.,* p. 1086.
40. ———. P. 1107.
41. ———. Pp. 1137–8.
42. ———. P. 1256.
43. Déscartes, René, *Philosoph. Werke.* Edited and translated by J. H. von Kirchmann,
    Heimann, Berlin, 1870; *sur la methode,* pp. 66–68.
44. Borst, A., *op. cit.,* p. 1272.
45. Hankamer, P., *op. cit.,* pp. 127 et seq.
46. Leibniz, Gottfried Wilhelm, *Werke.* Edited and translated by W. von Engelhardt and
    H. H. Holz, *Wiss. Buchgesellsch.,* Darmstadt, 1961, pp. 1, 21.
47. Borst, A., *op. cit.,* p. 1475.
48. Locke, John, *An Essay Concerning Human Understanding.* (1st ed., 1689.) Dickson and
    Elliot, Edinburgh, 1777; (6th ed), Book 2, Ch. 33, Book 3, Ch. 1, Sec. 1, Ch. 2, Sec. 1.
49. Locke, J. Book 3, Ch. 6, Sec. 44 et seq.
50. Borst, A., *op. cit.,* pp. 1396 et seq.
51. Condillac, Etiénne B., *Unterricht aller Wissenschaften f. den Prinzen von Parma.* Trans-
    lated from the French Typogr. Geselsch., Bern, 1777, Sprachlehre., pp. 4, 6.
52. Condillac, E. B., *op. cit.,* pp. 20, 23.
53. ———. Pp. 14, 18, 49.
54. ———. P. 19.
55. ———. P. 24.
56. ———. Pp. 18, 69–70.
57. Buffon, George L. de, *Historie d. Natur.* Translated by Haller, Grund and Holle, Ham-
    burg, 1752, Part 1, Vol. 2, p. 206, Part 2, Vol. 1, pp. 220 et seq.
58. Funke, Otto, *Neujahrsblatt literarischen Gesellschaft Bern.* Neue Folge Heft II. Francke,
    Bern, 1934, p. 32 et seq.

59. De Brosses, Charles, *Traité de la formation méchanique des langues et de principes physiques de l'etymologie.* Translated by M. Hissmann, Über Sprache und Schrift. Weygand, Leipzig, 1777, Vol. I, pp. 11, 12, 14, 310.

60. De Brosses, C., *op. cit.,* Vol. I, pp. 68, 75 et seq., 102 et seq., 135 et seq. Vol. II, p. 25 et seq.

See also Funke, O., *op. cit.,* pp. 41–54.

Borst, A., *op. cit.,* p. 1446 et seq.

61. Schmid, E. A., *Des Lord Monboddo Werk,* etc. Hartknoch, Riga, 1784, (Introduction by J. G. Herder), Book 1, p. 11. Book 2, Ch. 1. Book 3, p. 281.

Funke, O., *op. cit.,* pp. 54, 56, 82.

Borst, A., *op. cit.,* pp. 1413, 1441.

62. Ferguson, Adam, *An Essay on the History of Civil Society.* (1st ed., 1767.) Tourneisen, Basle, 1789, p. 4.

63. Ferguson, A., *op. cit.,* p. 5.

64. ———. P. 6.

65. ———. Pp. 5, 180.

66. Sturm, Wilhelm, *Herder's Sprachphilosophie....* Diss. University Breslau, 1917, pp. 5–6.

Borst, A., *op. cit.,* p. 1441 et seq.

67. Herder, Johann G., *Abhandlung ueber den Ursprung der Sprache ...* Voss, Berlin, 1772, pp. 119, 146, 177.

Sturm, W., *op. cit.,* p. 71.

Borst, A., *op. cit.,* p. 1523.

68. Jespersen, Otto, *Language: Its Nature, Development and Origin.* Allan & Unwin, London, 1922, pp. 36–65.

69. Gall, Franz J., *Anatomie et Physiologie du Systeme Nerveux en General et du Cerveau en Particulier.* 1810–1819. Schoell, Paris, Introduction.

70. Temkin, Owsei, *Bull. Hist. Med.* Vol. 21, No. 3, 1947, pp. 275–321.

Riese, Walter, *Bull. Hist. Med.* Vol. 21, No. 3, 1947, pp. 322–334. *J. Hist. Med.* Vol. 5, 1950, pp. 50–71; Vol. 6, 1951, pp. 439–470.

Ackernecht, Erwin H. and Vallois, H. V., *Franz Joseph Gall. . . . and His Collection.* Wisc. Stud. Med. Hist., No. 1, Madison, 1956.

Boring, Edwin G., *History of Experimental Psychology.* Appleton, New York (2nd ed.), 1950, pp. 386–88. (1st ed., 1929.)

71. Gall, F. J., *op. cit.,* Vol. 4, p. 3.

72. ———. Vol. 4, p. 68.

73. ———. Vol. 2, p. 173. Vol. 4. p. 62.

74. ———. Vol. 4, pp. 65, 68.

75. Bouillaud, Jean B., *Archives Generales de Medicine.* Paris, 1825, p. 44.

76. Head, Henry, *Aphasia and Kindred Kinds of Disorders.* Cambridge Univ. Press, 1926, p. 120.

77. Humboldt, Wilhelm von, *Werke,* Leitzmann (ed.), Behr, Berlin, 1915, Vol. 4 (1820–1822), pp. 8, 14.

78. Humboldt, W., *op. cit.,* Vol. 16 (1827–1829), p. 177.

79. ———. Vol. 6, p. 305.

80. ———. Pp. 21–27.

81. ———. Vol. 4, p. 242; Vol. 6, p. 145.

82. Schleicher, August, *Ueber die Bedeutung der Sprache fuer die Naturgeschichte des Menschen.* Boehlau, Weimar, 1865, pp. 8–9, 14–17.

83. Muller, Max, *Lectures on the Science of Language.* Longman, Green, London, 1862, pp. 22, 32, 349, 356, 386–388.

84. Whitney William D., *Max Mueller and the Science of Language.* Appleton, New York, 1892, pp. 23, 29, 74.

Jolly, Julius (ed. and Trans.), *Die Sprachwissenschaft W. D. Whitneys Vorlesungen.* Ackermann, Muenchen, 1874 (1st Eng. Ed., 1867), pp. 73, 553–557, 686.

85. Darwin, Charles, *The Descent of Man and Selection in Relation to Sex*. Random House, New York (1st ed., 1871), p. 467.

86. ———. Pp. 462–467.

87. Jackson, J. Hughlings, *Brain*, Vol. 38, p. 56 (1915).

88. ———. P. 133.

89. ———. Pp. 94–5.

90. ———. P. 67. See also Head, H., *op. cit.*, Vol. 1, pp. 138, 194, 224.

91. Jackson, J. H., *op. cit.*, p. 85.

92. Steinthal, Heyman, *Einleitung in die Psychologie und Sprachwissenschaft*. Duemmler, Berlin, 1871, pp. 42, 82–85, 369–370, 385–86.

93. Kussmaul, Adolf, *Die Stoerungen der Sprache* in Handb. d. Spec. Path. and Therap. H. V. Ziemssen (3rd ed.), Vogel, Leipzig, 1885. (1st ed., 1879.) Pp. 26, 33–34, 49.

94. Kussmaul, A., *op. cit.*, pp. 33, 110, 114, 127.

95. Wernicke, Carl, *Der aphasische Symptomkomplex*. Cohn and Weigert, Breslau, 1874, pp. 4, 36.

96. Freud, Sigmund, *Zur Auffassung der Aphasie*. Deuticke, Wien, 1891, pp. 56–57, 68.

97. Gabelentz, Georg von der, *Die Sprachwissenschaft*. Tauchnitz, Leipzig, 1891, pp. 14, 303.

98. Paul, Hermann, *Prinzipien der Sprachgeschichte*. Niemayer, Halle, 1880, pp. 1, 7.

99. Tylor, Edward B., *The Origin of Culture*. Part 1. "Primitive Culture." Harper and Row, New York, 1958 (1st ed., 1871), Chap. 5.

100. Wundt, Wilhelm, *Grundzuege der Physiologischen Psychologie*. 2te Auflage, 1880, Vol. 2, p. 438.

Credits

For permission to reproduce figures, the author wishes to make grateful acknowledgment to the following sources:

The Macmillan Company, New York, Fig. 1.1; S. Karger AG, Basel/New York and Dr. A. H. Schultz, Fig. 1.2 and Fig. 2.12; The Johns Hopkins University Press, Figs. 2.1 through 2.3; Springer-Verlag, Berlin and Prof. Dr. Curt Elze, Figs. 2.4 and 2.5; Gebrüder Borntraeger, Berlin, Fig. 2.6; Gustav Fischer Verlag, Stuttgart and Drs. Helmut O. Hofer and A. Dabelow, Figs. 2.7 through 2.11; S. Karger AG, Basel/New York, Figs. 2.13, 2.14, 2.16, 2.17, 2.20, and 2.23; and to Dr. K. Feremutsch for his permission to reproduce Fig. 2.23; Springer-Verlag, Berlin and Prof. Dr. H. Lullies, Fig. 2.15 and Fig. 3.1; *Acta Otolaryngologica* and Dr. Bertil Sonesson, Figs. 2.18 and 2.19; Masson & Co., Paris, and Dr. Henri Hécaen, Fig. 2.21; Macmillan & Co., Ltd., Fig. 2.22; The Clarendon Press, Oxford, and Prof. W. Ritchie Russell, Fig. 2.22; John Wright & Sons, Ltd., Fig. 2.24; *Journal of Speech and Hearing Research* and Dr. M. H. Draper, Fig. 3.2; *Journal of Psychosomatic Research* (Pergamon Press, Ltd.), *British Journal of Psychology,* and Dr. Frieda Goldman-Eisler, Fig. 3.3; *Acta Radiologica* and Dr. Lars Björk for the photographs in Figs. 3.4 and 3.5; Oberlin College, Ohio, and North-Holland, Publishers, Amsterdam, Fig. 3.6; Dr. Gunnar Fant, Director of the Speech Transmission Laboratory in Stockholm, Sweden, Figs. 3.7 and 3.14; *Journal of the Acoustical Society of America* and Dr. Colin Cherry, Fig. 3.19; Dr. A. W. F. Huggins, Fig. 3.20; *EEG and Clinical Neurophysiology* and Dr. Mary A. B. Brazier, Fig. 3.21; Harvard University Press and Dr. J. LeRoy Conel for the several illustrations in Fig. 4.6; McGraw-Hill Publishing Company and Dr. C. Miller-Fisher, Figs. 5.1 through 5.3; Ferdinand Enke Verlag, Stuttgart, and Dr. Bernhard Rensch, Fig. 6.5; The Macmillan Company, New York, Fig. 6.6; S. Karger AG, Basel/New York, and Dr. Godfrey E. Arnold, Fig. 6.8; S. Karger AG, Basel/New York, and Prof. Dr. R. Luchsinger, Fig. 6.8; George Allen and Unwin, London, and Prof. C. H. Waddington, Fig. 6.10; *Journal of Abnormal and Social Psychology* and the American Psychological Association, Table 7.3; Williams and Wilkins, Baltimore, and the Association for Research in Nervous and Mental Disease, Figs. 7.10 and 7.11, and for Tables 7.4 through 7.7; Indiana University Publications, Fig. 8.3; *Behavioral Science,* Fig. 8.4; *Perceptual and Motor Skills,* Fig. 8.6; and finally to the C. H. Stoelting Company, Chicago, for permission to photograph the several items of the Leiter Test appearing in Fig. 8.8.

470

Author Index

Subject Index

DATE			
JUL 16 '78			
NO 1 1 '80			
MR 25 '81			
MR 16 '87			
NO 12 '91			
DE 14 '93			